THE INTERNATIONAL
BUSINESS ENVIRONMENT

THE INTERNATIONAL BUSINESS ENVIRONMENT

Text and Cases

Anant K. Sundaram
University of Michigan/Dartmouth College

J. Stewart Black
American Graduate School of International Management
(THUNDERBIRD)

Prentice-Hall, Englewood Cliffs, New Jersey 07632

Library of Congress Cataloging-in-Publication Data

Sundaram, Anant K. (Anant Kumar)
    The international business environment: text and cases / Anant K.
Sundaram, J. Stewart Black.
       p.   cm.
    Includes bibliographical references and index.
    ISBN 0-13-110496-9
      1. International business enterprises--Management.
    2. International business enterprises--Management--Case studies.
    I. Black, J. Stewart. II. Title.
    HD62.4.S865   1995

    658'.049--dc20

                                          94-32778
                                            CIP

Editorial/Production Supervision: Publishers Services, Inc.
Acquisitions Editor: Natalie Anderson
Cover Design: Merl Krumper
Buyer: Patrice Fraccio

© 1995 by Prentice-Hall Inc.

A Simon & Schuster Company

Englewood Cliffs, New Jersey 07632

Printed in the United States of America

10 9 8 7 6 5 4 3 2 1

ISBN 0-13-110496-9

PRENTICE-HALL INTERNATIONAL (UK) LIMITED, *LONDON*
PRENTICE-HALL OF AUSTRALIA PTY. LIMITED, *SYDNEY*
PRENTICE-HALL CANADA INC., *TORONTO*
PRENTICE-HALL HISPANOAMERICANA, S.A., *MEXICO*
PRENTICE-HALL OF INDIA PRIVATE LIMITED, *NEW DELHI*
PRENTICE-HALL OF JAPAN, INC., *TOKYO*
SIMON & SCHUSTER ASIA PTE. LTD., *SINGAPORE*
EDITORA PRENTICE-HALL DO BRASIL, LTDA., *RIO DE JANEIRO*

Contents

Preface

The Rationale for the Book

In the past couple of decades, the phenomenon of globalization has progressed from buzzword to reality. Indeed, chances are low that a typical MBA today will work for an organization that is *not* a multinational enterprise (MNE); the notion of a purely domestic firm is fiction.

At the same time, there has been a debate in business schools about whether their curricula should have "separate international courses" or whether international material should be integrated into the "regular," functional area courses. Many business schools appear to view these approaches as being substitutive rather than complementary. The essence of this debate can be captured in one question: Are differences in business across borders those of degree or those of kind? The short answer is, both. There are many managerial issues confronting MNEs that are qualitatively no different from those that confront a non-MNE, and these issues are probably best dealt with in the regular, functional area courses. However, there are also managerial issues that are unique to MNEs and these, we believe, are best addressed in a separate course.

This book is based on the premise that there are two distinguishing aspects of business in today's global environment that present differences of kind, and therefore, will not fit as easily into the traditional functional areas of a business curriculum: They are multiple sources of external authority ("MA"), and multiple denominations of value ("MV"). These two aspects of the MNE environment cut across managerial issues in all functional areas, and have implications for internal organization across a broad range of firm attributes.

The emphasis of the book is to give students the tools to effectively and systematically analyze the various facets of the international business environment, and how they affect internal organization. It provides students with tools and perspectives to analyze the economic structure and stability of the countries and of the linkages between them; their conflicts resulting from issues over free trade and protectionism; their political and legal institutions, processes, and risks; their cultural norms, values, ethical systems, and customs; their competitive vulnerabilities and opportunities arising from the impact of exchange rates and international capital markets; and so on. As this list suggests, the material in this book requires the integration of theories and models from a wide variety of liberal arts disciplines, including political science, sociology, economics, finance, law, psychology, and religion. In the process, this book assumes that business schools must treat the two approaches—international issues within the functional disciplines and a separate international course—as being complements rather than substitutes.

What Differentiates This Book?

There are a number of excellent texts on international business in the marketplace, and one might legitimately ask, what makes this book different? We believe that the following attributes differentiate this book from its competitors:

1) Conceptual Underpinnings: This book "bites the bullet" on the question of what is unique about MNEs, and develops the argument (see Chapter 1) that the distinguishing features of this organizational form result from the *environment* in which they operate. This, in turn, leads us to a discussion of the two generic attributes of the environment—MA and MV—that lead to specific types of managerial challenges. The entire book is developed around the cohesive theme of systematically analyzing the different parts of MA and MV, and how the various aspects of this environment affect MNEs' internal organization.

2) Integration: The material in this book is integrative, in the sense that it combines insights from a number of different academic disciplines and functional areas. It shies away from unidimensional (e.g., purely economic or purely social) views of organizational imperatives, and in the process, motivates students to appreciate the challenges of managing a complex organizational form in an equally complex and rapidly changing environment.

3) Managerial Relevance/General Management Focus: The material in this book is based on the implicit assumption that ideas covered in an MBA curriculum must ultimately be managerially relevant. In other words, the presumption is that, from the standpoint of MBAs, all theory must ultimately lead to better managerial practice. In the process, the tone and content of the book adopts the viewpoint of the general manager of an MNE—that is, someone who is responsible for formulating and implementing global strategy. The cases also adopt this perspective.

4) Coverage of Issues: A number of topics are covered in the setting of this single textbook at a level of depth that instructors and students would typically have to search out from a number of different texts. Examples include treatment of economic exposure to exchange rates (Chapter 5), international law (Chapter 8), MNE social responsibility (Chapter 9), and economic cost benefit analysis (Chapter 12). Moreover, there are accompanying full-length cases dealing with each of these issues.

5) Conciseness: The chapters are written in the manner of a "scholarly reading" that an instructor might typically assign with a case. In other words, they are designed to be concise summaries of the theoretical ideas that are necessary for cogent student analysis of cases. Unlike typical textbooks, the chapters are not designed to "give answers" to students, but rather, they are designed to provide them with sufficiently detailed information to frame their case analyses in a systematic way. In the process, our objective is to have the students go considerably beyond attempting programmed or "textbook" solutions to complex analysis.

6) Classroom Tested, Full-Length, Current Cases: All the cases have been successfully tested in the classroom. Moreover, they are full-length, rather than "boxed" summaries based on news articles. The cases attempt to convey the true complexity of general management decisions in the MNE context. Moreover, every case is specifically tied to a chapter, and in the process, instructors can assign them together as a cohesive, and often standalone, unit. The cases are current—with one exception, every one is from the decade of the 1980s onward, and many are from the 1990s. The cases also cover high-profile current events such as the Boeing-Airbus and semiconductor trade disputes, the breakup of the former Soviet Union, the corruption scandals in Italy, the opening of China, the ABB merger, and so forth.

7) Supplements: An instructor's manual containing solutions to the problem sets and teaching notes for the cases provides a clear teaching plan that we have successfully used with MBA students.

Suggestions for Classroom Use

We have effectively used the contents of the book in a 22- to 24-session core (required) course on the international business environment. The book can also be used in a second-year elective course that deals with the environment of MNEs, or with issues of business, government, and international competition. Chapters 1 through 8, Chapter 12, and Chapter 15 can be used in a course dealing with international economics and competitive strategy. Similarly, Chapters 1–2, Chapter 5–11, and Chapters 13–15 can be used in a course dealing with management of the MNE. Since chapters and cases are closely integrated, specific chapters (and associated cases) can be assigned to specific sessions in a wide variety of courses dealing with global strategy. In all these instances, this book could also serve as a useful supplementary text.

We recommend that the material in this book be positioned in the MBA curriculum *after* students have had the opportunity to take courses dealing with basic functional issues.

Acknowledgments

We owe a tremendous debt of gratitude to Nick Hall (Tuck '95, now with Mercer Management Consulting) who brought to bear impressive scholarly and managerial acumen to developing a number of the cases in the book. His efforts resulted in the inclusion of some of the finest cases we have had occasion to teach. In addition to Nick, we are deeply grateful to Chris Pears (Tuck '94, now with Cargill Inc.) and to Michelle Sparrow (Tuck '93, now with the MBA Enterprise Corps in Budapest) for their contributions to the development of other cases in the book. We are extremely grateful to Professor Mark Eaker at University of Virginia for giving us permission to include his superb case on ABB.

The material here has been honed by a number of years of classroom testing at the Amos Tuck School and at the American Graduate School of International Management. We owe much thanks to the many generations of students who helped sharpen our insights on (and lent considerable managerial relevance to) the issues addressed in the book. Some of the cases were also classroom tested by Professor Susan Kimmel at University of Michigan, and we are grateful for that.

There are numerous scholars in the field of international business whose writings (or conversations with whom) have had a significant influence on many of the ideas and the arguments developed here. We owe a deep debt of intellectual gratitude to them. A partial list includes Nancy Adler at McGill University, Christopher Bartlett at Harvard University, Jean Boddewyn at City University of New York, Sumantra Ghoshal at INSEAD, Anil Gupta at University of Maryland, Mel Horwitch at Theseus Institute, Stephen Kobrin at University of Pennsylvania, Bruce Kogut at University of Pennsylvania, Donald Lessard at Massachusetts Institute of Technology, Tom Murtha at University of Minnesota, Edgar Schein at Massachusetts Institute of Technology, Lemma Senbet at University of Maryland, Alan

Shapiro at University of Southern California, and Bernard Yeung at University of Michigan. Of course, we alone remain responsible for any errors or omissions in the interpretation of their work and their insights.

We cannot thank the people at Prentice Hall enough. At a time when ideas concerning the MNE are undergoing a paradigm shift and many business schools are still grappling with the vexing issue of how to globalize their curricula, publishers are loath to make bold publishing decisions until after the intellectual dust settles. (Of course, by the time the dust settles, issues also sometimes become jaded in a fast-moving world.) Not so, the team at Prentice Hall—Jackie Aaron, Natalie Anderson, Valerie Ashton, Diane Peirano, Allison Reeves, and Garrett White—who nudged us to undertake this work, and often despite ourselves, convinced us that the project would be a worthy one. Having now completed it—and leaving aside any issues of how the marketplace might respond—we could not agree more. Finally, John Beasley provided outstanding (and patient) editorial services, and we are deeply grateful to him.

Our final thanks, of course, goes to you—that your curiosity has taken you this far. If you feel, as we do, that the contents of this book are worthy of your classroom, we are deeply grateful. However, even if your plan for it is primarily bookshelf adornment, we urge you to peer into the chapters and cases. Any feedback or criticism you can give us—and corrections, additions, or deletions you might suggest—will considerably strengthen future editions.

Anant K. Sundaram
University of Michigan/Dartmouth College

J. Stewart Black
American Graduate School of International
Management (THUNDERBIRD)

Author Biographies

Anant K. Sundaram (PhD, Yale '87) is Associate Professor of Business Administration at the Amos Tuck School, Dartmouth College, and Visiting Associate Professor of International Business at the School of Business Administration, University of Michigan. He has published numerous articles in the area of international corporate finance and international business, in journals such as the *Journal of International Money and Finance, Financial Management, Academy of Management Review,* and *Recent Developments in International Banking and Finance.* He is an editorial board member of the *Journal of International Finance* and *Global Competitor.* He has also published popular press articles in the *Wall Street Journal,* and has been quoted extensively on international business issues in *The New York Times, Boston Globe, Chicago Tribune, Fortune,* and *US News and World Report.* Professor Sundaram has consulted for numerous organizations worldwide, and has taught courses in finance, international finance, and international business in both the US and Europe.

 J. Stewart Black (PhD, UC Irvine '88) is Associate Professor of International Management at the American Graduate School of International Management (Thunderbird), and was previously an Associate Professor of Business Administration at the Amos Tuck School, Dartmouth College. He is the coauthor of two books: *Global Assignments: Successfully Expatriating and Repatriating International Managers* and *Organization Behavior,* and author of numerous articles in the area of international human resource management which have appeared in both managerial and academic publications: *Business Week,* the *Wall Street Journal, World, Personnel, Academy of Management Review, Academy of Management Journal, Journal of International Business Studies, Human Resource Management, Human Relations,* and *Group and Organization Studies.* He is editor of *Journal of International Management,* an editorial board member of the *Academy of Management Review,* and a member of the Executive Committee of the International Division of the Academy of Management. Professor Black has consulted for numerous organizations worldwide, and has taught extensively in both the US and Japan. He speaks Japanese fluently.

chapter 1

Introduction

What is a multinational enterprise (MNE)? Why is it an important organizational form to study? Do any features differentiate it from a non-MNE? If so, what are these features, and what are their implications?

In this chapter (and throughout the book) we address these key questions, and, in the process, set the tone and the context for this book. We shall argue that there are, indeed, differences of kind, as opposed to simply differences of degree, that distinguish MNEs from non-MNEs. Moreover, they result from the environment in which the MNE operates. Managing across borders requires the ability to deal with the challenges presented by these unique features of the MNE environment.

Few will debate the importance of MNEs in the world economy. *The Economist* reports that there are approximately 35,000 MNEs around the world today, controlling over 170,000 foreign affiliates. It estimates that roughly half of all cross-border corporate assets are accounted for just by the top 100 MNEs, and that the top 300 MNEs control 25% of all the world's productive assets. In 1970, half of the 7,000 existing MNEs were either American or British. In contrast, by 1993, about half of the 35,000 MNEs were American, Japanese, German, or Swiss. Increasingly, many of the MNEs originate from the newly industrializing economies of the Far East, Latin America, and South Asia.

Thus, while the presence and influence of MNEs are beyond debate, what remains contested is whether MNEs require separate study by scholars or students. If placing the words "international," "global," "transnational," or "multinational" before the word "enterprise" or "corporation" simply means that a few standard functions of an organization change to some small degree, then there is little reason to study these organizations separately. If, however, there are differences in kind—or, at least, the differences are substantial enough in degree—between MNEs and non-MNEs, then it is important for those preparing to become global managers to have an in-depth understanding of the unique aspects of operating in the international business environment.

A DEFINITION OF THE MNE

Before examining the aspects that distinguish MNEs from non-MNEs, it is useful to define what an MNE is. Although many scholars have attempted to grapple with a definition that captures the true richness of this organizational form, previous writings abound with conflicting, and sometimes competing interpretations.

Different scholars have used different attributes to characterize the MNE. Such attributes include the geographic scope of the firm's value chain (that is, the sequence of value-adding activities or functions within the firm), management styles, ownership of productive assets, commonality of strategy formulation and implementation worldwide, and organizational structure:

- A distinction is made between "global" and "multidomestic" MNEs, based on coordination and geographic configuration of the firm's value chain. MNEs with high coordination among and concentrated configuration of the different parts of the value chain are called "global," while those with low coordination among and dispersed configuration of the different parts of the value chain are called "multidomestic."

- A distinction is made on the basis of management styles in the MNE—geocentric (world oriented), polycentric (host-country oriented), or ethnocentric (home-country oriented). A firm's true degree of multinationality is measured by the extent to which its top executives think geocentrically.

- The MNE is defined as an organization that owns productive assets in different countries, and has common strategy formulation and implementation across borders.

- The MNE is defined as any firm that "owns" outputs of goods and services originating in more than one country.

- A distinction is made based on organizational structure: "global" (tightly controlled with a centralized hub structure), "multinational" (decentralized federations), and "transnational" (structures that permit retaining local flexibility while simultaneously achieving global integration).

As we examine these definitions, two observations can be made. One, they revolve around an organizing framework that suggests three "forms" of the MNE; two, there are certain underlying features of the MNE that appear to cut across the different forms. This latter observation will provide us the foundation from which a general definition of the MNE can be derived.

Considering the first observation, Table 1.1 provides an organizing framework that defines the three types of MNEs.

At one extreme are MNEs that are "global," which are primarily national corporations with tightly controlled foreign operations, characterized by ethnocentric management styles, high coordination among (and concentrated configuration of) the various elements of the firm's value chain, organizational structures like a centralized hub, and a common set of strategies worldwide. At the other extreme are MNEs that are "multidomestic." They are characterized by polycentric management styles, low coordination among and dispersed configuration of the various elements of the value chain, decentralized organizational structures that operate as loose federations, and a diverse and perhaps uncoordinated set of strategies worldwide.

In between are the more complex MNEs that might be called "transnational," which variously combine attributes that characterize the previous two forms. Such MNEs might be characterized as complex global, or networks of subsidiaries performing different

TABLE 1.1

Organizing Framework for Previous MNE Definitions

Source	Attribute	Global	←Transnational→		Multidomestic
Perlmutter (1969)	Management style	Ethnocentric	Geocentric	Geocentric	Polycentric
Kindleberger (1973)	Various functional and attitudinal attributes	National corporation with foreign operations	International	–	Multinational
Porter (1986)	Coordination and configuration needs	Global	Complex global	–	Multidomestic
Bartlett and Ghoshal (1989)	Network/interorganizational structure	Global	Transnational	International	Multinational
Ghoshal and Bartlett (1990)	Organizational structure	Centralized	Networks	Networks	Decentralized
Hedlund (1986)	Organizational structure	Hierarchy (H-form)	Heterarchy	Heterarchy	Hierarchy (M-form)

functions. Such manifestations would also be consistent with a geocentric management style, and there is a growing recognition that MNE organizational forms are tending in this direction. The reasons for this include decreasing costs of worldwide coordination, decreasing importance of the need for concentrated configuration of the firm's value chain, and the necessity of managing the imperatives global integration, local responsiveness, and diffusion of innovations simultaneously.

Regardless of the particular MNE organizational form, there are certain common themes that emerge from the various definitions: They are those of an entity which, viewed from the "home" (parent) perspective, sells and/or produces in at least one other sovereign "host" (subsidiary) country where the nature and extent of multinationality may be divided further to include certain specific attributes. The crucial thing to note is that attributes of specific interest—whether it be output, sales, investment, management styles, organizational structure, coordination and configuration, or commonality of strategy formulation and implementation—manifest themselves across sovereign boundaries. Using these insights, we can define the MNE as "any enterprise that carries out transactions in or between two sovereign entities, operating under a system of decision making permitting influence over resources and capabilities, where the transactions are subject to influence by factors exogenous to the home country environment of the enterprise."

This definition not only is inclusive of past definitions, but it contains features that describe both the environment in which the MNE operates (features that derive from the common attribute that transactions span sovereign boundaries) and its internal organization (features that depend on the system of decision making and influence over resources and capabilities).

The phrases used in the definition above are inclusive rather than exclusive. The notion of "enterprise" is broad enough to include all organizational forms from unitary organizations to the more fluid network relationships. "Transactions" is broad enough to encompass the exchange across borders of people, products, knowledge, capital, technology, and so forth. The notion of "sovereignty" is inherent to the etymology of the word "multinational." The fundamental element of the MNE is the obvious idea that relevant transactions taking place both within and outside the firm are conducted across national boundaries. "System of decision making permitting influence" refers to the firm's ability to coordinate and control organizational variables (for example, resources, subsidiaries, managers) and market variables (buyers, suppliers, competitors). "Subject to influence by factors" refers to the effect of exogenous or environmental variables on transactions (for example, exchange rates, political and regulatory systems, cultures, tariff and taxation systems).

DISTINGUISHING ASPECTS OF MNEs

The pervasive feature that affects almost any transaction undertaken by the MNE is the manifestation of sovereignty, or the relative authority of the sovereign state over exchange rates, politics, culture, regulations, and languages. We shall see that, merging the idea of sovereignty and the idea that transactions cross sovereign borders, there are two specific attributes that distinguish MNEs from non-MNEs. We shall call these: (1) "multiple sources of external authority" and (2) "multiple denominations of firm value."

Multiple Sources of External Authority (MA)

The overriding principle underlying cross-border relationships is that of sovereignty. The sovereignty of a nation-state is embodied in its authority to influence events within its legal territory, and its choice to be relatively immune to outside influences. This authority generally manifests itself in terms of laws and regulatory institutions, political institutions, official language(s), norms of behavior, culture, and so forth. Consequently, the MNE has exposure to multiple (and often conflicting) sources of external authority (hereafter, we refer to this as MA).

There are three aspects of MA that merit consideration: (1) the number of geographic locations that the firm operates in; (2) the variance in country environments resulting from operating in different geographic locations; and (3) the lack of a superstructure to mediate threats or opportunities that arise at the intersection of the variances in country environments. While (1) and (2) represent differences of degree, although substantial degree, between MNEs and non-MNEs, aspect (3) represents a difference of kind—that is, it is a distinguishing aspect of the MNE, and results from the environment or the context in which it operates.

Clearly, the issue of geographic dispersal and scope per se (and the related problems of communication and coordination) is not unique to MNEs. Many large firms face these problems even within a single sovereign country. Indeed, it is possible that problems of coordination and communication among sovereign boundaries can sometimes be no worse (or even perhaps easier) than those within sovereign boundaries. For example, an MNE that conducts activities between the US and Canada may have fewer communication problems compared to a non-MNE in a vast country such as India, where communications are poorly developed. Similarly, on the question of variances in country environments, one could argue that laws, institutions, and behavioral norms can also vary within a sovereign country. In this case, however, differences among sovereign countries are likely to be a matter of greater severity but analogous to differences among regions within countries. For example, there are cultural differences within the US between the East and West, or the North and South; however, research suggests that the cultural variation within countries is substantially less than between countries. Consequently, such between-country differences are likely to result in a substantially greater degree of environmental complexity and uncertainty for the firm, but may not raise issues that are categorically different from those in a non-MNE setting.

However, even though particular manifestations of external authority (for example, laws, political institutions, or cultures) may vary from region to region within the sovereign state, the existence of overarching and commonly applicable frames of reference provide a source of recourse in the event of conflicts. Firms can use such frames of reference as guides for strategy development and implementation. In the cross-sovereign setting, there are no commonly applicable legal, cultural, or political mechanisms that the firm can take recourse to in designing and implementing exchanges. Even if the issue of resolving conflicts arising from variances in specific country environments is manageable, the notion of sovereignty precludes the enforcement of resolutions without the common agreement of all sovereign entities involved (despite the existence of treaties or global institutions to the contrary).

Consequently, the distinguishing feature of the MNE environment arises at the intersection of differences in country environments. In the absence of commonly applicable and enforceable institutional mechanisms, all conflicts arising from cross-border transactions at this intersection of differences in sources of external authority create both opportunities and risks that non-MNEs do not face. The opportunities and risks arise as a consequence of the lack of any superstructure or supranational institutions to mediate conflicts.

Consider, for example, the case of legal norms and the risks and opportunities they create. As we shall see in Chapter 8, one of the fundamental principles governing the intersection of conflicting between-country legal norms is that of consent between the affected parties or the principle of reciprocal goodwill between nations, often referred to as the doctrine of "comity." Within-country laws have only prescriptive, and not enforcement, jurisdiction across countries.

This void in jurisdiction has often led to conflicts in areas such as antitrust (for example, the case of Laker Airways bankruptcy in 1982), multinational bankruptcy (for example, the case of BCCI failure in 1991), liability limitation (for example, the case of Union Carbide and the Government of India in relation to the Bhopal disaster in 1984, which we examine later in the book), as well as in the application of social, political, and national security norms between countries.

On the other hand, this void also provides the MNE with opportunities for regulatory arbitrage between borders. For example, race and gender discrimination laws that apply to firms in the US may not apply to US firms' operations abroad; thus, personnel policies that comply with US laws might be ignored by MNEs outside the US. Similarly, many strategies that might have the potential for violating US antitrust laws do not pose a problem when undertaken abroad.

In all these instances, the distinguishing feature in the transactions is not so much the differences resulting from the variance in country environments, but it is the void at the intersection of MA for resolving competing or conflicting demands.

The emergence and growing prominence of supranational institutions (for example, the GATT, or the International Court of Justice), cross-national trading arrangements (for example, EC 1992, the Andean Pact, NAFTA-North American Free Trade Agreement), and developments in capital markets (for example, Eurocurrency markets, capital market integration, harmonization of laws for securities issuance and trading) might be viewed as institutional mechanisms that have evolved to mitigate the problems at the intersection of multiple sources of external authority. These and other developments have softened the impact of sovereign authority, but, for the reasons mentioned previously, they have not eliminated it, since they are ultimately forums for *voluntary* mediation of disputes.

In summary, MNEs face multiplicity of authority (MA) that is broader than non-MNEs because of their geographical dispersal, deeper than non-MNEs because of the variances among country environments, and different from non-MNEs because of the absence of a mediating superstructure at the intersection of differences between country environments.

Multiple Denominations of Value (MV)

The second distinguishing aspect of MNEs results from the fact that there are multiple denominations, or numeraires, of firm value (hereafter we refer to this as MV). That is, the firm's cash flows are denominated in different exchange rates. This, in turn, results in three effects on the MNE: (1) "translation exposure," which is the problem of ex-post settling up and valuation of transactions already undertaken across multiple currencies;

(2) "transaction exposure," which is the problem of hedging known or anticipated cash flows against future exchange rate shifts; and (3) "economic exposure," which is the problem of the impact of unanticipated changes in real exchange rates on the firm's competitive position (these issues are covered in depth in Chapters 3 through 5).

As we shall see, translation and transaction exposures are primarily manifestations of differences in denominations of value. This is similar to the issues of geographic dispersal and differences in country environments discussed in the previous section. As in the case of differences in MA, translation and transaction exposures may result in a greater degree of environmental complexity and uncertainty but are unlikely to raise strategic management issues that are substantially different from those in a non-MNE setting. The problem of translation exposure to exchange rates (and the accounting rules to deal with it) are conceptually similar to the problem of inflation accounting that a non-MNE might face, just as the problem of transaction exposure and the associated financial hedging techniques are conceptually similar to the problem of having to hedge in, say, commodities markets by non-MNEs.

However, the distinguishing aspect of the MNE's environment, as we shall see in greater detail in Chapter 5, is the problem of economic exposure to exchange rates. As before, this problem occurs at the intersection of differences in currency values: Economic exposure is the consequence of breakdowns in the mechanism that works to equilibrate differences in real currency values across countries.

Since the advent of the floating exchange rate regime, economic exposure has been a source of both great risks and opportunities to MNEs. For example, US MNEs whose costs were substantially denominated in US dollars (for example, Caterpillar Tractor Co., Boeing Co., firms in the US semiconductor industry) found their competitive positions destroyed by the 35% real appreciation of the US dollar between 1981 and 1985 against the currencies of their competitors. Some of these same MNEs found that the subsequent reversal in the real value of the US dollar between 1985 and 1988 gave them a windfall of competitive opportunities that they had not seen in years. Nevertheless, many found that the cumulative organizational consequences of adverse economic exposure in the early 1980s were extremely difficult to reverse. Similarly, one of the reasons for inward direct foreign investment activity in the US during the second half of the 1980s was the real depreciation of the US dollar that led to lower costs of internally generated capital and higher net wealth perceptions on the part of foreign investors.

In summary, MNEs face a multiplicity in denominations of value (MV) that is broader than non-MNEs because of the number of currencies involved as transactions cross boundaries, deeper than non-MNEs because of the volatility of currency values, and different from non-MNEs because of the breakdown in equilibrium currency values at the intersection of these differences.

THE MANAGERIAL CHALLENGES AHEAD, AND OUTLINE OF THE BOOK

If one accepts the argument that MV and MA are distinguishing aspects of the MNE environment, then managers within MNEs face two key challenges. First, MNE managers must gain an in-depth understanding of these distinguishing aspects of the international environment. In the absence of this understanding, managers must muddle through in an international environment that is becoming increasingly complex and unpredictable. At a basic level, this means that managers must understand the forces that drive MV and MA.

Second, MNE managers must make the specific links between these factors and how they affect strategy formulation and implementation in the MNE. In other words, it is not sufficient simply to understand the environment, but we must also have the ability to see the specific ways in which it affects the MNE, or how these issues matter when they arrive at the "factory gate." Both are necessary for effective management across borders. This book attempts to give managers the tools to do precisely this.

Figure 1.1 graphically summarizes the structure of the book. Chapter 2 examines the underlying macro forces that have shaped globalization—the expansion of MNEs and the internationalization of business in general. This chapter provides the general context in which the subsequent chapters and cases can be understood better.

Chapters 3, 4, and 5 provide the fundamentals of MV, that is, the role of exchange rates on MNE operations. Chapter 3 examines the basics of foreign exchange markets, and develops the theories that are necessary to appreciate the influence of exchange rates. Chapter 4 then deals with the issue of transaction exposure to exchange rates, and how MNEs can cope with them, while Chapter 5 does the same with the issue of economic exposure to exchange rates.

The succeeding chapters provide an in-depth understanding of MA, from a variety of perspectives. Chapter 6 provides a backdrop of the theories of international trade. Given that governments ultimately determine the extent to which goods, services, people, knowledge, or capital can flow freely across national borders, this chapter provides the economic context within which these issues can be understood. Chapter 7 then examines how these ideas and theories have shaped the laws and institutions that govern the conduct of international trade, both in the US and abroad.

Chapter 8 explores the regulatory environment of international business and addresses many of the issues that we talked about earlier in this chapter, notably the concern of the "void at the intersection of sovereign boundaries." Chapter 9 explores a related set of issues at the intersection of individual, organizational, and government roles relative to social responsibility, liability, and ethical conduct. Given that multiple sources of authority can provide conflicting norms concerning responsible or ethical behavior, this chapter provides some frameworks that managers can use as a guide to think through various situations in which such norms are in conflict.

Chapter 10 provides a framework for analyzing the risk factors of a country in which an MNE decides to enter, expand, or exit operations. Chapter 11 continues this general thrust but explores the specific issue of how managers can effectively analyze the *political* risk that might be related to the firm's current or potential operations in a given country.

Figure 1.1 Structure of the Book

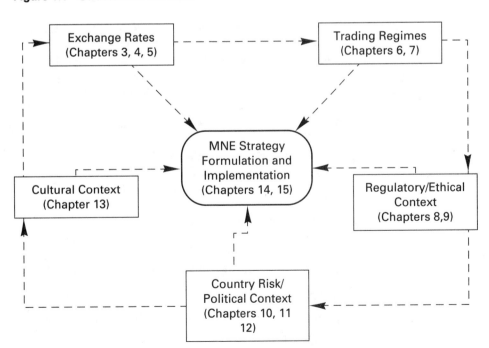

Chapter 12 turns the tables and examines how governments analyze firms, and the conflicts that can arise between the firm's analysis of a country in terms of a given project versus the government's analysis of the firm and the proposed project. Chapter 13 explores the role of culture as it affects an MNE's operations, and how it can be analyzed.

Chapters 14 and 15 address how all these considerations—exchange rates, trading regimes, trade laws and institutions, the regulatory environment, the ethical environment, country risk, political risk, and culture—affect strategy formulation and implementation in the MNE. These two chapters examine how an MNE, through its competitive strategy and organizational structure, can both react to and proactively prepare for environmental conditions.

Finally, with all these chapters, cases are included that place the reader in the position of having to analyze how to cope with MV and MA in the international environment. Thus, while the chapters provide a generally deductive means of conceptualizing ways in which MNEs deal with the international environment, the cases provide an inductive means of approaching this challenge.

CONCLUSION

There is little debate on the importance of MNEs and their role in the world economy. In the future, few managers will work in organizations that are "non-MNEs" or be unconcerned with how the international environment shapes businesses. Consequently, it is critical for management students to have an in-depth understanding of what distinguishes domestic and international environments, and to develop analytical and conceptual skills for dealing effectively with the unique aspects of the international environment—multiple sources of external authority and multiple denominations of value. The rest of the book deals with the development of these skills.

SELECTED BIBLIOGRAPHY

BARTLETT, C. A., and S. GHOSHAL. *Managing Across Borders: The Transnational Solution.* Cambridge: Harvard Business School Press, 1989.

GHOSHAL, S., and C. A. BARTLETT. "The Multinational Corporation as an Interorganizational Network." *Academy of Management Review* 15 (4) 1990: 603-625.

GHOSHAL, S., and N. NOHRIA. "Internal Differentiation Within Multinational Corporations." *Strategic Management Journal* 1 (1989); 323-337.

HEDLUND, G. "The Hypermodern MNC—A Heterarchy? *Human Resource Management* 25 (1986): 9-36.

HOFSTEDE, G. *Culture's Consequences.* Newbury Park, CA: Sage Publishing, 1980.

KINDLEBERGER, C. P. The Clash of Economics and Sociology and Politics in the Internationalization of Business. Reprinted in Kindleberger (ed.), *Multinational Excursions.* Cambridge, MA: MIT Press, 1984: 35-50.

"Multinationals." *Economist* (March 27, 1993), 5-8.

PERLMUTTER, H. V. "The Tortuous Evolution of the Multinational Corporation." *Columbia Journal of World Business* (January/February 1969): 9-18.

PORTER, M. "The Changing Patterns of International Competition." *California Management Review* 28(2) 1986: 9-38.

PORTER, M. *Competitive Strategy.* New York: Free Press, 1980.

SUNDARAM, A. K., and J. S. BLACK. "The Environment and Internal Organization of Multinational Enterprises." *Academy of Management Review* 17 (1992): 729-757.

chapter 2

Forces of Globalization

Few words in the language of business have been more overused—and perhaps misused—in recent times than "globalization." Much has been written and said on the topic, but it is a phenomenon that is rather simply described: Globalization is the process by which an activity or undertaking becomes worldwide in scope. The purpose of this chapter is to understand the consequences and the determinants of the process by which a firm's activities become worldwide in scope—why a firm becomes an MNE. We shall also attempt to understand *how* a firm pursues its entry into markets abroad.

By any stretch of imagination, economic activity in the post–World War II era has been characterized by unprecedented levels of globalization. Furthermore, the primary engine for globalization of economic activity has been the MNE. Consider the following facts:

- According to *BusinessWeek,* in 1993, the largest 1000 firms in the world—most of them MNEs—had combined assets of about $25 trillion, annual revenues of about $8 trillion, and a market value of about $7 trillion. In order to put these data in perspective, the "gross world product" that year was lower than $25 trillion.

- The largest fifty MNEs alone accounted for over $3 trillion in assets, of which approximately 40% was located outside the home country of the MNE.

- In 1993, almost $4 trillion in goods and services was traded across national borders—slightly less than 20% of world output; moreover, since the end of World War II, world trade has grown one-and-a-half times faster than world output. Almost half of world trade is now conducted by firms that can be characterized as MNEs.

- The annual value of cross-border mergers and acquisitions—an important means by which firms globalize—currently exceeds $50 billion, and in the late 1980s, it exceeded $100 billion per year. During the last fifteen years, it is likely that over $1 trillion in cross-border M&A activity took place.

- Cross-border equity flows exceeded $1.7 trillion in 1993, accounting for about 15% of the worldwide trade in equity.

What explains this dramatic growth in the worldwide scope of multinational economic activity? What are the forces that propel MNEs to look globally for their markets, technologies, labor, and capital? What factors drive the MNE's decision of whether to export, or enter into a joint venture agreement, or directly invest in plant and equipment abroad? In this chapter, we examine the answers to these questions. But first, a bit of historical background.

A BRIEF HISTORICAL BACKGROUND

Globalization is not a twentieth-century phenomenon. Globalization of economic activity has been closely linked with the development and establishment of empires worldwide through international trade since the sixteenth century. Looking back over the last three centuries, it would be nearly impossible to separate the political and economic—in particular, international trade—histories of Western nations.

Empire building in the last three centuries was closely connected with the development of, and attempts to monopolize, international trade. The Spaniards and the Portuguese won trade routes from the Mediterranean powers in the fourteenth to the sixteenth centuries; subsequently, these routes were won over and monopolized by the British, the Dutch, and the French. Major areas of the world that started out as "economic" colonies (and monopolies carved out among the three trading powers) subsequently became political colonies (including North America).[1] Numerous wars were fought in Europe and elsewhere over international trading rights, trade routes, and maintenance of trading monopolies.[2] Driving these activities and the prevalent philosophy of political economy in those days was "mercantilism"—that is, the philosophy that, from the standpoint of a nation's welfare, it is better to export than to import.

By the late eighteenth century, propelled by the Industrial Revolution, Britain had become the undisputed world economic power. Economic historians have attributed a combination of factors, such as the technical progress and innovations in textiles, coal, iron, and steel, the harnessing of steam, the displacement of agricultural workforce to meet the needs of a fast-expanding industrial base, the Protestant ethic, riches plundered from colonies, and so forth, as among the reasons why Britain became the world's first industrial country. (For instance, by the mid-nineteenth century, Britain accounted for about 40% of the world export of manufactures.)

Globalization via the development and spread of the MNE through direct foreign investment is a more recent phenomenon. The earliest MNEs were mainly European firms, setting up manufacturing facilities in the colonies to extract primary resources for conversion to finished goods back home. However, by the mid-nineteenth century, many US firms began to globalize—for example, Singer Sewing Machines, which set up a joint venture in France in 1855, Westinghouse, which set up a plant in Paris in 1879, and Kodak, which set up a plant in London in 1889.[3] The expansion of US firms was furthered after World

---

[1]For instance, the Dutch and the British East India companies—perhaps among the earliest MNEs in the world—were closely connected with the colonization of South Asia.

[2]In the US, international trade played an important role in the Civil War, between the North and the South: The South, a leading exporter, had close trading relations with Britain from whom it imported finished goods, while the North was more industrialized and protectionist. The South hoped that Britain would intercede on its behalf in order to protect its trading interests, but that never happened!

[3]By the early twentieth century, there was considerable alarm in Europe over the "invasion" of US MNEs; two widely read—and some say, influential—books in the UK in the early 1900s were titled, *The Americanization of the World* and *The American Invaders* (see M. Wilkins, *The Emergence of the Multinational Enterprise,* Cambridge, MA: Harvard University Press, 1970).

War II when both European and Japanese industrial infrastructure was largely destroyed by the war. Resource transfers for rebuilding these economies through programs such as the "Marshall Plan" gave US firms the ability to consolidate their position even more firmly. Japanese firms were relatively late entrants into the world of MNEs. Although they were major exporters prior to World War II, most did not begin to set up subsidiaries abroad until well into the second half of this century.

Alongside the development of the MNE through direct investment abroad, the numerous international agreements and institutions that were set up after World War II acted as further catalysts to the process of globalization. Such institutions included the international fixed-exchange rate monetary arrangement under the Bretton Woods agreement, the International Monetary Fund (IMF), the World Bank, the General Agreement of Tariffs and Trade (GATT), and the World Court. Although these institutions represented the outcome of voluntary acceptance of worldwide agreements among member countries, they seemingly provided the basis for a more stable worldwide environment in which MNEs could conduct their business. Many of these agreements have subsequently broken down (for example, Bretton Woods), or are considered ineffective (the World Court), or have strayed from the original agenda that led to their creation (the IMF). Yet, by the 1970s, the process of globalization propelled by the MNE as an organizational form had broken free; it had acquired a life of its own and become irreversible. In terms of its ability to move knowledge, people, capital, goods and services, and technology across borders, the process of globalization, led by MNEs, had gone far beyond the reach of any national sovereign government or international agreement. To borrow a phrase from a famous scholar of international business, Raymond Vernon, the MNE had reached a level of maturity and influence worldwide whereby it could keep "sovereignty at bay."

THE DECISION TO GLOBALIZE

In their decision to conduct business abroad, all firms have to answer at least the following three questions: (1) Why should the firm go abroad? (2) How should the firm go abroad—should it be through exports, licensing, or joint ventures, or should it be through direct investment abroad? (3) Once abroad, how should the firm compete in the global economy? Obviously, answers to these questions are not simple, and, indeed, much of the rest of the book is concerned with them. However, in this chapter, we shall provide an overview of the answers to the first two questions: the why and the how of going abroad. (We shall specifically examine the third question—MNE competitive advantage—in Chapter 14.)

WHY SHOULD THE FIRM GO ABROAD?

Firms go abroad for both organizational and environmental reasons. There is a set of factors both internal to the firm and industry, as well as external to the firm, that make it necessary to consider globalizing. The main *internal organizational and industry* reasons for going abroad are those of: (1) exploiting worldwide market imperfections (including matching a rival's move); and (2) exploiting the opportunities that arise along the life cycle of a firm's product. The main *environmental or external* reasons for going abroad are: (1) responding to the macroeconomic imperatives for globalization; and (2) exploiting the competitive advantage of nations. We now discuss each of these ideas.

The MNE as Exploiting Market Imperfections: Seeking Markets, Efficiency, and Knowledge

Within the framework of the classical economic view of perfectly competitive markets, firms are price-takers whose prices equal marginal costs, and there is no economic profit to be had in equilibrium. In such a world, there is little incentive to enter or contest a new market, and there is no incentive to become a multinational. However, the essence of competitive advantage is a firm's ability to create and sustain economic rents in an imperfect marketplace for products and factors.

Thus, to the extent that firms globalize by seeking markets abroad, seeking to make themselves more efficient, or seeking new avenues for innovation and knowledge-creation, they must be doing so in order to exploit some imperfection in the markets for products, factors, and technology. Often, a firm has a source of *monopolistic advantage*—for example, a differentiated product—over local firms in a country that it has not exploited yet, creating opportunities for economic rents in that country. Similarly, there are *factor inputs (labor, capital) or raw materials (natural resources) that can be sourced or extracted cheaper* in foreign locations, and they provide the firm with the ability to lower its costs, thereby creating the opportunity for economic rents. Moreover, many firms are repositories of *firm-specific knowledge-based capital*—for example, R&D, patents, process innovations, marketing techniques, management cultures—that can be leveraged to earn economic rents in other parts of the world.

The three reasons mentioned above are *proactive* reasons for globalization. There is also a *reactive* reason of *oligopolistic interdependence*. In other words, most firms compete in markets that are dominated by a few firms, and their relative competitive position is affected by the actions undertaken by their oligopolistic rivals. If a firm's rivals are exploiting markets abroad, seeking efficiency, or exploiting their knowledge-based capital in foreign locations, the firm may be bound to follow suit; otherwise it would risk its competitive position in the industry.[4]

The MNE and the Life Cycle of Its Products

A comprehensive and dynamic "product life cycle" theory of Raymond Vernon links the development of a firm's product over its life cycle, the firm's knowledge-based assets, the nature of the firm's production and marketing process, and why firms go abroad. The theory makes two assumptions: (1) Innovations that lead to new products and processes are costly, and require large amounts of capital and skilled labor; and (2) The innovations in the product and its manufacturing process go through a "life cycle" that consists of three stages: introduction/growth, maturity, and standardization/decline.

Stage 1: Introduction/Growth. In their early stages of development, products typically require a large amount of skilled human and financial capital, both prominent in R&D as well as the setup of the manufacturing process. The product is likely to be nonstandardized, and the production process requires a great deal of coordination and high flexibility. As a result, costs of production are likely to be substantial, and the manufacturing takes place in the country of the parent (or innovating firm). Since consumers who buy the product are inclined to be "innovators," they probably base their purchase decisions less on price, and the price elasticity of demand is likely to be low. Profit margins are likely to be high, and the firm is apt to be a monopolist. At this stage of introduction and growth, the firm is likely to be nonmultinational in its production and sales of the product.

Stage 2: Maturity. By this stage, the development costs are likely to have been recouped, the need for product and process innovation declines as production and sales expand, and there are relatively smaller needs for skilled labor and capital compared to the introduction stage. The high margins attract competitors, and profit margins decline due to

---

[4]In a famous study done in the early 1970s, Frederick Knickerbocker found empirical support for the theory of oligopolistic reaction. In a sample of 187 US MNEs, he found that half of them went abroad in industry clusters around a three-year time frame; three-quarters of them went abroad in industry clusters around a seven-year time frame. Moreover, he found that entry concentration was positively related to industry concentration, suggesting that the more oligopolistic an industry, the more the reactive behavior by firms in that industry vis-à-vis entry abroad.

price pressure. Adding to the price pressure is the fact that the consumer base shifts to "imitators" whose price elasticity is likely to be higher. Lowering production costs and sustaining market share become important concerns. This, in turn, may lead the firm to start looking abroad for both its markets and its factors of production. The firm may export the product abroad, and may source raw material or factors from abroad.

Stage 3: Standardization/Decline.   At this stage, the product is completely standardized, and the industry itself becomes mature. Coordination needs in production are likely to be low, and labor requirements are for the relatively unskilled. Profit margins are likely to be razor-thin, and the concern becomes solely that of finding the cheapest way (and place) to manufacture: Thus, the firm sets up production facilities abroad. It is likely that the home country of the firm becomes a net importer of the product. At this stage, the firm may try to extend the life of the product by seeking markets in countries where the product is still likely to be relatively new, typically lower-income countries. Ultimately, the industry itself is in decline, and the firm has to make the appropriate decision of when and whether to exit, or to "milk" the product as a cash cow for funds to be used elsewhere. The process of innovation starts all over again, completing the cycle.

The product life-cycle theory therefore predicts that, initially, the comparative advantage will exist in the innovating country with export-based MNEs, but over time, as the product becomes standardized, the country of comparative advantage will shift to lower-factor cost locations. Moreover, the theory suggests that MNEs will start out as exporters, and increasingly move toward direct investment abroad.

The MNE and Macro Forces of Globalization

During the course of the last three decades, many forces in the larger global economy have made it imperative—and easier—for firms to go abroad. While we shall discuss many of these forces in more detail in subsequent chapters, we mention them here briefly. There are three main macro forces that propelled the process of globalization of firms in the last few decades: (1) globalization of capital markets (including the growth and volatility of currency markets and interest rates); (2) the declining costs of transportation and communication, and the growth and reach of information technology; and (3) the growth of regional and international trading arrangements.

The last decade and a half has witnessed unparalleled growth in the volume and sophistication of global financial markets, for both regular (or direct) securities such as equity, bonds, and loans, as well as in derivatives such as options, futures, and swaps. In many instances, these markets offer more liquid and flexible sources of capital for MNEs than do many domestic capital markets.[5] The origins of the global capital market can be traced to: (1) the development of eurocurrency markets in the early 1960s, which created a pool of capital outside the regulatory purview of any sovereign authority (a "eurocurrency" is either a deposit or loan made in a currency outside the country to which that currency belongs; for instance, a dollar loan that is made to an Australian borrower from Singapore would be an example of a eurodollar loan); and (2) the breakdown of the Bretton Woods agreement of fixed-exchange rates in the early 1970s, which led not only to the development of a massive foreign currency market (see Chapter 3), but also to the development of markets for derivative financial instruments to cope with the exchange rate and interest rate volatility that resulted from the floating exchange rates. While these markets did not necessarily *cause* firms to initially undertake their globalization decision, they certainly *eased*

---

[5]As of the end of 1992, there was $1.5 trillion in eurobonds outstanding (compared to $250 billion in 1982), nearly $7 trillion in global derivatives (compared to almost nothing a decade and a half ago), and *daily* foreign currency trading volume exceeded $900 billion. As we mentioned previously, annual cross-border equity flows now exceed $1.7 trillion (this market grew at a compound annual growth rate of 28% during the period 1980-1990).

the process considerably. Better access to financing sources and hedging instruments made it possible for many firms to match the currency denomination of their assets and liabilities worldwide.

The decline in transportation and communications costs in the last sixty years, as well as the growth in information technology in the last two decades, further propelled globalization. According to a study done by the Institute for International Economics in Washington, DC, a three-minute transatlantic telephone call now costs 1.5% of what it cost in the 1930s; similarly, the average cost of air transport is 18% of what it was sixty years ago, and the average cost of ocean freight and port charges is 50% of what it was sixty years ago. The role of the growth in computer technology as well as worldwide information transmission and communication (whether through global media such as CNN, or the development of the fax machine and satellite technology) in "making the world a smaller place" are well-known.

The third important set of macro forces that propelled globalization includes worldwide agreements such as those with GATT, as well as the moves toward the unification of Europe (under the umbrella of what came to be known as EC'92), and trade agreements such as the US–Mexico–Canada North American Free Trade Agreement (for details of these, see Chapter 7).

The MNE and the Competitive Advantage of Nations

Recently, scholars have turned their attention to the issue of whether and how nations themselves compete, and how they provide the context in which firms undertaking the process of globalization are helped or hindered. Developed in their most comprehensive form by Michael Porter, these ideas are based on the assumption that comparative advantage and factor endowments are not just inherited or given at the country level, but rather, created by the firms that undertake innovation in these countries. Porter argued that, in the process, a pattern of country-based competitiveness emerges, and identified four determinants of this competitive advantage of nations:

1. *Factor Conditions:* Do the nation's factors of production help a firm compete successfully in a given industry? Moreover, does the nation provide a context in which these factors can be continuously upgraded and deployed in new ways?

2. *Demand Conditions:* Are local markets highly demanding of the firm in terms of price and nonprice factors, as well as in the quality of what it produces and sells?

3. *Related and Supporting Industries:* Are there related and supporting industries, as well as suppliers, that enable the firm to maintain close working relationships, have proximity to those suppliers, and ensure timeliness of product and information flows?

4. *Firm Structure, Strategy, and Rivalry:* Do the firms in the local economy have structures and strategies that make them flexible and effective competitors? Is there vigorous rivalry among firms in various industries, and do local laws and institutions (for example, antitrust laws) encourage such rivalry?

Porter argues that a country context that can offer affirmative answers to all these questions is likely to be one in which globally competitive firms emerge and flourish. While there are as yet no comprehensive empirical tests of whether and the degree to which each of these factors affects a firm's ability to compete globally, it would appear that there are many industries in which at least anecdotal evidence supports Porter's hypotheses. Examples include the semiconductor and the software industries in the US, the electronics and automotive industries in Japan, and the footwear industry in Italy.

HOW THE FIRM SHOULD GO ABROAD: THE MODE OF FOREIGN ENTRY

We have discussed why firms decide to globalize and what factors propel them to go abroad; however, the issue of "how" they globalize—that is, the mode of entry abroad once they decide to globalize—still remains to be addressed. In any decision to go abroad, the choice typically comes down to one of three approaches: (1) Produce at home and export abroad; or (2) Enter into a contractual agreement, such as licensing a technology or enter into a management contract, without actually owning significant amount of assets abroad; or (3) Own and control assets abroad, by having a joint venture, or through majority ownership (where the entry mode may involve either building *de novo,* or acquiring a foreign asset); this third choice is also sometimes referred to as "direct foreign investment" (DFI). These choices are summarized in Figure 2.1.

Figure 2.1   The Foreign Entry Decision

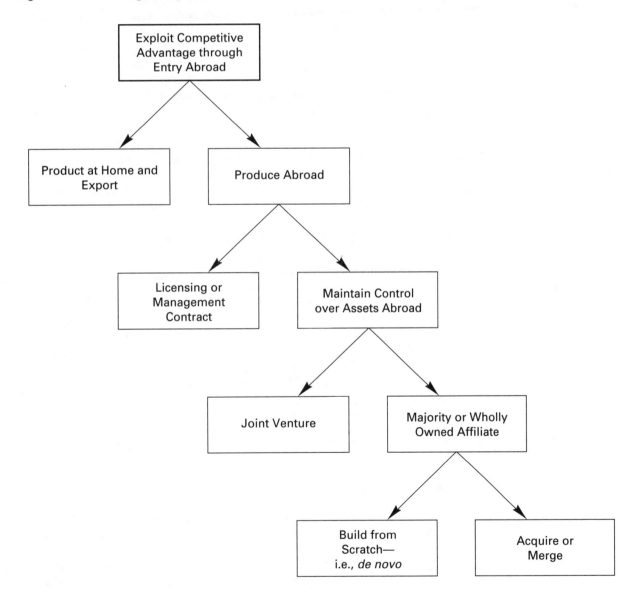

Adapted from G. Dufey and R. Mirus, "Foreign Direct Investment: Theory and Strategic Considerations," School of Business Administration, University of Michigan, May 1985 (mimeo).

There are two sets of ideas that provide guidelines for firms in making their foreign entry decision: (1) the theory of internalization, based on the economics of transactions costs of activities undertaken by the firm; (2) the impact of the two environmental variables that are unique to the MNE, MA, and MV (defined in Chapter 1).

MNEs and Internalization of Transactions in the Choice of Mode of Entry

Under the assumption that parties to any transaction are basically driven by the imperative of self-interest maximization, and that there is likely to be information asymmetry between the parties, the theory of transaction cost economics (TCE) argues that transactions (defined to be transfers of goods and services across a "technologically separable interface") in market settings may be prone to friction and failure, resulting in transaction costs for firms undertaking them. Transactions or exchanges that are more likely to entail such costs are characterized by three attributes: (1) They have *asset specificity*—the asset involved in the transaction cannot be redeployed to alternative uses or users without loss in value; (2) There is the likelihood of a greater *frequency of interaction* between the parties to the transaction; and (3) There is *uncertainty* surrounding the outcome of an arms-length transaction. The greater the asset specificity, the higher the frequency of interaction, or the greater the uncertainty, the greater the transaction cost. If the potential cost of undertaking such transfers through markets exceeds the costs of undertaking them within the firm, parties to the transaction will have the incentive to "internalize" such transactions within the firm.

The logic of TCE is a dominant paradigm that explains patterns of MNE entry abroad. The TCE logic is that the MNE will "internalize" through direct foreign investment (ownership and control of assets abroad) in situations where arms-length contracting modes (that is, export or contractual modes of entry) are prone to failures. In particular, the MNE will internalize through the DFI entry mode when its investment abroad is primarily in the form of knowledge-based assets such as technology, managerial skills, corporate culture/shared values, organizational structure, and so forth that result in high asset specificity. The incentive to internalize through DFI would be correspondingly greater if the potential frequency of interactions with buyers in the foreign country is likely to be greater (for example, if the firm plans a foreign presence for the long haul), and if there is a great deal of uncertainty surrounding outcomes in arms-length relations in the particular host country (for example, if exporting, management or licensing contracts are difficult to write, verify, and enforce in the particular host country).

In summary, a firm will have the incentive to enter abroad through DFI when the basis of its competitive advantage is derived from nontransferable or nonmarketable sources, such as technology, brand equity, R&D and innovation, proprietary information about a product or process, and so forth. In such instances, there is the likelihood that exporting or licensing may not be effective in transferring the competitive advantage, or even if it were, there is the likelihood that the knowledge embodied in the asset or the product may be diffused too easily, without the firm being able to capture any rents from it.

MNEs and the Role of MA and MV in the Choice of Mode of Entry

Although internalization may argue for a particular mode of entry, factors in the MNE environment, notably multiple sources of external authority (MA) and multiple denominations of value (MV), can constrain or alter the choice of the particular mode. In the presence of high MA, the MNE should seek to minimize its asset commitments in a specific host country, given the greater likelihood of asset and cash flow vulnerability to the authority of the sovereign state. Therefore, when MA is high, the MNE should choose export of contractual modes of entry, even if internalization considerations argue otherwise; when MA is low, the MNE should choose the DFI mode of entry.

MV, however, has the opposite set of implications. When the degree of MV is high, firms with most of their assets in the home country and with relatively high ratios of export-to-investment abroad will be vulnerable to unanticipated real exchange rate shifts (see Chapter 5 for more details). The greater the concentration of productive assets in one location, the greater the fluctuations in asset values and prices of its exports that would result from swings in real currency values. Since the primary risk of MV arises from unanticipated changes in currency values, it is not possible for the firm to protect itself against this risk through traditional techniques of financial hedging. Protecting against MV will require the firm to diversify its investment base so as not only to diversify the value of its assets, but also to have the ability to shift its production and export worldwide from multiple locations in response to adverse or favorable currency movements, which may often require having to carry excess capacity worldwide. Clearly, then, a high degree of MV would favor the DFI mode of entry, in order to take advantage of the benefits from asset diversification. However, if MV is low, there is little value to asset diversification, and therefore, the MNE would prefer export and contractual modes of entry in order to avoid the costs of carrying excess capacity worldwide.

The Complex MNE: Nonsequential Entry

While the ideas we have discussed are implicitly based on the notion of a single-product firm competing in a clearly defined industry group, it is important to recognize that many modern MNEs are complex organizations—multidivisional, multiproduct firms competing simultaneously in multiple-industry categories. The factors that propel globalization and lead firms to make particular choices of entry mode can, however, be aggregated to the firm level. For instance, an MNE in say, three industries A, B, and C may export product A from country X, license product B in country Y, and decide to produce product C in country Z, where these choices may be determined by a set of firm- or industry-specific factors relevant to products A, B, and C. For example, product A may be at the growth stage of the life cycle, product B at the maturity stage, and product C at the decline stage. In that sense, many MNEs viewed as a "snapshot" will appear to be a collection of seemingly differentiated activities that are dispersed worldwide. Yet, they simply represent an aggregation of a set of individual decisions that are based on considerations that we have discussed.

However, even in the case of a single-product firm, we have implicitly assumed that entry abroad takes place sequentially and in stages, with the firm first testing the waters abroad by exporting, and, as it finally evolves into a mature MNE, deciding to undertake DFI abroad. It is important to recognize that this is a stylized representation. Even a single-product MNE can often look like a complex organization, and at any given point in time, it would project a set of differentiated activities being undertaken worldwide. The reason is simple: How firms go abroad, or their mode of entry, is also determined by location- or host country-specific factors, notably MA and MV. In other words, even if the firm is producing only product A, it may be exporting to country X, licensing in country Y, and producing in country Z, since the combination of MA and MV may be different in the different countries (for instance, high MA and low MV would lead the firm to consider exports as the mode of entry, while low MA and high MV will lead the firm to consider DFI as the mode of entry). In other words, entry can be nonsequential, depending on the characteristics of the location.

SUMMARY

In this chapter, we examined the forces that propel firms to go global—to become MNEs—and, once they have made the decision to do so, the choices they have as to the mode of entry abroad, and what factors determine these choices. The decision to go global is affected by a set of factors internal to the firm and its industry, such as monopolistic advantage, oligopolistic reaction, and the stage in the life cycle of the firm's product. It is also affected by a set of factors external to the firm and its industry, such as globalization of capital markets, the growth and declining costs of transportation and communication technologies, regional trading arrangements, and indeed, factors that determine the "competitive advantage of nations." Once the firm has made the decision to go abroad, its choice of whether to export, enter into contractual agreements, or undertake DFI abroad is determined by internalization considerations as well as the environmental variables, MA and MV. Finally, it is important to recognize that many MNEs combine varying degrees and types of globalization—that is, they look like complex organizations undertaking different activities in different locations—resulting from the tradeoffs between firm-specific and location-specific factors.

SELECTED BIBLIOGRAPHY

BODDEWYN, J. J., and T. BREWER. "International Business Political Behavior: New Theoretical Dimensions." *Academy of Management Review* (1994), 119-143.

BUCKLEY, P. J., and M. CASSON. *The Future of the Multinational Enterprise.* London; Macmillan, 1976.

CALVET, A. L. "A Synthesis of Foreign Direct Investment Theories and Theories of the Multinational Firm." *Journal of International Business Studies* (1981), 43-60.

CASSON, M. "Transaction Costs in the Theory of the Multinational Enterprise." In A. M. Rugman, ed., *New Theories of the Multinational Enterprise.* New York: St. Martin's Press, 1982.

DUFEY, G. AND R. MIRUS. "Foreign Direct Investment: Theory and Strategic Considerations." School of Business Administration, University of Michigan, 1985 (mimeo).

DUNNING, J. H. "Explaining Changing Patterns of International Production: In Defense of the Eclectic Theory." *Oxford Bulletin of Economics and Statistics* (1979), 269-296.

HENNART, J. F. *A Theory of the Multinational Enterprise.* Ann Arbor: University of Michigan Press, 1982.

HYMER, S. H. *The International Operations of National Firms: A Study of Direct Foreign Investment.* Cambridge, MA: MIT Press, 1976.

KINDLEBERGER, C. P. *American Business Abroad.* New Haven: Yale University Press, 1969.

KNICKERBOCKER, F. T. *Oligopolistic Reaction and the Multinational Enterprise.* Boston; Harvard Business School, 1973.

PORTER, M. E. *The Competitive Advantage of Nations.* New York: Free Press, 1991.

ROOT, F. *Entry Strategies for International Markets.* Lexington, MA: Heath, 1987.

ROOT, F. *International Trade and Investment.* Cincinnati: South-Western Publishing, 1989.

RUGMAN, A. M. "Internalization as a General Theory of Direct Foreign Investment: A Reappraisal of the Literature." *Weltwertschaftliches Archiv* (1980), 365-379.

SUNDARAM, A. K., and J. S. BLACK. "The Environment and Internal Organization of Multinational Enterprises." *Academy of Management Review* (1992), 729-757.

TEECE, D. "A Transaction Cost Theory of the Multinational Enterprise." In M. Casson, ed., *The Growth of International Business;* London: Allen & Unwin, 1983.

VERNON, R. "International Investment and International Trade in the Product Life Cycle." *Quarterly Journal of Economics* (1966), 190-207.

VERNON, R. *Sovereignty at Bay: The Multinational Spread of US Enterprises.* New York: Basic Books, 1971.

VERNON, R. and L. T. Wells Jr. *The Manager in the International Economy.* Englewood Cliffs, NJ: Prentice-Hall, 1968.

WILKINS, M. *The Emergence of the Multinational Enterprise.* Cambridge, MA: Harvard University Press, 1970.

WILLIAMSON, O. E. *Markets and Hierarchies: Analysis and Antitrust Implications.* New York: Free Press, 1975.

WILLIAMSON, O. E. *The Economic Institutions of Capitalism.* New York: Free Press, 1985.

chapter 3

Foreign Exchange: The Basics

In this chapter, we introduce one of the most pervasive and influential features of the international environment in which MNEs operate: the market for national currencies, or the foreign exchange market. As we shall see in subsequent chapters, foreign exchange markets create a qualitatively new set of issues for MNEs, including the different types of exchange rate exposure for a firm's operations. First, however, it is necessary to understand some of the underlying forces in the foreign exchange market and some of its basic institutional features.

We will begin by defining some of the commonly used and necessary terminology. We will then discuss the purchasing power parity theory, one of the most important ideas underlying the theory and practice of international finance and foreign exchange markets. The purchasing power parity theory enables us to understand the distinction between nominal and real exchange rates, a distinction whose importance will become clear in subsequent chapters. These ideas will be integrated with those relating to the influence of interest rates, which will lead to two other crucial underpinnings of international finance theory, the covered interest parity theorem and the uncovered interest parity theorem. Using these ideas, we will summarize the variables that influence the value of currencies in the medium term and examine the reasons why they are argued to do so. After providing brief descriptions of the key institutional features of currency markets, we will end this chapter with definitions of the different types of exchange rate exposure that MNEs face. (Chapters 4 and 5 will elaborate on the more pervasive types of exchange rate exposure—transaction exposure and economic exposure—and the ways in which MNEs can deal with them.)

It is important to keep one thing in mind: We believe that the role of an MNE manager is *not* to forecast exchange rates but to, first, appreciate the fact that the uncertainty induced by this aspect of the international environment is real and ubiquitous, and, second, manage and plan for the effects of this uncertainty on the operations and performance of the firm. This, in turn, requires us to understand the different ways in which MNEs are exposed to exchange rates.

For the purposes of this discussion, and unless otherwise mentioned, the United States will be considered the "home country" and the US dollar ($) the "home currency." France will be considered the "foreign country" and the French franc (FF) the "foreign currency." This discussion is, of course, generalizable to any pair of countries.

BASIC DEFINITIONS

The foreign exchange rate is the nominal price of one nation's money in terms of another, that is, the number of US dollars it takes to buy each French franc.[1] The price of one currency in terms of another can be quoted either directly or indirectly. A direct quote expresses the foreign exchange rate in terms of the number of units of home currency it takes to buy each unit of foreign currency (the same concept as, say, the number of dollars it takes to buy one hamburger). From the US perspective, a direct quote would be written $/FF. An indirect quote is the reverse—the number of units of foreign currency it takes to buy each unit of home currency (the number of hamburgers per dollar), which would be written FF/$. To avoid confusion, it is extremely important that we remember which of the two quotation methods is being used; otherwise, just about everything we do in international finance would become topsy-turvy. In our discussion of these basic ideas, we will use the direct quote ($/FF) throughout. (The effects of using the indirect quote are shown in the appendix to this chapter.)

The two commonly observed foreign exchange rates are the spot rate (which we shall denote as e_0 or, when there is no scope for confusion, just e) and the t-period forward rate (which we shall call e_t). The spot rate is today's exchange rate, or the number of dollars you have   to pay to buy each FF.[2] In actuality, this transaction is formally settled two business days after the date on which the spot transaction is entered into.

The t-period forward rate is the exchange rate available today for transactions that you may wish to make at time t. That is, you can enter into an agreement today to, say, deliver FF100 ninety days hence, at the 90-day forward rate known to you today (no money changes hands until the ninetieth day). So, for example, you would pay $(100*e_{90})$, 90 days from now. Typically, maturities are 30, 90, 180, or 360 days. Forward rates are crucially important in managing a problem that MNEs face known as transaction exposure to exchange rates, which we will examine more thoroughly in Chapter 4.

The forward rate is conceptually similar to the futures rate. Many of the differences between the two are institutional. Therefore, while actual forward rates may differ slightly from actual futures rates due to these institutional features (and because there are some minor valuation differences induced by the effects of interest rate uncertainty), for our purposes, we will use the two concepts interchangeably.

These two types of exchange rate, however, are different from the expected future spot rate, which we will express as $E(e_0{}^t)$. This rate reflects the expectation the market has about the price of a currency t days from now. $E(e_0{}^t)$ is, of course, only an expectation and is not known with certainty. We will see later that the forward rate and the expected future spot rate should be (in theory) closely related.

DEPRECIATION, APPRECIATION, PREMIUM, AND DISCOUNT

Using the direct quote, a currency is said to undergo a depreciation when there is an increase in e, and appreciation when there is a decrease in e. To repeat:

e increases => home currency depreciation

e decreases => home currency appreciation

---

[1]The nominal price is distinct from the real price, as will be made clear shortly.

[2]In the real world, there are bid-offer spreads in currency quotations, that is, a rate at which the foreign exchange market will buy ("bid") currencies from you and a rate at which it will sell ("offer") currencies to you. Bid-offer spreads are quite small for the heavily traded currencies. In order to keep the development of ideas conceptually simple, we ignore bid-offer spreads.

For example, in our hamburger economy, if the price of hamburgers (FF) goes up (the equivalent of an increase in e), we would say that the dollar has depreciated vis-à-vis the hamburger (FF) or that the hamburger (FF) has appreciated against the dollar. To be more specific, suppose the initial exchange rate is \$0.15/FF and this changes to \$0.20/FF. The number of cents we put out to buy each FF has gone up (e has increased), and this means that FF has become 5 cents more expensive with respect to the dollar—that is, the dollar has depreciated.

A foreign currency is said to be at a forward premium if

$$e_t > e_0 \tag{1}$$

that is, its forward rate is higher than the spot rate. If the inequality is reversed, we say that the foreign currency is at a forward discount. Note that the FF being at a forward premium is semantically equivalent to the dollar being at a forward discount and vice versa. The actual percentage annualized premium (or discount) is

$$\% \text{ fp} = (100)[(e_t - e_0)/e_0][360/t] \tag{2}$$

where t is the time-period forward.

PURCHASING POWER PARITY

The theory of purchasing power parity (PPP), perhaps one of the most influential ideas in all of economics, establishes a formal link between a country's price level or inflation rates (relative to another country's) and the prevailing exchange rate between the two countries. There are two well-known versions of this theory, the absolute version and the relative version.

The absolute PPP relationship says that

$$P = eP^* \tag{3}$$

where P is the domestic price level, P^* is the foreign price level, and e is the exchange rate (direct quote). If you think about it for a moment, all that PPP is about is the absence of arbitrage opportunities in a frictionless (and undifferentiated) goods market—that is, it says that the exchange rate (price levels) will adjust to eliminate discrepancies in price levels (exchange rates) for similar commodities between two countries. Consider an example. Suppose a ton of widgets costs \$1 in the United States and 7FF in France, and the exchange rate is \$0.10. For a US buyer of widgets, the FF price at the current exchange rate is only \$0.70 per ton, and thus cheaper. This will increase the demand for French widgets and decrease the demand for US widgets, raising their FF price and lowering their US price. Further, in the process of buying the French widgets, US buyers will be supplying dollars and demanding francs, leading to appreciation of the franc and depreciation of the dollar. In equilibrium, then, the theory says that US and French widget prices and the \$/FF exchange rate will adjust, resulting in PPP.

A less stringent definition of PPP is called relative PPP (or RPPP), which expresses this arbitrage relationship in terms of price levels and exchange rates today (time 0) relative to our expectation for some future point in time (time 1). It is

$$[P_1/P_0] = [e_1/e_0][P_1^*/P_0^*] \tag{4}$$

where P, P^*, and e are as above, and the subscripts 1 and 0 refer to, say, tomorrow and today, respectively. It is easy to see (if you take logarithms and juggle things around slightly) that we can also express the RPPP relationship approximately (the symbol $\approx$ means approximately equal to):

$$\Delta e \approx \Delta P - \Delta P^* \tag{5}$$

where

Δe = expected percentage change in exchange rates

ΔP = expected percentage change in domestic prices (i.e., domestic inflation rate)

ΔP^* = expected percentage change in foreign prices (i.e., foreign inflation rate)

What we have also just seen is one simple model for predicting future exchange rates. If we can reasonably predict US inflation rates and French inflation rates, RPPP tells us that the predicted percentage change in the $/FF rate is approximately equal to the estimated US inflation rate minus the estimated French inflation rate.

Now we are ready to define real exchange rates. As you probably guessed, we can define real exchange rates using both absolute and relative PPP. The definition, using absolute PPP, is

$$s = [eP^*/P] \tag{6}$$

where s is the real exchange rate, e is the nominal exchange rate, and P and P^* are as defined above.

A similar definition, using relative PPP, is

$$\Delta s \approx \Delta e + \Delta P^* - \Delta P \tag{7}$$

where Δs refers to the percentage change in the real exchange rate.

There is also an effective exchange rate, which is a multilateral rate that measures the overall nominal value of the currency in the foreign exchange market. For example, the effective US dollar exchange rate combines many bilateral exchange rates using a weighting scheme that reflects the importance of each country's trade with the United States. Several institutions (for example, the International Monetary Fund, the Federal Reserve Board, and Morgan Guaranty Trust Bank) regularly calculate and report the effective exchange rates. There is also a real effective exchange rate, adjusting for multilateral PPP relationships.

EXCHANGE RATES AND NOMINAL INTEREST RATES

The relationship between exchange rates and nominal interest rates is captured in two simple propositions: (1) the covered interest parity theorem, which deals with arbitrage in international financial markets, and (2) the speculative efficiency hypothesis, which deals with speculation in international financial markets. Each of these is described below.

Covered Interest Parity Theorem

Covered interest parity is the mechanism through which an equilibrium relationship is established between spot and forward exchange rates, and domestic and foreign interest rates. This relationship is also sometimes referred to as the interest rate parity theorem or the covered interest arbitrage condition. In addition to the notation developed thus far, suppose r_d stands for the domestic (US) t-period nominal interest rate, and r_f stands for the risk-equivalent foreign (French) t-period nominal interest rate. At any given point in time, we can observe e_0, e_t, r_d, and r_f. Is there an equilibrium relationship among these four variables? And, if this equilibrium relationship is not met, is there an arbitrage opportunity? The answer to both questions is "yes."

Let us illustrate this issue with a simple example. Suppose that the \$/FF spot exchange rate (e_0) is 0.15 (that is, it costs 15 cents to buy each FF) and the 180-day forward rate (e_t) is 0.145 (that is, the FF is at a forward discount vis-à-vis the dollar). Let us also suppose that the relevant annual interest rate in the US is 10 percent and that the corresponding French interest rate is 20 percent—that is, the 180-day interest rates are 5 percent and 10 percent, respectively.

Suppose we did the following:

Borrow	\$[X/1.05] in the US markets for 180 days (so that we repay \$$X$ in 180 days);
Convert	it into [X/(1.05)(0.15)] FF;
Invest	this amount in the FF markets to get [(X)(1.1)/(1.05)(0.15)] FF at the end of 180 days;
Sell Forward	this amount today, to guarantee ourselves \$[(X)(1.1)(0.145)/(1.05)(0.15)] 180 days from now;
Repay	the \$$X$ we owe the US bank we originally borrowed from.

The profit from this transaction is

$$X(1.0127) - X = X(0.0127) \tag{8}$$

For example, if we started with a borrowing of \$10 million, we would have netted an almost riskless profit of \$127,000—not bad for a day's work!

The profit relationship above can be reexpressed in terms of our symbols as

$$(X)[e_t(1 + r_f)/e_0(1 + r_d) - 1] \tag{9}$$

However, if everybody else in the market started doing exactly the same thing, such arbitrage profits would be driven to zero. Why this would happen is easy to see. If everyone goes through the same set of transactions,

- r_d will increase because of increased demand for domestic funds,
- r_f will decrease because of increased supply of foreign funds,
- e_0 will rise because of the spot conversion demand for FF (by supplying dollars), and
- e_t will fall because of the increased supply of forward FF (and demand for forward dollars),

thereby driving the profit in expression (9) to zero.

Thus, in a no-arbitrage equilibrium, we can equate expression (9) to zero. Then, canceling out X and rewriting the expression in (9), we have

$$[e_t/e_0] = [1 + r_d]/[1 + r_f] \tag{10}$$

This is called the covered interest parity (CIP) condition, which we can restate in a more simplified (and approximated) form. Subtracting 1 from both sides in expression (10), we have

$$(e_t/e_0) - 1 = [(1 + r_d)/(1 + r_f)] - 1$$

or

$$(e_t - e_0)/e_0 = (1 + r_d - 1 - r_f)/(1 + r_f) \qquad (11)$$

where the term $[(e_t - e_0)/e_0]$ is the percentage forward premium on the foreign currency.

We can juggle things around a bit and rewrite the above as:

$$r_d - r_f = (e_t - e_0)(1 + r_f)/(e_0)$$
$$= [(e_t - e_0)/e_0] + [(e_t - e_0)r_f/e_0] \qquad (12)$$

Now, note that the second term on the right side is one that multiplies two "percentages" and is thus a very small number that can usually be ignored. Ignoring it, then, we have a simplified (and approximated) restatement of the covered interest parity condition:

$$(e_t - e_0)/e_0 \approx r_d - r_f \qquad (13)$$

or, the percentage forward premium on the foreign currency is approximately equal to the domestic nominal interest rate minus the foreign nominal interest rate.

Empirical studies generally show that the covered interest parity relationship holds up quite well, particularly when measured using Eurocurrency interest rates. With increased global capital market integration (that is, increased capital mobility between countries), the relationship is becoming more true of pairs of domestic interest rates as well, at least in the industrialized countries. Indeed, bankers often use the CIP model to quote forward rates, a rare example of a model driving reality (rather than the other way around!).

Speculative Efficiency Hypothesis

In this discussion of the theory of speculation in foreign exchange markets, we will assume risk-neutral speculators, by which we mean speculators who care only about *expected* returns and not about the standard deviation (risk) in returns. This theory could also be applied to risk-averse cases, but with no significant gain in insights for our present purposes.

The concept of speculation is really quite simple. If you expect a currency (or anything else) to appreciate in value, you want to buy into it (be "long" in it); if you expect it to depreciate, you want to get out of it ("short" it).

Recall that $E(e_0^t)$ is the future spot rate you expect will be realized at time t. Recall that this is an unknown variable. All we have today is an *expectation* of what the value of the currency is going to be when date t rolls around.

The concept of speculation stated above translates more formally into the following:

If $e_t > E(e_0^t)$, get out of FF (the foreign currency).

If $e_t < E(e_0^t)$, get out of $ (the domestic currency).

In the first case, our expectation is that the forward rate overpredicts the future spot rate for FF and underpredicts the future spot rate for $. Thus, we want to buy into $ (and out of FF).

An example will perhaps make this clearer. We know that the 180-day forward rate on FF is 0.14. Suppose that we think that the actual future spot rate is going to be 0.15 (that is, we think that the forward rate known to us today *underpredicts* the expected future spot rate). Using the decision rule above, we want to get out of \$ and into FF. Here is why: We buy FF forward at 14 cents; when the 180th day comes around, if our expectations are realized, we can sell these FF for 15 cents. We would have made a profit of 1 cent on every FF we bought. (As an exercise, work out what would happen if, instead, $e_t = 0.15$ and $E(e_0{}^t) = 0.14$.)

Now, if others in the market also form the same expectation (in efficient markets, there is no reason to assume that they aren't equally smart), they will start buying FF forward and pushing up the price. In fact, and even if no one else in the market shares our expectation, our going into an "equilibrated" market with a sudden and sizeable demand for forward FF will have a similar effect. In the process, e_t will rise until

$$e_t = E(e_0{}^t) \tag{14}$$

(it goes home).

Likewise, when the forward rate *overpredicts* the expected future spot rate, we will demand forward \$ (and supply forward FF), so that e_t is driven down until the equality in expression (14) is again attained.

This relationship—that the forward rate is the best unbiased predictor of the future spot rate—is called the speculative efficiency hypothesis.

Uncovered Interest Parity Theorem

If (14) is true, we can conceptually substitute $E(e_0{}^t)$ in place of e_t in the covered interest parity condition, with the rather interesting implication that

$$[E(e_0{}^t) - e_0]/e_0 \approx r_d - r_f \tag{15}$$

or, that the expected future (percentage) depreciation of the domestic currency is equal to the domestic nominal interest rate minus the foreign nominal interest rate. (Note that the expected future depreciation of the domestic currency is semantically equivalent to the expected future appreciation of the foreign currency.) This relationship is called the uncovered interest parity theorem.

Empirical tests generally show that the forward rate is not a very good predictor of the level of the future spot rate (it explains about 10% of the change in the actual future exchange rates). However, evidence is also strong that the forward rate does a better job of predicting at least the *direction* of changes to future spot rates than do about two-thirds of the better known foreign exchange forecasting services, making it one of the best unbiased predictors around.

THE FOREIGN EXCHANGE MARKET

The market for foreign exchange is the largest market in the world. Transactions in the foreign exchange market are estimated to exceed \$900 billion daily. The market operates almost twenty-four hours a day, so that somewhere in the world, at any given time, there is a market open in which you can trade foreign exchange. For example, trading starts in Sydney; before Sydney closes, trading opens in Tokyo, Hong Kong, and Singapore; before Singapore closes, trading opens in Bahrain; and so on. Nearly nine-tenths of the trades across the world involve the US dollar.

The most important participants in the market are banks. Traders in the major money center banks are constantly buying from and selling to each other; in fact, deals between banks, so-called "direct deals," account for nearly 85% of the activity in foreign exchange markets. Foreign exchange is traded "over the counter" via telephone and computer communications among banks, and not in organized exchanges such as stock exchanges.

The three common types of transactions are spot, outright forward, and swap transactions. Spot transactions involve buying or selling at today's exchange rate (the deposit transfer between the buyer's bank and the seller's bank actually occurs two business days later). Outright forward transactions involve agreement on a price today for settlement at some date in the future. Swap transactions involve an agreement to buy or sell in the spot market, with a simultaneous agreement to reverse the trade in the outright forward market. Approximately 65% of trades take place in the spot markets, 33% in swap markets, and only about 2% in the outright forward markets.

DETERMINING THE VALUE OF EXCHANGE RATES

There is a large volume of research on the underlying fundamentals that determine currency values. In the very short run (hour to hour, or even over a day or two), such fundamentals do not seem to matter much, since currency trading and speculation are driven almost entirely by technical considerations (this is consistent with the fact that direct deals account for a large proportion of foreign exchange transactions). In the medium to long term (one to five years), however, there is general agreement that the following factors are determinants of the direction in which—if not the level to which—currency values move: a country's level of economic activity (GNP or GDP), its money supply and demand (M^s and M^d), its nominal and real interest rates (r^n and r^r), its economic productivity (η), its inflation rate (ΔP), and its trade or current account balances (the value of exports minus the value of imports, or $X - M$).

In general, the effects of these variables on the future value of a currency (everything else remaining equal) and the reasons for these effects are hypothesized as follows:

- GNP increase: Increases a currency's value, since there is likely to be greater transaction demand for that country's currency.
- M^s increase: Decreases a currency's value, since there is greater supply of the currency; increased money supply could signal higher inflation.
- M^d increase: Opposite effect of M^s increase.
- r^n increase: Decreases a currency's value, through uncovered interest parity; intuitively, it could signal an increase in the inflation rate.
- r^r increase: Opposite effect of r^n increase, since it increases the inflation-adjusted yield from securities denominated in that currency.
- η increase: Increases a currency's value, because it signals GNP increase and r^r increase.
- ΔP increase: Decreases a currency's value, through PPP.
- $X - M$ increase: Increases a currency's value, since it increases the demand for that currency (to pay for its exports) and decreases the demand for the other country's currency (because of reduced imports).

Of course, it is important to keep in mind that none of these variable changes occurs in isolation, and so the effect of an individual variable may be difficult to discern. In addition, actual changes in these variables are often not necessary for currency values to change—a credible expectation by the market that these changes will occur may be sufficient (and it is difficult to pin down exactly when the expectations of market participants actually change). Finally, there may be significant currency movements even when expectations regarding a particular country's fundamentals do not change; all that may be necessary is for the market's expectations regarding a fundamental in the other country to change. It is for these reasons that foreign exchange forecasting is an exercise that is, at best, tenuous and, at worst, somewhat pointless.

Therefore, the list of variables and the effects indicated above should be used with a fair amount of caution. The role of an MNE manager is not to forecast exchange rates; rather, it is (a) to appreciate the fact that the uncertainty induced by this aspect of the international environment is real and ubiquitous, and (b) to manage and plan for the effects of this uncertainty on the operations and performance of the firm. This, in turn, requires us to understand the different ways in which MNEs are exposed to exchange rates.

TYPES OF MNE EXCHANGE RATE EXPOSURE

There are three types of impact of exchange rates on the operations and performance of MNEs: translation, transaction, and economic exposure (also sometimes called operating or real exposure). A stylized graphical description of the three types of exchange rate exposure is shown in Figure 3.1.

Figure 3.1   Types of Exchange Rate Exposure of MNEs

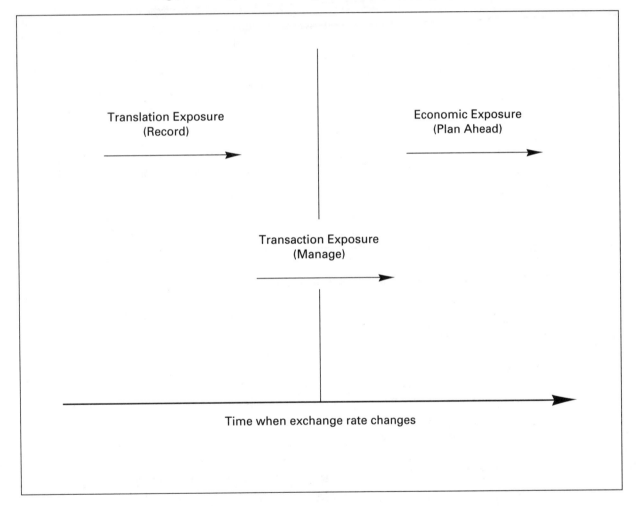

Translation exposure deals with the ex post impact of nominal exchange rate changes on the consolidated financial statements of MNEs. There are well-known accounting rules (e.g., the Financial Accounting Standards Board Rule 52, or "FASB 52" in the US) to deal with such currency translation issues. Since the issue is primarily one of "How shall I record the effect of foreign exchange movements on my operations?" we shall not deal with them here.

The second type of exposure, transaction exposure, results from the fact that firms enter into transactions of known ex ante value (in domestic currency terms) prior to—but have to settle these transactions after—an exchange rate change. These are exchange rate effects resulting from outstanding obligations across borders that have to be *managed* during the life of these obligations, rather than just recorded using accounting methods. The two common types of transaction exposure incurred by firms are (1) those relating to payables and receivables outstanding, and (2) those relating to borrowing (debt issuance) or lending (debt investment) abroad. We shall deal with transaction exposure—in particular, the payables/receivables and the debt issuance/investment cases—in Chapter 4.

The third category, economic exposure, results from the fact that the firm's expected cash flows experience unexpected changes in the real exchange rate. More precisely, if we define a firm's cash flow as π, where π is the sum of domestic and foreign cash flows (and hence a function of the real exchange rate), then a firm is said to have economic exposure to exchange rates if $\partial\pi/\partial e$—that is, the sensitivity of cash flows to real exchange rate changes—is not equal to zero. While translation and transaction exposures need not affect real cash flows (since the ex ante domestic currency value of the exposure is known, and hence can be hedged), we shall see that economic exposure has to be dealt with typically through variables such as pricing, sourcing from different locations, diversifying the manufacturing base geographically, and so forth, rather than through financial hedging techniques; that is, these are exchange rate exposures that have to be *planned for*, rather than just managed or recorded. This is dealt with in Chapter 5.

APPENDIX

A Restatement of Some of the Key Relationships Using the Indirect Quote

It might be useful to see comparisons of some of the important formulae with direct versus indirect quotes. In the real world, you should have the ability to deal with both perspectives, since some currencies are quoted one way (e.g., £) and others the opposite way (e.g., ¥). Further, you will be confronted with these differences from one article to another, one textbook to another, etc.

The best strategy, therefore, is not to try to memorize any of the formulae, but to develop the ability to derive them from first principles, given the particular currency quotation (e.g., you may be told that you are dealing with $1.7/£ in one problem, but ¥125/$ in another problem).

	Direct Quote ($/FF)	Indirect Quote (FF/$)
Appreciation of $:	e decreases	e increases
Depreciation of $:	e increases	e decreases
APPP:	$P = eP^*$	$P^* = eP$
RPPP:	$\Delta e \approx \Delta P - \Delta P^*$	$\Delta e \approx \Delta P^* - \Delta P$
Forward Premium:	$e_t > e_0$	$e_t < e_0$
CIP:	$(e_t - e_0)/e_0 \approx r_d - r_f$	$(e_t - e_0)/e_0 \approx r_f - r_d$
UIP:	$[E(e_0{}^t) - e_0]/e_0 \approx r_d - r_f$	$[E(e_0{}^t) - e_0]/e_0 \approx r_f - r_d$

Foreign Exchange Problem Set*

1) Understanding Foreign Exchange Basics

Consider the following foreign exchange quotations from the *Wall Street Journal* of Wednesday, July 29, 1992, and some additional data provided. Based on these, work through the questions that follow.

CURRENCY TRADING

EXCHANGE RATES

Tuesday, July 28, 1992

The New York foreign exchange selling rates below apply to trading among banks in amounts of $1 million and more, as quoted at 3 p.m. Eastern time by Bankers Trust Co., Telerate and other sources. Retail transactions provide fewer units of foreign currency per dollar.

Country	U.S. $ equiv. Tues.	Mon.	Currency per U.S. $ Tues.	Mon.
Argentina (Peso)	1.01	1.01	.99	.99
Australia (Dollar)	.7443	.7457	1.3435	1.3410
Austria (Schilling)	.09649	.09594	10.36	10.42
Bahrain (Dinar)	2.6522	2.6522	.3771	.3771
Belgium (Franc)	.03297	.03278	30.33	30.51
Brazil (Cruzeiro)	.00026	.00026	3838.00	3872.00
Britain (Pound)	1.9295	1.9195	.5183	.5210
30-Day Forward	1.9193	1.9089	.5210	.5239
90-Day Forward	1.8974	1.8877	.5270	.5297
180-Day Forward	1.8672	1.8578	.5356	.5383
Canada (Dollar)	.8418	.8414	1.1880	1.1885
30-Day Forward	.8402	.8398	1.1902	1.1907
90-Day Forward	.8378	.8373	1.1936	1.1943
180-Day Forward	.8348	.8342	1.1979	1.1987
Czechoslovakia (Koruna)				
Commercial rate	.0372162	.0371885	26.8700	26.8900
Chile (Peso)	.002811	.002835	355.80	352.75
China (Renminbi)	.182815	.182815	5.4700	5.4700
Colombia (Peso)	.001722	.001722	580.64	580.64
Denmark (Krone)	.1764	.1754	5.6675	5.7005
Ecuador (Sucre)				
Floating rate	.000693	.000693	1443.00	1443.00
Finland (Markka)	.24780	.24649	4.0355	4.0570
France (Franc)	.20098	.19998	4.9755	5.0005
30-Day Forward	.19978	.19881	5.0056	5.0300
90-Day Forward	.19751	.19653	5.0630	5.0882
180-Day Forward	.19437	.19340	5.1449	5.1705
Germany (Mark)	.6791	.6754	1.4725	1.4805
30-Day Forward	.6753	.6715	1.4808	1.4891
90-Day Forward	.6684	.6648	1.4962	1.5043
180-Day Forward	.6584	.6548	1.5188	1.5272
Greece (Drachma)	.005516	.005491	181.30	182.10
Hong Kong (Dollar)	.12924	.12919	7.7375	7.7405
Hungary (Forint)	.0131527	.0131389	76.0300	76.1100
India (Rupee)	.03565	.03565	28.05	28.05
Indonesia (Rupiah)	.0004927	.0004927	2029.51	2029.51
Ireland (Punt)	1.8121	1.8026	.5518	.5548
Israel (Shekel)	.4156	.4065	2.4062	2.4600
Italy (Lira)	.0008975	.0008924	1114.24	1120.55
Japan (Yen)	.007848	.007843	127.42	127.50
30-Day Forward	.007843	.007838	127.50	127.58
90-Day Forward	.007836	.007831	127.62	127.69
180-Day Forward	.007833	.007830	127.67	127.72
Jordan (Dinar)	1.5277	1.5277	.6546	.6546
Kuwait (Dinar)	3.4206	3.4206	.2924	.2924
Lebanon (Pound)	.000503	.000503	1990.00	1990.00
Malaysia (Ringgit)	.3999	.4000	2.5005	2.5003
Malta (Lira)	3.3445	3.3445	.2990	.2990
Mexico (Peso)				
Floating rate	.0003211	.0003211	3114.51	3114.51
Netherland (Guilder)	.6021	.5989	1.6610	1.6698
New Zealand (Dollar)	.5460	.5461	1.8315	1.8312
Norway (Krone)	.1728	.1718	5.7885	5.8195
Pakistan (Rupee)	.0400	.0400	25.00	25.00
Peru (New Sol)	.8390	.8390	1.19	1.19
Philippines (Peso)	.04090	.04090	24.45	24.45
Poland (Zloty)	.00007713	.00007717	12965.01	12959.01
Portugal (Escudo)	.007990	.007949	125.16	125.80
Saudi Arabia (Riyal)	.26738	.26738	3.7400	3.7400
Singapore (Dollar)	.6196	.6190	1.6140	1.6155
South Africa (Rand)				
Commercial rate	.3630	.3623	2.7548	2.7598

$/FF exchange rate (direct quote) exactly one year ago: $0.18000/FF.

Inflation rate in the US, July '91-July '92: 5%.

Inflation rate in France, July '91-July '92: 3%.

*This problem set was developed by Associate Professor Anant K. Sundaram as a basis for class discussion. © 1992.

1a) Consider the *WSJ* data for France. From the US perspective, what is the direct quote of the FF *spot* exchange rate on 7/28/92, and what is the indirect quote?

1b) (*Use direct quotes only*) What are the 30-, 90-, and 180-day *forward* exchange rates on the FF?

1c) Is the FF at a forward premium or a forward discount relative to the US$? Explain. What is the percentage forward premium or discount on the 90-day FF?

1d) $/FF exchange rate was $0.18000/FF exactly one year ago. Comparing against the $/FF exchange rate for 7/28/92, during the past year, did the dollar depreciate or appreciate? By what percentage?

1e) Inflation rates during the past year in the US were 5%, and inflation rates in France were 3%. Would the theory of RPPP have predicted a dollar depreciation or dollar appreciation over the past year?

1f) (*Using the data from questions 1d and 1e*) Compared against the actual change in $/FF, did the US$ undergo *real* appreciation or a *real* depreciation? By what percentage?

1g) Suppose you export $1,000,000 million worth of garage openers to a buyer in France for a total FF price of FF4,975,620, but your buyer in France will make the payment only 90 days from now. Suppose further that the buyer will make her payment with a cheque drawn in FF (and assume no transaction costs).

   i) Suppose the actual exchange rate 90 days from now is $0.22000/FF How many dollars will you get 90 days from now?

   ii) Suppose the actual exchange rate 90 days from now is $0.19000/FF. How many dollars will you get 90 days from now?

   iii) Suppose you do not like the exchange rate uncertainty. Given the data [from the *WSJ*], can you think of a way to get rid of the uncertainty—that is, hedge your receivable? What would you do?

2) From base price levels of 100 in 1981, German and US price levels in 1988 (both measured using consumer price indices) stood at 163 and 219, respectively. If the 1981 $/DM exchange rate was $0.31/DM, what should the exchange rate be in 1988? In fact, the exchange rate was $0.52/DM. List at least three reasons that might account for this discrepancy.

3) Suppose the $/¥ exchange rate moves from $1 = ¥135 at the beginning of the year to $1 = ¥122 at the end of the year. At the same time, the US price index rises from 130 to 145, and the Japanese price index moves from 110 to 115. What is the percentage real change in the value of the yen? Is this a real appreciation or depreciation?

4) Suppose we observe the following values in the international money markets:

Spot = $0.50/DM

Forward (1 yr) = $0.52/DM

DM Interest Rate = 8% per year

$ Interest Rate = 13% per year

     Suppose there are no taxes or transaction costs. Do covered interest arbitrage profits exist in the above situation? Describe the flows to take advantage of the arbitrage opportunity.

     Questions (5)-(10) require you to pick the correct statement from among the listed choices, and provide an explanation for your choice.

5) Assume that both uncovered interest parity (UIP) and relative purchasing power parity (RPPP) hold at all times, for all countries. Then, it must be true that

    a) Real interest rates in all countries are zero.

    b) Real interest rates in all countries are equal.

    c) Nominal interest rates in all countries are equal.

    d) Real interest rates in all countries will be equal to the percentage difference between the current spot rate and the expected future spot rate.

    e) Nothing necessarily is implied about interest rates.

6) Suppose that the ¥/$ exchange rate is 200, and the 90-day interest rates are 8% per annum for the Japanese yen, and 10% for the US dollar. Then, the 90-day ¥/$ forward rate is (closest approximation):

    a) ¥201

    b) ¥196

    c) ¥99

    d) ¥204

    e) None of the above

7) In the early 1980s, US nominal interest rates (as proxied by long-term government bond yields) were 13%, and the yields for risk-equivalent bonds in Germany and Japan were 10% and 6%, respectively. By 1991, these rates were, respectively, 7% (US), 10.5% (Germany), and 7% (Japan). Based on this data, *BusinessWeek* concluded that ". . . US firms used to have a cost of capital disadvantage relative to their German and Japanese competitors, but by 1991, their cost of capital differential had substantially narrowed."

    a) This assertion is likely to be correct.

    b) This assertion is likely to be incorrect.

    c) This assertion is incorrect, since Germany now has a wider, not narrower, cost of capital differential compared to the US.

    d) Both (b) and (c) are correct.

    e) This assertion can be correct or incorrect.

8) Ms. Wong, an arbitrager for Hong Kong and Shanghai Banking Corp., arrives at work Tuesday morning to be faced with the following quotations:

Spot exchange rate = ¥135/$

180-day forward exchange rate = ¥134.5/$

Six-month Eurodollar interest
rate (annualized) = 8%

Six-month Euroyen interest
rate (annualized) = 5%

    Given these quotations, and assuming that she has a credit line (at the given interest rates) to borrow either ¥135 million or $1 million, and assuming no transaction costs, she

    a) has no opportunities available to make arbitrage profits.

    b) can make an arbitrage profit of ¥1,505,000.

    c) can make an arbitrage profit of ¥2,505,000.

    d) can make an arbitrage profit of $8,295.

    e) can make an arbitrage profit of $9,295.

9) On November 7, 1984, Fuji Bank revealed that Mr. Jahimu Nakazawa, the chief foreign exchange trader in its New York branch, lost ¥11.5 billion ($47.91 million based on the previous day's exchange rates) resulting from his speculation using the three-month ¥/$ forward exchange rate over the summer (he had bought 1150 forward contracts). During the summer, Mr. Nakazawa forecasted that near-term inflation in the US would be significantly higher than in Japan, and based his trades on this expectation (the spot ¥/$ exchange rate then was ¥226/$). He had seriously violated Fuji's

internal rules on trading limits, but Fuji says that it failed to detect this because his branch's computer system was being replaced and the bank's accounting system had become ". . . temporarily confused."[1]
Given Mr. Nakazawa's expectations three months ago, he is likely to have

a) bet on a dollar appreciation (relative to the forward rate), and bought dollars forward for yen.

b) bet on a dollar depreciation (relative to the forward rate), and bought dollars forward for yen.

c) bet on a yen appreciation (relative to the forward rate), and bought yen forward for dollars.

d) bet on a yen depreciation (relative to the forward rate), and bought yen forward for dollars.

e) done none of the above.

10) In 1988, Walt Disney was considering raising ¥25 billion by issuing a financial instrument called the "dual-currency bond" to finance its growing worldwide entertainment operations. Dual-currency bonds are debt instruments denominated in one currency paying coupons in that currency, but paying the principal in another currency. Walt Disney was considering a three-year yen/dollar dual-currency bond with the following features: It would be issued at par, pay an annual coupon of 8% in yen, and the final total principal repayment would be US$ 116 million (rather than the yen face value).

   i) From the issuer's perspective, this dual-currency bond can be described as

     a) a straight yen bond plus a long-dated forward contract to buy US$ for ¥215.5.

     b) a straight yen bond plus a long-dated forward contract to sell US$ for ¥215.5

     c) a series of call option contracts with a long-dated forward contract.

     d) a series of forward contracts with a long-dated call option contract.

     e) none of the above.

   ii) From a yen investor's perspective, everything else remaining constant, a decrease in the spot ¥/$ exchange rate—i.e., a depreciation of the US dollar—would lead to the following impact on the value of the dual-currency bond:

     a) a decline in the value of the dual-currency bond

     b) an increase in the value of the dual-currency bond

     c) no impact on the value of the dual-currency bond

     d) offsetting impacts on coupon payments and principal payment parts of the dual-currency bond

     e) both (c) and (d)

---

[1]A postscript: Mr. Nakazawa was ultimately fired, and Fuji's board of directors took a 20% pay cut for the next six months to demonstrate their shame.

chapter 4

Foreign Exchange: Transaction Exposure

With floating exchange rates, a new type of risk was introduced into foreign transactions undertaken by MNEs—currency risk. (When exchange rates were fixed, currency risk was almost synonymous with country risk.) Since it is normal to enter into agreements to pay or receive money at some future date relative to the date on which transactions are made, participants on both sides expose themselves to potential losses (or gains) arising from currency fluctuations. Such exposure—arising from contractual agreements entered into before an exchange rate change, but settled after—is called transaction exposure to exchange rates.

The basic approach to dealing with transaction exposure is through hedging strategies. Hedging is the means by which risk associated with future cash flows is eliminated: In the process, the company buying the hedge transfers risk to the entity selling the hedge. Hedging is particularly common among MNEs; a recent study shows that over four-fifths of treasurers of companies that are engaged in international trade hedge their transaction exposure. There are various ways to hedge foreign currency transactions, but the three common approaches are those that involve (1) forward exchange rates, (2) futures exchange rates, and (3) foreign currency options.

In this chapter, we deal with the use of forward exchange rates for hedging both receivables and payables in some detail. We then briefly describe the use of foreign currency futures markets (which, you will recall, is conceptually similar to forward markets), and provide a short introduction to the use of foreign currency option markets for hedging. We also consider some of the other common techniques that MNEs use to manage their transaction exposure. Finally, we examine another broad type of transaction exposure that most MNEs face: that from lending and borrowing decisions made across different currencies. We provide some benchmarks for how firms can go about making those decisions.

FORWARD MARKETS

Forward contracts are the most common hedging instrument used by MNEs, particularly to hedge receivables and payables. The attractive feature of forward contracts is that, unlike exchange-traded contracts (for example, futures contracts), they can be tailored to suit the individual firm's needs.

Hedging Receivables

Suppose that we had a receivable of X FF, due in, say, 180 days. We decide not to wait out the 180 days because, given exchange rate fluctuations, this might be unacceptably risky. What should we do?

There are two choices: Do a forward cover or do a spot cover (also sometimes called money market cover). The simpler of the two is the forward cover. All we have to do today is sell forward the X FF we know that we are going to get 180 days hence, at the quoted forward exchange rate e_t (direct quote). We can then guarantee ourselves

$$\$(X)(e_t) \tag{1}$$

where $t = 180$, and e_t is the 180-day \$/FF forward rate.

Alternatively, we can use the spot cover, which is a little more complicated, but worth the effort if it is likely to make us better off. Suppose we (or our bank, on our behalf) could borrow in the French financial markets at a 180-day interest rate r_{tF} and lend (invest) in the US at interest rate r_{tUS}. These interest rates could be different from those that determine covered interest parity (why?); you can think of them as borrowing and lending rates, respectively.

We could then

Borrow $\quad X/(1+r_{tF})$ FF, so that we have to repay the FF lender X FF 180 days from now;

Convert $\quad$ this into US\$ today at the spot rate e, giving us $(X)(e)/(1+r_{tF})$ dollars today;

Invest $\quad$ these dollars in the US financial markets, to guarantee ourselves

$$\frac{(X)(e)(1 + r_{tUS})}{(1 + r_{tF})} \tag{2}$$

dollars 180 days from now.

If the dollar revenues from the spot cover exceed those from the forward cover, we would go with the spot cover. That is, by comparing expressions (1) and (2), and canceling out the common term X, and taking e to the right-hand side, if

$$(1 + r_{tUS})/(1 + r_{tF}) > (e_t)/(e) \tag{3}$$

we use the spot cover in hedging receivables.

On the other hand, if

$$(1+r_{tUS})/(1+ r_{tF}) < (e_t)/(e) \tag{4}$$

we use the forward cover in hedging receivables.

Note that, if our lending and borrowing rates are the same as those that determine covered interest parity, equality would obtain between the left- and the right-hand sides in (3) and (4), and we would be indifferent between spot and forward covers.

Hedging Payables

Now let us suppose that we had a payable to make, instead. That is, we know that, 180 days from now, we have to pay a French exporter Y FF. As before, we can examine both spot and forward covers. The sequence of transactions is, however, slightly different. Suppose that r_{tUS} and r_{tF} are as before. The forward cover will then be to

Invest $[(Y)(e_t)/(1 + r_{tUS})]$ to guarantee ourselves $(Y)(e_t)$ dollars 180 days from now;

Sell Forward   this amount in the FF markets today, to guarantee ourselves that we will have $(Y)(e_t)/e_t = Y$ FF 180 days from now.

The spot cover, on the other hand, is,

Convert $[(Y)(e)/(1 + r_{tF})]$ dollars into FF, to get $[Y/(1 + r_{tF})]$ FF;

Invest   this amount in the FF financial markets at the 180-day FF interest rate so that we have $[(Y)(1 + r_{tF})/(1 + r_{tF})] = Y$ FF, 180 days hence.

In this case, we would be interested in the option that minimized the amount of dollars that we put aside today to meet our FF payable. Doing a bit of juggling and canceling as we did before, we can conclude that, if

$$(1 + r_{tUS})/(1 + r_{tF}) < (e_t)/(e) \tag{5}$$

we use the spot cover in hedging payables.

On the other hand, if

$$(1 + r_{tUS})/(1 + r_{tF}) > (e_t)/(e) \tag{6}$$

we use the forward cover in hedging payables.

Note that this is the exact reverse of the decision rule for the receivables case, which leads us to wonder what we would do when we have both receivables and payables.

Receivables and Payables

When payables equal receivables, if they are in the same currency and for the same maturity, they hedge each other and, thus, the optimal hedging strategy is to do nothing. Otherwise, all you would be doing is incurring transactions costs. Normally, an MNE is likely to have differing amounts of both, in which case, the MNE should hedge the netted out payable or receivable.

FOREIGN CURRENCY FUTURES

The first exchange-traded foreign currency futures contract was introduced on the International Monetary Market (IMM)—now part of the Chicago Mercantile Exchange (CME)—in 1972. Seven currencies were traded and, since then, others have been added. The CME remains the most active market in these contracts, although a number of other exchanges have launched their own contracts—for example, Philadelphia Board of Trade, Singapore Monetary Exchange, and Sydney Futures Exchange.

Futures contracts are conceptually similar to forward contracts in that, in theory, they too obligate the buyer of the contract to buy foreign currency from the seller at a specified price on a specified future date. However, there are some important institutional differences:

- Futures contracts are "marked to market," which implies that there are daily cash flows. In a forward contract, no money changes hands until the contract expires, and, as a result, interest rate volatility could be a potential source of valuation differences between forwards and futures.
- In futures contracts, both amounts and maturities are standardized. This is not the case with forwards, which can be tailored contracts.
- Futures are traded on organized exchanges; forwards are OTC contracts.
- Futures have a secondary market; forwards typically do not.
- Futures are delivered at expiration only in about 5% of the cases; forwards are delivered in about 90% of the cases.
- Futures are used frequently for speculative purposes (that is, betting on the direction of futures price movements).

Hedging with Futures Contracts

The underlying principle of hedging with futures is quite straightforward: Whenever an underlying asset is likely to lose its value, you should get into a futures contract on that asset, which will gain in value. In other words, if you have a long position on an underlying asset, you should have a short position on the futures contract on that asset (and vice versa). Consider an example. Suppose you have an FF receivable—you then have a long position on FF during the maturity of the receivable. You would offset the exchange rate risk of this long position by taking a short position on an FF futures contract for equivalent maturity. Thus, if the FF loses value, your futures contract would gain value.

Of course, this assumes that there is a perfect negative correlation between the values of spot and futures contracts. Although this correlation is often high, it is rarely perfect. As a result, there is what is referred to as basis risk—or the risk that the movement between spot and futures prices is not exactly one for one. In actuality, this risk is usually small for most of the heavily traded currencies.

Although foreign exchange futures contracts offer liquid markets for hedging foreign exchange movements, their inflexibility and the difficulties involved in managing basis risk make them somewhat more difficult than forward contracts to use for specific corporate hedging purposes.

CURRENCY OPTIONS

Option contracts give the buyer of the contract the right, but not the obligation, to buy or sell something. The holder (buyer) of a currency option has the right, but not the obligation, to exchange a fixed amount of one currency for another at a fixed exchange rate (strike or exercise price) on or before a predetermined future date. An option to buy foreign currency is a call option ("I call it in"), and an option to sell, a put option ("I put it to you"). Since all foreign exchange transactions involve buying one currency by selling another, a call option on the foreign currency is the same as a put option on the domestic currency.

Options that can be exercised only at maturity are called European options, while those that can be exercised any time up to (and including) maturity are called American options. This right to exercise the option comes with an option premium or option price (usually paid two working days after the deal), and represents the maximum loss to the buyer, and thus, also the maximum profit to the seller.

There are three basic types of currency options:

Options on Spot: These are options to buy or sell spot foreign currency and can be either American or European options.

Options on Futures: These are options to go long (call) or short (put) an exchange-traded currency futures contract, and are typically American options.

Futures-Style Options: These are basically speculative contracts where investors are speculating on the direction of the option price: The buyer agrees to pay (receive) a daily cash flow equal to any decrease (increase) in the market value of the option, in addition to which there is an option to buy or sell the underlying currency. Premiums are paid only at exercise, and are marked-to-market daily.

The currency option that is usually used for hedging purposes is the option on spot exchange rates.

Using Options on Spot to Hedge

Since they offer downside protection, buying options is basically like buying insurance: Under certain circumstances, you never need to use insurance—it "expires worthless"—but when things go bad, it has value. The basic idea behind hedging with options is as follows. When you have foreign currency to sell (that is, the case of receivables) and you want to protect some floor value of the foreign currency in domestic currency terms, you would buy a put option. When you have foreign currency to buy (that is, the case of payables) and you want to put a ceiling on the value of the foreign currency in domestic currency terms, you would buy a call option.

Let us see this with an example.[1] Suppose you had a receivable for FF10 in one month, and as a US exporter, you want to ensure that its value does not fall below $2. Let us suppose that it would cost you ¢1 to buy a put option on FF1 at an exercise price of ¢21 each. You would then buy 10 put options on the FF (that is, options to sell the FF), at an exercise price of ¢21 each. Thus, if the value of FF settles below ¢21 at maturity, you can sell your 10FF to guarantee yourself $2.10. This covers not only the ¢10 you paid to buy the option, but also the $2 you wanted to get out of your receivable. (Notice, however, that the option was not free: You have to pay ¢10 for the right to guarantee yourself at least $2.) If the FF value is greater than ¢21 one month from now, you would let the option expire worthless, since you can get more than ¢21/FF (that is, more than $2 on your receivable) by selling your FF in the market at the then-prevailing spot rate. In summary, you can use put options to put a floor price on the domestic currency value of foreign exchange:

Floor price = Exercise price of the put – Price of the put

Similarly, suppose you had a payable for FF10 in one month, and, as a US importer, you want to ensure that the total amount of dollars you pay does not exceed $2. Let us suppose that it would cost you ¢1 to buy a call option on FF1 at an exercise price of ¢19 each. You would then buy 10 call options on the FF (i.e., options to buy the FF), at an exercise price of ¢19 each. If the value of FF goes above ¢19, you can still buy your 10FF for the total exercise price of $1.90. Adding the ¢10 you paid to buy the 10 call options, your total dollar outlay would be $2. If the FF value falls below ¢19 one month from now, you would let the call option expire worthless, and be happy with the smaller amount of dollars you need to pay by buying your FF in the market at the then-prevailing spot rate. In summary, you can use call options to put a ceiling price on the domestic currency cost of foreign exchange:

Ceiling price = Exercise price of call + Price of the call

[1]The floor and ceiling prices we will calculate are approximate, for two reasons: (1) we ignore transaction costs, and (2) since option premiums are paid up front while options are exercised at maturity, we have to make a slight adjustment for the time value of money. We assume away these two factors in order to develop the hedging logic in the simplest possible way.

Of course, this assumes that you pay a fair price for these options. There are well-known models (for example, the Black-Scholes model and its variants) for pricing each type of option, and these can be found in any textbook on international finance.[2]

A wide range of products is now available, and more are being researched and developed. Various payoff structures, each with several names, have been developed to get over investors' unwillingness to pay up-front premiums. These can delay the premium payment until maturity (for example, "Boston" options), reduce the premium by giving up some of the benefit (participating forwards), or get rid of it all together (cylinder options). Nearly all these more complex instruments are just combinations of call and put options (and sometimes spot and forward currencies) in varying amounts and/or different exercise prices.

OTHER WAYS TO MANAGE TRANSACTION EXPOSURE

Although foreign exchange forwards and currency options are the most popular ways for most MNEs to hedge their transaction exposure, they are especially useful when the contracts outstanding are relatively short term in nature—for example, less than one year's maturity. In addition, for MNEs that have many such contracts outstanding, the transaction costs associated with these forms of hedging, although reasonable, can quickly add up.

Reducing the Transaction Costs of Hedging

The three most common ways by which MNEs seek to reduce transaction costs in hedging are by (1) matching foreign assets/revenues to foreign liabilities/expenses, (2) invoicing in the home currency, and (3) putting currency adjustment clauses in outstanding contracts. Matching of assets and liabilities, and of revenues and expenses, involves looking for opportunities for natural hedges. For example, an MNE that exports a large amount to a particular country may look for ways to import intermediate inputs and raw materials from that country; an MNE with long-term assets in a foreign country may look for ways to issue debt denominated in that country's currency (see below for ramifications of the debt decision). Invoicing in the home-country currency is another way that MNEs seek to reduce transaction exposure (particularly those MNEs who incur most of their costs in the home currency). However, while this may sound like a simple policy, it can introduce other kinds of problems, notably of economic exposure to exchange rates (see Chapter 5): For example, if the invoicing is done in dollars and if the dollar appreciates in real terms, demand abroad for the exporter's products would fall. Finally, currency adjustment clauses would require the MNE to write into contracts ways in which the foreign buyer (or seller) would compensate the firm in the event that the exchange rate moves above or below a certain amount.

Long-Term Hedging: Currency Swaps (Advanced Section)

The most common approach to dealing with transaction exposures in the medium and long terms is through the use of currency swaps. In a currency swap, the MNE typically agrees to make periodic payments, based on either fixed or floating interest rates, to a counterparty, who in turn makes periodic payments to the MNE in a different currency. The payments are based on notional principal amounts, which are fixed at the initiation of the swap. There are many uses for currency swaps. Borrowers with funding advantages in different markets can exchange these benefits to gain attractive funding costs in nondomestic currencies. Swaps

---

[2]Because it would require considerable digression and substantial notation, we shall not develop this model here. For those readers who are already familiar with the Black-Scholes model in the context of equity options, an important point to note is that, unlike the standard model, the option pricing model for foreign currencies requires the use of two interest rates—domestic and foreign—rather than one (recall the connection between the two interest rates from covered interest parity in Chapter 3).

can also be useful in the management of existing liabilities and assets, in hedging currency exposure associated with acquisitions, divestitures, and management of subsidiaries abroad, and in circumventing foreign exchange regulations. Unlike forwards, swap markets are liquid out to around 10 years, and swaps as long-dated as 30 years are not unheard of. Also, because there is a liquid two-way market, cross-currency swaps can be tailored to meet the requirements of almost any MNE. Many major corporations, financial institutions, governments, and governmental entities worldwide currently use these instruments.

Example of a Currency Swap. Suppose a French company would like to borrow floating-rate US dollars to finance a foreign investment, but is not very well known outside France. There is a similar US company, which would like to borrow fixed-rate French francs (FF). An intermediary may get involved in putting the two companies together through the following kind of currency swap: The French company issues a fixed-rate FF bond, turns the FF proceeds over to the US company, and agrees to pay the US company its dollar coupon on principal obligations on US dollar floating rate debt that the US company would issue (and whose proceeds would be turned over to the French company). The US company has the fixed-rate payment commitment in the swap deal, and is said to be "long" the swap (while the French company, which has a floating-rate payment commitment in the swap deal, is said to be "short" the swap).

Valuation of Swaps. The value of a swap at any time is simply the value of the portfolio that is long one bond and short the other: That is, it is the difference between the values of the two bonds. In a currency swap, this change in value is dependent on two factors: interest rate changes and exchange rate changes.

The general effects of these changes are as follows: (1) A change in interest rates would affect the long side of the swap, primarily, since that is the side that has a fixed-payment obligation; the value of floating rate debt is affected to a far lower degree by interest rate changes (since coupon payments on floating rate debt change as the interest rate changes). For example, an increase in interest rates would make the long side better off, since that party is committed to making lower fixed-coupon payments than what the market currently requires; similarly, a decrease in interest rates makes the long side worse off, since it is locked into paying a higher fixed coupon than what the market currently requires. (2) A depreciation of one of the currencies makes the party who is getting the coupon payments in that currency worse off; on the other hand, an appreciation makes that same party better off.

Consider the long side in the previous example—the US firm. Suppose US dollar interest rates fall, and nothing happens to FF interest rates. Since the US firm has a dollar floating-rate asset, its asset value does not change (approximately speaking); on the other hand, since FF interest rates do not change, the value of its fixed-rate FF liability does not change either. Therefore, in this instance, the value of the swap does not change on account of the interest rate change. However, suppose the US dollar depreciates against the FF. This depreciation must mean that the party receiving the dollar coupons and paying the FF coupons—the US firm—is made worse off by the extent of the depreciation.

BORROWING OR LENDING ACROSS CURRENCIES

A common problem that we face in the multinational context is how do we compare between an $X\%$ US dollar loan, against, say, a $Y\%$ French loan? If we are borrowing money (that is, issuing bonds), which is cheaper? If we are lending money (buying bonds) which will give us a greater return?

We will develop the analysis below on the assumption that tax rates on current and capital gains are the same between the US and France. Assume that a firm considers issuing an N-year bond (that is, it wants to borrow money). It is considering the US (dollar;

\$) and France (French franc; FF) as two possible places to issue its bonds. The bonds yield r_{US} and r_{FF}, respectively, and are sold at par. Interest is paid at the end of each year, and the principal will be paid as a lump sum at the end of year N. The US dollar is expected to undergo a cumulative depreciation against the French franc of $(e_N - e_0)/e_0 = (\Delta e)_N$, over the entire period 0 to N. We can then compute the average annual (expected) depreciation (call it Δe). Δe can be computed either as an arithmetic mean $(\Delta e)_N/N$, or as a geometric mean (the Nth-root of $\{1+(\Delta e)_N\}$). Given our continuing assumption of direct quotes, recall that Δe will be a positive number.[3]

It can then be shown that the equivalent dollar yield of French franc financing is equal to

$$r_{FF}(1 + \Delta e) + \Delta e \tag{7}$$

where Δe is the annual expected depreciation of the US dollar.[4] The intuition is that, since the dollar is expected to depreciate against the French franc, the market will expect a higher dollar coupon (relative to the French franc coupon, r_{FF}) so that it can be induced to hold the dollar bond.

Thus, for the yield on the dollar bond to equal the yield on the FF bond on an exchange rate–adjusted basis (from the market's standpoint), the market should require a dollar coupon (call it r_{US}^*) given by

$$r_{US}^* = r_{FF}(1 + \Delta e) + \Delta e \tag{8}$$

for it to be indifferent between the two. Now, if we can issue at a coupon rate below r_{US}^* in the US (given our view of Δe), then we would prefer to issue the bond in the US. (Suppose you are trying to choose between issuing a 10-year bond in the US with a yield-to-maturity of 9%, and an equivalent-risk 10-year UK bond with a yield-to-maturity of 13%. Assume that both bonds pay coupons annually, and are issued at par. The current \$/£ exchange rate is \$1.7/£, and you expect the US dollar to appreciate to \$1.3/£ 10 years from now. Where would you issue the bond?)

SUMMARY

In this chapter, we examined the role of transaction exposure to exchange rates—the exposure to MNEs resulting from contractual agreements entered into before a probable future exchange rate change, but settled after the future exchange rate change—and the ways in which MNE managers can hedge it. For short-term transaction exposure, the most common approach uses forward markets. Managers also use the futures markets, although these are somewhat less flexible than forward markets. Currency options provide another increasingly popular means of short-term transaction exposure hedging. Managers also attempt to manage transaction exposure by matching assets and liabilities or revenues and expenses abroad, by invoicing in the home currency, or by putting currency adjustment clauses in outstanding contracts. The most commonly used financial technique for hedging long-term transaction exposure is currency swaps. Finally, using some of the analytical ideas developed in this chapter and in Chapter 3, we examined how managers can compare lending and borrowing opportunities across various currencies.

---

[3]If the US dollar is expected to appreciate, Δe will be a negative number.

[4]Note that $\Delta e=(e_1-e_0)/e_0$, and is basically the "expected percentage depreciation of the domestic currency."

Piermont Inc.*

On Monday, 31 August, Danielle Webster received the good news. It came in the form of a faxed contract from Germany and was signed by Ansgar Vorstmann, the German distributor she had first met four months ago. The contract confirmed an order for 250 of Piermont's frozen yogurt dispensers and represented $908,000 worth of business. This was Piermont's first major foreign order and a great coup for Danielle, President and CEO of the $8 million manufacturer.

The fax indicated that a first payment of DM 147,000 was being wired to Piermont's bank the next day. This was the first time that Piermont had conducted business in another country and Danielle hoped to minimize any problems. Given the recent confusion with the European ERM, she knew there had been a great deal of Deutschemark (DM) exchange rate volatility since she had first signed the deal with Vorstmann back in June.

THE PIERMONT FROZEN YOGURT COMPANY

Piermont Frozen Yogurt was started in 1981, in a small town on the New Hampshire–Vermont border, just as the health craze was taking hold and people were turning to low-fat foods as part of a healthier lifestyle. The company was started by Danielle and a fellow engineer after they both left their previous jobs as production engineers at a New England ice-cream manufacturer. They developed some unique designs for small-scale mixing and dispensing machinery and designed most of the production equipment themselves.

*The case was developed and written by Nick A. Hall under the supervision of Associate Professor Anant K. Sundaram as a basis for class discussion. © 1993.

The firm was successful in its early stages because they combined a low-fat product with imaginative, premium flavors. However, distribution quickly became expensive outside the New England area and a number of large ice-cream manufacturers moved into the market, squeezing Piermont's profits and putting the company at a disadvantage due to its comparatively lower volume of production. The company, meanwhile, continued to develop its mixing and dispensing machinery to the point where it was selling the dispensing equipment to local catering firms and restaurants, along with the yogurt product. The company realized that it had some unique skills in this area.

In 1986, the company started full-scale production of frozen yogurt dispensing machinery, adding assembly line staff and expanding their manufacturing facilities. They continued to concentrate on restaurants, fast-food outlets, and small-scale producers, and they used the Piermont reputation for premium frozen yogurt as leverage to their industrial sales. Within two years, the catering equipment business exceeded two million dollars in revenues, and Piermont stopped selling frozen yogurt altogether. Four years later, they were distributing over most of the country, producing about two thousand units a year.

As the country went into recession in the early 1990s, sales went flat and rising costs resulted in the company suffering two years of minor losses. Danielle decided to develop some of Piermont's overseas contacts to bolster the flattening sales. Three of the food-chains to whom they had sold dispensers in the United States had subsequently sent their Piermont equipment overseas—saying that they couldn't obtain the same quality in a compact unit compared to that provided by their Piermont equipment. Sensing a potential market, Danielle contacted Ansgar Vorstmann, a catering equipment distributor in Bremen, to talk about using the German company as a Piermont distributor.

The two met in Boston in the Spring of 1993 and discussed a possible deal in some detail. Vorstmann said that he was impressed with the quality and reputation of the Piermont product and thought it had great potential in the German market. However, his firm had not dealt with foreign suppliers before and he was wary of doing business in US dollars because of the high level of exchange rate uncertainty. Danielle assured him that Piermont would be happy to conduct all transactions in DM and Vorstmann requested a firm offer.

On 16 June 1993, Danielle faxed an offer to Vorstmann for 250 of their restaurant-style dispensers at a total price of DM 1,476,862 to be delivered over a period of six months. The offer stipulated a down payment of DM 147,000 at the time that the offer was signed. This payment would be followed by one of DM 591,000 three months later, after delivery of the first 120 units, and the balance of DM 738,862 six months after signing the contract. Danielle had priced the entire order using the June 14, 1993, spot exchange rate of 1.6265 DM to the dollar (see *Exhibit 1*).

EXHIBIT 1

The June Calculation

Offer Price Calculation	
Cost to Piermont	$825,500
Desired profit	$82,500
Total dollar price	$908,000
Spot exchange rate	1.6265
Deutschemark price	1,476,862

FALLING PROFITS

Glancing over the fax, Danielle thought about what she had read in the press over the last two months. The dollar had strengthened against the Deutschemark during this period and she recalculated the new revenue from the contract, with the spot exchange rate listed in that day's *Wall Street Journal* (see *Exhibit 2*). To her dismay, she realized that the exchange rate shift had reduced the company's expected revenues by $24,181—29% of the anticipated profit margin—and she wondered what she could do to prevent further erosion of profits due to the DM exchange rate movement. She decided to contact her banker for advice.

The bank suggested that she had three courses of action. She could do nothing and convert the money at the prevailing spot rate as and when the receivables were paid off. As long as the rate didn't fall too far, Piermont would still stand to make something on the deal. Or, she could cover the risk with a financial hedge either in the forward exchange markets or in the money markets.

Doing Nothing

This would mean the subsequent payments would be converted into dollars at whatever the DM spot rate was at the time. The exchange rate could easily move back up to its original value of 1.6265, but, it could also become more unfavorable.

Hedging in the Forward Exchange Markets

If Piermont took this choice, it would enter into a forward contract to sell the DM 591,000 in 90 days and the DM 738,862 in 180 days. The bank quoted a price of 1.6857 DM/$ for the 90-day contract and 1.6964 DM/$ for the 180-day contract. The company would then be guaranteed these rates when the payment was received from abroad. Danielle could use these proceeds to finance the working capital required to complete the production of the units, and repay part of another outstanding $308,000 short-term loan.

Hedging in the Money Markets

To use the money markets, Piermont would take out two DM loans—one of 90-day maturity and the other of 180-day maturity—so that the principal plus the accrued interest would equal the DM payments to be received. The bank quoted DM interest rates of LIBOR plus 150 basis points for the loans (see *Exhibit 3*). Again, Piermont could then use these proceeds to finance its working capital needs and repay part of the outstanding short-term loan.

Danielle thought that they would need about $500,000 in working capital to finance the production and she had planned to draw this down from their existing line of credit. The

EXHIBIT 2
Currency Trading Exchange Rates on Monday, August 31, 1993

| Country | US $ equiv. | | Currency per US $ | |
	Mon.	Fri.	Mon.	Fri.
Germany (Mark)	.5984	.6008	1.6710	1.6645
30-Day Forward	.5966	.5988	1.6763	1.6699
90-Day Forward	.5932	.5956	1.6857	1.6791
180-Day Forward	.5895	.5918	1.6964	1.6899

Source: *Wall Street Journal.*

outstanding loan of $308,000 was part of a $950,000 line of credit that Danielle had arranged with the bank. The interest charged was prime plus 150 basis points and this was adjusted quarterly. Currently, the prime rate was 6%. The banker told Danielle that any additional, unused proceeds could be invested in a Eurodollar time deposit in London (interest rate data shown in *Exhibit 3*).

EXHIBIT 3

Selected Interest Rates on Monday, August 31, 1993

Interest Rates	*Now*	*3 months*	*6 months*
US dollars			
Eurodollar rates (LIBOR)		3.19%	3.40%
Dollar CDs		3.00%	3.10%
Prime rate	6.00%	6.00%	6.00%
Deutschemarks			
Eurocurrency (LIBOR)		6.56%	6.38%
Prime rate	9.50%	9.50%	9.50%

Source: *The Financial Times.*

TOO MANY OPTIONS

That afternoon, Danielle discussed the deal with Piermont's CFO who mentioned the additional possibility of using a DM options contract. They both wondered what the benefit of doing so would be, and turned to the *WSJ* again. Danielle noticed a list of Deutschemark options prices (see *Exhibit 4*) and she wondered why the banker hadn't discussed that as another possible path for Piermont to take.

The next day, Piermont's account received the proceeds from the down payment, which had been sold at a spot price of 1.6767 for $87,672. This meant Piermont had already lost $2,706 of the profit they had anticipated. Danielle had to make some quick decisions before exchange rate movements turned this profitable piece of business into a loss-making one.

EXHIBIT 4

Currency Trading Options Prices on Monday, August 31, 1993

Strike Price	Expiration	Vol.	Last	Calls Vol.	Puts Last
German Mark					
62,500 German Mark–cents per unit					
50	Sep	1	9.72	. . .	. . .
62,500 German Marks EOM–cents per unit					
59	Sep	. . .	. . .	31	0.44
62,500 German Marks European style					
55.5	Oct	. . .	. . .	50	0.06
56	Oct	. . .	. . .	100	0.10
57.5	Sep	. . .	. . .	100	0.03
58	Sep	. . .	. . .	100	0.06
59	Dec	. . .	. . .	22	1.33
59.5	Oct	16	1.10	5	0.88
60	Sep	20	0.36	. . .	. . .
61	Sep	40	0.10	. . .	. . .
62	Sep	20	0.04	. . .	. . .
62,500 German Marks–cents per unit					
52	Dec	. . .	. . .	157	0.06
55	Dec	. . .	. . .	3	0.23
56	Sep	50	3.85	. . .	. . .
56	Dec	. . .	. . .	5	0.40
57	Sep	50	2.85	. . .	. . .
57	Dec	. . .	. . .	20	0.66
57.5	Sep	20	2.35	. . .	. . .
57.5	Oct	. . .	. . .	40	0.32
58	Sep	20	1.87	5	0.05
58	Oct	14	1.92	119	0.43
58	Dec	4	2.26	5	1.00
58.5	Sep	20	1.40	. . .	. . .
58.5	Oct	7	1.68	100	0.60
59	Sep	. . .	. . .	151	0.20
59	Oct	. . .	. . .	403	0.71
59	Dec	3	1.69	15	1.25
59.5	Sep	453	0.56	410	0.40
59.5	Oct	16	1.11	. . .	. . .
60	Sep	42	0.38	19	0.64
60	Oct	300	0.85	100	1.31
60	Dec	. . .	. . .	161	1.98
61	Sep	. . .	. . .	2	1.40
61	Oct	190	0.44	. . .	. . .
61	Dec	8	0.87	. . .	. . .
61.5	Oct	19	0.31	. . .	. . .

Source: *Wall Street Journal.*

case 3

The World Wildlife Fund and Debt-for-Nature*

When lenders and debtors began to look for solutions to the emerging debt crisis among less-developed countries (LDCs) they created bridge loans, rollover contracts, and multi-year reschedulings. In short, they created anything which temporarily stabilized their relationships. The focus has now shifted toward innovative contractual agreements—agreements which perform various kinds of "swaps" to recapitalize LDC debt.[1] An increasingly popular type of contract in this financing rubric is the exchange of one form of paper for another, using available market mechanisms. Broadly stated, such exchanges can take the form of either "debt-for-debt" swaps or "debt-for-equity" swaps.

Although specific forms which such swaps can take vary from one contract to another, they all have certain common features. Typically the debtor country may have neither the ability nor the willingness to pay off, for example, a dollar debt, but it may be able to offer to its creditors something in exchange for their voluntarily canceling those dollar debts. What makes this possible is a small secondary market for LDC debt in which such debt sells for substantially below its face value.

The amount of this discount varies from country to country. Outside investors can buy this dollar debt at a market-determined discount. In turn, the debtor country is usually willing to convert limited amounts of such dollar debt into local-currency debt (or equity) at or near 100% of its face value. The investor can make approved investments in its domestic economy. Such swaps provide an innovative tool for financing projects in heavily indebted LDCs, and have recently received a fair amount of attention.[2]

---

*This case was developed by Anant K. Sundaram, Associate Professor of Business Administration, as a basis for classroom discussion. © 1990.

[1]Donald R. Lessard, "Recapitalizing the Third World—Toward a New Vision of Commercial Financing for Less Developed Countries," Working Paper No. 1946-87, Sloan School of Management (mimeographed, 1987).

[2]See, for example, Steve M. Rubin, "Debt Equity Swaps in the Philippines," *Multinational Business,* 1987, No. 4, pp. 13-22. Also see: Michael Blackwell and Simon Nocera, "The Impact of Debt to Equity Conversion—An Explanation and Assessment of Debt-equity Swaps," *Finance and Development,* Vol. 25, No. 8, June 1988, pp. 15-17. Also see: Joseph Ganitsky and Gerardo Lema, "Foreign Investment through Debt-equity Swaps," *Sloan Management Review,* Winter 1988, pp. 21-29. Also see: S.L. Mintz, "Dancing the Debt Swap Tango," in *Corporate Finance,* September 1988, pp. 50-55.

The World Wildlife Fund (WWF) is considering buying Ecuadorian debt at a discount from a US bank. This purchase finances a conservation project in local currency for a private Ecuadorian nature conservancy group, Fundacion Natura (FN). The example lends itself to general application in that WWF is analogous to the parent company of a multinational enterprise, and FN can be viewed as its subsidiary. The objective of the parent company (WWF) is to maximize the cash flow to its subsidiary (FN); the objective of the Ecuadorian government is to reduce its external indebtedness by supplanting some of the foreign-currency debt with domestic-currency debt; and the objectives of the bank selling its debt at a discount are many—these might include reducing debt exposure to meet regulatory standards, and cleaning up its books by reducing the amount of doubtful debt. Done in reasonable amounts such deals might represent a positive-sum game for all the players.[3]

WWF AND THE ECUADORIAN GOVERNMENT

WWF, based in Washington, D.C., is a leading private organization working internationally to protect endangered wildlife and wildlands. WWF, with 650,000 US members, has 23 national organizations worldwide and an international office in Gland, Switzerland.

In October 1987, William K. Reilly, then president of WWF, was considering a "debt-for-nature" swap. Debt-for-nature swaps are a proposal for saving some of the most biologically valuable real estate in the world—tropical forests. WWF had $330,000 that it wanted to make available to Fundacion Natura. The proceeds would benefit conservation activities in Ecuador, all aimed at strengthening the country's system of national parks and reserves. WWF sought to purchase portions of the debt at a discount from commercial lenders and then, in cooperation with Ecuador, to convert those debt purchases into conservation projects jointly agreed upon by WWF and FN. These funds would be used to manage park lands and conduct environmental education and training programs. Ecuador, which is the size of Colorado, has twice the number of bird species found in the United States. It has a variety of ecosystems ranging from the Galapagos Islands to high Andean plains to Amazonian forests.

MECHANICS OF THE SWAP

The currency of Ecuador is sucre, and it is currently valued at 250 sucre to the US dollar. In the last few years, the sucre has depreciated against the US dollar at an average annual rate of 31%, and the average annual inflation rate during this period has been around 33%.[4] Ecuadorian dollar debt was selling for about 33 cents on the dollar in secondary markets for LDC debt, and Reilly was assured by a leading US bank of being able to obtain this rate for the proposed transaction. The government of Ecuador was willing to supplant this dollar debt with a sucre bond of eight years' maturity, and was willing to pay an annual coupon of 2% plus the prevailing rate of inflation. This coupon was below the current market interest rate for an equivalent instrument in Ecuador. Given the positive-sum nature of such swaps, it is usual for local governments too to take something off the top. The deal was simply this: With, say, $1, WWF could purchase $3 of debt from the US bank, and exchange this at prevailing currency rates (250 sucre to $1) into sucre bonds issued by the Ecuadorian government. The government would be willing to pay a coupon of 2% plus inflation rate

---

[3]Of course, one must be a little skeptical of positive-sum games in efficient financial markets. There are a number of negatives as well to such deals. In terms of first-order effects, most of these concern the borrowing country or the bank. For example, deals done in large amounts can have inflationary consequences in the borrowing country; large excess demand or excess supply can drive up or drive down the value of such debt in the secondary markets, with important balance sheet consequences.

[4]International Monetary Fund, 1987; various issues of International Financial Statistics.

for the next eight years, with the principal repaid at the end of the eighth year (assume, for simplicity, that all payments are made annually).

Ecuadorian inflation in October 1987 was about 29 percent annually. The prevailing market interest rate (for an 8-year loan) which Ecuadorian banks are willing to offer for dollars converted into sucre at today's exchange rate is not readily known. In the United States, WWF can get 8% (annually) for an equivalent investment in dollars. The US inflation rate, as of October 1987, was 4% annually.

Specific questions arise from this, the most basic of which is: Is this swap a good deal, or should WWF simply go ahead and invest the $330,000 (on behalf of FN), in a US bank? How should they go about getting a "benchmark" answer to this question? How will this compare with an Ecuadorian investment at market rates? Several ancillary questions arise as well. What if Ecuadorian or US inflation rates went up? How will this relate to exchange rate changes in the future? What will that do to the spending power of FN, given that the swap is being made at currently prevailing exchange rates? What other factors can affect the economics of the deal? More generally, what are the risk factors to consider, and how can WWF assess them?

Prior to doing anything else, and in order to clarify his thinking, Mr. Reilly first laid out the various options he had available in making the decision whether or not to swap—these options are shown in *Exhibit 1*.

EXHIBIT 1
World Wildlife Fund

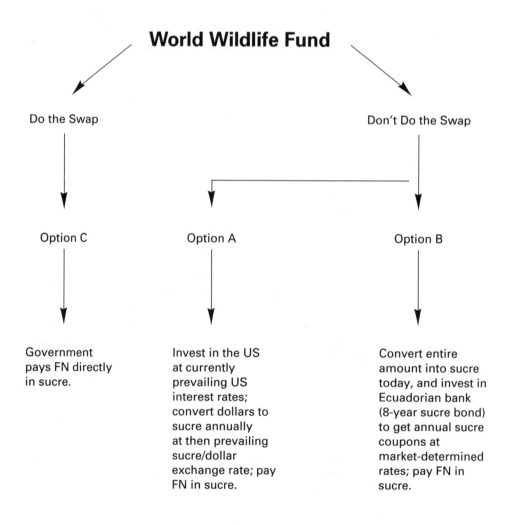

World Wildlife Fund

Do the Swap

Don't Do the Swap

Option C

Option A

Option B

Government pays FN directly in sucre.

Invest in the US at currently prevailing US interest rates; convert dollars to sucre annually at then prevailing sucre/dollar exchange rate; pay FN in sucre.

Convert entire amount into sucre today, and invest in Ecuadorian bank (8-year sucre bond) to get annual sucre coupons at market-determined rates; pay FN in sucre.

chapter 5

Exchange Rates: Economic Exposure

Since the advent of floating exchange rates, there have been major variations from PPP, and substantial real currency movements over the medium term have been common. For example, during the period 1977–1981, the US dollar depreciated over 10% in real terms against a weighted average basket of the rest-of-the-world currencies, subsequently appreciated by over 35% during the period 1981–1985, and then depreciated again by about 35% between 1985 and 1988. The period 1988–1991 saw relative stability. However, since mid-1992, the dollar has appreciated in real terms against most of the European currencies, and depreciated against the Japanese yen.

The impact of such currency movements on price, cost, and competitive adjustments by multinational enterprises (MNEs) has only recently received any careful academic attention. In the management literature, the impact of real currency movements on firm cash flows is referred to as the problem of "economic exposure" to exchange rates. In this chapter, we systematically examine how firms can manage their economic exposure through (1) their revenue/pricing decisions abroad, (2) their cost/sourcing decisions abroad, and (3) the competitive strategies they adopt both at home and abroad.

DEFINITIONS

As we discussed in Chapter 3, there are three types of impact of exchange rates on the performance of MNEs: translation, transaction, and economic exposure (also sometimes called operating or real exposure). Translation exposure deals with the ex post impact of nominal exchange rate changes on the MNE's consolidated financial statements. Transaction exposure results from the fact that firms enter into transactions of known ex ante value (in domestic currency terms) prior to an exchange rate change, but have to settle these transactions after the exchange rate change.

The third category—economic exposure—results from the fact that the firm's expected cash flows experience unexpected changes in the real exchange rate. More precisely, if we define a firm's cash flow as π, where π is the sum of domestic and foreign cash flows (thus, a function of the real exchange rate), then a firm is said to have economic exposure to exchange rates if $\partial\pi/\partial s$—that is, the sensitivity of cash flows to real exchange rate changes—is not equal to zero (where s is the real exchange rate, expressed as the number of domestic currency units required to buy each unit of foreign currency, or the direct quote).

While translation and transaction exposures need not affect real cash flows (since the ex ante domestic currency value of the exposure is known, and hence can be hedged), we shall see that economic exposure typically has to be dealt with through variables such as pricing, sourcing from different locations, diversifying the manufacturing base geographically, and so forth, rather than through financial hedging techniques.

In the economics literature, the consequence of pricing decisions resulting from real exchange rate changes is referred to as "pass-through" (or, sometimes, "pricing-to-market"): that is, the extent to which a firm passes through the impact of any currency changes to its customers.

REVENUES AND PRICING STRATEGIES

The Pricing Strategy Choices

Assume that the firm in question is a foreign firm (say, Japanese) selling domestically (say, exporting to the US), competing against other domestic (US) firms. If the foreign currency (the yen) depreciates against the domestic currency (the dollar), then a skimming pricing strategy will involve maintaining the dollar price at the predepreciation level, but letting the yen price rise (thereby yielding extra yen profits on each unit sold), while a penetration pricing strategy will involve lowering the dollar price and maintaining the yen price at the previous level (thereby gaining extra market share from the increased domestic demand resulting from lowered dollar prices). If the yen appreciates against the dollar, foreign firms would be adopting the equivalent of a skimming pricing strategy when they maintain the yen prices at, or close to, the preappreciation level and let the dollar prices rise; they would be adopting the equivalent of a penetration or market share pricing strategy when they maintain dollar prices at, or close to, the preappreciation level, and let the yen prices fall.

An Example. Suppose Honda Motor Company is selling its Civic model in the US for, say, $10,000, and the initial exchange rate is $1=¥100. The yen price of a Honda Civic is, therefore, ¥1,000,000. Suppose the yen depreciates by 25 percent, so that the new exchange rate is $1=¥125. If Honda maintains the US $ price of Civics at $10,000, it would obtain a yen revenue of ¥1,250,000 on each car that it sells in the US. One could reasonably presume that demand does not change much in the US, since consumers are still paying the same dollar price that they paid prior to the yen depreciation. Thus, the real depreciation of the yen combined with maintenance of the price in the foreign currency could lead to a 25% increase in revenues, with all of this excess revenue going toward profits. This is what we call a skimming pricing strategy in face of a real depreciation of the home (in this case, Japanese) currency. At the other extreme, Honda could adopt a different pricing strategy: It could maintain the yen price of Civics at ¥1,000,000 (thus making at least as much profit as it did on each unit sold prior to the depreciation of the yen), so that the US $ price of each car falls by the full extent of the depreciation, to $8,000. The drop in price should, under normal circumstances, lead to an increase in US demand for Civics, and thus presumably an increase in Honda's market share in the US. This we shall call a market share or penetration pricing strategy in the face of a real depreciation of the home currency. (Suppose, instead, that the yen appreciated by 25%. Using the same example, work out the intuition for skimming and penetration pricing under an appreciation scenario.)

Pricing Strategy and Pass-through. In the economics literature, this pricing issue manifests itself in the concept of pass-through, where the focus of attention is the degree to which the effects of an exchange rate change are passed through to a firm's export price. If the exchange rate change is reflected in a one-for-one change in prices abroad, then it is referred to as full pass-through; if none of the exchange rate change is reflected in prices abroad, it is referred to as no pass-through. More precisely, if s is the exchange rate as defined previously, P^f is the foreign firm's price expressed in domestic currency terms (therefore, the foreign currency price is P^f/s), then the phenomenon of pass-through is the response of domestic currency prices of the foreign firm to changes in the real exchange rate, or dP^f/ds (that is, the rate of change of P^f with respect to s).

A convenient way of expressing pass-through is as a coefficient—in percentage (elasticity) terms:

$$\text{If } (dP^f/ds)(s/P^f) = 1, \text{ then there is full pass-through}$$

$$\text{If } (dP^f/ds)(s/P^f) = 0, \text{ then there is no pass-through}$$

Another concept that is sometimes used in the literature is that of pricing to market: If there is less than full pass-through, firms may be adopting pricing strategies suited to features of particular markets, in response to an exchange rate change, and thus are said to be pricing to market.

Note, from this discussion, that the relationship between pricing behavior in response to economic exposure and pass-through is dependent (though only definitionally) on whether the currency undergoes an appreciation or depreciation. If the domestic currency depreciates, then no pass-through will be consistent with full skimming pricing, and full pass-through will be consistent with full market share (or penetration) pricing. If the domestic currency appreciates, the reverse relationship holds. Table 5.1 summarizes these definitional linkages.

TABLE 5.1

The Relationship between Terminologies: The Exporter's Viewpoint

Currency	Movement	Pass-through	Pricing
Depreciation		No pass-through	Skimming pricing
		Full pass-through	Penetration pricing
Appreciation		No pass-through	Penetration pricing
		Full pass-through	Skimming pricing

With respect to the concept of pricing to market, given a depreciation of the domestic currency, anything less than full penetration pricing (that is, full pass-through) will imply that there is pricing to market.

In the popular press, there is a general sense that many US firms chose to pursue a skimming strategy when the US dollar depreciated after 1985, while Japanese firms chose to pursue a market-share strategy when the yen similarly depreciated between 1981 and 1984. An article in the *Wall Street Journal* (May 15, 1987), for example, suggested that the norm for US firms operating in Japan has been to go for ". . . profits rather than market share." An editorial in *BusinessWeek* (August 27, 1987) chastised US firms for such pricing strategies in Japan: ". . . [S]uch a (pricing) approach is short term, whereas US manufacturers should be trying to grab a bigger share of the market. . . if they show price restraint now, they may win bigger markets and profits later." Similar criticisms were leveled in 1993, when the US dollar depreciated in real terms by more than 15 percent relative to the yen.

The prescription is not always that simple. As we shall see below, the optimal responses can (and should) vary from industry to industry (and even firm to firm); thus, it is difficult to draw generalizations.

The Choice between Skimming and Penetration Pricing

Suppose, for specificity, that the yen has undergone a depreciation against the dollar. At the new exchange rate, also suppose that the Japanese firm maintains the yen price of its exports, letting the dollar price of its products fall to the full extent of the depreciation (in other words, the firm decides to pursue a market-share pricing, or a full pass-through strategy).

Depending on the price elasticity of demand for the firm's product, this would increase the demand, and would lead to an increase in the market share for its product in the US (assuming, of course, that not all of its competitors' currencies were similarly affected). While the firm could have lower average dollar profit on each unit sold in the US, the increase in volume sold may compensate for this, resulting in a total revenue and profit that makes up for the reduced average profit. However, it is possible that the firm may have scale economies resulting from the increased volume (for example, because it may have excess capacity, or it might be able to take advantage of the learning curve by producing extra units, or there may be cost savings through access to fixed distribution and transportation costs, and so forth). Such scale economies would mitigate the reduction in dollar profit margin (or may even increase the profit margin), thus enhancing the total yen profit potential from the increased volume (relative to the case of constant returns to scale).[1]

There are other factors to consider as well. First, we have to form a judgment on whether the depreciation is expected to be a temporary phenomenon. For example, what if, a few months later, the yen appreciated back to its original level? If this happened, the exporter might have to raise its dollar prices in order to return to its original level of profitability (or not make losses at the current yen price). Whether or not it can do so will depend on a number of factors, including its ability to create entry barriers (is the product differentiated, does the firm have blocking access to distribution channels?), whether and how consumers will react to price fluctuations (are consumers likely to be put off by the uncertainty at the point of purchase resulting from price changes that occur every time exchange rates fluctuate?), and the competitive structure of the product market (Is the firm a monopolist, a perfect competitor, or an oligopolist? If an oligopolist, does it compete in a market based on prices or quantities? Does it compete in a market with "aggressive" competitors or "passive" competitors?[2] See the section below on competitive strategies). Second, a firm may make a rational penetration pricing decision taking all the factors we have discussed into account, but it has to consider whether the distribution channels in the importing country would simply soak up the difference, so that the consumer does not see any significant dollar price reduction. If this happened, then the firm would see no benefits from pursuing penetration pricing strategy. Also, sometimes firms compete as though "market share matters" (and only indirectly, profits). In such an instance, there would clearly be the incentive to pursue a penetration pricing strategy.

Invoicing strategies also matter. If exporting firms invoice in their home country currency (in this case, the yen), the depreciation translates to a full market-share pricing strategy by default (since the firm would not change its yen prices, the dollar prices would

---

[1] A convenient way to capture this effect would be to think in terms of the concept of "quantity elasticity of average costs": i.e., what percentage decrease in average costs you can expect to achieve for each percentage increase in volume of units produced.

[2] In the industrial organization literature, aggressive competitive responses are referred to as product markets characterized by strategic complements (SC), while passive competitive responses are referred to as product markets characterized by strategic substitutes (SS). Whether SC or SS obtains in product markets is dependent on three factors: the nature of the demand function, the nature of the cost function, and the conjectures that competitors make about each other's behavior in response to any changes in strategy.

automatically fall). Similarly, if firms invoice in the currency of the country that they are exporting to, then they are de facto adopting a skimming strategy.[3]

In the case of a skimming pricing strategy following a depreciation, the exact reverse of many of the considerations that we discussed above will apply: Firms will have the incentive to skim if, for example, demand elasticities and scale economies are low, the product is undifferentiated, entry barriers are low (and the depreciation is expected to be temporary), competition is in strategic complements, and so forth.

Conclusions on Pricing Strategies

We have seen that the optimal pricing response of firms to unanticipated changes in real exchange rates should be a function of the following factors: (1) the demand elasticity, (2) the nature of returns to scale (the quantity elasticity of average costs), (3) whether the currency change is expected to be temporary or permanent, (4) whether the firm can create entry barriers, (5) whether the product is differentiated, (6) how distribution channels and consumers will react to price cuts, (7) whether "market share matters," and finally (8) the currency invoicing strategies used. In addition, the nature of product-market competition—whether competitors will react passively or aggressively to any pricing moves—will play an important role, as discussed later in the chapter.

COST AND SOURCING STRATEGIES

The Sourcing Problem in the Face of Currency Movements

In many ways, cost-minimizing strategies in the face of a real currency movement are the reverse of those related to pricing strategies, in that a similar underlying set of variables affect strategic choices. First, note that currency movements matter for the MNE's costs only in situations where the firm sources some or all of its inputs (for example, raw material, intermediate products, labor, technology) from abroad. If the MNE buys its inputs solely in the domestic markets, any direct currency effects are unlikely. Most import-based MNEs—particularly those that rely on natural resources such as petroleum and minerals (firms in oil, steel), and commodities (firms in food processing, textiles), as well as firms that tend to outsource their component and parts supplies from abroad (firms in computers, commercial aircraft, automobiles)—are often equally affected by currency movements on the cost side as they are on the revenues side.

If the MNE's home currency appreciates against the supplier's currency, cost management is less of a problem, and indeed, becomes more of an opportunity for managing additional profits arising from cost reduction. The reason is that, under an appreciation, the MNE has to pay out fewer units of its home currency to buy the same amount of inputs denominated in the foreign currency. There is, however, the issue of whether the MNE should pass on any of the currency-related savings to its input suppliers.

Factors Affecting Cost-based and Sourcing Strategies

The difficult cost management issue arises from a depreciation of the home currency (against supplier currencies), and is as follows: (1) Given that most MNEs have input sourced from abroad, how much of the home currency depreciation can be passed through to the suppliers of these inputs? (2) In the event that pass-through of costs to suppliers is difficult, how much can be passed through to consumers through price increases? (3) In the

---

[3]There is some evidence to suggest that in the 1970s and early 1980s, US firms mostly invoiced in dollars, while German and Japanese firms invoiced in the currency of the country that they were selling to. But US firms' invoicing strategies changed in the latter half of the 1980s.

event that both (1) and (2) are difficult to accomplish, what are the options available for diversifying into new sourcing alternatives from more favorable currency areas? The answers to these questions depend on (a) the buyer power that the MNE exercises over its suppliers, (b) the nature of the contracting relationship between the supplier and the MNE, (c) the currency invoicing strategies used, (d) the availability of alternate suppliers of inputs, and (e) the permanence of currency movements.

Clearly, the ability of the MNE to pass through the impact of a depreciation on to its suppliers will depend on the power it has over its suppliers, as well as the nature of contracting with its suppliers. The higher the buyer power of the MNE, the greater its ability to insulate its costs from the impact of currency movements; however, the more formal and long term the contracting between the firm and its suppliers, the lower its ability to insulate its costs from the impact of currency movements. Similarly, if the firm invoices its supplies in its home currency, it obviates the problem and lowers the impact of currency movements; on the other hand, if it invoices its supplies in the seller's currency, any impact of currency movements are passed through directly to the MNE's costs.

What if an MNE has little power over its suppliers, or is unable to undertake spot contracting with its suppliers, or operates in a supplier market in which the invoicing is done in the seller's currency? The first option is to examine whether the impact of the cost increase resulting from the currency depreciation can be passed through to its customers; the decision variables in this case revert to those we discussed under pricing and revenue strategies in the previous section. A more stable—and longer-term—option is for the MNE to diversify its supplier base across at least two or three major currency areas (for example, the US dollar, German DM, and Japanese yen currency blocs). This sourcing flexibility is particularly crucial if the currency movement can be expected to be more than temporary—can say, be expected to last two or three years (not an unusual scenario if the events of the past decade are any guide).

COMPETITIVE STRATEGIES

The most subtle problem induced by real currency movements is that of assessing how the MNE's competitors are affected by economic exposure, and equally importantly, how they are likely to react to any competitive moves the MNE makes. This, in turn, depends on (1) whether the competition is from a similar or different currency area, (2) the market structure in the MNE's product market, and (3) the MNE's strategic orientation.

Currency Area of Competition

Often, firms do not pay sufficient attention to how real currency movements can affect their major competitors. Consider an MNE in country A selling in country B, and competing against an MNE from country C also selling in that market. There may be no exchange rate changes between the currencies of A and B, but C's currency could undergo a real depreciation against B's. Even if A was doing everything right, it might suddenly discover that its competitive advantage is being steadily eroded in B's market because of its competitor's economic exposure to exchange rates. An example that comes to mind is firms in the US semiconductor industry in the early 1980s (whose cost base was largely domestic), who watched their competitive advantage being eroded (in part) by the depreciation of the Japanese yen. The major Japanese producers of semiconductors were able to price far below the US producers—in both Europe and in the US—which facilitated their rise to market leadership during the mid-1980s.

There is a somewhat more subtle issue. Economic exposure can occur even if an MNE has few competitors based in other countries and its competition is mostly from other domestic producers whose economics are affected similarly by currency movements. Quite apart from the fact that such a competitive scenario is rarely the case in the globalized economy confronting most firms, a firm that responds faster and more effectively than its domestic competition through the types of pricing and sourcing strategies we have previously discussed will clearly have a significant first-mover advantage.

Finally, a firm can have exposure to real currency movements even when it does not export (or produce) abroad, or does not source from abroad, if most of its competition is located abroad and their economics are affected by currency movements. An example is the steel industry in the US. Despite the fact that most of their inputs are sourced and output sold domestically, US steel firms saw their competitive positions erode in the early 1980s, in part because of currency-induced advantages accruing to their competitors from Brazil and South Korea.

The prescription is simple. Look for currency effects even when you think they are nonexistent. There is much to said for performing a systematic audit of not only how one's own economics are affected, but also how one's competitors' economics are likely to be affected by currency movements. Even if it appears that their economics are no differently affected, the MNE must examine whether it can move faster than its competition in dealing with the impact of economic exposure.

Market Structure (Advanced Section)[4]

Let us consider the pricing and revenue responses under some specific competitive scenarios. The conclusions are fairly straightforward for an exporter who is a monopolist (as well as a monopolistic price discriminator), and a perfect competitor. Starting with the case of a monopolist, its profit function, in foreign currency terms, may be expressed as:

$$\pi^* = P^*(q)q - c^*(q)$$

where $P^* = P^f/s$ (as noted before), π^* is the foreign currency profits, q is the quantity sold abroad, and $c^*(q)$ is the cost as a function of the quantity sold. If first derivatives are denoted as $P^{*'}$ and $c^{*'}(q)$[5], then the first-order condition for the optimum is

$$\partial\pi^*/\partial q = P^*(q) + P^{*'}(q)q - c^{*'}(q) = 0$$

which we can reexpress as[6]

$$P^*(q)/c^{*'}(q) = 1/(1 - [1/\mu])$$

where μ is the price elasticity of demand. If there is constant demand elasticity (that is, μ does not change when price changes), and constant marginal costs ($c^{*'}(.)$ is invariant to changes in quantity), then the equilibrium foreign currency (yen) export price is invariant to the exchange rate change. However, since $P^* = P^f/s$, this must imply that the export price expressed in domestic currency (US dollar) will fall (rise) by the full extent of the depreciation (appreciation): in other words, there will be full pass-through when the firm is a monopolist facing constant elasticity of demand and has constant returns to scale.

The case of the monopolist can be further generalized by considering the implications of particular types of demand and cost functions. For example, it would be straightforward to show that if demand elasticity is constant and marginal costs are increasing (that is, there is decreasing returns to scale), there will be less than full pass-through. If demand

---

[4]All but the last paragraph in this section can be skipped without loss of continuity for those unfamiliar with calculus.

[5]Note that $c^{*'}(q)$ is the marginal cost. If $c^{*'}(.)$ is greater (lesser) than zero, marginal costs are increasing (decreasing) and the monopolist has decreasing (increasing) returns to scale; if $c^{*'}(.)$ is constant—i.e., it does not change as the quantity produced changes—then marginal costs are constant, and there is constant returns to scale.

[6]This expression should be familiar to you, from your microeconomics course, as the well-known "Lerner index" of market power.

elasticity is constant and marginal costs are decreasing, there will be greater than full pass-through (the pass-through coefficient will be greater than one).

The intuition for the case of a monopolistic price discriminator is just an extension of that for the case of the monopolist: There will be as many Lerner indices as there are markets across which price discrimination occurs. Depending on the particular demand and cost function in each market, the extent of pass-through may vary (that is, there may be pricing to market), but it will be the same as though the firm were a monopolist in that particular market.

If the exporter is a perfect competitor, it would face infinitely elastic demand—it would be a price taker—in the market it is exporting to. In this case, the price in the export market will remain the same regardless of what the exporter does. Therefore, the foreign currency price of exports will remain unaffected by the real exchange rate change, and there will be no pass-through if the firm is a perfect competitor in world markets.

Finally, it is instructive to look at an example of imperfect competition. Let us consider the case of Cournot (that is, quantity) competition. The profit functions for the domestic (π) and foreign (π^*) firm, respectively, are as follows:

$$\pi = P(Q)q - c(q)$$

$$\pi^* = [P(Q)q^*/s] - c^*(q^*)$$

where $P(.)$ is the domestic price, $Q = q + q^*$ is the total quantity sold in the domestic market, q is the domestic firm's quantity, q^* the foreign firm's quantity, and $c(.)$ and $c^*(.)$ are the domestic and foreign firm's cost functions, respectively. Note that the foreign firm's revenue is expressed in foreign currency terms.

Assume, for simplicity, that the domestic and foreign firms have similar cost functions, and that marginal costs are constant. Then the first-order conditions for the Cournot equilibrium are:

$$\pi' = P(Q) + P'(Q)q - c'(q) = 0$$

$$\pi^{*'} = P(Q) + P'(Q)q^* - sc^{*'}(q^*) = 0$$

Solving the first-order conditions above, we can see that

$$dP/ds = [P'(Q)c^{*'}(q^*)]/[3P'(Q) + QP''(Q)]$$

where $P''(.)$ is the second derivative of prices with respect to quantity. It can then be shown that the pass-through coefficient, $(dP/ds)(s/P)$ will lie between zero and one: That is, it will always be positive, but less than one. Translated, it suggests that with Cournot competition, the pass-through will be less than that of the case of a monopolist, but greater than that of a perfect competitor.

In the case of Bertrand (that is, price) competition, a similar result will obtain, but the extent of pass-through will be closer to the perfectly competitive case—the pass-through coefficient will be lower than that of Cournot competition.

We can derive the following insights from the discussion of the various competitive scenarios. If the exporter is a monopolist with constant returns to scale facing constant elasticity of demand, there will be full pass-through; for the polar case of an exporter who is a perfect competitor, there will be no pass-through. The case of the monopolistic price discriminator would be similar to that of the monopolist, but the nature of pass-through may vary in each market depending on the demand and cost function relevant to a particular market. In product markets characterized by imperfect competition, the pass-through coefficient will generally be between zero and one: If there is aggressive competition (the product market is characterized by strategic complements, as is the case more often when there is price competition), the extent of pass-through will be closer to zero, while if there is passive competition (the product market is characterized by strategic substitutes, as is the case more often when there is quantity competition), then the extent of pass-through will be closer to one.

Strategic Orientation

Real currency movements can affect not only the firm's pricing and sourcing decisions, but also larger decisions such as (1) modes of entry—whether to export, license, or invest directly abroad, (2) configuration of activities—where and how to concentrate or disperse the MNE's value chain, and (3) the firm's competitive strategy.

When the MNE has a high degree of economic exposure, concentration of its productive assets in one currency location will leave it vulnerable to greater fluctuations in its asset values and its export prices resulting from swings in exchange rates. Protecting against this would require the firm to diversify its investment base so as not only to diversify the value of its assets, but also to have the option to shift its production worldwide from multiple locations. This may require the MNE to carry adequate manufacturing capacity— and perhaps even considerable slack—in at least two or three major currency areas. In this sense, MNEs in industries that are highly prone to the effects of real currency movements may have to move in the direction of becoming direct investors abroad, rather than merely exporters producing and selling from a home base (as many Japanese firms did with respect to the US in the 1970s, versus the 1980s), or even merely licensors of technology abroad (as many US firms did with respect to Japan in the 1970s, versus the 1980s).

A related insight applies to the MNE's decision to configure its value chain. When economic exposure is high, dispersing the firm's value chain would serve to diversify the firm's risks arising from unfavorable exchange rate movements relative to otherwise concentrated value activities. The problem goes a step further: Diversifying a value chain alone is often not sufficient. To the extent that a value chain is dispersed but differentiated, each differentiated activity is then subject to risks similar to those for the full range of value chain activities located within one country. Thus, a high degree of economic exposure may require the MNE not only to disperse its value chain, but also to carry out undifferentiated activities in each location; in short, despite internal (and industrial) economics that might argue for a global value chain configuration, the MNE may have to pursue a multidomestic approach (with apparent slack) in order to insulate itself from the effects of currency movements.

Finally, it is of consequence whether or not the MNE competes on the basis of cost- or value-based strategies. In general, MNEs pursuing cost-based, rather than value-based, strategies are likely to be more vulnerable to economic exposure. Cost-based strategies are generally likely to have lower per-unit margins, resulting in a smaller pricing leeway. Consequently, if there is an unanticipated real appreciation of the currency in which costs are denominated, there is a high risk that profit margins will be reduced further. Even worse, an appreciation could push the firm's costs above the world price the market will bear, resulting in negative profit margins. This risk is much lower for value-based strategies, given the likelihood of higher profit margins. The nature of competitor reactions also matters less when the MNE pursues value-based strategies. Overall, then, a high risk of economic exposure should lead MNEs to explore means to differentiate themselves in their product market (even if industry economics might argue otherwise).

SELECTED BIBLIOGRAPHY

Baron, D. P. "Fluctuating Exchange Rates and the Pricing of Exports." *Economic Inquiry* 14 (1976).

Bulow, J., J. Geanokoplos, and P. D. Klemperer. "Multimarket Oligopoly: Strategic Substitutes and Complements." *Journal of Political Economy* 93 (1985).

DORNBUSCH, R. "Exchange Rates and Prices." *American Economic Review* 77 (1987).

FISHER, E. "A Model of Exchange Rate Pass-through." *Journal of International Economics* 26 (1989).

FROOT, K., and P. D. KLEMPERER. "Exchange Rate Pass Through When Market Share Matters." *American Economic Review* 80 (1990).

JORION, P. "The Exchange Rate Exposure of US Multinationals," *The Journal of Business* 63 (1990).

KNETTER, M. "Price Discrimination by US and German Exporters," *American Economic Review* 79 (1989).

KOGUT, B. "Normative Observations on the International Value-added Chain and Strategic Groups." *Journal of International Business Studies* (Fall 1984).

KOGUT, B., and N. KULATILAKA. "Multinational Flexibility and the Theory of Direct Foreign Investment." Working Paper #88-10, Reginald S. Jones Center, University of Pennsylvania, 1988.

KRUGMAN, P. "Pricing to Market When the Exchange Rate Changes." NBER Working Paper No. 1926 (1986).

LESSARD, D., and E. FLOOD. "On the Measurement of Operating Exposure to Exchange Rates: A Conceptual Approach." *Financial Management* (Spring 1986).

LESSARD, D., and J. B. LIGHTSTONE. "Volatile Exchange Rates Can Put International Operations at Risk." *Harvard Business Review* (July-August, 1986).

LUEHRMAN, T. "The Exchange Rate Exposure of a Global Competitor." *Journal of International Business Studies* 21 (1990).

PORTER, M. "Changing Patterns of International Competition." *California Management Review* (Winter 1986).

SUNDARAM, A., and J. S. BLACK. "The Environment and Internal Organization of Multinational Enterprises." *Academy of Management Review* (October 1992).

SUNDARAM, A., and V. GOVINDARAJAN. "Strategic Implications of a Currency Devaluation." *Journal of Corporate Finance* (Winter 1989).

SUNDARAM, A., and V. MISHRA. "Economic Exposure to Exchange Rates: A Review." The Amos Tuck School Working Paper, March 1990.

SUNDARAM, A., and V. MISHRA. "Currency Movements and Corporate Pricing Strategies." In *Recent Developments in International Banking and Finance,* ed. S. Khoury, Volume IV-V. New York: Elsevier, 1991.

Economic Exposure to Exchange Rates: Problem Set*

1) Given an appreciation of the US dollar, an exporter from the US that fully passes through the exchange rate is
   a) adopting a penetration pricing strategy abroad
   b) adopting a skimming pricing strategy abroad
   c) adopting a pricing strategy that is somewhere midway between skimming and penetration pricing abroad
   d) None of the above

2) It is end-1984, and Jaguar PLC, a UK-based manufacturer of luxury high-priced automobiles was reconsidering its pricing strategy in the US market. In their London offices, CFO John Edwards was getting advice from his economic advisors—and he himself was convinced—that the sustained real appreciation of US dollar had begun to run out of steam, and the currency value was about to reverse course.

Customers in this segment of the market do not make purchase decisions solely on the basis of price, but they do shop around. To the extent that price changes take place in this market, one firm usually plays the role of price leader—in the US market, Daimler Benz seems to play this role.

Jaguar sold over 50% of its cars in the US, and its production costs and factories are almost completely UK-based; further, labor accounts for a significant portion of the cost base for luxury cars. In the recent past, Jaguar has performed extremely well in the US market, thanks in large part to the substantial real appreciation of the US dollar against all European currencies. While the strong dollar gave Jaguar the opportunity to cut its prices, it had not done so (nor had its competition).

*This case was developed by Associate Professor Anant K. Sundaram as a basis for class discussion. © 1990. Revised 1993.

Mr. Edwards knew that the projected depreciation of the US dollar would seriously cut into his profitability, and some upward revision of prices would be required if the depreciation did happen. For starters, he had to make a broad assessment of the nature of Jaguar's economic exposure to exchange rates.

2a) Given the facts above, Mr. Edwards should worry about his exposure to:
  a) the US dollar only
  b) the UK pound only
  c) the German DM only
  d) both (a) and (b)
  e) (a), (b), and (c)

2b) Assuming that a real depreciation of the US dollar is imminent, the scenario of exchange rate changes that would result in the "best case" competitive environment for Jaguar is
  a) the US dollar depreciates equally against the pound and the DM
  b) the US dollar depreciates against the pound, but less so against the DM
  c) the US dollar depreciates against the pound, but the pound depreciates against the DM
  d) the US dollar depreciates against the pound, but the pound appreciates against the DM
  e) not dependent on the value of $/DM

3) Airbus Industrie, the European consortium of aircraft manufacturers, buys jet engines from the US. The US dollar was depreciating in real terms against European currencies between 1985 and 1988. According to a story in the *Wall Street Journal*, ". . . as a result of the weaker dollar, the cost of a major component, jet engines, is declining for Boeing's biggest competitor, giving it a competitive advantage over Boeing." Assess this assertion.

4) A country's "terms of trade" is defined as the weighted average price of its exports divided by weighted average price of its imports. When this ratio declines, economists say that a country's terms of trade "worsen" (although the implication is that the country becomes more competitive in its export market, relative to its imports). Consider a situation in which a country exports its goods at the average home price level P, and imports its goods at the average foreign price level, P^*. Everything else remaining equal, a real appreciation of the home currency will
  a) make its terms of trade worse
  b) make its terms of trade better
  c) have no impact on its terms of trade
  d) make its terms of trade better or worse depending on UIP
  e) make its terms trade better or worse, depending on the international Fisher effect

5) Suppose that consumer price indices for traded goods in countries A and B went up by 10% and 6%, respectively, while during the same period, indices of production costs went up 7% and 6% respectively. A's exchange rate (relative to B's currency) depreciated in nominal terms by slightly less than 4% during this period. Country A's trade unions claim that this means that the export sector has become more profitable, implying that wages should rise.
  a) The trade union's claim is correct
  b) The trade union's claim is incorrect, because exchange rates moved as predicted by RPPP, and there is no real exchange change
  c) The trade union's claim is incorrect, because costs in country A rose faster than those in country B
  d) The information given is not sufficient to assess whether the claim is correct or incorrect

6) A US firm sells all its products in Germany, at a price of DM 2 per unit. It incurs all its costs in the US, and these costs work out to $0.85 for each unit produced (returns to scale are constant). The firm invoices its sales in DM. The initial exchange rate is $0.5/DM. A few months later, it discovers that it is making a loss of $0.05 (i.e., 5 cents) on each unit sold in Germany. This must be because
   a) The US$ depreciated by 20% relative to the DM
   b) The US$ depreciated by 25% relative to the DM
   c) The US$ appreciated to by 20% relative to the DM
   d) The US$ appreciated to by 25% relative to the DM
   e) There isn't enough information to make an assessment

Campbell Soup Company in Japan*

Campbell professes to have a long-term commitment to the Japanese market as part of its strategy ". . . to be the strongest competitor wherever and in whatever form soup can be sold. . . " It has adapted its products to Japan, using shiny-topped cans that Japanese consumers prefer, and has developed a new soup variety, "corn potage," exclusively for this market.

Although the company presently imports all its products from the US, there are indications that, as the brands become firmly established, the company intends to produce locally in order to lower the significant transportation costs for canned, water-based food products.

Campbell's main product, soup, is essentially undifferentiated in its basic form. However, Japanese consumers like to purchase those American products that have a reputation for consistent good quality and value (which Campbell already enjoys in the US). Thus, there is the opportunity for Campbell to position itself as "America's soup," with the connotations of heartiness and richness which are gaining acceptance with Japan's changing dietary habits.

Studies show that the price elasticity of demand for branded consumer products such as soup is likely to be at the higher end—typically in the range of 1.5 to 2. Returns to scale are significant, since Campbell has excess capacity in its US plants for supplying the Japanese market. Total cost as a percentage of selling price is approximately 85%. In export markets for soup, transportation costs account for a significant proportion of total costs. Campbell is a vertically integrated producer (vegetables to cans), and is considered the technological leader in soup production. In Japan, the company has been successful in securing key distribution channels needed for wide-scale product availability.

In 1987, Campbell sold approximately 100 million cans of soup in Japan, accounting for 15.6% of the market share. Its leading competitors are Sapporo Grand Hotel (19%), Knoru (a subsidiary of Ajinomoto, 13.3%), Heinz (11.3%), and UCC (10%). Though the canned soup market is oligopolistic, it forms a small portion of the total soup market. Miso (a traditional Japanese soup) and other forms of packaged soup are substantially larger markets, and are dominated by giants such as Ajinomoto.

Since the second half of 1986, the US dollar has undergone a real depreciation against the Japanese yen with the currency value changing from ¥165$ to ¥122/$, creating substantial economic exposure for Campbell's operations in Japan (relative inflation rates in the US and Japan remained low and roughly constant during this period). The company has not changed its retail prices for soup in Japan in over a year. Consequently, the EVP of international operations was offered a major strategic choice on the pricing front—should Campbell pocket extra cash with a profit-skimming pricing strategy or should it use the opportunity to gain market share in Japan with a penetration pricing strategy?

*This case was developed by Associate Professor Anant K. Sundaram as a basis for class discussion. © 1990. Revised 1993.

E. I. DuPont de Nemours & Company in Japan*

DuPont has signalled its commitment to serving the Japanese market. This is made visible by its newly built $85 million technical center outside of Tokyo and a 20-story downtown office building bearing its corporate logo. A large portion of DuPont's sales in Japan (two-thirds in 1986) come from joint ventures with Japanese partners. The company is recruiting from Japanese colleges, and already enjoys a reputation as one of the best foreign companies that a Japanese person can work for.

DuPont sells two types of products in Japan—specialty products that require customer support and service, and commodities like Titanium Dioxide (TiO_2) which are in short supply worldwide. Most of DuPont's Japanese customers are plastics, electronics, or paint manufacturers. Since many of the specialty chemicals are proprietary products, barriers to entry in this industry are fairly high.

Demand for DuPont's products appear to be fairly inelastic to prices. Japanese industrial customers, although conscious of price differentials, place even greater value on customer service, reputation, and a visible commitment to a long-term partnership.

Worldwide, the chemical industry has been operating at historically high capacity utilization rates (around 85%) in 1986-87, due to strengthening demand and the closure of bulk chemicals plants during the industry downturn of the '70s and early '80s. Of DuPont's approximately $1 billion in Japanese sales (1986), about 25% is imported directly from the US, and most of the remaining products are manufactured in Japan with its joint venture partners. Raw materials for Japanese manufacture, however, are mostly imported from other countries, since Japan has scarcity of mineral and natural resources. Twenty percent of DuPont's imports consist of TiO_2, and are used primarily for colored plastics and automotive paints.

Plants producing specialty chemicals are usually smaller than bulk chemicals factories. Production runs are small, making scale economies difficult to achieve. Total cost as a percentage of selling price is 85%.

Since the second half of 1986, the US dollar has undergone a real depreciation against the Japanese yen with the currency value changing from ¥165/$ to ¥122/$, creating substantial economic exposure for DuPont's operations in Japan (relative inflation rates in the US and Japan remained low and roughly constant during this period). Consequently, DuPont's EVP for international operations faces an important strategic choice in the Japanese market—should DuPont pocket extra cash with a profit-skimming pricing strategy or should it use this opportunity to gain market share with a penetration pricing strategy?

*This case was developed by Associate Professor Anant K. Sundaram as a basis for class discussion. © 1990. Revised 1993.

chapter 6

Theories of International Trade

The year 1993 witnessed two landmark events in the recent history of international trade: the passage of the North American Free Trade Agreement (NAFTA) by the US, Canada, and Mexico, and the conclusion (although not yet ratification) of the seven-year "Uruguay Round" of negotiations of the General Agreement on Tariffs and Trade (GATT).[1] Despite general consensus that these agreements would benefit the world economy in general and MNEs in particular, passage of both agreements was preceded by acrimonious debate in the media, by makers of public policy, and in academic realms.[2] While many CEOs of MNEs welcomed both NAFTA and GATT, many labor unions, consumer groups, and environmentalists were strongly opposed to their passage.

Such debates, which are more generally about the merits and demerits of "free trade," are not new. Indeed, they have been at the heart of Western economic thought (and even the intellectual development of capitalism) over the past two centuries. This chapter traces these intellectual developments, with a view to understanding the factors that drive international trade and the consequences of these factors for MNEs. It also examines the paradoxical impulses for protectionism that are inherent in the theories that extol the efficiency virtues of free trade. These impulses result from the distributional implications of free trade, as well as the factors that drive some segments of industry and society to demand protection from the effects of free trade. Such protection takes the forms of tariff barriers and non-tariff barriers, and we shall understand the implications of each form.

This chapter also looks at a phenomenon that has grown in both its application and its intensity during the past decade, namely, "strategic trade," and what drives governments and industries to try to "manage" their trading relationships with other countries.

There is a large body of institutions and laws—both bilateral and multilateral—that govern international trade and which constitute the specific environment in which MNEs manage their global trading relationships (these are examined in more detail in Chapter 7).

---

[1]We discuss both NAFTA and GATT in greater detail in Chapter 7.

[2]For instance, the debate between the US Vice President Albert Gore and independent politician Ross Perot, on NAFTA, had the single highest viewership for any program in the history of US cable television.

The ideas developed in this chapter are essential not only in order to understand and interpret this environment of institutions and laws, but also to trace the development of these institutions over the years, and their continued evolution into the future.

VIEWS OF US CEOS, THE PUBLIC, AND ECONOMISTS ON FREE TRADE

Before we get into the intricacies of theories of international trade, it is useful to see how different constituencies in the US respond to the issue of free trade versus protectionism.

In a *New York Times/CBS* interview conducted in July 1992, 490 CEOs were asked to choose between the following three statements: (1) "Free trade must be allowed even if domestic industries are hurt"; (2) "Trade restrictions are necessary to protect domestic industries"; (3) "Don't know/no answer." Nearly two-thirds of CEOs—61% to be exact—agreed with the statement that free trade must be allowed, and only 33% agreed that trade restrictions may be necessary. They were then asked to choose between whether (1) it is important to protect American industries and jobs by limiting imports, or (2) it is important to allow free trade so the public can buy good products at low prices. Only 29% of CEOs agreed with the statement that it is important to protect rather than have free trade; 61% agreed that free trade is more important than protection. Interestingly, the survey asked the same question of a broad cross-section of the US public, and the reaction was almost the opposite: 56% of the US public felt that protection by limiting imports may be more important than free trade, while 38% felt that free trade was more important.

In another survey that was conducted in the late 1970s, 100 top US economists were asked to agree or disagree with the proposition, "Tariffs and import quotas reduce general economic welfare." The responses, from a profession (probably justifiably) famous on its inability to agree on just about anything, were as follows: "Generally Agree," 81%; "Agree with Provisions," 16%; "Generally Disagree," 3%.[3]

Clearly, the data above suggest that decisions makers in the private sector are for "free trade" while the public at large have some qualms. Yet, as we shall see, demands for protection—for example, petitions to various arms of the government that oversee matters of trade—often tend to come from decision makers in the private sector, especially those firms and industries that are likely to be adversely affected by more open trade (for example, the automobile and semiconductor industries in the 1980s). Thus, there appears to be some inconsistency between the views expressed by the CEOs and their practice when their firms or industries are affected.

THE CLASSICAL THEORIES OF TRADE: ABSOLUTE ADVANTAGE AND COMPARATIVE ADVANTAGE

In 1776, Adam Smith noted that, if a country could produce a good cheaper than other countries, it had an *absolute advantage* in the production of that good; he then argued that, in order to maximize national income, countries should produce and export surpluses of what they have absolute advantage in, and buy whatever else they need from the rest of the world. In this way, he theorized, specialization, and hence efficiency, would be encouraged as a result of the increased competition and scale economies. Of course, the question that was left unanswered was, "What if a country had absolute advantage in all products, or even worse, in no products at all?" The theory would imply that the former country need not trade, while the latter could not trade!

Forty years later, David Ricardo unambiguously answered the question with what has become one of the most important ideas in all of economics: He showed that both countries should, and indeed, will trade in order to increase their national welfare, as long as each has

---

[3]See J. R. Kearl et al., "A Confusion of Economists?" *American Economic Review* (May 1979): 30.

a *comparative advantage* in the production of one good versus another. In other words, incentives for trade would exist even when one country has absolute cost advantage in everything or another country has the absolute cost advantage in nothing. The key, he noted, was that a country should have the ability to produce one good, relative to another good, that is *different* from another country's relative ability to produce the same two goods. The best way to see this argument—before we see the intuitive reasoning behind this powerful idea—is through an example.

An Example of the Comparative Advantage Argument

Let us assume that there are two countries—say, the US and France—both of which can produce beef and wine; assume that returns to scale are constant, and the factor of production used in producing these two goods (say, land) can be costlessly transformed from producing beef to wine and vice versa. Let us further assume, for the sake of argument, that France has the absolute advantage in the production of both goods. Specifically, if the US used all its factor of production (say, land) in producing wine, it could produce 25 bottles of wine, while if it used all of its factor of production in producing beef, it could produce 50 pounds of beef. Similar figures for France are 150 bottles of wine and 60 pounds of beef, respectively. (That is, France can produce more of both beef and wine compared to the US.)

Note the following: For every pound of beef that France chooses not to produce, it releases land that can be used to produce $150/60 = 2.5$ bottles of wine. (We can think of this as a relative price of beef with respect to wine: In France, each pound of beef costs 2.5 bottles of foregone wine.) Similarly, for every pound of beef that the US chooses not to produce, it releases land that can be used to produce $25/50 = 0.5$ bottles of wine. (In the US, each pound of beef costs half a bottle of foregone wine.) In this example, compared to the US, beef is more expensive in France relative to wine (since you have to give up 2.5 bottles of wine); the reverse is true in the US. Suppose the initial, "no-trade" production and consumption of beef in the two countries is 40 pounds in the US and 20 pounds in France. This would, in turn, mean that the US has available land that can now be used to produce and consume $(50 - 40)*0.5 = 5$ bottles of wine (think through why this is the case). Using similar arguments, France has available land that can be used to produce and consume $(60 - 20)*2.5 = 100$ bottles of wine. Table 6.1 summarizes these transactions.

TABLE 6.1

Initial (Pretrade) Production

	Beef	Wine
US	40	5
France	20	100
Total	60	105

Let us now suppose that the two countries can agree to trade with each other at a price that is somewhere between 2.5 and 0.5 bottles of wine for each pound of beef—say, one bottle of wine per pound of beef. (Where this price will actually be in the posttrade equilibrium is subject to considerations that may include the bargaining ability and power of the players, the nature of demand, and so forth; in order to develop the idea of comparative advantage further, just assume that the players settled on this price.) At this new price of one bottle of wine for each pound of beef, the US has the incentive to sell its beef for French wine, since for each pound of beef sold, it can get twice the amount of wine that it did before (that is, one bottle rather than 0.5 bottle of wine per pound of beef foregone); France has the incentive to sell its wine for US beef, since for each bottle of wine sold, it can now get two-and-a-half times the amount of beef that it did before (that is, one pound rather than $1/2.5 = 0.4$ pounds of beef per bottle of wine foregone).

Assume that neither country wants to reduce its production and consumption from the pretrade level: that is, the US still wants to produce and consume 40 pounds of beef, and France still wants to produce and consume 100 bottles of wine. Here is what they can do: Rather than producing any wine at all, the US can produce 10 more pounds of beef (its remaining production possibility after consuming 40 pounds) and sell it to France for 10 bottles of wine; similarly, France can export 10 bottles of wine for 10 pounds of US beef. (It can continue to produce and consume 100 bottles locally; with the additional 10 bottles of export-related wine production, it can use its land to still produce 16 pounds of beef for domestic consumption.) The net result of this trade is as follows: The US can consume 40 pounds of beef and 10 bottles of wine (compared to 5 bottles pretrade); France can consume 100 bottles of wine and 10 + 16 = 26 pounds of beef (compared to 20 pounds pretrade). The bottom line, Ricardo observed, is that trade makes both countries better off compared to a no-trade equilibrium. Moreover, it enabled one country (in this case, the US) to specialize in the production of one of the goods (in this case, beef).

The basis for this welfare improvement was that the two countries had differential *relative* advantages in their production possibilities. Despite the fact that France could, overall, produce more beef, the US had a relative advantage in the production of beef. For each bottle of wine that was given up, the US could produce 1/0.5 = 2 pounds of beef, while France could only produce 1/2.5 = 0.4 pounds of beef. The reverse is true in the case of relative advantage for wine production. Posttrade production and consumption of beef and wine are summarized in Table 6.2.

TABLE 6.2

Posttrade Production (Price is one bottle of wine = one pound of beef)

	Beef		Wine	
	Domestic	Import	Domestic	Import
US	40	0	0	10
France	16	10	100	0
Total	56 +	10	100 +	10
	= 66		= 110	

Intuition Behind the Idea of Comparative Advantage

The following stylized example (and the questions that follow) illustrates the intuition behind the idea of comparative advantage in simple terms. Let us suppose that, when you get to be the CEO, you are aware that, along the way, you also acquired the skills to become the fastest typist in your company. Your available time is finite, and you can use it up in either running the company or in typing (or some combination of the two). Further, assume that for each unit of time spent on either activity, you can create substantially greater value by running the company rather than typing. How would you prefer to spend your time? Would you hire a typist to do your typing even if that person were slower than you (assuming that the typist is worse at running the company than at typing)? If you answered, "running the company" and "yes," respectively, you have grasped the intuition behind Ricardo's principle of comparative advantage!

Some Crucial Assumptions Underlying the Ricardo Model

The Ricardian theory of comparative advantage relies on a number of assumptions. The more important ones are: (1) Production technologies in both countries exhibit constant returns to scale; (2) Factors of production can be easily and costlessly moved from one sector to the other as the country specializes through trade, and there is a fixed supply of the factors of production; (3) The underlying market structure driving production is based on perfect competition; and (4) There is no technological innovation, and there are no technological spillovers. Moreover, the basis for one country's comparative advantage over another (that is, what causes the differences in production efficiencies) is left undeveloped in this model.

Clearly, some of these assumptions—in particular, assumptions (3) and (4)—are strong. Despite these strong assumptions, however, few theories in the course of the history of economic thought approach the importance of the principle of comparative advantage—notably in the way it has influenced academics, policymakers, and the international laws and institutions that govern the structure and conduct of international trade. Moreover, the simplicity and elegance of the underlying insight have outlived the numerous criticisms that have been leveled against it.

FACTOR ENDOWMENTS AND COMPARATIVE ADVANTAGE: THE HECKSCHER-OHLIN THEORY

In 1933, drawing upon the work of Eli Heckscher, Bertil Ohlin took the Ricardian model a significant step further, by linking the source of a country's comparative advantage to the endowment of its factors of production. This theory, known as the Heckscher-Ohlin model of international trade (or simply, the H-O model) is probably the most widely accepted form of the comparative advantage theory today.

The H-O model focussed on two assumptions: (1) Goods differ in how much they use of certain types of factors of production—that is, different goods have different factor intensities; for instance, the manufacture of textiles is labor intensive, while the manufacture of semiconductors is capital intensive. (2) Countries differ with respect to their factor endowments; for instance, one might reasonably argue that India has an abundant supply of labor relative to capital, while the reverse is true of the US. Further, H-O assumed (as Ricardo did) that markets are perfectly competitive and factors are perfectly mobile, but it relaxed the assumption of constant returns to scale in order to allow for decreasing returns to scale. Putting these assumptions together, the main proposition of the H-O model is the following: *A country exports those goods that use intensively its relatively abundant factor of production.* That is, countries export those goods that they are best suited to produce, given their factor endowments.

Using the examples above, H-O would argue that a country such as India would export labor-intensive goods (and import capital-intensive goods), while a country such as the US would export capital-intensive goods (and import labor-intensive goods).

As with Ricardo's theory of comparative advantage, there are some potential weaknesses underlying the theory: (1) Endowments are supposed to be given, when they can often be created (for example, through innovation); in other words, H-O assumes a static supply of factor endowments. (2) If some countries kept to their static endowment–determined advantages, they might be stuck with a second-rate economy in the long run. (3) In an empirical insight that later came to be known as the "Leontief Paradox," economist Wassily Leontief found that, contrary to predictions suggested by the H-O model, US exports were less capital intensive than US imports. All these shortcomings led economists to a number of other, more realistic approaches to modeling international trade (as we will see below). However, the central insight of H-O regarding the link between factor endowments and factor intensity remains widely accepted.

SOME IMPLICATIONS OF THE THEORIES OF COMPARATIVE ADVANTAGE (OR HOW FREE TRADE ALSO CREATES THE INCENTIVE FOR PROTECTION)

Both the Ricardian and the H-O theories have some powerful implications. These implications, paradoxically, lead to equally powerful incentives—and in some cases, commonly used arguments to justify demands—for protection from the forces of free trade.

The first major implication of free trade is *factor price equalization:* International trade will tend to equalize factor prices across countries that trade. The reason is simple. The more trade that occurs in a particular good from a country, the greater the demand for the factors used intensively in the production of that good and the less the demand for the other factor. As a result, the price of one of the factors will be driven up and the other driven down. The exact opposite will happen in the other country. As a consequence, factor prices will be driven toward equalization in the two countries. For example, in the country that exports labor-intensive goods, the relative wages of labor will rise. Similarly, international trade will tend to drive the costs of capital closer together in the countries that trade.

The second major implication has come to be known as the *Rybczynski Theorem:* An increase in the endowment of one of the factors will reduce the production of goods that intensively use the other factor. For example, if the US is capital rich, and innovation increases the productivity of capital, then labor-intensive industries in the US will get hurt. Again, the reason is simple. With an increase in its capital endowment, the US can now produce and export more capital-intensive goods; this would lower the demand for labor, since resources will move away from the labor-intensive sectors of the economy (and, by definition, the capital-intensive sectors use relatively less labor). Indeed, in developing countries that specialize in labor-intensive goods, the reverse implication is even more surprising: An increase in the productivity of labor—for example, through better education and training or better provision of health care—will hurt capital-intensive sectors in those economies!

If these two implications are true, then we are likely to observe demand for protection from the effects of free trade from precisely those sectors in the economy that are hurt. Thus, demands for protection are likely to come from segments that represent labor in capital-intensive economies, and segments that represent capital in labor-intensive economies. This may explain why, in countries such as the US, labor unions often strongly oppose agreements such as NAFTA.[4] It may also explain why developing countries tend to be the ones that usually have stricter controls on cross-border capital flows. But this suggests another important corollary to the factor price equalization and Rybczynski theorems: *Demands for protection are most likely to arise from the less efficient sectors in an economy.*

This takes us to another implication of comparative-advantage theories, an implication that has come to be known as the *Stolper-Samuelson Theorem:* Any protection—for example, a tariff—will increase the income of factors of production used intensively in the good that receives protection; in the process, the relative income of the factor of production used in the other good will fall. For example, in countries such as the US, there will be cries for—and hence the incentive for—protection from labor-intensive sectors; such policies will prop up incomes in those sectors, but in the process they will hurt the capital-intensive sectors and, hence, capital. The reverse will be true in labor-intensive economies such as the developing countries: Efforts at protecting capital (for example, capital controls) would actually end up hurting labor in those economies.

There are three main insights to take away from this discussion. One, the incentives (and some might argue, the logic) for protection are inherent in arguments for free trade. Two, demands for protection will usually arise from the less efficient sectors in an economy. Three, protection will usually end up hurting the more efficient sectors in an economy.

As with many other arguments in economics, the logic for free trade is a conditional one. It simply says that, if a nation wants to increase its economic efficiency, then the avenue for doing so is by focusing on its comparative advantage and trading with other nations. But policymakers also often worry about nonefficiency aspects of free trade—in particular, aspects such as distributional (or "equity") considerations, short-term unemployment, preservation of a "way of life," and so forth. But the question that they—and the MNEs that benefit from such protection—then have to confront is whether global

---

[4]This is not to suggest that CEOs of the negatively affected industries didn't oppose agreements such as NAFTA. They, too, had the incentive to do so, and made sure that their anti-NAFTA views were heard in the US Congress.

economic competition makes loss of jobs (and attendant ways of life) inevitable, and if so, whether it is better to recognize and manage the inevitable transitions and dislocations that are bound to occur sooner or later.[5]

FORMS OF PROTECTION

There are two broad types of barriers to international trade: tariff barriers and nontariff barriers.

Tariff Barriers

Tariff barriers are types of direct price protection, and take three common forms: ad valorem duties, specific duties, and compound duties. An *ad valorem duty* is a tax that is imposed as a percentage of the value (price) of the imported or exported good; a *specific duty* is a flat tax (that is, constant dollar amount of tax) that is imposed regardless of the value of the imported or exported good; a *compound duty* is one that combines ad valorem and specific duties.

In the last few decades, with the success of GATT (more on this in the next chapter), tariff barriers have become less important as a form of protection than nontariff barriers, or forms of indirect, nonprice protection of exports and imports.

Nontariff Barriers

The most common form of nontariff barrier is the *quota,* or a quantitative restriction on the volume of imports. One well-known example of this is the textile quotas (called the "multifiber agreement") that were imposed by industrialized countries against textile imports from developing countries. (This quota was allowed by GATT for over forty years, until the recent round of negotiations.) A recent variant on quotas is the *voluntary export restraint* (VER), whereby the exporting country is gently warned that it had better "voluntarily" restrain its exports to the importing country. During the 1970s and 1980s, the VER was a common form of protection used against Japan in products ranging from steel, to machine tools, to automobiles, to semiconductors, among others.

The 1970s and 1980s also saw the increasing application of another form of nontariff barrier, *antidumping restrictions,* particularly by the US and the European Union (and usually against Japan and other exporting countries in the Far East). This form of protection seeks to prevent exporters from "dumping" their products—selling their products at "less than fair value"—in the importing country (again, more on this in Chapter 7). The net result is for the exporters' prices to be increased in the importing country.

The use of direct and indirect *subsidies*—that is, a government's attempt to lower a firm's or industry's costs by direct or indirect use of public funds—is another common form of nontariff barrier. Famous examples of subsidies include the case of Airbus Industries (see Case 9), where Boeing alleges the use of European taxpayer funds for Airbus in order to make Boeing a less competitive firm in the worldwide market for commercial airframes; or, the subsidies by the French government to its farmers and film industry, an issue that nearly prevented the recent GATT agreement from being concluded.

Governments also use other forms of nontariff barriers: local content requirements, technical standards and health regulations, and procurement policies. *Local content requirements* are efforts to promote import substitution by specifying that a certain portion of the value added must be produced inside the country; for instance, the European Union has established strict local content rules (with specific timetables) for Japanese cars manu-

[5]There is also a related "public choice" issue of concentration/dispersion of costs and benefits that often gives elected representatives the incentive to respond to pleas for protection. The benefits of protection are typically concentrated and visible in particular sectors, while the costs are typically dispersed and diffused across many sectors. This is the classic situation in which interest-group politics tend to prevail.

factured in Europe. *Technical standards and health regulations* relate to regulations of matters such as consumer safety, health, the natural environment, labeling, packaging, quality standards, and the like. The US, for instance, prohibits imports of many types of agricultural products on such grounds; Japan refused to import US skis for a number of years on grounds that Japanese snow was different from US snow; the European Union recently imposed restrictions imports on US beef fed on growth hormones, despite well-established research (and approval from the US Food and Drug Administration) that these hormones pose no health risk. Examples such as these are endless. Governments also adopt *procurement policies* that typically favor domestic producers: For instance, the US government has "Buy American" regulations to give US producers up to a 50% price advantage on Defense Department contracts. Such policies are common in almost every country.

IMPACT OF PROTECTION ON NATIONAL WELFARE: THE CASE OF TARIFFS

Relative to the free-trade equilibrium, the net impact on society of the imposition of any of these types of protection is, on balance, negative, as we shall see using the case of price restrictions (tariffs). Once we have understood how the welfare of various constituencies is affected by tariff barriers, the analysis can be applied with minor twists to many of the other cases.

Consider the traditional partial equilibrium framework from basic microeconomic theory, with quantities on the horizontal axis and prices on the vertical axis (Figure 6.1). Let the downward-sloping line dd represent domestic demand for a product, and ss the domestic supply. Define the world price of the product as p_w, and assume that p_w is lower than some domestic (no-trade) price p_d (presumably this has to be the case in order for domestic consumers to want to import the foreign product). The initial, free-trade domestic consumption of the product is given by the distance Q_2, which is the sum of domestic production (Q_1) and volume imported ($Q_2 - Q_1$). Domestic consumer surplus is shown by the region A, domestic producer surplus is shown by the region B, and the total welfare is A + B.

Figure 6.1   Impact of Free Trade (at world price lower than domestic price) on Domestic Consumer and Domestic Producer Welfare, and Volume of Trade

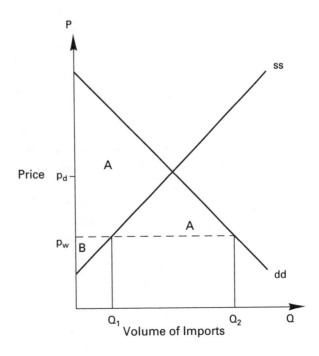

Suppose the domestic government imposes a tariff at rate τ; then the new domestic price of the product will be $p_w(1 + \tau)$. At this new higher price, domestic consumers demand less, and the total quantity demanded falls to Q_4 (see Figure 6.2); however, at this protected higher price, domestic producers have the incentive to supply more, and their production rises to Q_3. The volume of imports shrinks to the distance $Q_4 - Q_3$. What about welfare effects?

First, domestic consumer surplus falls from A to A' ; two, domestic producer surplus rises from B to B' ; three, the domestic government gets a tariff revenue represented by the rectangle C' (which is equal to $p_w\tau*(Q_4 - Q_3)$). In addition, there are now two "deadweight loss" triangles represented by the areas D' and E' , which accrue to no one. The post-tariff total welfare is less than the free-trade total welfare, since A' + B' + C' is less than A + B.

Figure 6.2 Impact of a Tariff on Domestic Consumer and Domestic Producer Welfare, and Volume of Trade

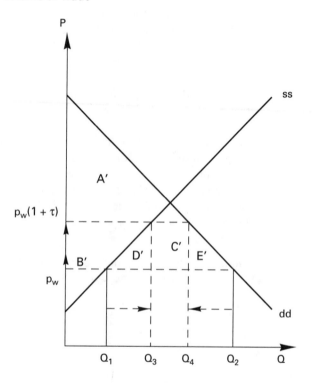

Summing up, the net effects of a tariff, relative to a free-trade equilibrium, are as follows:

- The volume of international trade declines;
- The volume of domestic production rises, and domestic producer surplus also rises as a result of the import price protection that domestic producers receive;
- The volume of domestic consumption falls, and domestic consumer surplus falls;
- The domestic government gets tariff revenue, but deadweight losses are created;
- Overall national welfare falls, because of the deadweight losses from the tariff. In other words, the sum of gains in domestic producer surplus and government tariff revenue does not make up for the consumer welfare losses resulting from the tariff.

As an exercise, extend this analysis to the case of: (1) quotas (or other quantitative restrictions, such as VERs); (2) antidumping restrictions; and (3) subsidies.

NEWER THEORIES OF INTERNATIONAL TRADE: STRATEGIC TRADE[6]

With the dramatic growth in trade in the last few decades, and the growth in the role of MNEs in international trade, there has been a resurgence of interest in taking a fresh look at theories of international trade. In the last two decades, a new set of models has come into being, using the perspectives of game theory and theories of industrial organization. While there is no one overarching model, this broad collection of theories and ideas has come to be known as "strategic trade theories." Most of the models of strategic trade are motivated by the attempt to relax (and explore systematically the implications of) the seemingly restrictive assumptions of the Ricardian and H-O models, such as those relating to perfectly competitive markets, constant or decreasing returns to scale, product homogeneity, perfect factor mobility, no externalities or spillover effects, and so forth. In the process of doing so, a fresh new set of insights relating to international trade and trade policy has emerged.

The essence of almost all the new models of trade is the recognition that industries are characterized by any or all of the following features: scale economies (both dynamic and static), product differentiation, imperfect competition, externalities and spillovers, and, in cases, irreversible investments. Some of the main insights from this literature are as follows:

1. *Increasing returns to scale* provide a justification for trade for reasons other than comparative advantage, since firms will have the incentive to produce and export in order to lower costs by attaining greater scale economies; an example of an industry where this is an important issue is the commercial airframes industry.

2. *Product differentiation* can result in intraindustry trade, since, within the same industry, the same product can have different brand identities; for example, the US will export certain types of automobiles (Ford Escort) and it will import other types of automobiles (BMWs).

3. *Imperfect competition* creates rents, and trade policy could shift rents from the foreign country to the home country. For example, the imposition of quotas will increase domestic prices and thus can create rents for foreign producers; the home-country government may try to counterbalance it with a subsidy to domestic producers, so as to put price pressure on foreign producers.

4. *Externalities and spillover effects* (particularly in innovation and R&D) may sometimes provide a justification for industry protection for reasons other than industry infancy or national security. For instance, if the process innovations in commodity chip production can create spillovers in the manufacture of specialized chips, then the government may have an incentive to protect the manufacture of commodity chips.

5. *Irreversible investments* induce an asymmetry between entry and exit costs, and can therefore lead to "hysteretic"[7] responses to price or quantity shifts. For instance, firms in the US earth-moving equipment industry (for example, Caterpillar Tractor Company) lost substantial market share in the early 1980s when the US dollar appreciated 35% in real terms against the Japanese yen. Yet, firms could not exit markets because the costs of reentry (for example, rebuilding distribution networks) would be prohibitive. Thus, they had to stay on in many markets despite the fact that they were incurring losses.

---

[6]Some commentators split hairs between the phrases "managed trade" and "strategic trade." We shall use these two terms interchangeably.

[7]Hysteresis is the phenomenon whereby the demand or supply function is elastic in one direction and inelastic in the other. For example, demand may be elastic to price increases, but inelastic to price decreases.

As with conventional trade models, models of imperfect competition in international trade predict an increase in domestic producer surplus (and a decrease in domestic consumer surplus) as a result of price or quantity restrictions. However, the literature is eclectic on the impact of protection on foreign producer surplus. We may argue, for instance, that when domestic and foreign goods are substitutes, both price and quantity restrictions should, in general, increase the welfare of foreign producers. The reasoning is that trade restraints alter the nature of interaction between firms in a collusive direction, and thereby raise equilibrium prices and profits for all firms—that is, trade restrictions result in a collusion that the firms themselves were not able to achieve, since they impede the ability of firms to compete effectively.

The insights developed in the literature on strategic trade have been quite influential in shaping the evolution and application of US trade laws against its foreign competitors, particularly during the 1980s. Policymakers increasingly use these arguments to justify imposition of barriers to international trade. Chapter 7 deals with the important US trade laws in this regard, the agencies involved, and examples of industries where they have been applied. However, the GATT has also come to grips with many of these insights, and the Uruguay round concluded in 1994 marks a significant step in multilateral attempts to combat many of these incentives to imposition of trade barriers.

SUMMARY

This chapter examined the factors that drive international trade, as well as the consequences of these factors for the economy in general and MNEs in particular. The fundamental idea that governs international trade is that of comparative advantage (and its variants, such as the H-O model).[8] Despite the seemingly strong assumptions underlying the models that argue for free trade, the idea of comparative advantage is perhaps one of the most powerful and influential to have come out of the economics literature. We saw, however, that the efficiency consequences of trade may often be in conflict with its equity consequences, thereby—paradoxically—creating the incentives for protection from those segments of the economy that are adversely affected by trade. Such protection takes the form of tariff and nontariff barriers, many of which we examined in this chapter. More recent approaches to international trade (and protection) adopt the viewpoint of "managed" or "strategic" trade policies, which seek to maximize the home country's welfare at the possible expense of foreign countries' welfare. These ideas are important for managers of MNEs because they have influenced a large body of laws and institutions that govern the conduct of international trade, and thus the trading environment of MNEs. We turn to these in Chapter 7.

SELECTED BIBLIOGRAPHY

BHAGWATI, JAGDISH. *International Trade: Selected Readings.* Cambridge, MA: MIT Press, 1981.

BHAGWATI, JAGDISH. *Protectionism.* Cambridge, MA: MIT Press, 1991.

THE ECONOMIST. "A Survey of World Trade," September 22, 1990.

FEENSTRA, ROBERT. "How Costly Is Protectionism?" *Journal of Economic Perspectives* 6 (1992): 159-178.

[8]Indeed, the recent idea of "the core competence of the corporation" may be thought of quite simply as the notion of comparative advantage as applied to firms. It comes down to the following idea: Instead of spreading your resources thin, focus on, leverage, and derive value from the firm's core competencies (comparative advantage), and leave it to other firms to do likewise with theirs.

HABERLER, GOTTFRIED. "Survey of International Trade Theory." In *Special Papers in International Economics,* No. 1. Princeton, NJ: Princeton University Press, 1961.

HECKSCHER, ELI. "The Effect of Foreign Trade on the Distribution of Income." In *Readings in the Theory of International Trade.* American Economic Association, 1949 (originally published in Swedish, in 1919).

KRUGMAN, PAUL. "Is Free Trade Passé?" *Journal of Economic Perspectives* 1, No. 2 (1987).

KRUGMAN, PAUL. "Does the New Trade Theory Require a New Trade Policy?" *World Economy,* 15 (1992): 423-441.

KRUGMAN, PAUL, and E. HELPMAN. *Market Structure and Foreign Trade: Increasing Returns, Imperfect Competition, and the International Economy.* Cambridge, MA: MIT Press, 1985.

OHLIN, BERTIL. *Interregional and International Trade.* Cambridge, MA: Harvard University Press, 1933.

RICARDO, DAVID. *On the Principles of Political Economy and Taxation.* New York: E.P. Dutton 1912 (originally published in 1817).

SMITH, ADAM. *An Inquiry into the Nature and Causes of the Wealth of Nations.* New York, Random House, 1937 (originally published in 1776).

SUNDARAM, ANANT. "Market Value Impact of the US–Japan Semiconductor Trade Agreement." The Amos Tuck School Working Paper, December 1993.

case 7

International Trade: Problem Set*

Questions 1–4 require you to pick the most appropriate answer from the choices listed. You should provide a brief explanation, calculation, or diagram (as necessary) to support your choice.

1) Two countries, A and B, can use available factors production to produce aircraft and/or wheat. If A used all its resources to produce aircraft, it could produce 100 aircraft; instead, if it used all its resources to produce wheat, it could produce 500 tons of wheat. It could also produce all combinations in between. In the case of B, it could use all its resources to produce either 25 aircraft or 125 tons of wheat, or all combinations in between. Returns to scale are constant, and all production will be consumed. In this situation

  a) A will completely specialize in aircraft production (and partly in wheat) and B will completely specialize in wheat; A will sell aircraft to B in return for some wheat.

  b) A will completely specialize in wheat production (and partly in aircraft) and B will completely specialize in aircraft; A will sell wheat to B in return for some aircraft.

  c) It is difficult to tell, because we are not given initial production data.

  d) It is difficult to tell, because we are not given a price at which trade will take place.

  e) Both (c) and (d) are true.

  f) A and B have are unlikely to have an incentive to trade with each other.

2) Assume that the Heckscher-Ohlin theory and its corollaries hold. Suppose that the US is a relatively capital-abundant and labor-scarce country, and that textiles are a labor-intensive industry. Then, a tariff imposed on textiles imported into the US

  a) will hurt the textile sector.

  b) will hurt the capital-intensive sectors of the economy.

*This problem set was developed by Associate Professor Anant K. Sundaram, as a basis for class discussion. © 1994.

   c) will hurt trade unions in the US.

   d) will have no impact on capital-intensive sectors of the economy.

   e) will have no impact on the textile sector.

3) An important difference between tariffs and quotas (assuming that the quota being considered is a tariff-equivalent one) is that

   a) Quotas lead to lower consumer surplus.

   b) Quotas lead to lower deadweight costs.

   c) Quotas lead to higher producer surplus.

   d) Quotas lead to the transfer of a part of the producer surplus from the domestic economy to the foreign economy.

   e) None of the above.

4) Consider a situation in which demand for an imported product—say semiconductors—is rising rapidly, while demand for another imported product—say, oil—is relatively static. The government is trying to choose between a tariff and a quota on these imports. Its main objective is to minimize the welfare impact on industries that use these imports (for example, computers and energy-related industries). The government has a preference to impose quotas since it believes that quotas are easier to administer and monitor compared to tariffs. If the government allowed you the choice of recommending a quota for one product and is willing to consider a tariff for the other product, you would

   a) recommend a tariff for oil and a quota for semiconductors.

   b) recommend a tariff for semiconductors and a quota for oil.

   c) be indifferent as to the choice of form of protection.

   d) recommend a quota in both cases.

5) *The Principle of Comparative Advantage—In a Different Context!!*

Two companies—let us (creatively) call them Firm A and Firm B—are examining opportunities to borrow money in markets for fixed-rate and floating-rate bonds. They are both willing to consider either type of instrument, since they are of the opinion that the prices being offered to them by the market are fair. The prices (yields-to-maturity) associated with their choices are as follows:

	Firm A	*Firm B*
Fixed rate	12%	10%
Floating rate	8%	5%

Clearly, Firm B has the *absolute* borrowing cost advantage in both markets.

   a) However, does one firm have a comparative advantage for one type of instrument versus the other? If so, which firm, for which instrument?

   b) Can these two firms exploit their comparative advantage to borrow on behalf of each other, and swap their borrowing with the other firm, so that both are made better off? Describe how, and provide an example of the gains that could occur (assume that there are no default risks with either party).

chapter 7

The Trading Environment of International Business: Laws and Institutions

During the course of this century, numerous laws and institutions have come into existence to regulate world trade. Such laws and institutions—at both the national and international levels—constitute an important part of the environment in which MNEs conduct their worldwide business. Managers of MNEs must be familiar with these laws not only because they are a means to seek redress from "unfair" competitive practices, but also because such laws are often invoked against them. The institutions that we discuss below—such as the US Department of Commerce, the Office of the US Trade Representative in the US, and the GATT and the European Commission outside the US—sit in judgment over the application and enforcement of these laws.

In this chapter, we discuss three specific sets of laws and institutions governing and overseeing world trade, and examine how they affect the MNE's trading environment: (1) those regulating international trade into and out of the US, and affecting MNEs on a *bilateral* basis; such laws are administered and enforced by various arms of the US government; (2) those regulating international trade worldwide, and affecting MNEs on a *multilateral* basis; such laws are administered and enforced by the General Agreement of Tariffs and Trade, or GATT (soon to be renamed the World Trade Organization, or WTO); and (3) those regulating international trade at a *regional,* multicountry level, and enforced by a group of countries as a "customs union" or a "free trade area"—the two most important of these being the European Union (EU), and the North American Free Trade Agreement (NAFTA).

BILATERAL TRADE LAWS: AN OVERVIEW OF UNITED STATES INTERNATIONAL TRADE LAW

Since the end of World War II, although tariff barriers fell worldwide, the scope and creativity in the application of nontariff barriers increased substantially. The impressive growth in world trade has been accompanied by an equally impressive increase in the number of commercial disputes between countries. There are many statutes in US commercial policy that provide specific types of action and potential relief for US MNEs in such instances. These statutes form an important part of the international trading environment of

MNEs, whether such MNEs belong to the US or they are MNEs undertaking business in the US (or even just competing against US firms in other markets).

The US constitution grants the Congress—and not the president—the authority ". . . to regulate commerce with foreign nations," including the right to impose import tariffs. During this century, such congressional authority has manifested itself in the form of various key laws and bills, or trade statutes. The following are some of the more widely applied statutes (and sections), along with their commonly used names and reasons for application:

<table>
<tr><td colspan="4" align="center">**WIDELY APPLIED TRADE STATUTES**</td></tr>
<tr><td>STATUTE</td><td>SECTION</td><td>COMMONLY REFERRED TO AS:</td><td>REASON FOR APPLICATION</td></tr>
<tr><td>Tariff Act of 1930</td><td>337</td><td>Unfair import practices</td><td>Methods of competition that injure a US industry; usually applied in the case of patent infringements</td></tr>
<tr><td>Tariff Act of 1930</td><td>332</td><td>Investigation</td><td>Investigations of the effect of foreign trade on US firms and industries</td></tr>
<tr><td>Tariff Act of 1930</td><td>731</td><td>Dumping</td><td>Foreign firms selling products in the US at "less than fair value" and injuring domestic industries</td></tr>
<tr><td>Tariff Act of 1930</td><td>701</td><td>Countervailing duty</td><td>Imports into the US that receive subsidies from foreign governments</td></tr>
<tr><td>Trade Expansion Act of 1962</td><td>232</td><td>National security</td><td>Imports that threaten national security</td></tr>
<tr><td>Trade Act of 1974</td><td>301</td><td>Unfair practices outside US</td><td>A practice abroad that burdens or restricts US firms' ability to undertake business there; violation of a trade agreement</td></tr>
<tr><td>Trade Act of 1974</td><td>201</td><td>Escape clause</td><td>Imports that cause injury to domestic firms</td></tr>
</table>

We shall discuss some of these laws (and responsible agencies) in greater detail below.

Key US Government Agencies Responsible for US Trade Laws

Dozens of government agencies are involved in the regulation of international trade, but three are particularly important: The Department of Commerce (DOC), the International Trade Commission (ITC), and the Office of the United States Trade Representative (USTR).

The Department of Commerce: The DOC performs a wide array of services in the international trade arena. In trade remedy, the DOC is responsible for the determination and subsequent enforcement of punitive duties in antidumping and countervailing duty cases.

The International Trade Commission: The ITC is a quasi-judicial, independent, bipartisan agency established by Congress with broad investigative powers on matters of trade. The Commission is presided over by six commissioners, appointed by the president. In its adjudicative role, the ITC investigates and decides on the matter of "injury" to a domestic industry. The injury determinations are made by polling the six commissioners, with a tie vote indicating an affirmative decision.

The Office of the United States Trade Representative: The USTR is part of the Executive Office of the President, and the position of Trade Representative is a cabinet-level position. The USTR formulates trade policy and negotiating positions for the US government. The USTR also presides over investigations under Section 301 of the trade law.

Key Terminology in US Trade Laws

Some terminology will be useful in understanding the subtleties of the various statutes. Although the words will be familiar, these terms have precise legal meanings. Often, the outcome of a specific case can rest on the legal interpretation of these terms:

Like Product: Under any industry-specific investigation, the relevant product must be precisely defined. For example, an investigation involving cement defined the like product as "gray portland cement and clinker." This definition excludes other types of cement (such as hydraulic), but includes an essential factor input in cement production (clinker).

Domestic Industry: The precision of the like product definition is crucial in determining what firms make up the domestic industry. In general, firms within the United States who manufacture the like product are part of the domestic industry. However, a firm that merely assembles or installs the like product in this country—while importing the actual product or components—might not be considered part of the domestic industry.

Standing: Many of the laws presented here are initiated through petitions filed with the government on behalf of the domestic industry. These petitions may be filed by any firm, trade association, or labor union that is representative of the domestic industry. Such groups enjoy legal "standing," but while these groups can submit a petition on behalf of their industry, any investigation will be terminated if it is determined that most of the industry opposes the petition.

Injury: In most trade remedy actions, the US domestic industry must establish that it has been "injured" in some way. In the statutes, injury is a concept whose meaning has been left deliberately vague. As a result, agencies possess great latitude in evaluating injury and often impose different thresholds of injury for different industries. Furthermore, different statutes contain slightly different definitions of injury and also may treat the issue of causation differently. Not all injury tests are created equal: for instance, the "serious" injury test is the most stringent, while "material" injury is defined as injury that is "not insignificant" (for examples, see below).

AN OVERVIEW OF FOUR KEY US TRADE STATUTES

The descriptions that follow go beyond textbook definitions of the laws and attempt to describe the process of trade remedy. The laws governing US trade may appear to be straightforward, but careful attention to the concepts described reveals important complexities.

Section 201: "Escape Clause"

Section 201, the so-called "escape clause" statute, is designed to respond to situations in which increased imports cause "serious injury" to a domestic industry. The statute is based on Article 19 of the GATT, which allows for countries to "escape" from their GATT obligations in the event that these obligations introduce overwhelming competition with respect to a specific product. Unlike other major trade laws, §201 responds to situations that do not necessarily involve "unfair" practices.

To initiate a case, any party with legal standing files a petition with the International Trade Commission (ITC) describing the effects of increasing imports on the industry. Investigations can also be requested by the president, USTR, or Congress. To be found eligible for relief under Section 201, an industry must be found by the ITC to meet the following criteria:

- Imports are increasing as a result of unforeseen developments,
- The industry has been "seriously injured," and the imports represent a substantial cause (no less than any other cause) of the injury.

The ITC generally issues its determination within 120 days. If the ITC determines that an industry qualifies for relief under §201, it forwards its affirmative recommendation for action to the president. The president can refuse to provide relief, however.

Presently, the statute itself is rarely used. In the early 1980s, however, much of the high-profile trade litigation occurred in §201 settings. For example, in 1984, the United States steel industry (carbon and alloy steel) pursued a §201 case that ultimately resulted in voluntary export restraints (VERs) in the steel industry. These agreements affected billions of dollars of trade annually. Other §201 investigations were conducted concerning automobiles, color television sets, and motorcycles.

In 1984, and again in 1988, §201 was revised in such a way that litigation became both more onerous and less likely to succeed. Accordingly, the number of §201 cases has fallen drastically. In 1990, for example, only Keystone Camera filed for relief, and their request was unanimously denied by the ITC commissioners.

Section 301: Unfair Practices Outside the United States

Section 301 is designed to allow the United States to redress any foreign government practices that are "unjustifiable, unreasonable or discriminatory" and which "burden or restrict US commerce." The statute encompasses trade in both goods and services. In §301 cases, the "unfair" action occurs outside the United States.

It is important to distinguish between regular Section 301 and the so-called "Super-301." Regular 301 actions involve a particular product, while Super-301 involves an overall pattern of unfair practices by a foreign government. Furthermore, regular 301 cases can either be initiated by a private petition or self-initiated by the US Government, while Super-301 cases were only self-initiated. Super-301 was effective for only 2 years, 1989 and 1990, although there are currently proposals before the Congress to reinstate it.

Parties with standing file a §301 petition with the Office of the United States Trade Representative (USTR). The USTR has 45 days after receiving the petition to decide whether to initiate an investigation of the complaint. Once an investigation has begun, it may take from 12 to 18 months depending on whether a GATT dispute settlement mechanism is available. The object of the investigation, which typically involves intensive negotiations with the government of the other country, is to secure removal of the offending practice.

Some examples of successful §301 actions are semiconductors (citing Japan in 1985), wine (citing Korea in 1988), and market access barriers (self-initiated against a wide range of such barriers in China, 1991 to 1992, and recently against Japan, in 1994).

Title VII Cases: Antidumping and Countervailing Duty (CVD)

Title VII of the Tariff Act of 1930 defines two specific conditions of trade that are generally considered "unfair." These are dumping (Section 731) and unfair subsidies (Section 701, called "countervailing duty" investigations). Punitive responses to these unfair practices are sanctioned by GATT.

The two types of Title VII cases are very similar, so we shall restrict our discussion to Section 731, the antidumping law.[1] These cases are unique in that they are simultaneously investigated by two government agencies, the Department of Commerce and the International Trade Commission.

Petitions are filed with the Department of Commerce, which rules on the sufficiency of the petition within 20 days. Petitions are rarely judged insufficient, partially because the Commerce Department will conduct "pre-filing" meetings to ensure the adequacy of the document. This ruling is intended to judge the completeness, and not the factual merit, of the petition. When the Department of Commerce approves the petition, a "preliminary" investigation begins at both agencies. The case terminates with a negative preliminary determination at the ITC; otherwise, both agencies conduct a "final" investigation. The entire process typically lasts about one year.

The ITC Investigation: The ITC is responsible for the injury determination. In Title VII cases (§731 and §701), the ITC must rule whether the domestic industry has been "materially" injured as a result of the unfair practice. This injury test differs substantially from that imposed in §201 investigations. First, "material" injury is defined to be less severe than "serious" injury. Furthermore, the unfair practice—not the imports—is considered to be the cause of the injury, and need only be a cause of injury, not the most important cause. In fact, the ITC is specifically directed by Congress in the statute not to weigh causes of injury.

In an injury investigation, the ITC conducts a direct survey of all parties involved, both foreign and domestic. The ITC staff conducts on-site verification of the data submitted by the parties. As a result, the ITC routinely evaluates proprietary data on current business. Injury is evaluated using a number of indicators, including production, sales, employment, net income, return on assets, and ability to raise capital.

The Department of Commerce Investigation: The Commerce Department is responsible for calculating the "dumping margin" in antidumping cases, and the "actionable subsidy" in countervailing duty cases. The department will analyze six months of proprietary sales data for the largest exporting companies in determining the extent of sales made at "less-than-fair value" (LTFV). There can be tremendous debate over accounting issues and calculation methodologies and, especially, as to what constitutes "fair value." The Department uses the following hierarchy in calculating fair value: (1) home market sales of identical or similar merchandise, (2) export sales to third countries of identical or

---

[1]The most significant difference between the two is that, in dumping investigations, the Department of Commerce determines the extent of pricing by foreign *firms* in the US below "fair value," while in CVD cases, the Department quantifies the "actionable subsidies" in percentage terms provided by a foreign *government* to its firms who are exporting subsidized goods to the US.

similar merchandise, or (3) constructed value, which is just a marked-up cost of production. The percentage dumping margin (or subsidy, in a CVD case) typically becomes the ad valorem tariff should both agencies rule affirmatively.

Relief will not be granted unless both agencies involved find affirmatively. If the ITC rules negatively, or the Commerce Department finds very low dumping margins, the case is terminated and no punitive duties are established. Dumping cases have become a popular instrument of remedy against unfair trade practices. Industries that have successfully obtained relief through the antidumping law include the small business telephone system industry (basically, AT&T) and the gray portland cement industry. Industries that have successfully obtained relief under the countervailing duty law include forged steel crankshafts and electrical conductor aluminum redraw rods.

Section 337: Unfair Practices of Import Trade

Section 337 complaints are submitted to the International Trade Commission (ITC). Under Section 337, the ITC applies US statutory and common law of unfair competition to the importation of products into the United States. Most complaints filed under Section 337 involve allegations of patent, copyright, or trademark infringement, but they can also include violations of US antitrust laws.

The ITC must complete its investigation and rule on whether there is a violation within 12 months (18 months for more complicated cases). If the ITC finds a violation, it can order the unfairly traded goods to be excluded from the United States. In cases involving patent, copyright, or trademark infringement, no injury test is required. However, in all Section 337 cases, the ITC considers general effects on public welfare, and all decisions are subject to presidential review. For instance, in 1989 alone, the ITC initiated 19 investigations under §337. Among those industries which successfully secured relief were small aluminum flashlights, light-duty screw anchors, and even Cabbage Patch dolls without adoption papers!

MULTILATERAL TRADE LAWS: AN OVERVIEW OF GATT

Founded in 1948 by two dozen industrialized countries, the objective of the General Agreement of Tariffs and Trade (GATT) is to reduce barriers to international trade. By 1994, GATT had nearly 120 member countries, and another 30 countries applied GATT rules to their trade. Over 90% of world trade is carried out by countries who are signatories to GATT. Unlike agencies such as the World Bank and the IMF, the GATT is not as much a physical institution as it is a comprehensive set of agreements and rules on world trade, administered and governed by a small secretariat in Geneva, Switzerland. Parties to GATT are governed by voluntary acceptance of its jurisdiction, and the organization does not have any formal enforcement powers. In other words, GATT is nothing more than an "agreement" among signatory countries to follow a collectively agreed-upon set of rules.

The workings of GATT are based on five underlying principles, which form the basis for almost all of its rules:

1. *Nondiscrimination:* This principle states that countries should not grant preferential treatment to any one group of member countries over other member countries. This is the basis for the "most favored nation" (MFN) rule, which simply means that every member country will be treated alike by all GATT members. In other words, MFN does not imply preferential treatment; rather it implies that every country should be treated as favorably as every other country.

2. *Reciprocity:* This means that if one country lowers its tariffs against another country, the other country should do likewise; any concession that is made will be reciprocated. Combined with the idea of MFN, it is the means by which GATT tries to get all members to lower their tariffs to each other.

3. *Transparency:* This principle asks countries that do impose protection to do so through tariffs, and not nontariff barriers or quantitative restrictions. Even if there are nontariff barriers, GATT urges their "tariffication," so that they can be made more transparent, and subsequently reduced through the principle of reciprocity.

4. *Dispute Settlement:* GATT members are expected to use the dispute settlement mechanisms of GATT. There is, however, no enforcement mechanism in the event that a member country refuses to abide by GATT rules in dispute settlement.

5. *Exceptions:* Countries are granted exceptions to GATT rules under special or emergency circumstances. These exceptions include special treatments for regional trading arrangements, for developing countries, for trade in certain industries such as agriculture and textiles, for dumping, for domestic firms seriously injured by imports, and for balance-of-payments difficulties.

Despite some criticisms of the rules and GATT's apparent lack of enforcement authority, these rules have combined to work remarkably well for world trade in the past few decades, at least in reducing tariff barriers worldwide. In 1947, the average tariffs on imported products worldwide stood at about 40%; by 1990, they had declined to about 5%. It is estimated that, by the year 2000, the average tariff will have fallen to about 2%.

These tariff reductions have been achieved through various "rounds" of negotiations among the member countries. The earliest round of negotiations was the "Geneva" round, in 1947; more recently, the sixth and seventh rounds of negotiations, the "Kennedy" round (1964-67) and the "Tokyo" round (1973-79) were particularly effective in achieving tariff reduction agreements.

The Uruguay Round

The most ambitious round of world trade negotiations, however, was the recent "Uruguay" round. Initiated in Punta del Este, Uruguay, in 1986, this round of negotiations went through repeated roller-coaster rides—at points, looking almost certainly like it would fail—but was finally concluded, nearly eight years later, in December 1993. On April 15, 1994, the signatory governments met in Marrakech, Morocco, and formally ratified the agreement.

The Uruguay round was considered ambitious in as much as it sought to address numerous issues that GATT had previously sidestepped since its creation in 1948. These issues included:

- Trade in services
- A consistent set of rules governing trade in intellectual property rights ("TRIPs")
- A consistent set of rules to govern trade-related investment measures ("TRIMs"), or direct investments abroad
- Trade in textiles, which had previously been protected (under the auspices of GATT) through the "multifiber agreement"
- Trade in agricultural products
- The creation of a new entity whereby GATT would be renamed the "World Trade Organization (WTO)" with improved dispute settlement processes, and improved "functioning of the GATT system" ("FOGS")

At the conclusion of the Uruguay round in December 1993, many of these issues were successfully addressed, resulting in a 22,000-page (385-pound) document. Jerry Junkins, CEO of the US company, Texas Instruments, sees the importance of the agreement as follows:[2]

---

[2]"Economic Well-being: A New Name for National Security," Advertisement Section, *New York Times,* April 15, 1994, p. A27.

For American business, the Uruguay Round means increased fairness and order in the marketplace, not a perfect marketplace. For Texas Instruments, the increase in trade resulting from a more open world market could translate into additional revenues of roughly $5 billion over the next ten years. Put another way, the implementation of the Uruguay Round agreement could contribute 6 percent of TI's revenues by the year 2004, and support 2000 to 3000 new jobs, most of them in the United States.

The specific achievements of the Uruguay round agreements, which will start to take effect starting 1995, are as follows:

- Agreements on services trade were reached in the areas of banking, insurance, and tourism; however, agreement in areas such as shipping, telecommunications, airlines, and audiovisual products were postponed.
- The new rules tighten antidumping laws and follow US practices in this regard (Section 731, which we discussed above) rather closely.
- The protection of intellectual property rights has been made uniform and substantially strengthened, in the areas of patents, copyrights, trademarks, industrial designs, trade secrets, and integrated circuits.
- The TRIMs text establishes GATT oversight in investment matters, and prohibits imposition of local content rules and trade-balancing rules.
- Industrialized countries agreed to a 10-year phase-out of the multifiber agreement, which was originally intended to protect the textile industries of the US, Japan, and Western European countries from low-wage textile exporters, primarily in Asia.
- Existing tariffs on both industrial and agricultural products will be cut by an average of 40%, most of them over 5 years starting 1995; in some industries, (for example, construction equipment, medical equipment, beer, steel, pharmaceuticals), tariffs are completely eliminated among major trading partners in the industrialized world; in electronics, tariff cuts range from 50% to 100% worldwide.
- Subsidies are more clearly defined and categorized, and these definitions and categories largely follow those used in relation to US countervailing duty laws (discussed earlier in this chapter).
- The agreement establishes international rules between governments regarding product and technical standards and in matters such as testing, inspection, certification.
- Most of the existing voluntary export restraints will be eliminated (although each country is allowed to "grandfather" one such agreement until 1999).
- A framework for the successor to GATT, the WTO, has been put in place.

It is estimated that the successful implementation of the Uruguay round agreements will result in approximately a 3.5% growth in gross world product during the next ten years; this translates to roughly an additional $235 billion in global income each year. From the standpoint of MNEs, the progress achieved in specific areas (and their implementation) during the course of the next few years bears careful scrutiny.

REGIONAL TRADING ARRANGEMENTS: THE EUROPEAN UNION AND NAFTA

Although there are numerous informal and formal regional trading arrangements among groups of countries all over the world, the two most prominent ones are the European Union (EU, formerly known as "EC92" or sometimes "1992") encompassing twelve European countries (with a few more slated to join in the near future) and the North American Free Trade Agreement (NAFTA) among the US, Mexico, and Canada. These two regional trading arrangements are prominent not only because the countries involved account for over 50% of world trade, but also because these trading arrangements are the farthest along in terms of formulation, ratification by member governments, and implementation.[3]

The European Union

A Brief History of the EU: The origins of the EU lie in the European Coal and Steel Community (ECSC) formed by France, Germany, Italy, Belgium, Holland, and Luxembourg in 1951. A significant step toward forming a common economic community occurred in 1957, when the same six countries signed a document called the "Treaty of Rome," which established the European Economic Community (EEC), and the Atomic Energy Committee (Euratom).

In 1967, these three entities—ECSC, EEC, and Euratom—merged to form the European Community (EC), with a view to push forward two primary aims that had been established with the Treaty of Rome: (1) to lay the foundations for a "closer union among the people of Europe," and (2) to establish a "common market" by the elimination of trade barriers. The 1967 merger agreement also laid the framework for the bureaucracy and the institutions (colloquially referred to as "Eurocrats") that would oversee the common market and the closer union. These included the European Commission, the Council of Ministers, the European Parliament, and the European Court of Justice. In 1972, the EC accepted three new members—Denmark, Ireland, and the UK—and Greece joined the EC in 1981; Spain and Portugal joined in 1986, bringing the total membership to twelve. In the meantime, in 1979, the then members created the European Monetary System (EMS), which attempted to limit currency fluctuations and bring inflation down among the member countries, by creating a system of quasi-fixed exchange rates (currencies could fluctuate within a narrow band, which, if violated, would require the concerned government to change its fiscal and/or monetary policies). They also created a new composite currency called the "ecu."[4]

EC92, the Internal Market, and the EU: The most significant step occurred in 1985 when the members of the EC agreed to the Single European Act (SEA; ratified in 1986), which agreed to "complete the internal market by 1992" (actually January 1, 1993) by removing physical and technical barriers to the movements of goods, services, and individuals, and fiscal barriers such as value-added taxes and excise duties. A white paper resulting from this agreement identified 282 specific proposals for implementation. The movement toward the adoption of these proposals, although not perfect, was remarkable; by 1992, more than 230 had been adopted by all the member countries.

The reason for this success (and its speed) is attributed to four principles espoused by the SEA: (1) The idea of *mutual recognition,* or the notion that, barring certain specific cases, law in one of the twelve member countries would be de facto recognized as valid law in the others; since this would mean that economic activity could follow the pocketbook inside the EC, it resulted in "competitive rulemaking" (rather than ponderous attempts at "harmonization") whereby each government competed with the other to deregulate so as to

---

[3]Although we deal with both EU and NAFTA under the umbrella of "regional trading arrangements," it is important to recognize that EU involves substantially more than just trade: Agreements among the twelve EU countries also include matters such as common social policy, defense policy, and foreign policy. More specifically, the EU is referred to in the theory and laws of international trade as a "customs union," while NAFTA is referred to as a "free trade area." A customs union is an agreement among several countries to eliminate internal barriers to trade and investment among themselves, and to erect, if necessary, a *common* set of barriers against nonmember countries; a free trade area, on the other hand, is an agreement among several countries to eliminate internal barriers to trade and investment among themselves, and to continue with their existing, *individual* set of barriers against nonmember countries.

[4]In 1992, the EMS broke down, under the weight of a severe currency crisis brought on by speculation and divergent government policies among member countries. However, the ecu still continues to be used as a composite currency, and its importance as a medium of exchange in the EC has grown.

make its own laws more attractive to businesses and consumers; (2) The idea of *setting no priorities*. Rather than setting specific timetables for countries to implement each of the 282 items, the EC adopted the idea that whatever was implemented would be fine, without setting any priorities; this had the effect of building a shared sense of success in the implementation (even though it was only in terms of total numbers), and built a quick history of seemingly effective cooperation; (3) The principle of *subsidiarity*, or the idea that all decisions would be made at the lowest appropriate level; this had the effect of making the process of integration a "bottom-up," rather than a top-down and seemingly bureaucrat-imposed, process; (4) The idea of a *qualified majority*, which gave the weaker countries a somewhat greater incentive to cooperate, and made it more difficult for larger countries to oppose particular proposals.

In December 1991, in the Dutch town of Maastricht, the twelve countries attempted to take the movement toward integration a step further, by trying to achieve a timetable for adoption of a common social, defense, and foreign policy, as well as the creation of a common currency and a common central bank for all of the EC. In the process, the EC would also be renamed the "European Union" (EU). By all accounts, the Maastricht proposals were a failure, and perhaps even set back the movement toward integration. The reasons for this were both endogenous and exogenous: (1) The fall of the Berlin Wall and communism, German unification, and the creation of a whole new set of independent states resulted in considerable disarray within the EC, by creating tensions between domestic policy and foreign policy in many of the member countries; (2) The currency system, EMS, collapsed under the weight of divergent macroeconomic policies among member countries and speculative attacks by foreign exchange traders; (3) The genuinely bottom-up process of integration that was set in motion by the SEA was seen as being reversed by bureaucratic interference over matters of social organization, politics, defense and foreign policy, and the like—in essence, matters of national culture and sovereignty; and (4) Europe slipped into a major recession in 1992, and with increasing unemployment and economic hard times, member countries became more inward-looking in their policy concerns—that is, the move toward integration, which had happened in the midst of economic good times, had never really been tested by a severe recession or a downturn.

In summary, currently the movement toward a "closer union" would appear to be stalled compared to the earlier enthusiasm and the genuine forward movement that took place in the late 1980s (leading some to make the comment that "the best years for 1992 were 1986-89"). However, the progress that has been achieved on the economic front has been remarkable.

From the standpoint of the manager of an MNE, it is this latter point that really matters. For all practical purposes, many MNEs treat the EU as one marketplace and geographic setting not only from the point of view of their distribution, sales, and marketing strategies, but also in terms of their plant location, R&D, product approval and testing, and sourcing strategies. Moreover, major trade laws and competition laws are largely harmonized in their application among the twelve countries. Many of these laws have evolved in the tradition of US laws on these matters. Indeed, for many MNEs, it is as important to have lobbyists and to attempt to influence regulation in Brussels (the home of the European Commission) as it is in Washington, DC. The economic changes that have taken place in Europe, resulting from the attempt to create a frictionless internal market, may be irreversible for all practical purposes. The continued evolution of these changes represents an important part of the European environment in which managers of MNEs will conduct business.

The North American Free Trade Agreement (NAFTA)

Originally initiated by the government of President George Bush, NAFTA was concluded by the Clinton administration after more than three years of work. The agreement, which covers the US, Mexico, and Canada, is fundamentally a trade and investment agreement with a view to reduce barriers to the flow of goods, services, and people among these three countries. The agreement covers only goods and services that are produced in North America or, if imported, goods and services that meet certain local content requirements; the nationality of ownership does not matter, as long as such local content requirements are met (for example, a Japanese company manufacturing its products in North America and meeting these standards will qualify for the same benefits as any American company).

The agreement covers areas such as tariff reduction, freer movement of professionals among the three countries, financial and direct investment matters, and consumer safety, and it includes escape clauses for "emergency actions" for injured industries. In addition to the basic agreements, there are "side" agreements that specifically cover issues relating to protection of labor and protection of the natural environment. Some of the specific objectives of NAFTA are the following:

- Substantial tariff reductions over a ten-year period. For instance, in agriculture, the countries will eliminate 57% of their tariffs immediately, and 94% after ten years. In automobiles, the US will eliminate tariffs on automobiles assembled in Mexico, and phase out tariffs on light trucks; Mexico will reduce its tariffs on US-built cars and trucks immediately from 20% to 10%, and phase out the rest over the next few years.

- More access to financial services. NAFTA will dismantle Mexico's ban on US banks and brokerage services. Over time, US banks will be allowed up to 25% of the Mexican market, and brokerages up to 30% of the Mexican market.

- Protection for investment. No investment can be expropriated without full compensation.

- Lowering barriers to movement of goods. Specifically, trucking traffic will be able to move easier across borders.

- The creation of a special office (based in Canada) to investigate environmental abuses, and one (based in the US) to investigate labor abuses. Both offices can impose fines or recommend trade sanctions for countries or industries that fail to enforce their own laws.

- The creation of a special fund for worker retraining and financial support in industries adversely affected by the passage of NAFTA.

- The creation of a North American Development Bank with capital of up to $4 billion, to assist in environmental cleanups and to provide trade adjustment assistance to communities adversely affected by NAFTA.

- The creation of a US–Mexico border environmental commission that could spend up to $8 billion to address air and water pollution, and clean up toxic waste dumps.

In summary, NAFTA is an attempt to move the economies of North America toward a scenario whereby a company that is based in any one of the three countries can freely conduct its business across all three borders, as long as certain basic standards relating to North American local content, labor standards, consumer safety standards, and environmental standards are met. There is already talk in Washington that the long-term objective of the agreement is to bring into its fold all of the countries in both North and South America.

SUMMARY

In this chapter, we examined the laws and institutions that govern the conduct of international trade in the US and North America, in Europe, and worldwide. These laws and institutions constitute an extremely important aspect of the cross-border trade and investment environment of MNEs worldwide. In the US, there are numerous trade laws covering specific aspects of international trade, while NAFTA expands the scope of some of these laws to all three North American countries; the European Union and its institutions do likewise in the case of Europe; the GATT, with its successfully concluded Uruguay round, provides the global framework within which MNEs conduct their business worldwide. In all three instances, the laws and institutions are not static—their continued evolution bears careful scrutiny, in terms of both the constraints and opportunities they create whereby MNEs deal with their global competition.

case 8

The Chips Are Down*

It was perhaps the biggest leap in technology since the invention of the transistor—a tiny silicon wafer, called a "chip," developed in part by Fairchild Semiconductors in California's Silicon Valley. It was capable of storing millions of bits of information and yet, would fit on a fingernail. The invention was another example of the vitality of US technology, as symbolized by California's Silicon Valley.

US manufacturers soon grew to be the global market leaders in semiconductors. In 1974, they had nearly three-quarters of the world market share (see *Exhibit 1*). By 1980, the US electronics industry—in significant part represented by the semiconductor industry—ran a trade surplus of close to $8 billion, accounting for over four-fifths of the overall favorable US trade balance.

Apart from the innovative ability of the Americans, numerous factors helped in the development of the semiconductor industry in the US. The largest user industry, computers, was still predominantly US-based; further, the market for computers was shifting to smaller personal computers and to workstations, the development and marketing of both of which were closely related to innovations in the semiconductor industry. Some of the finest research facilities and universities in the world are located in the US, providing a constant source not only of ideas, but also of skilled labor. Many US government agencies—notably the Department of Defense and NASA—were early and large consumers of (as well as providers of research funds for) semiconductors. Finally, from the late 1970s and onwards, there were thriving venture capital markets for small firms with innovative technologies in the US, at a time when such capital markets were unheard of in most other parts of the world.

By 1986, however, tables had turned. The US electronics industry, in line with the rest of the economy, was running a trade *deficit* of $8.6 billion. The segment of the electronics

*This case was developed by Associate Professor Anant K. Sundaram, as a basis for class discussion. © 1988. Revised 1993.

industry that was the worst affected by this turnaround was semiconductors. Many firms had gone out of business, an estimated 65,000 jobs were lost, and those firms that remained were running huge losses, estimated to be $2 billion in the years 1986-87.[1] US firms lost market share (see *Exhibit 1*) to more efficient (see *Exhibit 2*) Japanese semiconductor makers, and to manufacturers in the cheap-labor environments of South Korea, Taiwan, and Singapore.

EXHIBIT 1

Market Shares of Worldwide Merchant* Semiconductor Sales

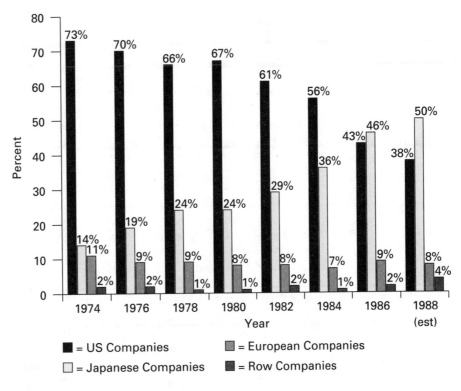

- ■ = US Companies
- ▨ = European Companies
- ☐ = Japanese Companies
- ■ = Row Companies

Source: "Status 1989: A Report on the Integrated Circuit Industry," Integrated Circuit Engineering Corporation, Scottsdale, AZ.

*"Merchant" producers (as opposed to "captive" producers) are those firms that sell at least 25% of their output outside the firm.

EXHIBIT 2

Yield Comparisons of US and Japanese Semiconductor Manufacturers

| | Typical Yields of Good Chips per Wafer (%) | |
	US	Japan
Start of wafer fabrication	100%	100%
After first quality check	66%	88%
After final wafer test	20%	57%
Saleable chips after assembly	17%	54%

Source: *BusinessWeek*, August 18, 1986.

[1] *Fortune*, April 13, 1987.

THE JAPANESE "INVASION"

There were a number of causes for this sudden and dramatic decline. First, the computer industry, which was the single largest user of semiconductors, saw a downturn in 1984. Second, the substantial real appreciation of the US dollar led to a relative decline in price competitiveness for US manufacturers of semiconductors in global markets. Third, there were increasing complaints from the users of US chips concerning the quality of US chips and service of US chip manufacturers. For example, chip customers charged that, lulled by their previous success, the ". . . arrogant and short-sighted US semiconductor firms have not serviced customers adequately."[2]

However, as the US chip industry saw it, the problem was simply the result of Japanese "unfair trade practices." US firms claimed that there was protectionism in the Japanese markets that blocked their access there, while in the US markets, they claimed that the Japanese firms were dumping the semiconductors—that is, selling their chips below "fair market value."

US manufacturers had a less than 10% share of a $6 billion Japanese chip market, the largest in the world.[3] US manufacturers asserted that they were being excluded from 70% of the Japanese markets through various forms of nontariff barriers, and could not make bids; the Japanese maintained that US chips did not meet Japanese specifications, and that US chips were of poor quality. The nontariff barrier charge was captured in a comment made by Steven Mihaylo, CEO of Inter-Tel Inc., of Phoenix, Arizona, who said, "We've found the Japanese very difficult to negotiate with; they've raised procrastination to an art form."[4]

On the price front, the US Semiconductor Industry Association claimed that the Japanese firms were selling at between 50 and 60% of their average cost of production, and accused them of conducting "bottomless auctions."[5] For example, between 1985 and 1986, the price of 256K EPROM (erasable, programmable, read only memory) chips had fallen from about $17.50 to less than $5. Similarly, the price of DRAM (dynamic, random access memory) chips had fallen 80% during this period, enough to drive Motorola, National Semiconductor, Intel, and Mostek out of the DRAM business (see *Exhibit 1*). George Schneer, a vice-president at Intel, recalled, "We announced our withdrawal from DRAMs on October 9, 1985; it sticks in my mind like Pearl Harbor."[6]

The Japanese claimed that the correct basis for pricing is marginal cost, a concept that was convenient given the fact that most Japanese chip-makers were vertically integrated, and had a substantial domestic (and within-firm) market to purchase their basic production (see *Exhibit 3* for a comparison of external dependence of US and Japanese firms on their semiconductor sales). The incremental costs in producing for foreign markets were, indeed, low. It was common for most large Japanese firms to have interconnected manufacturing structures called "keiretsu." Advantages of the keiretsu system include insulation against market instability, as well as provision of entry barriers against potential competitors.

Japanese firms also argued that rising global competition from countries such as Korea and Taiwan, combined with falling demand worldwide, was leading to excess capacity globally, and hence, falling chip prices.

US industry, however, claimed that these arguments were simply smokescreens for the Japanese to subsidize money-losing chip operations with profits from their other products. Texas Instruments (TI) was a case in point.[7] For decades, TI dominated the world

---

[2]*Barron's,* March 30, 1987.

[3]Unlike the US, where the market was largely in computer and defense-related industries, the market for semiconductors in Japan was largely in the electronics industry.

[4]*The Wall Street Journal,* March 30, 1987.

[5]*Fortune,* May 12, 1986.

[6]*Fortune,* op. cit.

[7]Most of TI's case is drawn from *New York Times,* July 1, 1987.

semiconductor industry because of its overwhelming strength in technology and manufacturing. But that success caused the company's leaders to believe that the company could do no wrong, according to its longtime employees. It also, reportedly, led to an insularity that left it out of touch with rapidly changing markets. "We were too damn arrogant," said William Weber, president of the semiconductor division. In a market that was becoming increasingly dominated by Japanese firms, the company began to lose money in 1985, and barely achieved breakeven in 1986. The changing course of events during these years is summarized in *Exhibit 4*.

EXHIBIT 3

Dependence on Semiconductor Sales: US and Japanese Firms

Japanese Firms	SC Sales as % of Total Sales	US Firms	SC Sales as % of Total Sales
NEC	18	AMD	89
Fujitsu	7	Fairchild	69
Toshiba	6	Intel	75
Hitachi	4	Motorola	31
Mitsubishi	3	National	85
Matsushita	2	Texas Instruments	36

Source: *New Scientist,* May 1986.

EXHIBIT 4

Rank of Leading Chip Manufacturers by Sales

Rank	1983	1985	1987
1	Texas Instruments	Nippon Electric	Nippon Electric
2	Nippon Electric	Fujitsu	Toshiba
3	Fujitsu	Texas Instruments	Hitachi

Source: *Dataquest.*

TI, however, decided not to take it lying down. It decided to fight back using all means available, including (a) suing eight chip manufacturers from Japan and one from Korea for patent infringements; at least six reached settlements with TI; (b) joining other US chipmakers in lobbying the Reagan administration for imposition of sanctions for "unfair" Japanese trade practices; (c) spending more than $1 billion in modernizing its production and R&D facilities; and, (d) entering into a conscious program of forging closer ties with suppliers and customers. In addition to all this, the dollar began to reverse course from its earlier substantial appreciation, and began to depreciate.

In 1987, the company turned around with a reasonable profit of $83.8 million on sales of $1.3 billion—but, not without some help from Washington.

LOBBYING AND THE CHIP PACT

By 1986, most of the major US chip manufacturers had set up shop in Washington, D. C. The American Electronics Association, based in Palo Alto, increased its Washington staff by 50%. A number of companies, including Hewlett-Packard and Intel, formed political action committees (PACs) to "funnel funds to favorite candidates."[8]

[8]*Fortune,* July 7, 1986.

Lobbying successes were soon evident. A trade bill was passed by the US House of Representatives in May that included a resolution to open up its semiconductor market. According to a report, 275 legislators were "jawboned" by TI, National Semiconductor, and others into going along with the resolution. Five days after that bill passed, Japanese negotiators sat down with their US counterparts, and came up with a preliminary trade pact that would allow US companies to increase their market share to 20% by 1991. The lobbyists also won in another key area—taxes. They won an extension of the tax credit for their R&D in the Tax Reform Act of 1986.

In addition, responding to the allegations of the US firms, the Commerce Department was pursuing antidumping actions against Hitachi, Fujitsu, NEC, Toshiba, Mitsubishi and Oki; Federal courts were hearing suits claiming damages from Japanese firms; the Justice Department was investigating allegations of predatory practices by Japanese firms; another Washington agency, the International Trade Commission, was considering a petition to ban imports of certain Japanese products.

The biggest victory came on July 31, when the Commerce Department concluded that Japanese companies were, indeed, "dumping" in the US markets, and that they were selling abroad at an average of 59.4% to 63.6% of their home price. It proposed duties to punish Japan for underpricing memory chips in the US. The Japanese government quickly responded, and after lengthy (and reportedly, often acrimonious) discussions, agreed to a bilateral trade pact on chips (called the "chip pact"). In return for these concessions, President Reagan announced that he would postpone the imposition of duties until such time as it could be determined that the Japanese had lived up to the chip pact. The major outcomes of the pact were:

a) the Japanese government will help police the price of chip exports;
b) a floor price would be established for chips sold in the US;
c) they would take steps to help US chipmakers increase their share of the Japanese markets, to 20%.

The last item was contained in a side letter to the agreement, and was considered quite novel in terms of a US trade agreement—never before had the US government asked a foreign country to guarantee market share; previous such agreements had usually sought access. The key paragraph of the side letter said:

> The government of Japan recognizes the US semiconductor industry's expectation that semiconductor sales in Japan of foreign-capital affiliated companies will grow to at least slightly above 20% of the Japanese market in five years. The government of Japan considers that this can be realized and welcomes this realization. The attainment of such an expectation depends on competitive factors, the sales efforts of the foreign-capital affiliated companies, the purchasing efforts of the semiconductor users in Japan, and the efforts of both governments.

In the meantime, Fujitsu, in an attempt to diversify its operations and obtain a US manufacturing base, made a bid to acquire 80% of Fairchild Semiconductor from its parent, Schlumberger (France). US chipmakers saw this sale as "reward for past unfair trade practices,"[9] and protested loudly to Washington. Commerce Secretary Malcolm Baldridge opposed the buyout on grounds this was the first step towards Japanese domination of the US semiconductor industry; Defense Secretary Caspar Weinberger opposed it on national security grounds, based on advice from the Department of Defense and the Central Intelligence Agency (30 to 40% of Fairchild sales were to DOD); the Justice department opposed it on grounds that it had potential antitrust implications. The outcome of all this pressure was exactly the one that US chipmakers wanted: Early in 1987, Fujitsu dropped its bid for Fairchild Semiconductor.

[9]*Business Week Industrial Edition,* March 30, 1987.

LAME DUCK AND DEAD DUCK

The US semiconductor industry was quite pleased with its lobbying successes. It had clearly obtained a short-term reprieve. Silicon Valley was beginning to perform better again. Production of US electronic equipment, major users of chips, was expected to increase 7.6% in 1987 and 10.3% in 1988.[10] User inventories were low after a two-year glut, and 1987 sales in the US semiconductor industry were expected to rise 20%.[11] Moreover, newer generations of computers required greater memory—for example, the original IBM PC, introduced in 1981, had 64,000 characters of internal memory, but recent models had anywhere from one to four million characters. The semiconductor industry association began talking about the formation of industry consortia to compete globally, and the setting up of a body called Sematech, which would be a joint, industry-government overseeing body. An analyst at Dataquest, a market research firm, said, "never have I seen America so bent on waging a multifront war."[12]

In the meantime, the European community protested loudly against the US-Japan chip pact, claiming that the pact calls for market access steps that favor US manufacturers, and that prices were being artificially propped up, thus hurting European electronics firms. The EC contended that this was a direct violation of well-accepted GATT principles, and appealed to GATT for a ruling. A ruling was not likely for at least another year.

Further, with Japan's $60 billion trade surplus that was showing no signs of abating, combined with its perceived recalcitrance on a whole host of trade issues—getting rid of tariffs on agricultural products, participation of US firms in the Kansai airport construction project, orders for US-made supercomputers, etc.—protectionist sentiment was running high in Congress, which was moving in the direction of passing a massive trade bill. Nine House committees had added or drafted a grab-bag of provisions. At least one presidential candidate, Richard Gephardt, was basing his campaign on the trade theme. All of this was exacerbated by the perception that Reagan's "lame duck" presidency was hamstrung by the Iran-Contra affair and hence, it was up to the Congress to take some action.

It was soon obvious that the chip pact was failing. The Japanese Ministry of International Trade and Industry (MITI) was given the task of making sure that Japanese firms were sticking to the 1986 pact. However, it soon became clear, contrary to US notions of MITI's power, that it had no control over Japanese manufacturers. It was unable to stop sales in third countries—small Japanese trading firms would simply buy cheaply at home where minimum price stipulations did not apply, and make money by selling them abroad at prices that would still constitute dumping under the chip pact. Further, Japanese producers were angry because floor prices meant that Korean firms were nibbling away at their markets. A fall in their US sales was leading to a glut at home, and further depressed prices. Many Japanese firms began to feel the pinch. When asked whether they would agree to production quotas established by MITI, one Japanese manufacturer said, "well, maybe."[13] Finally, there was no progress on the front of US manufacturers increasing their market share in Japan—the usual charges and countercharges did little to elucidate issues.

On March 27, 1987, there was cheering in Congress and in Silicon Valley. Reagan announced that Japan had failed to live up to the 1986 chip pact, and that, under Section 301 of the Trade Act, he was imposing 100% tariffs on a range of Japanese products, including film, computer disk drives, TVs and VCRs, and portable tape players. The duties would take effect on April 17. Clayton Yeutter, the US Trade Representative, said that ". . . this action probably constitutes the first step in a major reassessment of the longer term

---

[10]*Purchasing World,* August 1987.

[11]*Computerworld,* July 27, 1987.

[12]*Fortune,* April 13, 1987.

[13]*Business Week,* April 13, 1987.

economic relationship with the Japanese." Another trade official remarked, ". . . the Japanese have been nickel-and-diming us for years."[14]

Wall Street did not react too well to the news. The following morning, the Dow Jones industrial average dropped 80 points. Less than a month away, the Japanese prime minister Yasuhiro Nakasone was due in Washington on an important state visit. According to some newspaper reports, a grim joke that was apparently making the rounds in Washington, D. C., was, "If Reagan is a lame duck, Nakasone is a dead duck."

[14]*Wall Street Journal,* March 30, 1987.

Boeing versus Airbus: GATT and Mouse*

In June 1991 the dispute between the US and the European Community (EC) over the alleged infringement of international trade laws by Airbus Industrie rose to a new intensity. The US had recently threatened to bring a complaint against the governments of the four nations comprising the Airbus consortium—France, Germany, Britain, and Spain—before the Subsidies Committee of the General Agreement for Tariffs and Trade (GATT). Efforts by the EC to have the complaint brought under the jurisdiction of the more flexible Civil Aircraft Committee had failed.

After a meeting of the four nations comprising Airbus in Paris, French Transport Minister Paul Quiles told reporters: "We regret that a bilateral accord with the US has not been reached, but we hope for a positive response. . . to [our] proposal to hold multilateral talks under the [GATT] Civil Aircraft Code." Despite this apparently conciliatory tone, the four member countries said that Washington's allegations were excessive and that they were ready to defend, as one spokesman put it, "the jewel of the European aircraft industry." Others, however, believed that "the jewel" did not need defending. Raymond J. Waldmann, Boeing Commercial Airplane Group's Director of government affairs commented, "Airbus is 21 years old—no longer an infant industry dependent on the government; it is time for it to leave home."

The marked difference between the positions of the governments of the US and the EC (and of Boeing Company and Airbus Industrie) was the basis for a trade dispute that had been played out over the last five years and was still continuing. The solution to this dispute would be as much a matter of the governments' strategic trade policies, as it would be of the companies' business strategies. The question that would soon be facing the GATT was: Did certain types of financial support provided to Airbus by the EC governments constitute "unfair export subsidies?"

Simultaneously, the question facing Frank Shrontz, Chairman of Boeing, was to what degree, if at all, did this affect Boeing's strategy in a year when it had made record profits of $1.4 billion and faced a year-end order backlog worth $97 billion?

*This case was developed by Nick A. Hall under the supervision of Associate Professor Anant K. Sundaram as a basis for class discussion. © 1993.

THE AEROSPACE INDUSTRY

June 1991 was a turbulent time for the aerospace industry. The greatest order boom in the history of commercial aviation had been followed by its worst financial crisis. In August of the previous year, Saddam Hussein invaded Kuwait, and the ensuing Persian Gulf War precipitated a worldwide recession, sent fuel prices skyward, tourist traffic earthward, and hit commercial air travel hard. The three largest aircraft manufacturers—Boeing, McDonnell Douglas and Airbus—had anticipated strong demand growth through 1991, but now watched in dismay as first quarter orders all but disappeared.

Despite this short-term gloom, however, worldwide air traffic was predicted to grow by 5 to 6% annually through the 1990s, with US traffic growing slightly below average and international traffic slightly above (see *Exhibit 1*). This projected growth, together with the need to replace aging fleets and the increasing demands of noise regulators (implying a need for newer, reduced-noise models of aircraft) resulted in the three manufacturers having a combined order backlog equal to four years worth of production by the end of 1989 (*Exhibit 2*).

The building of aircraft is just one part of an industry that spans everything from making automatic cabin-doors to space satellites. The aerospace industry is split into three broad segments: defense contracts, space programs, and commercial aircraft. The industry is one of the most capital-intensive in the world. It combines the capital and labor requirements of heavy manufacturing with the research and development (R&D) requirements of a high technology industry. The aerospace share of total US private sector industrial R&D

EXHIBIT 1

World Air Travel Forecast

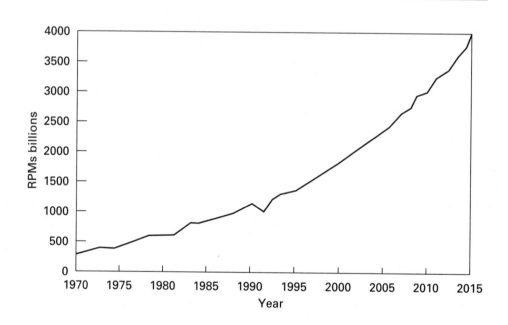

Source: Boeing Company.

Notes:

• This chart shows historical data up to 1991. The average growth rate until 1991 was 6.8% per year. From 1991 to 2000 the rate of growth is forecast at 5.9% per year. From 2000 onwards the rate of growth is forecast at 5.0% per year.

• RPMs: Revenue Passenger Miles

EXHIBIT 2

Civil Transport Aircraft Backlog

Year	1986	1987	1988	1989	1990
Total (units)	948	1,272	1,977	2,738	3,176
Value ($ millions)	22,264	32,371	58,457	89,069	112,339
Boeing					
B-727	0	0	0	0	754
B-737	269	342	488	739	250
B-747	84	120	153	165	333
B-757	63	67	205	344	192
B-767	35	44	91	192	34
Total	451	573	937	1,440	1,563
Airbus					
A300	14	31	58	68	78
A310	38	45	44	48	70
A320	236	294	420	445	526
A321	0	0	0	0	137
A330	0	12	12	110	138
A340	0	68	71	84	89
Total	288	450	605	755	1,038
McDonnell-Douglas					
DC-9/MD-80	203	213	346	423	400
DC-10	6	7	1	0	0
MD-11	0	29	88	120	175
Total	209	249	435	543	575

Source: "The Aerospace and Space Industry," *Standard & Poors Industry Surveys, Volume A-L, July 1991.*

expenditures is shown in *Exhibit 3*. This R&D, apart from providing tomorrow's large commercial aircraft designs, provides technology for the US defense and space programs.

The defense contract segment includes missile systems as well as military aircraft. In the US, Department of Defense contracts make up a substantial part of overall aerospace sales for the aircraft manufacturers Boeing and McDonnell Douglas, as well as for other industry suppliers such as General Electric (GE) and Pratt & Whitney (*Exhibit 4*).

Space programs are also heavy users of the industry's R&D expenditure. In the US, a large part of this R&D is done on behalf of NASA with federal financial support. Although it is difficult to identify specific sources of funding with specific uses in this segment, a total of $17.4 billion was provided through federal funding in 1990 alone.[1]

Despite direct and indirect support from governments, there still are large private capital requirements. The third industry segment, commercial transport aircraft, is no exception. The costs from design to launch of a new commercial jet, for example, can be around $4 billion.

In 1960 there were seventeen companies building commercial aircraft; by 1991, this had whittled down to only three: Boeing and McDonnell Douglas in the US, and Airbus

[1] "The Aerospace and Space Industry," *Standard & Poors Industry Surveys, Volume A-L,* July 1991.

EXHIBIT 3

R&D Expenditure by Industry

Industry	R&D in 1990	R&D as % of Total	Sales in 1990	R&D as % of Sales	Profits in 1990	R&D as % of Profits
Computers & office equipment	$15,954	23%	$201,434	8%	$17,783	90%
Automotive	10,710	15%	290,467	4%	493	2172%
Health care	8,535	12%	97,871	9%	17,811	48%
Electrical/electronics	7,042	10%	128,724	5%	8,308	85%
Chemicals	5,160	7%	131,388	4%	12,626	41%
Aerospace	3,916	6%	105,920	4%	4,327	91%
Conglomerates	3,669	5%	135,734	3%	10,720	34%
Manufacturing	3,238	5%	110,146	3%	7,236	45%
Telecommunications	3,179	5%	87,791	4%	10,454	30%
Fuel	2,713	4%	400,782	1%	29,163	9%
Consumer products	1,935	3%	137,518	1%	14,834	13%
Leisure	1,798	3%	35,170	5%	1,435	125%
Food	526	1%	75,432	1%	5,915	9%
Housing	506	1%	28,140	2%	1,700	30%
Metals and mining	406	1%	38,452	1%	2,355	17%
Paper & forest products	392	1%	35,946	1%	2,682	15%
Service industries	116	0%	13,792	1%	246	47%
Containers/packaging	94	0%	9,985	1%	386	24%
Nonbank financial	89	0%	13,196	1%	1,047	8%
Publishing & broadcast	13	0%	434	3%	(1)	-2150%
Total	69,989		2,078,319		149,520	

Source: "R&D Statistics," *Business Weekly/Quality,* October 25, 1991, pp. 169-216.

Notes:

• All figures in millions of dollars.

• Data only contain private investment in R&D. Government expenditure is excluded.

• The values for R&D as a % of profits for the automotive and publishing industries should be considered outliers, due to their unusually low profit during the year.

EXHIBIT 4

Sales in the US Aerospace Industry

EXHIBIT 4a   Sales in the US Aerospace Industry, by Product

Year	Total	Military Aircraft	Civil Aircraft	Missiles	Space	Nonaero-space
1990	131,430	38,347	31,356	10,601	29,221	21,905
1989	117,566	38,867	22,135	11,215	25,755	19,594
1988	114,562	41,867	19,019	10,270	24,312	19,094
1987	110,008	43,723	15,465	10,219	22,266	18,335
1986	106,183	40,687	15,718	11,964	20,117	17,697
1985	96,571	36,752	13,730	11,438	18,556	16,095
1984	83,486	31,215	10,690	11,335	16,332	13,914
1983	79,975	30,058	12,373	10,269	13,946	13,329
1982	67,756	24,502	10,982	10,368	10,514	11,390
1981	63,974	19,635	16,427	7,640	9,388	10,884

Industrie in Europe. The steady reduction in the number of manufacturers worldwide resulted from firms dropping out due to bankruptcy, or exiting the industry in anticipation of heavy losses. The last company to exit the commercial aircraft segment was the US manufacturer, Lockheed, in 1981, soon after it launched the L-1011. This model was aimed at the same market segment as the McDonnell Douglas DC-10 (which was introduced at the same time). A rule of thumb in the industry is that it is necessary to sell about 400 units of production to break even, and around 700 units to earn normal industry margins. The size of the L1011/DC-10 market segment was not enough to support two manufacturers, and Lockheed lost. The US government eventually stepped in to prevent Lockheed from going under entirely. Lockheed lobbied the government for a federal rescue package, arguing that the loss of the firm would have a severe impact on the US aerospace industry. After passing the legislation by one vote, the US Senate agreed to provide a federal loan guarantee of $250 million to allow Lockheed to withdraw from commercial aircraft manufacture and concentrate on its military and space programs.

The necessity of producing a large number of units to make a decent return is due to the steep learning curve in aircraft manufacture. As more units are produced, unit costs are reduced and labor productivity improves. Profits are dependent on widening profit margins late in the production cycle. A second source of profits is the market for aircraft spares and maintenance, which might continue for a decade or more after an aircraft is sold.

All three manufacturers market their aircraft worldwide, and a substantial portion of Boeing and McDonnell Douglas's output goes abroad (geographic market shares for each manufacturer are shown in *Exhibit 10*). *Exhibit 5* shows the size of these exports and their effect on the US trade balance.

EXHIBIT 4b Sales in the US Aerospace Industry, by Customer

| | | Aerospace Products & Services | | | Nonaerospace |
| | | Government | | Commercial | |
Year	Total	DoD	NASA		
1990	131,430	56,784	11,981	40,760	21,905
1989	117,566	58,457	9,638	29,877	19,594
1988	114,562	61,327	7,899	26,242	19,094
1987	110,008	61,817	6,813	23,043	18,335
1986	106,183	59,161	6,236	23,089	17,697
1985	96,571	53,178	6,262	21,036	16,095
1984	83,486	45,969	6,063	17,540	13,914
1983	79,975	41,558	5,910	19,178	13,329
1982	67,756	34,016	4,899	17,451	11,390
1981	63,974	27,244	4,709	21,137	10,884

Source: "The Aerospace and Space Industry," *Standard & Poors Industry Surveys, Volume A-L, July 1991.*

EXHIBIT 5

US Trade Balance and Aerospace Trade Balance

Year	Total Balance	Balance	Aerospace Exports	Imports
1990	(101,010)	26,050	36,810	10,760
1989	(109,399)	22,083	32,111	10,028
1988	(118,526)	17,860	26,947	9,087
1987	(158,207)	16,019	23,924	7,905
1986	(162,281)	12,802	20,704	7,902
1985	(136,627)	12,592	18,724	6,132
1984	(110,932)	10,082	15,008	4,926
1983	(60,710)	12,619	16,065	3,446
1982	(35,182)	11,035	15,603	4,568
1981	(30,051)	13,134	17,634	4,500

Source:"The Aerospace and Space Industry," *Standard & Poors Industry Surveys, Volume A-L, July 1991.*

Selling commercial aircraft is a long drawn-out process and most manufacturers concentrate on just a few large airlines. Although the larger airlines might source their fleets from multiple manufacturers, they like some degree of homogeneity in their fleets; hence the initial order for a few planes is likely to be followed by subsequent orders for additional units. From a marketing perspective, airlines form a tight-knit informational community and a new aircraft's quality and reputation is rapidly disseminated to others in the market.

BOEING CORPORATION

The Boeing Company, located in Seattle, Washington, was founded in 1916 by a wealthy timberman, William E. Boeing, and a Navy officer, G. Conrad Westervelt. The company has grown to be the largest private commercial aircraft manufacturer in the world and, for much of the 1980s, the only profitable one. In 1990 it employed 39,700 people and made profits of $1.4 billion on $27.6 billion in sales. The last ten years of financial results for both Boeing and its main US rival, McDonnell Douglas, are shown in *Exhibit 6*.

The commercial aircraft segment has two key operating characteristics: range and seating capacity. The range varies from short-haul planes such as the Boeing 737-200, with a range of 1,600 to 2,000 nautical miles,[2] to long-range planes like the 747, flying for up to 6,000 nautical miles. The seating capacity in a single model may change considerably depending on the configuration of first-class, business-class, and economy-class seating but capacity varies broadly from planes with less than 150 seats to the 747 jumbo-jet seating around 400 passengers. Boeing's current product-line and the equivalent models from Airbus and McDonnell Douglas are shown in *Exhibit 7*.

Boeing's products are split between space, military, and commercial aircraft. Although the commercial side of the business is profitable, the military side currently loses money. Recently, given the post–Cold war military needs, some of Boeing's military contracts have been winding down, with projects such as the Minuteman missile, the B52 bomber program, and the KC-135 headed for oblivion. Faced with the general downturn in military spending in the 1980s, Boeing sales representatives bid aggressively for the few remaining contracts in the market. These were on a fixed price basis and the result was that Boeing found itself holding on to a number of loss-making projects—such as the rebuilding of Air Force One, the President's plane. Although there were some potentially stronger contracts on the horizon (Boeing had just won a half share with Sikorsky for a military helicopter deal and a third of the Advanced Tactical Fighters program), full production and subsequent profits for these contracts are not expected to be realized until 1996 at the earliest.

Military programs are important to Boeing as they have absorbed a substantial portion of the early costs of commercial aircraft development. The 707 and 367-80 ("dash-eighty") are good examples. Boeing sold 732 units of these planes between 1956 and 1965 on military contracts, after which it was modified and sold to commercial carriers. The 707 established Boeing's lead in the marketplace, which it has kept ever since. Yet another example is provided by two of Boeing's factories in Renton and Wichita, both of which were paid for by the US government as part of military programs, but are now used to manufacture parts for the 737 and 757 aircraft. Sales to the military segment over the last few years are summarized in *Exhibit 8*.

Boeing's strategy consists of five aspects: to be a technology leader, to be a low-cost leader, to market its products on a global basis, to build a large customer base, and to develop "derivative" products from each basic design. It had considerable success with the 707 derivatives, the 707-100 and the 707-320, selling a total of 1,010 units by 1977. The 727 was a similar success with 1,832 units sold by 1984.

The funding provided by these successes proved critical for one of the most important of Boeing's projects, the 747. The project was initiated by the Pentagon, who approached three companies with the idea of building a "jumbo jet," a long-haul aircraft that was far larger than any then available in the market. Boeing and Lockheed were awarded the contracts and Boeing selected Pratt & Whitney to make the engines.

---

[2]One nautical mile equals 1.1508 miles.

EXHIBIT 6

US Aerospace Companies—Financial Data

EXHIBIT 6a Boeing Company Annual Income Statements 1981–1990 (dollars in millions)

Year ended December 31	1990	1989	1988	1987	1986	1985	1984	1983	1982	1981
Sales	27,595	20,276	16,962	15,355	16,341	13,636	10,354	11,129	9,035	9,788
Cost of goods sold	23,355	17,302	14,316	13,028	13,885	11,781	8,707	9,629	7,422	7,898
Gross Profit	4,240	2,974	2,646	2,327	2,456	1,855	1,647	1,500	1,613	1,891
Selling, general & administrative expense	2,032	1,766	1,631	1,617	1,363	886	926	803	1,039	1,174
Operating income before depreciation	2,208	1,208	1,015	710	1,093	969	721	697	574	717
Depreciation, depletion & amortization	678	627	567	501	463	386	365	365	350	291
Operating Profit	**1,530**	**581**	**448**	**209**	**630**	**583**	**356**	**332**	**224**	**426**
Interest expense	28	24	26	27	27	20	36	42	43	29
Nonoperating income	470	365	398	476	425	300	249	185	183	294
Pretax income	1,972	922	820	658	1,028	863	569	475	364	691
Total income taxes	587	247	206	178	363	297	(218)	120	72	218
Minority interest	0	0	0	0	0	0	0	0	0	0
Income before extraordinary items	1,385	675	614	480	665	566	787	355	292	473
Extraordinary items	0	298	0	0	0	0	0	0	0	0
Net Income	**1,385**	**973**	**614**	**480**	**665**	**566**	**787**	**355**	**292**	**473**
Earnings per share (primary)—excluding extra items	4.01	1.96	1.79	1.38	1.90	1.67	2.40	1.09	0.89	1.45
Earning per share (fully diluted)—including extra items	4.01	2.82	1.79	1.38	1.90	1.64	2.29	1.09	0.89	1.45
Dividends per share	0.95	0.78	0.69	0.62	0.53	0.46	0.41	0.41	0.41	0.41

EXHIBIT 6b

Boeing Company Balance Sheets 1981–1990 (dollars in millions)

Year ended December 31	1990	1989	1988	1987	1986	1985	1984	1983	1982	1981
Assets										
Cash and equivalents	3,326	1,863	3,963	3,435	4,172	3,209	1,595	1,095	294	920
Net receivables	2,057	1,855	1,651	2,369	1,201	885	777	541	550	534
Inventories	3,332	4,942	2,947	3,509	3,105	2,672	3,798	3,526	4,543	3,268
Total current assets	8,770	8,660	8,561	9,313	8,478	6,766	6,170	5,162	5,387	4,722
Gross plant, property & equipment	9,711	8,318	7,127	5,813	5,247	4,628	4,156	3,921	3,680	3,399
Accumulated depreciation	4,633	4,168	3,715	3,259	2,931	2,633	2,363	2,096	1,780	1,480
Net plant, property & equipment	5,078	4,150	3,412	2,554	2,316	1,995	1,793	1,825	1,900	1,918
Other assets	743	468	635	699	274	485	522	484	306	313
Total Assets	**14,591**	**13,278**	**12,608**	**12,566**	**11,068**	**9,246**	**8,485**	**7,471**	**7,593**	**6,954**
Liabilities										
Long-term debt due	4	5	7	14	14	18	15	17	20	17
Notes payable	0	0	0	0	0	0	0	65	138	0
Accounts payable	2,586	1,967	1,964	1,844	1,716	1,473	1,555	1,394	1,793	1,633
Taxes payable	479	252	144	515	1,563	1,129	853	4	42	77
Accrued expenses	1,405	1,305	1,046	948	1,575	1,226	973	845	783	783
Other current liabilities	2,658	3,144	3,544	3,743	791	571	644	880	811	742
Total Current Liabilities	**7,132**	**6,673**	**6,705**	**7,064**	**5,659**	**4,417**	**4,040**	**3,205**	**3,587**	**3,251**
Long-term debt	311	275	251	256	263	16	284	301	315	327
Deferred taxes	161	174	205	192	219	326	322	743	666	499
Investment tax credit	14	25	43	67	101	123	144	184	212	222
Equity										
Common stock	1,746	1,164	776	776	776	776	488	488	488	483
Capital surplus	581	572	565	559	562	571	355	350	345	346
Retained earnings	4,840	4,452	4,137	3,760	3,497	3,018	2,854	2,203	1,984	1,827
Less: Treasury stock	194	57	74	108	9	1	2	3	4	0
Total Equity	**6,973**	**6,131**	**5,404**	**4,987**	**4,826**	**4,364**	**3,695**	**3,038**	**2,813**	**2,655**
Total Liabilities & Equity	**14,591**	**13,278**	**12,608**	**12,566**	**11,068**	**9,246**	**8,485**	**7,471**	**7,593**	**6,954**

Source: Boeing Company.

EXHIBIT 6c

McDonnell Douglas Company Annual Income Statement (dollars in millions)

Year ended December 31	1990	1989	1988	1987	1986	1985	1984	1983	1982	1981
Sales	16,246	14,581	15,069	13,289	12,772	11,618	9,819	8,242	7,412	7,454
Cost of goods sold	13,234	11,693	11,612	10,360	10,070	9,103	7,599	6,542	5,911	6,155
Gross Profit	3,012	2,888	3,457	2,930	2,702	2,515	2,220	1,700	1,501	1,299
Selling, general & administrative expense	2,073	1,965	2,118	2,013	1,829	1,614	1,440	1,094	1,017	903
Operating income before depreciation	939	923	1,339	917	874	901	780	606	485	396
Depreciation, depletion & amortization	533	487	496	397	369	312	286	211	173	142
Operating Profit	**406**	**436**	**843**	**520**	**504**	**588**	**494**	**395**	**312**	**254**
Interest expense	613	568	348	129	102	95	62	10	27	70
Nonoperating income expense	9	12	12	55	60	48	42	50	40	47
Special items	600	0	0	0	0	0	0	0	0	0
Pretax income	402	(120)	507	446	462	541	474	435	325	232
Total income taxes	127	(83)	157	133	185	196	148	161	110	55
Income before extraordinary items & discontinued operations	275	(37)	350	313	278	346	325	275	215	177
Extraordinary items	0	179	0	0	0	0	0	0	0	0
Discontinued operations	31	77	0	0	0	0	0	0	0	0
Net Income	**306**	**219**	**350**	**313**	**278**	**346**	**325**	**275**	**215**	**177**
Available for common	275	(37)	350	313	278	346	325	275	215	177
Savings due to common stock equivalents	0	0	0	0	0	0	0	0	1	1
Adjusted available for common	275	(37)	350	313	278	346	325	275	215	178
Earnings per share (primary)— excluding extra items & discontinued operations	7.180	-0.970	9.130	7.750	6.860	8.600	8.100	6.910	5.440	4.440
Earnings per share (primary)— including extra items & discontinued operations	7.990	5.720	9.130	7.750	6.860	8.600	8.100	6.910	5.440	4.440
Earnings per share (fully diluted)— excluding extra items & discontinued operations	7.180	-0.970	9.130	7.750	6.860	8.600	8.070	6.910	5.440	4.440
Earnings per share (fully diluted)— including extra items & discontinued operations	7.990	5.720	9.130	7.750	6.860	8.600	8.070	6.910	5.440	4.440
Dividends per share	2.820	2.820	2.560	2.320	2.080	1.840	1.620	1.420	1.240	1.060

EXHIBIT 6d

McDonnell Douglas Balance Sheet (dollars in millions)

Year ended December 31	1990	1989	1988	1987	1986	1985	1984	1983	1982	1981
Assets										
Cash & equivalents	226	119	115	53	78	79	34	407	287	15
Net receivables	3,781	4,030	3,606	1,445	1,463	1,267	946	605	541	501
Inventories	6,201	5,128	4,279	3,794	3,294	3,056	2,584	1,905	2,436	2,488
Prepaid expenses	146	199	289	105	106	73	36	23	16	9
Other current assets	0	0	0	0	0	0	0	0	0	0
Total current assets	10,354	9,476	8,289	5,397	4,941	4,475	3,599	2,940	3,279	3,014
Gross plant, property & equipment	6,416	5,979	5,771	4,545	4,144	3,549	3,076	2,434	1,833	1,585
Accumulated depreciation	3,163	2,738	2,652	2,155	1,938	1,621	1,359	1,029	886	754
Net plant, property & equipment	3,253	3,241	3,119	2,390	2,207	1,928	1,718	1,405	947	831
Investments at equity	0	0	0	213	173	162	152	142	223	324
Intangibles	0	50	83	0	0	0	0	0	0	0
Deferred charges	0	0	0	0	0	0	0	41	36	40
Other assets	1,358	630	394	536	590	703	722	263	138	154
Total Assets	14,965	13,397	11,885	8,536	7,911	7,268	6,191	4,792	4,622	4,364
Liabilities										
Long-term debt due	545	413	221	38	43	32	61	18	34	23
Notes payable	1,573	1,868	1,020	786	199	362	602	0	0	244
Accounts payable	1,333	1,276	1,177	1,064	997	968	833	569	636	612
Taxes payable	1,000	979	1,471	1,027	1,017	916	857	732	683	614
Accrued expenses	1,485	1,164	974	519	536	478	366	313	317	283
Other current liabilities	0	0	0	1,364	1,515	1,275	1,089	1,032	1,063	863
Total current liabilities	5,936	5,700	4,863	4,797	4,307	4,031	3,807	2,664	2,732	2,639
Long-term debt	3,466	2,654	2,387	769	759	603	41	60	70	71
Other liabilities	2,049	1,756	1,449	0	0	0	0	0	0	0
Equity										
Common stock	38	38	38	41	41	40	40	39	39	39
Capital surplus	283	281	277	421	417	406	393	372	362	342
Retained earnings	3,193	2,968	2,871	2,623	2,387	2,189	1,911	1,656	1,439	1,273
Less: Treasury stock	0	0	0	115	0	0	0	0	21	0
Total Equity	3,514	3,287	3,186	2,970	2,845	2,635	2,344	2,068	1,820	1,654
Total Liabilities and Equity	14,965	13,397	11,885	8,536	7,911	7,268	6,191	4,792	4,622	4,364

Source: McDonnell Douglas.

EXHIBIT 7

Civil Aircraft Industry—Product Lines

Manufacturer Aircraft model	Seating (average)	Range (approximate)	Comments
Boeing			
737-200	110	2,100 to 2,600	737 is a narrow-bodied, twinjet
737-300	128	1,800 to 2,800	
737-400	150	2,500 to 2,900	Stretched version of the -300
737-500	108	3,400	Replaces the 737-200
727-200	156	1,900 to 2,700	Trijet, discontinued in 1984
757-200	194	3,200 to 4,600	Narrow-bodied
767-200	224	3,600 to 7,000	
767-300	269	3,600 to 7,000	
747-100	366	to 6,300	
747SP	276	to 7,600	
747-200	366	to 6,100	
747-300	400	to 5,600	
747-400	412	8,400 to 9,700	Advanced flight-deck version
Airbus			
300-600	270	3,200 to 3,700	
310-200	220	4,399 to 4,456	Wide-bodied
310-300	220	5,090 to 6,172	
320-100	150	to 2,015	Narrow-bodied
320-200	150	to 3,305	
321-100	186	2,671 to 2,752	Proposed for 1994
330	335	5,360 to 5,490	Proposed for late 1992
340-200	262	to 8,695	Proposed for late 1992
340-300	295	to 7,770	Proposed for late 1992
McDonnell Douglas			
MD-80	150	1,800 to 3,260	
MD-87	130	2,731 to 4,203	
DC-10	330	to 6,600	
MD-11	323	4,079 to 5,760	
MD-12	400	to 7,000	Studying development

Source: *Jane's All The World's Aircraft 1990-1991,* 81st Edition, Jane's Information Group and Boeing Company.

Notes:

• Seating capacity varies depending on the mix of first-class, business-class, and economy seating. In most cases the seating capacity quoted is for a standard mix of classes.

• Ranges are expressed in miles.

The size of the 747 project nearly bankrupted Boeing during the development process. It pulled through with an aggressive program of cost cutting and eventually emerged with lower costs and a more productive workforce. Today, Boeing is still the only manufacturer to offer a commercial aircraft the size of the 747.

Boeing has a number of development projects underway for new aircraft. Its principal new commercial aircraft project is the 767-X or 777 (the "seven cubed"), a twin jet wide-body plane that is expected to seat up to 400 passengers. The 777 is aimed at a range segment between the 767-300 and 747-400. Development of the new model was initiated without the usual level of advance orders for new planes, with just one confirmed order from United Airlines. The 777 would compete against the proposed Airbus A330 and A340. Although it has a specification similar to the A330/A340, the two companies have very different launch strategies. Airbus is pursuing the strategy of upgrading existing engines for the new planes, and as a result, the first A330s are expected in 1993. Boeing, on the other hand, is building the 777 with newly designed engines and hence the first 777 is not expected to be airborne until 1995.

EXHIBIT 8

US Sales by Segment

Year ended December 31	Boeing			McDonnell Douglas		
	1990	*1989*	*1988*	*1990*	*1989*	*1988*
Revenues						
Commercial transportation products/services	$21,230	$14,305	$11,369	$ 5,812	$ 4,511	$ 4,637
Military transportation products/systems	4,123	3,962	3,668	5,830	6,124	6,288
Missiles and space	1,739	1,467	1,457	3,188	2,761	2,390
Financial services				619	497	449
Other industries	503	542	468	797	688	671
Operating revenues	27,595	20,276	16,962	16,246	14,581	14,435
Corporate income	448	347	378	9	8	3
Total revenues	$28,043	$20,623	$17,340	$16,255	$14,589	$14,438
Operating profit						
Commercial transportation products/services	$ 2,189	$ 1,165	$ 585	$ (177)	$ (167)	$ 110
Military transportation products/systems	(299)	(559)	(95)	46	207	418
Missiles and space	(119)	85	124	167	116	179
Financial services				100	77	74
Other industries	(66)	26	(28)	49	17	(44)
Operating profit	1,705	717	586	185	250	737
Corporate income	448	347	378	714	259	(20)
Corporate expense	(181)	(142)	(144)	(386)	(373)	(200)
Earnings before taxes	$ 1,972	$ 922	$ 820	$ 513	$ 136	$ 517

Boeing also experimented with a 150-seat plane called the 7J7 that would compete in the short-to-medium range segment and projected that it would enter service in 1992. This project was undertaken in collaboration with Japanese aerospace manufacturers who were trying to break into the commercial aircraft segment through alliances with the US, after several unsuccessful attempts to go it alone. The Japanese Civil Transport Development Corporation (CTDC) consisted of three heavy manufacturing firms: Mitsubishi, Kawasaki, and Fuji Heavy Industries who were supported by loans from the Japanese Ministry for Trade, MITI. Unfortunately, the potential market for the 7J7 began to look questionable in the mid-1980s. The 7J7 faced competition from the new 150-seat Airbus A-320 as well as an active market in used 727s (which it was intended to replace). After three years of development and a $100 million investment, plans for the 7J7 were shelved in 1988.[3] Despite this, Boeing continued to look for other ways of working with Japanese component manufacturers.

Finally, Boeing is considering the development of a "super-jumbo" to replace the 747. The last model of 747, the 747-400, was plagued with problems. Boeing miscalculated the problems with upgrading the technology and the result was that the design was late in being certified and it was rushed through production. Some customers subsequently complained of the airplane's poor quality. Boeing is now working on a stretched version of the 747 with around 412 seats which might partially satisfy the "super-jumbo" market segment, and there are also tentative plans for a 787, another jumbo jet that could seat up to 600 passengers.

[3]"Bright Smiles, Sweaty Palms," *Business Week,* February 1, 1988.

AIRBUS INDUSTRIE

Airbus Industrie was formed 20 years ago in an attempt by European governments to recapture the dominance in aircraft manufacture that they had enjoyed in the prewar years. Headquartered in Toulouse in southern France, the consortium began in 1970 with France's Aérospatiale and West Germany's Deutsche Airbus. They were later joined by British Aerospace and CASA of Spain.

Airbus is an example of a special form of French partnership known as a Groupement d'Intérêt Economique ("grouping of economic interests"). The partnership is not required to disclose financial results and the four partners incorporate all financial transactions into their own accounts. There is no formal sharing of revenues or costs, as each partner simply charges the consortium a "fee" for their work and the final profits or losses are divided between the partners at the end of each year. Since commercial aircraft transactions worldwide are denominated in US dollars, Airbus accounts are also denominated in dollars.

Although the group got off to a shaky start, Airbus Industrie eventually made a success with their first product—the A300 twin-jet wide-bodied plane. At that time, well over half of all air traffic was for journeys under 2,500 nautical miles. The A300 was aimed at this short-to-medium range market and offered lower life-cycle costs than similar products from US manufacturers (for a description of the Airbus product line see *Exhibit 7*). They had considerable success selling to the European flagcarriers, most of whom are still fully or partially nationalized airlines. By 1990, Airbus's share of commercial airplane deliveries stood at almost 20% (see *Exhibit 9a*)

Airbus's strategy is to maintain a high degree of flexibility to meet customer demands worldwide. The Consortium coordinates overall development and production and manages marketing and after-sales service. Meanwhile the actual engineering, production, and financing is done at the partner level. The Consortium is expected to provide a source of technological expertise, a positive trade balance, and substantial employment for each nation, and hence, is considered an important national project. Development programs are backed by government loans known as "launch aid."

EXHIBIT 9
Market Share Data

EXHIBIT 9a Share of Total Units Delivered:

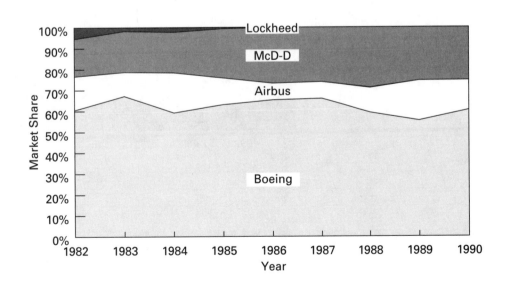

EXHIBIT 9b   Market Share of Value of Aircraft Delivered:

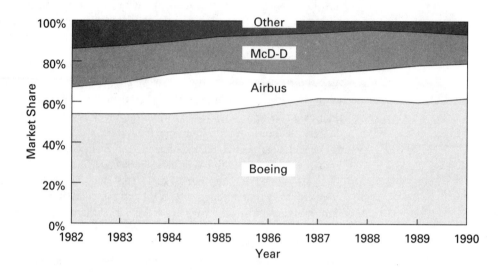

EXHIBIT 10

US Deliveries by Geographic Share

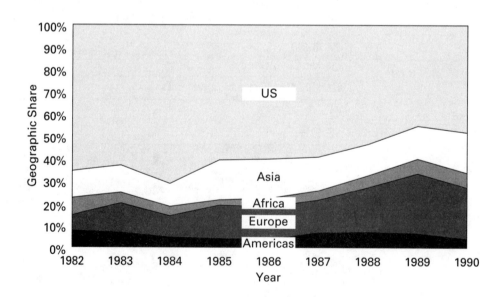

Source: Aerospace Facts and Figures, various years.
Notes:
• "Asia" includes Oceania.
• "Africa" includes the Middle East.
• "Americas" is Canada, Greenland, and Latin America.

European governments vigorously defend these loans with a variety of arguments: First, they maintain that the loans would be paid back (it is estimated that sales of 360 A300s and 360 A310s would be needed to provide the profits to repay the debts in full). Second, they claim that the use of government support, far from distorting the industry, actually corrected for the existing distortion as a result of Boeing's dominant position. The Europeans claim that Boeing's dominance resulted in monopolistic pricing on 747s and a slow introduction of new technologies such as the "fly-by-wire"[4] techniques employed on the A320s. Third, the Europeans argue that even if their loans ended up as a subsidy to Airbus, it was a small amount compared to the massive "indirect" subsidies to Boeing from military contracts and from the use of Federal funds for R&D programs. For example, during the first half of the 1980s, NASA spent nearly $1.5 billion on R&D programs with US aerospace companies, the results of which were then used in civil aviation programs.[*]

Over the years, the fortunes of Airbus have become entangled with those of the US. Not only are US airlines important customers of Airbus, but US suppliers also play an important part in the launching of Airbus planes. One-third of the value of the A300/A310 program and one-quarter of the A320 program come from US engine manufacturers such as Pratt & Whitney and General Electric. Airbus has also been known to use US military and space R&D: For example, the A300 was the first aircraft to exploit "supercritical airfoils," an invention patented by NASA (for which they paid NASA a royalty).

For Airbus, 1990 was a milestone year. At the Farnborough airshow that year, Jean Pierson, Airbus's managing director, announced that despite a depressed value of the dollar and a lower level of sales than 1989, the company expected to show its first profit.

The Airbus partners started to look to the future, in particular, for ways of breaking out from the short-to-medium range segment where they were concentrated. One project they have in mind is to produce an aircraft aimed at the jumbo market.

THE JUMBO WAR

An increase in air travel, combined with high levels of airport congestion imply that there is an opportunity for manufacturers to sell large-capacity aircraft to the airlines. It is generally believed that over the next ten years this market could be as large as 400-500 planes, each seating up to 800 passengers. Currently, the only plane that comes close to this size is Boeing's 747, first introduced in 1970. The 747 seats a maximum of 412 passengers and the current model, the 747-400, is priced at around $150 million.

Airbus has plans for a 600-700 seat super-jumbo aimed at the 747 market. Although the development costs for such a project would be huge—some estimates put it as high as $15 billion—it seems likely that the European partners will seek government launch aid in the same way they had for the A300 and A310.

Boeing could respond with its own stretched version of the 747, which, although it would not be as big as the proposed Airbus jumbo, could be built at considerably less cost. But Boeing currently has its development hands full with the 777, apart from which, many industry watchers thought that this was just too big a project for just one manufacturer to undertake.

---

[4]Fly-by-wire describes the technology of using electronic sensors and actuators instead of hydraulic hoses to control wing flaps.

[*]In a letter to the *Economist* on July 10, 1993, Robert Alizart of Airbus Industrie—responding to an article about the super-jumbo—wrote:

"The governments of all major developed countries have chosen for strategic reasons to support commercial aircraft manufacturing. The European governments prefer a system of direct, transparent and repayable launch-aid to the indirect, opaque, and largely non-repayable American system."

It was the prospect of a "jumbo war" between the two manufacturers that observers said caused the reawakening of the trade dispute between the US and EC governments.

THE BOEING-AIRBUS DISPUTE

Boeing and the US government have alleged since 1985 that the EC government support to Airbus represented an export subsidy. The first formal complaint made by the US government arose over an order for nineteen A-320 aircraft to Indian Airlines. The order, which was to be for twelve 757 aircraft from Boeing, was won by Airbus with the offer of attractive financing arrangements, including "free" leasing of interim 737s and A-300s until delivery of the new aircraft. Boeing and the US Government accused Airbus of selling the A-320s at less than cost, and putting political pressure on the Indian government, violating Articles 4 and 6 of the GATT (see *Exhibit 12a* for a summary of these articles).

Airbus Industrie argued that Boeing had also received subsidies, albeit indirectly, from the large defense contracts it enjoyed as well as from US tax breaks. Further, they noted that Boeing was also able to offer attractive financing deals with the aid of the US Export-Import (Ex-Im) Bank. During the 1980s, 60% of Boeing's exports were partially financed with the help of Ex-Im Bank funds. This represented 27% of the total funds loaned by the bank that year, leading some to dub it "the Boeing Bank."[5] Details of the Ex-Im Bank's loan authorizations are shown in *Exhibit 11*. Boeing's attractive deals didn't stop at financing arrangements. In 1988, there was controversy over a deal done with American Airlines which allowed the airline as little as a one month walk-away option.

The complaint was examined by the GATT Committee on Trade in Civil Aircraft during 1986, but did not result in a ruling. There was a widespread expectation that the US would take matters into its own hands and start to impose tariffs on European aircraft in retaliation. In 1988, however, with order backlogs overflowing and no shortage of demand in the industry, the US decided not to start a potentially costly trade war.

THE CURRENT SITUATION

In February 1991, the US lodged a new complaint with the GATT, focusing this time on a specific piece of financial support. It accused the German government of providing a subsidy of DM 390 million to Deutsche Airbus, the German part of the four-nation consortium.

In a change in tactics, the US government lodged the complaint with the GATT Subsidies Committee, rather than the Civil Aircraft Committee (which had dealt with the previous disputes). The EC governments were very unhappy with this change. Dieter Wolf, a German Economics Ministry official, explained later: "The Aircraft Code. . . gives governments more room for maneuver than the Subsidies Code" (The Civil Aircraft Code and Subsidies Code are summarized in *Exhibit 12*)

The alleged subsidy centered around a foreign-exchange rate guarantee made to Daimler-Benz when it purchased Deutsche Airbus GmbH in 1989. As part of a restructuring in the German aerospace industry, Daimler-Benz obtained an 80% interest in Deutsche Airbus GmbH, to be held by its subsidiary Messerschmitt-Bölkow-Blohm (MBB). It also took on all of Deutsche Airbus's commitments and costs, with the exception of the losses expected due to currency movements. The government provided Daimler-Benz with an exchange rate guarantee that amounted to some DM 390 million ($252 million) or about $2.5 million on each Airbus delivered in 1990.[6]

---

[5] Aerospace and Defense," *Forbes,* January 4, 1982, pp. 195-196; and "Sea-change in the Air" *The Banker,* December 1987, pp. 90-93.

[6] "GATT Trade Body Agrees to Set Panel to Rule on Airbus Subsidy," *The Reuter Library Report,* March 6, 1991.

EXHIBIT 11

Export-Import Bank Authorizations in Support of Aircraft Exports

Year	Total Authorizations	Support for Aircraft Exports			
		Total	% of Total Authorizations	Commercial Jet Aircraft	Other Aircraft
Loans					
1981	5,431.0	2,576.6	47.4%	2,550.3	26.3
1982	3,516.0	263.9	7.5%	199.1	64.8
1983	845.0	396.7	46.9%	383.6	12.9
1984	1,465.0	608.0	41.5%	531.8	76.2
1985	659.0	39.7	6.0%	12.6	27.1
1986	578.0	54.6	9.4%	46.4	8.2
1987	599.0	17.0	2.8%	13.3	3.7
1988	685.0				
1989	695.0	166.4	23.9%	158.0	8.4
1990	614.0	5.0	0.8%		5.0
Guarantees					
1981	1,506.0	562.6	37.4%	533.4	29.2
1982	727.0	104.2	14.3%	78.4	25.8
1983	1,741.0	629.6	36.2%	601.3	28.3
1984	1,333.0	355.5	26.7%	293.5	62.0
1985	1,320.0	322.4	24.4%	288.9	33.5
1986	1,128.0	329.2	29.2%	277.4	51.8
1987	1,506.0	808.3	53.7%	808.3	15.8
1988	601.0	89.2	14.8%	73.4	15.8
1989	1,293.0	496.4	38.4%	390.4	106.0
1990	3,333.0	1,666.3	50.0%	224.7	1,441.6

Source: Aerospace Facts and Figures 1991/1992, p. 134.

Notes:

- Amounts shown are in millions of dollars.
- "Commercial Jet Aircraft" includes complete aircraft, engines, parts, and retrofits.
- "Other Aircraft" includes business aircraft, general aviation aircraft, helicopters, and related goods and services.
- "Loans" are commitments for financing by the Export-Import Bank to foreign buyers of US equipment and services.
- "Guarantees" provide assurance of repayment of principal and interest on loans made by private lending institutions for major export transactions. Excludes insurance.

In a statement to the trade press in February, an official from the office of the US Trade Representative (USTR) said: "[It] recently became clear that the German program was more extensive than previously indicated and extended to German component suppliers as well as Deutsche Airbus. . . This money is in addition to $5.8 billion in government subsidies that has been committed to the Airbus program by the German government over the last 20 years. . . Total support by Airbus partner governments now comes to more than $13.5 billion, or $19.4 billion if interest costs to the governments are included."[7] A spokesman for McDonnell Douglas said: "A subsidy of that magnitude has a serious impact on international trade," and Boeing commented that this alleged subsidization of exchange rates "undercuts the balance of payments process."

The EC's response was to request that the complaint be heard by the Civil Aircraft Committee rather than the Subsidies Committee. They argued not only that the payments constituted allowed support under the aircraft code, but also that government payments were not strictly export subsidies since they applied to all the output from Deutsche Airbus. On April 11, however, a GATT panel agreed to take the complaint before the GATT Subsidies Committee.

[7]"US EC Escalate Battle over Airbus Exchange Rate Subsidy," *Aviation Daily,* Vol. 303, No. 33, p. 311, February 15, 1991.

EXHIBIT 12a

Articles 4 and 6 of the Agreement on Trade in Civil Aircraft

Article 4 Government-Directed Procurement, Mandatory Sub-Contracts, and Inducements

4.1. Purchasers of civil aircraft should be free to select suppliers on the basis of commercial and technical factors.

4.2. Signatories shall not require airlines, aircraft manufacturers, or other entities engaged in the purchase of civil aircraft, nor exert unreasonable pressure on them, to procure civil aircraft from any particular source, which would create discrimination against suppliers from any Signatory.

4.3. Signatories agree that the purchase of products covered by this Agreement should be made only on a competitive price, quality, and delivery basis. In conjunction with the approval or awarding of procurement contracts for products covered by this Agreement a Signatory may, however, require that its qualified firms be provided with access to business opportunities on a competitive basis and on terms no less favorable than those available to the qualified firms of other Signatories.[1]

4.4. Signatories agree to avoid attaching inducement of any kind to the sale or purchase of civil aircraft from any particular source which would create discrimination against suppliers from any Signatory.

Article 6 Government Support, Export Credits, and Aircraft Marketing

6.1. Signatories note that the provisions of the Agreement on Interpretation and Application of Articles VI, XVI, and XXIII of the General Agreement on Tariffs and Trade (Agreement on Subsidies and Countervailing Measures) apply to trade in civil aircraft. They affirm that in their participation in, or support of, civil aircraft programmes they shall seek to avoid adverse effects on trade in civil aircraft in the sense of Articles 8.3 and 8.4 of the Agreement on Subsidies and Countervailing Measures. They shall also take into account the special factors which apply in this area, their international economic interests, and the desire of producers of all Signatories to participate in the expansion of the world civil aircraft market.

6.2. Signatories agree that pricing of civil aircraft should be based on a reasonable expectation of recoupment of all costs, including nonrecurring programme costs, identifiable and pro-rated costs of military research, and development on aircraft, components, and systems that are subsequently applied to the production of such civil aircraft, average production costs, and financial costs.

Source: US Treaties and Other International Agreements, Volume 31, Part I 1-1014 TIAS 9605-9628, Department of State, Washington D.C.

EXHIBIT 12b

Articles 8 and 11 of the GATT Subsidies Code

Article 8 Subsidies—General Provisions

1. Signatories recognize that subsidies are used by governments to promote important objectives of social and economic policy. Signatories also recognize that subsidies may cause adverse effects of the interests of other signatories.

2. Signatories agree not to use export subsidies in a manner inconsistent with the provision of this Agreement.

3. Signatories further agree that they shall seek to avoid causing, through the use of any subsidy:

   (a) injury to the domestic industry of another signatory

   (b) nullification or impairment of the benefits accruing directly or indirectly to another Signatory under the General Agreement, or

   (c) serious prejudice to the interests of another Signatory.

[1]Use of the phrase "access to business opportunities. . . on terms no less favorable" does not mean that the amount of contracts awarded to the qualified firm of one Signatory entitles the qualified firms of other Signatories to contracts of a similar amount.

4. The adverse effects to the interests of another Signatory required to demonstrate nullification or impairment or serious prejudice may arise through:
   (a) the effects of the subsidized imports in the domestic market of the importing Signatory,
   (b) the effects of the subsidy in displacing or impeding the imports of like products into the market of the subsidizing country,
   (c) the effects of the subsidized exports in displacing the exports of like products of another Signatory from a third-country market.

Article 11 Subsidies Other than Export Subsidies
1. Signatories recognize that subsidies other than export subsidies are widely used as important instruments for the promotion of social and economic policy objectives and do not intend to restrict the right of Signatories to use such subsidies to achieve these and other important policy objectives which they consider desirable. Signatories note that among such objectives are:
   (a) the elimination of industrial, economic, and social disadvantages of specific regions,
   (b) to facilitate the restructuring, under socially acceptable conditions, of certain sectors, especially where this has become necessary by reason of changes in trade and economic policies, including international agreements resulting in lower barriers to trade,
   (c) generally to sustain employment and to encourage retraining and change in employment,
   (d) to encourage research and development programmes, especially in the field of high-technology industries,
   (e) the implementation of economic programmes and policies to promote the economic and social development of developing countries,
   (f) redeployment of industry in order to avoid congestion and environmental problems.
2. Signatories recognize, however, that subsidies other than export subsidies, certain objectives and possible forms of which are described, respectively, in paragraphs 1 and 3 of this Article, may cause or threaten to cause injury to a domestic industry of another Signatory or may nullify or impair benefits accruing to another Signatory under the General Agreement, in particular where such subsidies would adversely affect the conditions of normal competition. Signatories shall therefore seek to avoid causing such effects through the use of subsidies. In particular, Signatories, when drawing up their policies and practices in this field, in addition to evaluating the essential internal objectives to be achieved, shall also weigh, as far as practicable, taking account of the nature of the particular case, possible adverse effects on trade. They shall also consider the conditions of world trade, production (e.g., price, capacity utilization, etc.) and supply in the product concerned.
3. Signatories recognize that the objectives mentioned in paragraph 1 above may be achieved, *inter alia,* by means of subsidies granted with the aim of giving an advantage to certain enterprises. Examples of possible forms of such subsidies are: government financing of commercial enterprises, including grants, loans, or guarantees; government provision or government-financed provision of utility, supply distribution, and other operational or support services or facilities; fiscal incentives; and government subscription to, or provision of, equity capital.

   Signatories note that the above forms of subsidies are normally granted either regionally or by sector. The enumeration of forms of subsidies set out above is illustrative and nonexhaustive, and reflects these currently granted by a number of Signatories of this Agreement.

   Signatories recognize, nevertheless, that the enumeration of forms of subsidies set out above should be reviewed periodically and that this should be done, through consultations, in conformity with the spirit of Article XVI:5 of the General Agreement.
4. Signatories recognize further that, without prejudice to their rights under this Agreement, nothing in paragraphs 1-3 above and in particular the enumeration of forms of subsidies creates, in itself, any basis for action under the General Agreement, as interpreted by this Agreement.

Source: TIAS 9619, *United States Treaties and Other International Agreements,* Volume 31 Part 1 1979 1-1014 TIAS 9605-9628, Department of State, Washington D.C.

THE DISPUTE ESCALATES

One month later, the US announced it was considering widening the scope of the complaint to encompass the other three European governments.[8] The US Commerce Department claimed that altogether the four governments had provided up to $26 billion (in real terms) in subsidies to Airbus since 1970. In response, the EC said it would not block the resolution of the dispute within the GATT, but called again for the hearing to be made before the Civil Aircraft committee.

The EC also repeated a proposal they had made in February, just before the US lodged the complaint against Germany. The proposal called for the scrapping of all subsidies, direct and indirect, in world trade of commercial aircraft and a cap of 45% on development subsidies. But the US rejected the proposal, calling instead for a 25% cap.

On May 31, the United States filed a "request for consultations" with GATT over launch aid provided to the four European partners in Airbus. After the filing, the French Foreign Trade Minister, Jean-Noel Jeanneny, was asked if the issue of aircraft subsidies would be linked in any way to the issue of agricultural subsidies during the forthcoming Uruguay round of GATT negotiations: "You cannot isolate them," he said, "they are tied together."

SHRONTZ CONSIDERS BOEING'S STRATEGY

Frank Shrontz wondered how Boeing's future would be affected by the outcome of these talks. He didn't relish the prospect of a trade war with the EC, but could he really compete against a firm like Airbus which had the backing of its governments' deep pockets? He also had to bear in mind that Airbus was not his only competition: the Soviet Union has a skilled aerospace workforce that had been manufacturing military aircraft for many years, and is now turning to the commercial segment. Japan is building up its aerospace industry, and makes a potentially formidable competitor as well as an attractive partner. Finally, at home, McDonnell Douglas cannot be ignored.

"How important is Boeing's lobbying in Washington?" Shrontz asked himself. Is the position being taken by the US government in Boeing's best interests or, instead, should Boeing be seeking subsidies of its own? As Shrontz commented to a *Forbes* reporter in early May, "Just think [of] what we could have done with a $10 billion plus subsidy." Boeing's current financial position looked strong, but Shrontz pondered the direction of the company's strategy and how well placed it was for the future.

---

[8]US Considers Escalating Airbus Action," *Flight International,* May 22, 1991, Reed Business Publishing.

chapter 8

The Regulatory Environment of International Business

"The law is the law," wrote W. H. Auden, quoting a judge of whom he once asked what the judge meant by "law." Auden's quote provides a simple and appealing framework for dealing with legal issues in the domestic context, but in the cross-border context, things are a bit more complicated. In any cross-border transaction that has potential legal consequences—that is, in just about every transaction an MNE undertakes—the three underlying, vexing questions that managers of MNEs often face are the following: (1) Which law prevails? (2) In which court is it adjudicated? and (3) What is the enforcement mechanism across borders?

In order to put the answers to these questions in their appropriate context, we need to understand some of the important principles and practices governing the application of international law to cross-border business transactions. In this chapter we first examine a few general principles underlying jurisprudence, or philosophy of law, in all legal settings. We then consider how principles of jurisprudence vary across the different parts of the world. When these standards clash, as they often do, there are a few governing principles of international law that are brought to bear in the resolution of disputes, and we shall examine these. We shall then argue that, at some point, there is a *void* at the intersection of sovereign boundaries in terms of the application of international law to cross-border disputes, and we examine the main areas where this regulatory void creates potential problems for MNEs. We end this chapter by pointing out how MNEs deal with some of these vexing legal issues—albeit imperfectly—in practice.

A fundamental theme of this chapter is the following: While the global corporation has nudged economic activity toward borderlessness, it runs the risk of being frustrated by (and frustrating, as well) the reality of a legal and political world that still comprises over 170 nations, all of whom, in the eyes of international law, have equal sovereign authority. This sovereign authority is manifest in the commonly accepted notion that the "state" has the authority to influence events within its geographic and legal boundaries, but can itself choose to be relatively immune to influence by outside authority. This, in turn, raises a challenge that is common to the legal environment in which MNE managers operate: Unlike the case of domestic transactions, there is no supranational authority that can ultimately *enforce* (although such an authority might *mediate*) judgments that resolve conflicts and dissensions arising at the intersection of sovereign boundaries. In other words, enforcement in international law (short of war) is ultimately a matter of voluntary acceptance of jurisdiction.

SOME GENERAL PRINCIPLES OF LAW

The former US supreme court judge Oliver Wendell Holmes Jr. once observed that "law embodies the story of a nation's development through many centuries." In other words, the law and the legal system of a nation are inseparable from its history, its culture, and its customs. The reason for this is that law is an enforceable body of rules that govern the conduct of individuals in a society, not only in terms of their relationships with each other but also with the "society" as a whole. On the one hand, this body of rules provides certain rights, protections, and freedoms to each individual. On the other hand, it specifies the boundaries that may not be crossed in such relationships, and specifies penalties for the violation of these boundaries.

Basic Features of Law in Any Society

The basic features of law in any nation are the following: (1) It is a means to preserve the social order, and to specify the penalties for the violation of such order; (2) It is a means to provide a basic—albeit broad—model of conduct, at least to the extent that certain types of conduct are considered illegal; (3) It establishes the nature of property and other rights in a society, and thereby narrows the range of uncertainty in expectations; this uncertainty reduction is a necessary condition for the design and implementation of economic, political, and social exchange in any society; (4) It acts as a compromiser, by mediating the views of different segments of society into one common set of enforceable rules.

In most countries, the law is not monolithic—embodying solely a commonly accepted and unchanging set of rules; laws are usually the result of a compromise of ideas that are in conflict, and they change over time. While people in a society can agree on the need for laws, they differ on what the law should be and how it should be implemented. These differences are embodied in the different values and beliefs that each member or segment of society holds important to himself or herself. It is the incorporation of these values and beliefs—collectively, the culture, customs, and history of a society—that makes both the structure and the implementation of laws different in different countries.[1]

Types of Law in Different Parts of the World

There are at least three broadly different types of law in the different parts of the world: common law, civil law, and religious law.

The system of *common law* is one that is built on tradition and the notion of *stare decisis* ("let the decision stand") or, the notion of precedence. This system of law is based on the premise that it is not possible to codify every possible contingency, and it lays out certain general statutory principles (in some instances, these statutory principles can be unwritten, as in the UK).[2] These principles are used by courts to interpret, reinterpret, and apply the law as it evolves into a more perfect system over time. Courts in the common law

---

[1] The study of these different value and belief bases of law is referred to as "jurisprudence," or the study of legal philosophy.

[2] The system of common law originated in the UK around 1066, when William the Conqueror attempted to bring one common set of laws to the then disparate kingdom of England. Courts were ordered to respect local customs *and* the decisions of courts in other parts of England (which would be based on their local customs) in framing judgments. The idea was that, over time, a consistent set of decisions would evolve throughout the kingdom.

system generally place a great deal of emphasis on precedence, and it is a system of law that seeks to achieve consistency in the application of law in the nation. The US and most of the Anglo-American countries, by and large, follow the common law system.

Civil law is a more codified form of the law, where courts tend to follow statutes that are typically intended to cover every possible contingency. This system of law is based on the belief that such contingencies can be specified, and that courts have little role in *interpreting* the law; rather, the job of the courts is to *apply* the law. Most countries in continental Europe (for example, France, Germany, and Spain) follow the system of civil law. Countries in the Far East, such as Japan, South Korea, and Taiwan, also tend to follow systems of civil law, although many of the provisions of law are less codified than in continental Europe.

Many countries—notably the Islamic countries—follow *religious law.* Religious law is based on sacred texts, religious tenets, and interpretations of these texts and tenets by the religious hierarchy of the nation. Such law usually covers all aspects of life, from dress codes to business contracts. Most countries that have religious laws also tend to rely on some form of civil law; rarely do countries combine religious law and common law.

Some Important Differences in the Application of Common and Civil Laws

There are some important differences between the common and civil law systems in the way that trials take place and judgments are awarded. The following features typically separate the civil law system from the common law system: In civil law systems, (1) The right to a civil jury does not exist; (2) Courtroom arguments tend to be less adversarial; (3) Contingency fees for lawyers are not allowed (or are considered unethical): If plaintiffs sue, they must keep in mind the costs of litigation (for instance, in Japan, lawyers are paid an up-front 8% of the recovery amount sought by the plaintiff); (4) There are typically court-imposed limits on damage awards (in Japan, for example, damages cannot exceed $150,000 in wrongful death cases; in Europe, although there are limits on damages, the limits are fairly high—it can run into the millions of dollars); (5) Typically, punitive damages (or more generally, noneconomic damages for factors such as pain, suffering, and anguish) are not allowed; (6) US-style discovery procedures, where both parties' lawyers have access to the information that the other party will use in trial, are typically not allowed; often, parties go to trial without knowing what the other side will present (the idea behind this is that plaintiffs must be certain about their evidence and their claims before they go to trial, and should not indulge in "fishing expeditions);" and (7) Typically, class action suits are not allowed to be brought.[3]

Although these are important differences, their practical impact for corporations among the industrialized countries is minimal, as far as minor offenses are concerned.

Some Common Categories of Law

Despite these differences, there are a few common classifications of law in any society. These are as follows:

- *Criminal versus civil law:* Criminal laws deal with "wrongs done to society," while civil law deals with wrongs done to individuals in a society. The important difference is that violations of criminal law result in penalties (for example, fines to the

---

[3]Perhaps reflecting these differences, the US has a substantially larger number of lawyers, lawsuits, lawyer fees, and damage awards compared to most other industrialized nations. In 1991, the US spent approximately $100 billion on legal services (about 2% of its GNP), an amount that is much larger than that of any other country in the world. Compared to about 100 lawyers per 100,000 people in Japan, 190 in Germany, and 50 in France, the US has over 300 lawyers per 100,000 people. Singapore is the only country with more lawyers per 100,000 people: about 400.

state, imprisonment) while violations of civil law result in payments to the affected party. In reality, many violations, particularly those by corporations, tend to be violations of both.

- *Substantive versus procedural law:* Substantive law deals with the content of law, while procedural laws deal with how the content of the law is implemented (for example, how the violator is served notice, the process of "discovery" or gathering of data for legal arguments, the actual conduct of the trial, and so forth).

- *Public versus private law:* Public law is the law that is enacted by the state (which, in certain countries, may include the clergy), while private law is the set of rules agreed upon by any two (or more) private individuals or groups. Public laws are statutory and include laws embodied in documents such as the Constitution, as well as in the various codified laws at the federal, state, and local levels. Private law is created by parties to a private contract (such contracts would, however, generally have to be consistent with and not violate the principles of public law in any society). Most of the dealings that a corporation has with its stakeholders (employment contracts, warranties to customers, contracts with debtholders, and the like) are in the realm of private law.

BASIC PRINCIPLES OF INTERNATIONAL LAW FOR BUSINESS[4]

Compared to domestic laws, international law is less coherent since its sources embody not only the laws of the individual states concerned with any dispute, but also any treaties (multilateral, bilateral, or universal) or conventions (for example, the Geneva Convention on human rights, or the Vienna Convention on diplomatic security). In addition, international law contains an international code of "custom," or the unwritten boundaries of behavior that result from repeated interactions among "civilized nations."

The International Court of Justice (an arm of the United Nations, located in The Hague, the Netherlands) lays down the following as the sources of international law:

1. International conventions, whether general or particular, establishing rules expressly recognized by the contesting states;
2. International custom as evidence of a general practice accepted as law;
3. The general principles of law recognized by civilized nations;
4. Judicial decisions and the teachings of the most highly qualified publicists of the various nations, as subsidiary means for the determination of rules of law.

There are six broad and related principles governing the conduct of international law: (1) the concept of sovereignty and sovereign immunity; (2) international jurisdiction; (3) the doctrine of comity; (4) the Act of State doctrine; (5) the treatment and rights of aliens; and (6) the appropriate forum for hearing and settling disputes. We consider each.

Sovereignty and Sovereign Immunity

The principle of sovereignty underlies all international law. In times of peace, every state has the sovereign right to existence, legal equality, jurisdiction over its territory, ownership of property, and diplomatic relations with other states. This, in turn, implies sovereign immunity, or that one country's court system cannot be used to rectify injustices in, or

---

[4]International law makes a distinction between the "Law of Peace" and the "Law of War." The Law of Peace establishes the rights and duties of states at peace with one another—that is, having a normal relationship. The Law of War lays down rules constraining what countries can do to one another during times of war. Our concern here is with the former.

impose penalties on, another country (unless the other country consents). The statute that deals with sovereign immunity in the US is the Sovereign Immunities Act of 1976. Some of its important provisions are as follows:

- Sovereign countries cannot be subjected to the decisions of US courts for their acts;
- This holds whether or not such acts are illegal in the US or illegal even according to the principles of international law;
- However, a distinction is made for commercial transactions of a sovereign nation: Any economic exchange that is voluntarily agreed to by the county (for example, a debt contract, sale by a state trading agency) can be brought to trial in the US if the contract specifies this contingency beforehand.

International Jurisdiction

International law specifies three types of jurisdiction—the nationality principle, the territoriality principle, and the protective principle.

The *nationality principle* holds that every country has jurisdiction over its citizens no matter where they are located. Under this principle, for example, a US manager who violates the Foreign Corrupt Practices Act while traveling abroad could be found guilty in the US.

The *territoriality principle* holds that every nation has the right of jurisdiction within its legal territory; this jurisdiction applies even if the act was committed within the state's territory, but had an effect outside the state's territory. For example, if a firm located in the US incurred foreign product liability through a sale it made from the US, citizens of the foreign state could potentially sue the company in a US court (but the US court could potentially throw it back to the other country using *forum non conveniens,* or "you have the wrong court" as an excuse; see below). However, this principle does not apply if the action took place outside the country, even if it had an effect within the country: For example, if an advertising campaign abroad had negative spillover effects in the US, the company could not sue the foreign party in the US. In many instances, there are aspects of both the cause and the effect in both territories; in this situation, conflicts lodge in the void at the intersection of sovereign boundaries.

The *protective principle* holds that every nation has jurisdiction over behavior that adversely affects its national security or its government's operations, even if the conduct of that behavior took place outside the country and was conducted by a citizen of another state.

Most courts applying rules of international law tend to use the territoriality principle.

The Doctrine of Comity

Under the rules of sovereignty, there is a custom of international etiquette called "comity," or mutual respect for each country's laws, institutions, and governments in the matter of their jurisdiction over their own citizens. Although not a part of "law," it is an important part of international custom, and US courts, in particular, place great emphasis on this doctrine in the decisions they make with respect to international disputes.

The Act of State Doctrine

Under this principle, all acts of the governments of other states in their own territory are considered valid by US courts, even if such acts are illegal or inappropriate.

This includes cases in which the foreign government expropriates or nationalizes another country's assets located within its territory (although this doctrine is often challenged in such instances). However, under the Foreign Assistance Act of 1962, the US Congress requires the president to suspend all assistance to countries that have expropriated

US assets (including, in some instances, when the country imposes prohibitive discriminatory taxes on the US MNE located abroad). Such actions are also dealt with through bilateral treaties. Further, the federal agency, Overseas Private Investment Corporation, sells insurance against expropriation in low-income countries in which US firms do business. Recently, many US firms have bought such insurance for their investments in Eastern Europe and the former Soviet Union.

It should be recognized that host countries are free to set their limits for repatriation of MNE's profits. Such actions are considered acts of state, and cannot be challenged in US courts.

The Treatment and Rights of Aliens

Countries can refuse to admit foreign citizens and can impose special restrictions on their conduct (for example, their rights of travel, where they can stay, what business they can and cannot do, and so forth); countries also have the right to deport aliens. Special laws can be set up for treatment of aliens, who do not necessarily have the right of appeal, unless allowed to do so. In other words, there is no presumed equality in international law between "natives" and foreigners.

The Appropriate Forum for Hearing and Settling Disputes

This is a principle of US justice as it applies to international law. US courts, at their discretion, can dismiss cases brought before them by foreigners under the principle of *forum non conveniens*. Courts are, however, bound to examine issues such as where the plaintiffs are, where the evidence will be gathered, and where the property to be used in restitution is located. A famous example of the application of this principle was in the case of Union Carbide and the Bhopal disaster, where a New York court of appeals sent the case back to India (by adding the additional condition that the judgments of the Indian courts would be binding on Union Carbide; see Case 11).

THE VOID AT THE INTERSECTION OF SOVEREIGN BOUNDARIES

The structure of principles governing international law leave considerable room for confusion for MNEs, particularly with respect to those transactions and exchanges that involve causes and effects in both the home *and* the host country. First of all, when this happens, the application of the territoriality principle may break down, since issues do not fall within borders as cleanly as courts would like. Second, sovereign immunity from with the Act of State doctrine limits the ability of a country's courts to intervene in the impact of actions of another country. Third, while international legal institutions such as the International Court of Justice (the "World Court") do exist, any judgments they render are nonenforceable since they are forums for voluntary mediation of disputes. Fourth, the notion of comity, which is taken quite seriously by US courts, often limits the restitution that plaintiffs can seek. Fifth, the notion of *forum non conveniens* makes it possible that cases can get shuffled around back and forth between the two countries. Finally, the differences between legal systems—in the way in which trials are conducted, discovery procedures done, and judgments awarded—leave open considerable room for delays and uncertainties.

The combination of all these results in a situation in which the manager of an MNE can get caught in a void at the intersection of sovereign boundaries. Contract enforcement rules that are implicit in non–cross-border transactions do not necessarily exist in cross-border settings. Where, in particular, can these problems arise, and what can MNE managers do to mitigate this problem?

The following two sections address these questions.

AREAS OF PARTICULAR CONCERN TO MNEs

With the increased role of cross-border flows of capital, technology, people, knowledge, and other resources, there are many instances in which the actions undertaken or conduct in one country can affect citizens in another country. The particular areas of concern to MNE managers are the following: (1) international antitrust issues; (2) multinational bankruptcy; (3) product, process, and environmental liability across borders; (4) trade disputes; (5) protection of intellectual property; and (6) the tradeoffs between business in the host country and national security or foreign policy issues in the home country.

International Antitrust Considerations

There is wide variance in the existence and application of antitrust laws among different countries. Moreover, given the increasingly global nature of competition and strategic alliances, actions that are taken in other countries can have an impact on the home country, and vice versa.

Consider the case of the discount-price transatlantic airline, Laker Airways, in the 1980s. Forced into bankruptcy in 1982, it filed an antitrust suit in the US against two US airlines, as well as four European airlines, claiming that their predatory pricing strategies drove it out of business. Laker claimed that since US consumers were affected by this predatory pricing, the issue should be of concern to US regulatory authorities and should be tried in the US courts. A countersuit was filed by the European carriers in a British court claiming that US courts had no jurisdiction over them, and the British court issued an injunction prohibiting Laker from taking action in the US. In response, Laker filed a counter-countersuit in another US court, which sided with Laker. In response, some of the European carriers appealed, and so it went, until Laker ultimately went bankrupt and settled out of court with the defendants.

Similarly, there has been much recent concern over the effect that vertical *keiretsus* in Japan have on US businesses through what the US government considers anticompetitive practices. The US Justice department is testing the limits of the applicability of international law by trying to bring cases against some of the Japanese firms involved.

US antitrust laws do provide that a foreign firm can be sued in the US if its practices—even if undertaken abroad—have anticompetitive effects in the US.[5] However, as happened in the case of Laker, such a suit can be appealed, with the result that such cases become a dispute between the courts of the two countries. The effect is often one of confusion and delay, with out-of-court settlements.

Multinational Bankruptcy

The second major area in which international legal waters remain largely untested is the area of multinational bankruptcy. Suppose a firm is domiciled in one country, but its actions abroad result in bankruptcy; moreover, suppose there is an asymmetry between the amount of assets and liabilities across countries (say, most of the assets are in the home country, but liabilities are in the foreign country). Who gets paid, under what rules of priority, and who decides? The short answer is that nobody is really sure, since the definitions, procedures, and rules of bankruptcy and liquidation vary widely across countries.

Consider, for instance, the recent collapse of the Bank of Credit and Commerce International (BCCI) or the case of the Maxwell Communications Corporation. With BCCI, there is considerable asymmetry in the location of the depositors and the recoverable assets.

---

[5]Under US antitrust law, it is not illegal for a US firm to undertake an action that can have anticompetitive effects abroad. However, US laws are undergoing evolution: Recently, joint ventures between large US firms have been allowed for reasons of global competition. For example, General Mills was allowed to acquire RJR Nabisco's food businesses since it was felt that it would enable them to compete more effectively against rivals such as Nestle.

The question of which country's central bank decides who gets what is still wide open, several years after the incident. There is similar (but perhaps less of a) confusion in the case of Maxwell. Both cases could potentially drag on for years, and the outcomes are uncertain.

As cross-border business activity grows, the question of multinational bankruptcy, with the potential for MNEs being caught in the cross-border regulatory void, is particularly vexing.

Cross-border Liability

There are many instances in which cross-border activity imposes externalities and spillover effects across borders—for example, product liability, liability that results from defective processes, or liability involving the natural environment. Examples include the Union Carbide disaster in Bhopal (see Case 11), an oil spill that is caused by a firm in another country's waters, a nuclear disaster in one country that creates radiation in another (for example, the case of Chernobyl), or a defective product that is sold across borders (for example, the case of the US company, Piper Aircraft, whose plane crashed in Scotland because of a product defect). Every activity involving cross-border liability is potentially open for confusion because of the factors listed in the previous section, "The Void at the Intersection of Sovereign Boundaries." Indeed, all of the examples mentioned above resulted in some legal confusion or the other, with the substantive issues of law still left largely unresolved.

The extent and nature of cross-border liability—basic questions such as whether the MNE as a whole, or only the subsidiary that caused the damage, is liable, and whether and how the chain of control matters—remain wide-open issues in international law.

Trade Disputes

While this is a major area of concern for MNEs, as we saw in Chapter 7, there is a well-developed set of laws and institutions to deal with trade disputes, at both the international and domestic level (at least, in the industrialized world). Although such laws exist, they are a source of both opportunities and risks for MNEs. For details, refer again to Chapter 7.

Protection of Intellectual Property

Worldwide control over their patents, trademarks, brand equity, copyrights, and so forth is of crucial concern to MNEs. There are some international agreements (for example, the Madrid Agreement to facilitate international cooperation in intellectual property) and domestic laws (see Chapter 7 for US laws, such as Section 337, in this regard) that provide protection to MNEs. Moreover, there is a worldwide oversight organization and clearinghouse, called the World Intellectual Property Rights Organization. However, the existence and control of "gray markets"—international trade in goods and services without the consent of the owner of the trademark or copyrights—remains a major problem for MNEs. While there are evolving standards in various national courts for dealing with gray market goods, the application and enforcement of laws remain inconsistent and often ineffective.

Tradeoffs between Business Abroad and National Security/Foreign Policy at Home

The final area of great concern to managers of MNEs involves their being driven by local imperatives (either through choice, such as meeting the competition's moves, or through necessity, such as responding to the demands of the host-country government) to undertake actions that may conflict with national security or foreign policy goals of their home-country government. Such examples are numerous: the case of Dresser Industries caught between the US and French governments over its shipments to the Soviet Gas Pipeline project on which President Reagan applied sanctions (see Case 10); the alleged case of Cargill avoiding US laws to conduct business with Iraq using its subsidiary in the UK; the case of Toshiba shipping numerically controlled machine tools to the former Soviet Union, which allegedly enabled them to develop more silent nuclear submarines; and the prohibition by the US government of US firms from paying taxes to the government of Panama headed by Manuel Noriega.

Here again, the MNE may be caught in a situation in which the host and home-country governments, laws, institutions, foreign policy imperatives, national security concerns, and so on may be in legitimate conflict. The questions that arise, apart from issues of ethics and social responsibility (see Chapter 9), include: Whose laws should the MNE obey? In the event that the MNE perforce breaks one country's laws, where should the case be tried and which laws should apply? Even if both these questions are answered, is a judgment by the courts of one country applicable to the activities undertaken by the MNE in another country? Short of withdrawing from the dilemma by exiting the business—in which case, the MNE will conduct business in few places around the world—what can the manager of the MNE do, and who can he or she turn to?

All these are questions that the laws and institutions governing cross-border economic relations leave largely unanswered. However, the manager of an MNE can perhaps mitigate these concerns—albeit imperfectly—by adopting some practical guidelines in ex ante contract design. We turn to some of these below.

GUIDELINES FOR MANAGERS OF MNEs

Often, the primary solution to the problems previously detailed is for managers of MNEs to anticipate as many of them as possible, and to incorporate these possibilities and potential avenues for dispute resolution into contracts *prior to* undertaking any serious economic exchange. The important means by which many MNEs resolve international disputes is through *arbitration*. Many MNEs place clauses in contracts that require arbitration by specified international organizations, in addition to which they also specify which country's laws would apply and what language will be used. Another approach is to determine, ex ante, which courts' jurisdiction the parties to the contract will submit themselves to, in the event of a dispute; this avoids the lengthy litigation that surrounds the issue of whether or not jurisdiction belongs to a particular country's court *after* a problem has occurred.

The two commonly used organizations for international arbitration are the International Chamber of Commerce (ICC), located in Paris, and the International Center for Settlement of Investment Disputes (ICSID), an arm of the World Bank, located in Washington, DC. The ICC is most often used when parties on both sides of a contract are in the private sector; in a situation where a private party deals with nation states—particularly those in developing countries—many contracts choose the ICSID. In the event that courts are used, the commonly used courts in the US are the federal district courts.

In addition to contracts for dealing with normal cross-border business risks, MNE managers should also anticipate, and incorporate clauses relating to, other larger sources of risks such as war, terrorism, disruption of transportation and communication lines (for example, the shipping lines during the Gulf War), expropriation and other political actions that may be taken by the host state, and so forth. Such clauses are called *force majeure* clauses, and they specify many of the same contingencies as in the case of arbitration—for example, which courts, in what language, and whose law will apply.

While these are general approaches that managers of MNEs should adopt, there are ultimately certain limitations that result from many of the factors that we discussed earlier in the chapter. In most practical and day-to-day situations, however, these problems can be mitigated by careful ex ante contract design.

SUMMARY

In the past two decades, imperatives of borderless strategy formulation and implementation have repeatedly come into conflict with the regulatory and political reality of sovereignty. Inconsistencies in legal norms between countries as well the gray areas of international law have created both opportunities and risks for MNEs. As long as nation states continue to exist, attempts to take advantage of global corporate opportunities risk entering the regulatory void at the intersection of sovereign boundaries. Global managers would be naive to assume that the transition toward true borderlessness will be smooth, or that the laws of different nation states can be as easily navigated as in domestic cases.

In this chapter, we examined the range of regulatory issues that are of concern to MNEs, and the main principles of international law that relate to these concerns. While there are no simple solutions or "models" for MNE managers to follow in dealing with such concerns, careful contract design is the *sine qua non* of mitigating the impact of cross-border regulatory pitfalls.

SELECTED BIBLIOGRAPHY

EHLERMANN, C. D.   "Antitrust Issues in an International Dimension." *The University of Chicago Legal Forum* (1992): 241-262.

GITLIN, R. A., and E. D. FLASCHEN.   "The International Void in the Law of Multinational Bankruptcies." *The Business Lawyer* 42 (February 1987): 307-325.

JANIS, M.W.   "International Law?" *Harvard International Law Journal* 32(2) 1991: 363-372.

JOHN, K., L. W. SENBET, and A. K. SUNDARAM.   "Cross Border Liability of Multinational Enterprises, Border Taxes, and Capital Structure." *Financial Management* (Winter 1991): 54-67.

KINDLEBERGER, C. P.   "International Public Goods without International Government." *American Economic Review* 76(1) 1986: 1-13.

LECUYER-THIEFFRY, C., and P. THIEFFRY.   "Negotiating Settlement of Disputes Provisions in International Business Contracts: Recent Developments in Arbitration and Other Processes." *The Business Lawyer* 45 (February 1990): 577-623.

LIEBMAN, S. F.   "The European Community's Products Liability Directive: Is the U.S. Experience Applicable?" *Law and Policy in International Business* 18(4) 1986: 795-814.

NEALE, A. D., and M. L. STEPHENS.   *International Business and National Jurisdiction.* Oxford: Clarendon Press, 1988.

NEVEN, D., and G. SIOTIS.   "Foreign Direct Investment in the European Community: Some Policy Issues." *Oxford Review of Economic Policy* 9(2) 1992: 72-93.

PARK, W. W.   "Arbitration of International Contract Disputes." *The Business Lawyer* 39 (August 1984): 1783-1799.

PINCUS, L. B., T. H. PINCUS, and M. REID.   "Legal Issues Involved in Corporate Globalization." *Columbia Business Law Review* 2 (1991): 269-285.

SINGER, J. W.   "Sovereignty and Property." *Northwestern University Law Review* 86(1) 1991: 1-56.

SUNDARAM, A. K., and J. S. BLACK.   "The Environment and Internal Organization of Multinational Enterprises." *Academy of Management Review* 17 (1992): 729-757.

SWANSON, S. R.   "Comity, International Dispute Resolution Agreements, and the Supreme Court." *Law and Policy in International Business* 21(3) 1990: 333-365.

VERESHCHETIN, V. S., and R. A. MULLERSON.   "International Law in an Interdependent World." *Columbia Journal of Transnational Law* 28 (1990): 291-300.

WESTIN, E.   "Enforcing Foreign Commercial Judgments and Arbitral Awards in the United States, West Germany, and England." *Law and Policy in International Business* 19(2) 1987: 325-360.

Dresser (France) S.A. and the Soviet Gas Pipeline*

```
TELEX:  842-270772
TO:     R. E. TRON — DRESSER FRANCE
FROM:   J. R. BROWN JR. — DRESSER
DATE:   JUNE 21, 1982
CC:     J. J. MURPHY — DALLAS
        M. A. ZECH — COMPRESSOR GROUP — HOUSTON
        R. W. GAWRONSKI — COMPRESSOR GROUP — HOUSTON
        J. R. HUTTON — DRESSER MACHINERY INTERNATIONAL —
        HOUSTON
SUBJ:   YAMAL/URENGOY PIPELINE

CUT BACK ALL EXPENSES ON ABOVE SUBJECT. WILL FORWARD MORE
DETAILS ON EMBARGO BY PRESIDENT REAGAN, AS SOON AS IT IS
AVAILABLE. SUGGEST YOU CANCEL ALL OUTSTANDING ORDERS AND
REDUCE COSTS WHEREVER POSSIBLE. CALL IF YOU HAVE ANY QUES-
TIONS.[1]
```

Robert E. Tron, the President and General Manager of Dresser (France) S.A., looked at the telex in dismay: It referred to a contract to supply gas pipeline compressors to the proposed Soviet Urengoy-Uzgorod natural gas pipeline (SNGP) project. The contract was valued at 87 million French francs ($20 million) and represented 20% of Dresser France's current revenues. The consequences of abandoning the contract could be deleterious to the company's results, and mean the loss of hundreds of French jobs. But failure to comply with the request from Dresser Industries, its US parent, seemed to be out of the question, since this risked blanket export bans and denials of technology transfer from parent to subsidiary by

---

*This case was developed by Nick Hall under the supervision of Associate Professor Anant K. Sundaram as a basis for class discussion. © 1993.

[1]Case No. 632, Dresser (France) S.A. Motion to Vacate Temporary Denial of Export Privileges, Bureau of National Affairs.

the US government, under the Export Administration Act of 1979. Dresser France's long-term viability relied on the transfer of US technology for its research and development.

The telex resulted from a recent escalation in the US trade dispute against the USSR. At the end of last year, President Ronald Reagan had announced extensive economic sanctions against the Soviet Union protesting the Soviet Union's support of the current Polish military rule. These sanctions had included new requirements for export licenses for certain items of oil and gas equipment. Six months later, on June 18, Reagan extended the export ban to include the activities of foreign subsidiaries of US firms, and foreign firms licensing US technology.

Protests from various European governments against these developments were swift and loud. French Foreign Minister Claude Cheysson said of the western allies, "we no longer speak the same language" and described the relationship with the US as a "progressive divorce."[2] Many argued that the wider ban represented an infringement of their sovereignty, and that it hurt European business far more than American. Running beneath the general issue of the seemingly excessive US intervention was a specific point of contention over the Urengoy-Uzgorod pipeline itself, a project that the US government was anxious to undermine, against the wishes of the West Europeans.

It was inevitable that the political battles would eventually affect the operations of Dresser France, which was a major supplier to the Urengoy-Uzgorod project. And, if Robert Tron had any hope that the telex was an overreaction on the part of the US parent, it was rudely shattered 2 days later, when a second telex arrived confirming the instructions:

```
TO:   R. E. TRON — PARIS
CONFIDENTIAL
FROM: M. A. ZECH
DATE: JUNE 24, 1982
CC:   S. E. HANDEL
      N. J. KLIST
SUBJ: USSR PIPELINE, YOUR TELEX JUNE 24

I CONFIRM THE INSTRUCTIONS NOTED IN THE REF. TELEX.
1. NO EQUIPMENT FOR THE SUBJECT CONTRACT CAN BE SHIPPED FROM
   D. F. AFTER JUNE 22, 1982.
2. PROCEED WITH THE NECESSARY ACTION TO MINIMIZE COST ASSOCI-
   ATED WITH THE SUBJECT CONTRACT, INCLUDING CANCELLATION OF
   MATERIAL DELIVERY, WORK STOPPAGE AND PERSONNEL REASSIGN-
   MENT.
3. PLEASE DETERMINE TOTAL FINANCIAL IMPACT OF THE IMPOSED
   RESTRICTION.
```

Three compressors had been completed and were sitting at the dock in Le Havre awaiting loading aboard a Russian freighter. Tron ordered the compressors to be held, and canceled the customs documents. There were another 18 compressors under construction, and work on these was stopped and the workers reassigned. The management of Dresser France wondered if the work would ever be resumed.

DRESSER FRANCE

Dresser (France) S.A. was incorporated in France in 1956. It is owned by Dresser A.G. (Vaduz) in Liechtenstein which is, in turn, a wholly owned subsidiary of Dresser Industries, Inc. of Dallas, Texas. Dresser France operates a manufacturing plant at the port of Le Havre,

---

[2]"Pipeline Politics: The Complex Political Economy of East-West Energy Trade," Bruce W. Jentleson, *Cornell University Press 1986,* Ithaca and London.

an economically depressed area with high unemployment. Dresser is a major employer in the area, with 800 people directly employed in the plant itself and another 390 employed in subcontracted businesses or related industries.

The Le Havre plant manufacturers a variety of oil and gas mining equipment. Dresser-France reports to the Dresser Clark division in Olean, New York. Designs for its products are provided by the Olean staff and much of the technology used is provided by the US parent under an agreement signed in November 1976.

In September of the previous year, Dresser France had signed a contract with V/O Machinoimport, a Soviet trading company, and Creusot-Loire, a recently nationalized French company, to deliver 21 compressors to Machinoimport, to be used as part of the proposed Urengoy-Uzgorod natural gas pipeline project.

THE SOVIET NATURAL GAS PIPELINE (SNGP)

The SNGP was an ambitious project. Running over 3000 miles from Western Siberia to Western Europe it crossed the Ural mountains, the icy terrain of Siberia, over seven hundred rivers, and dense forest until it arrived in the heart of Europe. The pipeline would provide the means for the USSR to transport some of the vast natural gas reserves discovered in the frozen corner of the Yamal Peninsula to homes and factories in the West. It was intended to supply around 40 billion cubic meters per year, providing up to 30% of Western Europe's gas requirements within 10 years (see *Exhibit 1* for sizes of USSR natural gas exports). To many European companies, the project represented a huge business opportunity.

EXHIBIT 1

USSR Natural Gas Exports 1979–1981

Amounts in Terajoules	*1981*	*1980*	*1979*
World	2,080,000	2,014,440	1,643,000
USA	–	–	–
Europe	2,080,000	1,967,060	1,643,000
UK	–	–	–
Italy	211,650	233,440	217,120
W. Germany	414,810	379,150	352,570
France	161,710	138,390	94,310
E. Germany	221,020	209,540	150,020

Source: United Nations World Energy Book, 1982.

To build the pipeline meant relying on Western imports and financing. It was estimated that $25-30 billion of imports would be required in the form of gas compressors, computer control technology, and large-diameter pipe. The technology required to make very large-diameter pipe, capable of withstanding high pressures, was particularly vital. Western European companies had such technology, which was employed in a variety of other ways, including making submarine hulls.

Mannesman A.G., a German engineering company, estimated that 1,000 new jobs would be created by the project. For Creusot-Loire, a company that had just turned profitable in the last three years, work on the project would absorb half their personnel for the next few years. Italy would supply the large-diameter pipe. The French company Thomson-CSF would provide the computer system designed to automate the operation of the pipeline. The Thomson systems were considered state-of-the-art and used in a number of European defense applications. Finally, 120 gas compressors were required at regular intervals along the pipeline.

The gas compressors were based on US designs from General Electric (GE) that had been licensed to a number of European firms. Forty sets of gas compressors were due to come from Alsthom-Atlantique, which represented most of that firm's capacity. Twenty sets were to be supplied by the Italian engineering firm, Nuovo Pignone. Another twenty were to come from Mannesman A.G. and John Brown, a UK engineering firm. Finally, twenty-one sets were ordered under the contract with Dresser France.

US-SOVIET RELATIONS

The US government had changed its view of the SNGP over the last ten years. Prior to President Jimmy Carter's administration, US-Soviet policy toward the Soviet Union had sought to expand East-West trade in order to increase the economic dependence of the USSR on the West. There was an added incentive for the US in the case of the supply of soviet natural gas: Access to Soviet natural gas would be a means to escape the dependence on oil supplies from the increasingly unstable Middle East.

The US's views of the SNGP project soured with the invasion of Afghanistan by Soviet troops in 1980. US intelligence analysts urged that a reduction in OPEC imports should be replaced by new Western energy supplies, rather than risking dependence on an aggressive Warsaw pact. Attention turned to the implications of the pipeline as a source of hard currency and the effect on the Allied forces if countries relied too heavily on the Soviet source. In a Congressional testimony in 1981, Assistant Secretary of Defense Richard N. Perle articulated the fears the US had about the threats to the Western alliance:

> First, it will generate substantial hard currency earnings for the Soviet Union that will finance a number of Soviet developments inimical to our interests. With the pipeline in full operation, several billion dollars annually will flow into the Soviet treasury...
>
> Second, the revenues available to the Soviets will help to forge an economic link with Europe that will inevitably increase Moscow's influence among our allies. And where jobs and profits emanate from Moscow, it would be naive to believe that politics will stay far behind...
>
> Third we believe that Europe will incur a dangerous vulnerability to the interruption of supplies of natural gas from the Soviet Union... Even in the absence of a crisis severe enough to lead to a Soviet cutoff there is the day-to-day influence that must flow, like the gas itself, through a pipeline to which there will be no practicable alternative...
>
> Is there any doubt that our allies listen more carefully to kings and rulers who supply them with energy than to those who do not?

US-EUROPEAN RELATIONS

The Europeans, however, did not believe that the Soviet gas supply represented as much of a strategic threat as the Americans feared. The governments of many European countries had taken measures to reduce their exposure to the USSR. These included building gas storage facilities to buffer supplies against Soviet action and building generators to use coal as well as gas. Arrangements were also made with the Dutch and the Norwegians to provide backup sources of supply. European leaders were also unhappy about what they considered the US's hypocritical attitude East-West trade when it came to the US's own extensive grain exports to the Soviet Union (see *Exhibit 2* for details of US trade with the USSR).

The issue of US grain exports was the one exception to President Reagan's "get tough" policy. President Jimmy Carter had initiated the embargo of US grain to the Soviets as part of the US Cold War actions. However, with exports to the USSR representing 6.2%

of total US grain production, the Carter administration had found itself under considerable pressure from American farmers. Sympathetic members of congress argued that American farmers were bearing too heavy a burden of US foreign policy. Carter responded with some emergency farm subsidies but he maintained the embargo. Many observers saw this as one of the many reasons that contributed to Reagan's landslide victory in 1980.

Reagan lifted the embargo, and indeed, signed a new one-year grain contract on July 30, 1982, with the USSR. Reagan even made the promise that grain exports would never again be the subject of US economic sanctions.

Since the supply of foreign grain resulted in substantial savings for the Soviets,[3] the European governments had a difficult time reconciling this with the US concerns that gas contracts represented a dangerous source of hard currency.

EXHIBIT 2

US-USSR Trade Statistics, 1978–1981

	1981	1980	1979	1978
US Exports World:	$236,254	$224,237	$184,473	$142,054
US Exports: USSR				
Total	2,339	1,510	3,604	2,249
Agricultural	1,665	1,047	2,855	1,686
Nonagricultural	674	463	749	562
Oil and gas equipment (1)	64	51	164	83
US Imports: USSR				
Total	347	453	873	540
Agricultural	13	8	14	13
Nonagricultural	334	445	445	527
Gold bullion	22	88	88	287

Source: Economic Report of the President and Highlights of US Exports, US Bureau of Census, US Department of Commerce.

(1) These figures do not include shipments of pipeline, which were zero in the years listed.

REAGAN AND THE SOVIET PIPELINE

Throughout 1981, the US tried to stop European governments from signing gas import contracts and to impose tougher export controls, particularly on high-technology exports. At the Ottawa summit in July, President Reagan tried to persuade the German, French, Italian, and British governments from completing contracts to provide the 25 megawatt turbines the Soviets needed for the compressor stations. He did not succeed and a consortium led by Mannesman Anlagenbau of West Germany and Creusot-Loire of France signed a contract for turbines worth $1 billion. Nuovo Pignone of Italy also signed a contract for $1.1 billion, and John Brown Engineering of the UK, a subcontractor for the consortium, picked up the turbine spare parts contract, worth $60 million (see *Exhibit 3* for a summary of the major contracts signed during this time).

The President's attempts to dissuade the Europeans from buying Soviet gas were equally fruitless. In November, a US delegation traveled to Europe with an energy package to substitute American coal and Norwegian natural gas for the Soviet natural gas. But using American coal had a number of problems. The US was having problems shipping its current flow of coal, due to the congestion at ports, and there was some doubt that they could cope with any significant increase in supply. Also, the environmental movement was building in Europe, and governments were under pressure to move to the cleaner gas-fired generators or force utilities to undergo expensive upgrading of generators with scrubbers and

[3] Around $32 billion, according to a study by Wharton Econometrics.

emissions controls. Finally, the Norwegians were unenthusiastic about the idea of using their own gas reserves. The Norwegian government was trying to provide a gradual growth for Norway's energy industry and the American's scheme would have involved a sudden expansion in output.

For the governments in Europe, mired in recession for the last year (see *Exhibit 4*), the economic benefits of trading with the USSR far outweighed the foreign policy benefits of sanctions or the security concerns voiced by the US.

There was also the issue of export credits. A number of the contracts with the USSR were backed by financing arranged by the European governments. In 1978, a twenty-two nation agreement had established minimum rates of interest for all such export credits from OECD countries. Such an arrangement prevented foreign government from subsidizing export business with cheap credit—as long as all the nations signing the agreement cooperated. However, some governments had been undercutting the minimum rates for credit to the USSR. The Soviets had exploited such defections and played one government off against another, to drive down the rates as low as possible.

EXHIBIT 3

Major Contracts Signed by European Firms in 1981

Amounts in millions of dollars

Company	Country	Contract	Value
Althsom-Atlantique	France	40 spare turbine rotor kits	40
Creusot-Loire	France	19 refrigeration stations	225
Thomson-CSF	France	Computer control equipment	350
Italsider	Italy	400K tons wide-diameter pipe	230
Nuove Pignone	Italy	19 compressor stations	1,100
John Brown Engineering	UK	Turbine spare parts	60
Plenty	UK	Fuel gas conditioning facilities	30
Redifusion	UK	Computer information system	15
Ruston Gas Turbines	UK	45 gas turbine sets	30
Mannesman/Creusot	W. Germany/France	22 compressor stations	1,000
Liebhen	W. Germany	323 truck-mounted cranes	150
Mannesman/Thyssen	W. Germany	1.2M tons wide-diameter pipe	690

Source: "Pipeline Politics."

EXHIBIT 4

Economic Statistics for Selected Countries 1979–1981

Unemployment

	1981	1980	1979	1978
United States	7.6%	7.1%	5.8%	6.1%
France	7.7%	6.5%	6.1%	5.4%
West Germany	4.2%	3.0%	3.0%	3.4%
Italy	4.2%	3.9%	3.9%	3.7%
United Kingdom	11.3%	7.3%	5.7%	6.3%

Source: Economic Report of the President, 1982

GNP Growth Rate

	1981	1980	1979	1978
United States	2.0%	−0.2%	3.2%	4.8%
France	0.3%	1.6%	3.5%	3.7%
West Germany	−0.3%	1.8%	4.3%	3.6%
Italy	−0.2%	4.0%	4.9%	2.7%
United Kingdom	−0.8%	−1.7%	1.4%	3.3%

Source: Economic Report of the President, 1982.

THE REAGAN SANCTIONS

On December 13, 1981, martial law was imposed in Poland by General Jaruzelski's army in an attempt to control the labor movement, Solidarity. There was little doubt that the Polish forces were receiving support from Moscow. On December 29, Reagan made the following announcement of economic sanctions:

The Soviet Union bears a heavy and direct responsibility for the repression in Poland. For many months the Soviets publicly and privately demanded such a crackdown. They brought major pressures to bear through now-public letters to the Polish leadership, military maneuvers, and other forms of intimidation. They now openly endorse the suppression which has ensued.

Last week, I announced that I had sent a letter to President Brezhnev urging him to permit the restoration of basic human rights in Poland as provided for in the Helsinki Final Act. I have also informed him that, if the repression continued, the United States would have no choice but to take further concrete political and economic measures affecting our relationship.

The repression in Poland continues, and President Brezhnev has responded in a manner which makes it clear the Soviet Union does not understand the seriousness of our concern, and its obligations under both the Helsinki Final Act and the U.N. Charter.

I have, therefore, decided to take the following immediate measures with regard to the Soviet Union:

—All Aeroflot service to the United States will be suspended.

—The Soviet Purchasing Commission is being closed.

—The issuance or renewal of licenses for the export to the USSR of electronic equipment, computers, and other high-technology materials is being suspended.

—Negotiations on a new long-term grains agreement are being postponed.

—Negotiations on a new US-Soviet maritime agreement are being suspended, and a new regime of port-access controls will be put into effect for all Soviet ships when the current agreement expires on December 31.

—Licenses will be required for export to the Soviet Union for an expanded list of oil and gas equipment. Issuance of such licenses will be suspended. This includes pipelayers.

—US-Soviet exchange agreements coming up for renewal in the near future, including the agreements on energy and science and technology, will not be renewed. There will be a complete review of all other US-Soviet exchange agreements.[4]

Of the $300 million in sales revenue lost as a result of the sanctions, it was estimated that $200 million was in oil and gas equipment. The Commerce Department felt that this would have a substantial impact on the progress of the SNGP.

Others, however, were not so sure and were concerned that US business might be sacrificed for nothing. Armco International, for example, lost a $353 million contract after Carter's export license suspension in 1979. The business went to a French company. Many urged the government to get European agreement to prevent the Soviets substituting European goods for American ones. Bo Denysyk, the Deputy Assistant Secretary of Commerce, said that the Commerce Department was asking allies to support the sanctions but that no official agreements had yet been made.

The concerns of US businesses were by no means tempered when the Europeans refused to join the US in its pipeline sanctions. Instead, they limited their action against the Soviets to some minor economic sanctions and a communiqué condemning Moscow for its

[4]Text of Reagan's Announcement of Sanctions, *The New York Times,* December 30, 1981.

support of the suppression in Poland. Soon after this, the French signed their natural gas import contracts and, in early February, they extended their low-interest credit terms for $850 million to also include a $140 million down payment.

At the June Versailles summit, Reagan turned again to the issue of export credits and hoped to get agreement from the seven nations to limit financing arrangements on the pipeline. But the Europeans were not willing to be moved and the best that could be achieved was a loosely worded accord that said the allies agreed "to pursue a prudent and diversified economic approach to the USSR and Eastern Europe, consistent with our political and security interests."[5]

But even the accord quickly disintegrated when, after various diplomatic understandings had taken place, President Mitterand declared that France "would not support economic warfare against the Soviet Union and is not bound by the summit declaration to cut the amount of credit extended to Moscow." Later, the German Finance Minister echoed the French President's sentiments.

On June 18, President Reagan announced that he was extending the US sanctions to American companies' activities overseas and to foreign companies using American technological licenses. The new sanctions would be immediate and retroactive—requiring companies to cancel contracts that were already signed. The Reagan Administration made no pretense that these sanctions were designed specifically to delay the pipeline project. Lionel H. Olmer, Undersecretary of Commerce for International Trade Administration, predicted that the actions would delay the pipeline by at least two years. He said that the sanctions would cost US companies some $1.2 billion of business over the next three years.[6]

In describing the enforcement of these new sanctions Mr. Olmer said that the process would begin with a warning letter to the violator, who would then be placed on a "denial list," prohibiting the company "from receiving any export of any goods or data from the United States, irrespective of whether it's related to oil or gas." Criminal penalties could then be issued and fines of up to $100,000 levied on the violator. The Undersecretary did not, however, say how these fines would be collected from a foreign company.

THE EUROPEANS' REACTION

The reaction from the European governments took Washington by surprise. Probably the most muted comment came in the joint statement issued by the 10 EEC partners: "This action, taken without consultation with the Community, implies an extraterritorial extension of US jurisdiction, which in the circumstances is contrary to the principles of international law." British Prime Minister Margaret Thatcher said that "It is wrong for one very powerful nation [to try to prevent the fulfillment of] existing contracts that do not, in any event, fall under its jurisdiction." A West German political commentator in *Der Spiegel* summed up the European feeling when he said "The Americans were treating us as if we were not sovereign states. We could not sit still and let them run our lives for us."

THE FRENCH GOVERNMENT RESPONDS

In July, a few weeks after the sanction extentions, Robert Tron sent the following letter to Demag A.G. indicating they were unable to deliver a further five compressors destined for the pipeline head station:

[5]"Pipeline Politics."

[6]"US to Penalize Those Violating Curbs on Soviets," *The New York Times,* June 24 1982.

Demag A.G
4100
Wolfgang Reuter Plats
Postfach 10 01 41-43
Attn: Mr. W. Rodenbeck
Subject:URENCOT-USSR Pipeline

License agreement between DRESSER INDUSTRIES and DRESSER FRANCE dated November 1, 1976

Our license agreement provides that we are prohibited from selling or shipping to any country to which our licenser may be barred from selling or shipping by the government of the US.

Our Licenser has advised us that, as a result of the amendment to a regulation of the Oil and Gas Controls to the USSR issued by the US department of Commerce on June 22, 1982, we were not authorized to ship any equipment manufactured under the License Agreement, in connection with this YAMAL/URENGOY pipeline project.

We, therefore, are prohibited from supplying the equipment under your P.O.N deg. 143-143-81, D.F. contract N deg. 7251.

Yours truly,

R.E. Tron

One month later, however, Tron was contacted by Jean-Pierre Chevenement, Minister of State at the French Ministry of Research and Industry. Chevenement made it clear that the French government wanted the contract for the pipeline to be fulfilled and he asked Tron to keep him informed of any decisions Dresser management made about the compressors. Chevenement also hinted that, if necessary, the French government were prepared to take "administrative or statutory measures" to ensure that the deliveries were made.

Chevenment's statement was no idle threat. A French "actes du gouvernement" was all that was required to force Dresser France to comply, or face criminal prosecution which could mean fines and imprisonment for the company executives. In addition, it was possible that the government could nationalize Dresser-France.

Tron decided to take advice from his counsel. Despite the strong words from the French authorities to fulfill his contractual obligations, his counsel advised him that this did not constitute a binding order from the government. If Dresser-France did deliver the compressors, however, this would certainly contravene US law. Acting on this advice Tron ordered the packing company not to release the compressors for shipment. He then wrote to the French Minister of State to tell him what he had done (*Exhibit 5*).

As if to confirm Tron's decision, a telex arrived the following day from the Deputy Assistant Secretary of Export Enforcement, United States Department of Commerce, indicating that the US authorities were aware of the potential compressor deliveries. The telex reminded Tron that he was bound by Section 387.1 of the Export Administration Act of 1979 (se*e Exhibit 6*) and "formally" advised him of his obligations under the Export license agreements (see *Exhibit 7* for a copy of the telex).

Four days later, officials from the French Ministry of Research and Industry called on Tron at Dresser-France's headquarters and handed him the following communication. It confirmed his worst fears:

Republic of France
Requisition Order for Services
Pursuant to Ordinance No. 59-63 of January 6, 1959, concerning requisitions of goods and services;

Pursuant to Decree No. 62-367 of March 26, 1962, being a public regulation for the implementation of the Ordinance of January 6, 1959, concerning requisitions of goods and services;

Dresser France S.A., having its principal office 5 rue d'Antony, 94563 Rungis, in the person of its legal representative Mr. Tron, is obligated:

—to complete the manufacture and delivery of all compressors and other equipment provided for in contract No. CL C 102 dated September 28, 1981, which binds such corporation with Vneshnetorgovoie Obiedinenie Machinoimport and to the company known as Creusot-Loire;

—to complete the transfers of technology and the manufacture and delivery of all compressors, rotors and other equipment provided for in the contract dated June 16, 1978, which binds such corporation to the company known as Demag.

Failure to comply with this order would cause the penalties provided under article 31 of the Law of July 11, 1928, as amended, to become applicable.

Done in Paris, this 23rd August 1982

Jean-Pierre Chevenement
Seal of the
Ministry of Research & Industry
The Minister of State

EXHIBIT 5

Tron's Letter to the Minister of State (translated from the French)

Minister of State
Minister of Research & Industry
101 rue de Grenelle
75007 Paris   August 17, 1982

Dear Mr. Minister:

We beg to refer to the problems raised by the implementation of the export by our company of pipeline boosters for the construction of the Urengoy Gas Pipeline.

We have noted the position expressed in your letter of August 10, 1982. We are most desirous of meeting our contractual commitments but we have a serious problem in this respect due to the present circumstances.

Our company, a grand-daughter company of Dresser Industries, Inc., a US company, manufactures pipeline boosters from French material and labor based on technology and data received from the US under a license agreement with Dresser Industries, Inc.

Such technology and data were received prior to December 30, 1981, and prior to the imposition of sanctions by the United States Government on trade with the Soviet Union. We have thus been in a position to fulfill our contractual obligations until the imposition of the most recent sanctions by the United States Government.

At the present time, three of the pipeline boosters, which were near completion when the recent sanctions were imposed, are ready for shipment.

Naturally, we fully intend to comply with the laws and regulations of France. We however have been advised by counsel that if we were to ship these pipeline boosters under contract, this would raise serious questions under US law and could in the future place in jeopardy our company's access to the technology licensed to it by Dresser Industries, Inc. Further, we have been advised that neither the communique of July 21, 1982, from the French Government nor your letter to us dated August 10, 1982 constitute a binding order of the French Government requiring shipment of the materials.

I would like to assure you that the primary concern of the Management of Dresser, France, which has some 1000 people on its payroll—not to mention people on subcontractors' payrolls—in an area plagued by unemployment, is to ensure the continued existence of the company and to provide continued employment of as many people as possible both at our Le Havre plant and at our subcontractors' plants. Any action on our part which would result in an inability of our US parent company to continue to supply needed technology would force us to cease all operations in a very short time.

In view of the uncertainty of our position, we have been led to instruct the company in charge of storage in Le Havre harbor not to release the goods for shipment to the USSR pending further advice.

Materials for completion of the remaining pipeline boosters scheduled for 1982 and 1983 shipments have been received in our factories and the factories of our suppliers, but manufacturing progress has been halted as a result of the US sanctions.

We have been informed that a Soviet vessel has been dispatched to arrive in Le Havre August 24-27 for the purpose of loading the three completed pipeline boosters mentioned above.

We shall welcome any suggestions you may have regarding possible resolution of this difficult question, and would be honored to meet with you at your convenience to discuss the various aspects of this matter.

Respectfully,

R.E. Tron
President

Source: Bureau of National Affairs, Case No. 632.

EXHIBIT 6

Extracts from the Export Administration Act Regulations

Section 387.1 Sanctions
(a) Criminal
(1) Violations of Export Administration Act.

    i. *General.* . . . whoever knowingly violates the Export Administration Act ("the Act") or any regulation, order, or license issued under the Act is punishable for each violation by a fine of not more than five times the value of the exports involved or $50,000, whichever is greater, or by imprisonment for not more than five years, or both.

    ii. *Willful violations.* Whoever willfully exports anything contrary to any provision of the Act or any regulation, order, or license issued under the Act, with the knowledge that such exports will be used for the benefit of any country to which exports are restricted for national security or foreign policy purposes except in the case of an individual, shall be fined not more than five times the value of the exports involved or $1,000,000, whichever is greater; and in the case of an individual, shall be fined not more than $250,000, or imprisoned not more than 10 years, or both. . .

(b) Administrative

    1. *Denial of export privileges.* Whoever violates any law, regulation, order, or license relating to export controls or restrictive trade practices and boycotts is also subject to administrative action which may result in suspension, revocation, or denial of export privileges conferred under the Export Administration Act (See Section 388.3 et seq.)

    3. *Civil Penalty.* A civil penalty may be imposed for each violation of the Export Administration Act or any regulation, order, or license issued under the Act either in addition to, or instead of, any other liability or penalty which may be imposed. The civil penalty may not exceed $10,000 for each violation except that the civil penalty for each violation involving national security controls imposed under Section 5 of the Act may not exceed $100,000. . .

Source: Export Administration Regulations, January 25, 1983.

EXHIBIT 7

Copy of Telex to Robert Tron from the US Department of Commerce

```
ATTN:  MR MARCEL CHAMBEZ
       DRESR A 200277F
       232 0249
       USDEPTCOM WSH AUG 19 1982
TO:    ROBERT TRON, PRESIDENT, DRESSER FRANCE CIDEX L 192
       SILIC
       5 RUE D ANTONY
       94563 RUNGIS, FRANCE
```

THE OFFICE OF EXPORT ENFORCEMENT, INTERNATIONAL TRADE ADMIN-
ISTRATION, U.S. DEPARTMENT OF COMMERCE, IS RESPONSIBLE FOR THE
ENFORCEMENT OF THE EXPORT ADMINISTRATION ACT OF 1979, AS
AMENDED, AND ITS IMPLEMENTING REGULATIONS.

IT HAS COME TO THE ATTENTION OF THIS OFFICE THAT YOUR FIRM
MAY BE INTENDING TO EXPORT ITEMS WHICH FALL WITHIN THE GUIDE-
LINES ESTABLISHED UNDER THE REGULATIONS, RESTRICTING THE
EXPORT AND REEXPORT OF OIL AND GAS GOODS AND TECHNICAL DATA.
ACCORDINGLY, WE ARE TAKING THIS OPPORTUNITY TO ADVISE YOU FOR-
MALLY OF THE ADMINISTRATIVE AND OTHER SANCTIONS WHICH ARE
AUTHORIZED BY SECTION 307.1 OF THE REGULATIONS AND THE EXPORT
ADMINISTRATION ACT OF 1979 IF THESE GOODS OR TECHNICAL DATA
ARE EXPORTED WITHOUT ANY REQUISITE APPROVAL OF THE OFFICE OF
EXPORT ADMINISTRATION.

ANY QUESTIONS YOUR FIRM MAY HAVE ABOUT LICENSING REQUIRE-
MENTS OF ANY PENDING OR ANTICIPATED EXPORT TRANSACTION MAY BE
DIRECTED TO THE OFFICE OF EXPORT ADMINISTRATION OR THE UNITED
STATES EMBASSY.

SINCERELY,
THEODORE W. WU
DEPUTY ASSISTANT
SECRETARY FOR EXPORT ENFORCEMENT

Source: Bureau of National Affairs, Case No. 632.

Dresser-France was now in the unenviable position that whatever it did, it would be breaking some law. In addition, without the flow of designs and technology from the Dresser Clark division, the future of Dresser-France would be in serious question. The Clark compressors and follow-on spare parts business were expected to constitute 64% of Dresser-France's revenues next year (see *Exhibit 8* for financial statements of Dresser Industries). The company had recently started manufacturing drilling rigs using manufacturing equipment from the Ideco division of Dresser Industries and this business was estimated to bring 30% of sales revenues next year. The combined value of the business threatened by the loss of the flow of technical data and designs from the US would amount to $150 million.

The management of Dresser Industries, Inc, and Robert Tron had to decide what to do, and in coming to the decision, whose laws they were going to follow. Should the French subsidiary abide by the laws of its operating country, or by the laws of its parent's country?

Robert Tron picked up the file of correspondence that he had accumulated over the last two months. It included a number of letters from customers expressing concern about the ability of Dresser-France to deliver on their contracts without the technical backing from its US parent. Slowly, he walked down the hallway to a meeting with the executive officers of the company. Outside the gates of the Le Havre plant, French workers were protesting the Reagan sanctions and the devastating effect they were having on French jobs. Meanwhile, at the dock, the Soviet vessel *Borodine* sat waiting for its cargo of compressors destined for Riga.

EXHIBIT 8

Selected Financial Statements for Dresser Industries

Financial Summary

Year ended October 31	*1981*	*1980*	*1979*	*1978*
Summary of Operations				
Net sales and revenues	4,615	4,016	3,457	3,054
Cost of sales and service	3,047	2,704	2,329	2,033
Interest expense	53	48	51	52
Earnings before taxes	529	448	407	379
% of sales	12	11	12	12
% of average shareholders' investment	30	29	31	33
Income taxes	212	187	179	175
Net earnings	317	261	228	204
% of sales	7	7	7	7
% of average shareholders' investment	18	17	17	18
Total dividends paid	52	44	40	36
Segment Revenues				
Petroleum operations	2,063	1,604	1,101	886
Energy processing & conversion	901	725	750	709
Refractories & minerals operations	439	461	425	344
Mining & construction equipment	578	575	586	567
Industry specialty products	713	719	658	572
Less intersegment revenues	79	67	62	25
Net sales and service revenues	4,615	4,016	3,457	3,054
Segment Operating Profit				
Petroleum operations	394	248	153	147
Energy processing & conversion	101	101	141	145
Refractories & minerals operations	37	54	64	41
Mining & construction equipment	(10)	39	47	57
Industry speciality products	46	62	60	57
Less corporate expenses, net	39	55	57	68
Earnings before taxes	529	448	407	379

Source: Dresser Annual Reports 1980 and 1981.

chapter 9

The Ethical and Social Responsibility Environment of International Business

Should an MNE have the same high-level safety standards in all its worldwide operations, even if laws and regulations in host countries do not require high standards? Do all employees, regardless of nationality or employment location, have the same rights? Should managerial actions that are illegal or morally unacceptable in one country be allowed in another country in which they are legal or acceptable? Should MNEs maintain the same environmental standards in all countries? Should managers consider the interests of stakeholders such as employees, customers, and general citizens over those of shareholders? Questions such as these confront MNE managers on a regular basis, and they form the substance of MNE social responsibility and ethical behavior for managers in the international business environment.

Both social responsibility and managerial ethics focus on the "oughts" of conducting business in an international environment. While absolute statements of right or wrong (as opposed to what is legal or illegal) are difficult, it is possible to articulate general frameworks of social responsibility and ethics. An understanding of these frameworks not only helps future global managers examine and understand their personal views but also can enable them to understand and work more effectively with others who take different approaches.

MNE SOCIAL RESPONSIBILITY

The topic of MNE social responsibility essentially addresses the extent to which firms have the responsibility to consider the interests of society across national borders. While a variety of more fine-grained approaches to the topic exist, an examination of two fundamental perspectives provides a sufficient foundation for managers to reflect on their positions on the issue, and how they might effectively interact with others who hold differing perspectives.

The Efficiency Perspective

Perhaps no contemporary person presents the efficiency perspective of social responsibility more clearly than does Milton Friedman.[1] Quite simply, according to Friedman, the business of business is business. As Friedman is a contemporary exemplar of the efficiency perspective, Adam Smith is perhaps the earliest advocate of this approach.[2] Smith concluded that the best way to advance the well-being of society is to place resources in the hands of individuals and to allow market forces to cause them to effectively allocate scarce resources in order to satisfy societal demands.

When the manager of the business is also the owner, the self-interests of the manager are best achieved by serving the needs of society. If society demands that a product be made within certain environmental and safety standards, it is in the best interests of the manager to produce the product accordingly. Otherwise, customers are likely to purchase the product from a competitor. Thus, to the extent that a large number of customers for the owner's products place high value on environment, safety, or other concerns often associated with social responsibility, it will be in the owner's self-interest to incorporate those values into his or her products and operations. Complying with the widely shared and deeply held social values of customers will increase the likelihood that they will purchase from firms incorporating their values into operations and products.

Managers as Agents. The corporate form of organization is characterized by the separation of ownership (shareholders) and control (managers). Managers serve as agents of owners who are considered "principals." Friedman argues that managers should "conduct business in accordance with [owners'] desires, which will generally be to make as much money as possible while conforming to the basic rules of society, both those embodied in law and those embodied in ethical custom." Thus, from Friedman's perspective, managers have no obligation to act on behalf of society if it does not maximize the value of the corporation for the shareholders. For example, packaging products in recycled paper should be undertaken only if doing so maximizes shareholder wealth. If undertaking such action satisfies or benefits one particular segment of society but does not maximize the return to shareholders, not only do managers not have any responsibility to carry out such new packaging programs, but according to Friedman, they have a responsibility *not* to undertake such action—precisely because it does not maximize shareholder wealth. Similarly, charitable donations by the corporation are not the responsibility of management. Instead, management should maximize the return to shareholders, who are then free to spend, save, or donate their returns as they see fit.

Figure 9.1 provides a simple illustration of different situations that arise from the intersection of societal and shareholder interests. Simplified, managerial actions can either benefit or hurt one or both groups. According to Friedman, managerial actions that benefit both society and shareholders are nothing more than the fulfillment of agent responsibilities. Consequently, such actions should not be labeled "socially responsible." Managerial actions that hurt both the shareholders and society should not be labeled "socially irresponsible" but should be thought of as simply mistakes. Clearly, then, it is the off-diagonal cells that are of primary issue. According to Friedman, managerial actions that hurt shareholders and benefit society are not *socially responsible* but are *managerially irresponsible,* because as agents, managers have a duty to maximize shareholder value. Managerial actions that benefit shareholders and hurt society, or segments within it, are not *socially irresponsible,* but are *managerially responsible* and constitute prudent actions that managers, as agents, have an obligation to pursue.

[1]Milton Friedman, "The Social Responsibility of Business Is to Increase Its Profits," *New York Magazine,* September 13, 1970, 32-33, 122, 126.

[2]Adam Smith, *An Inquiry into the Nature and Causes of the Wealth of Nations,* eds. R. H. Campbell and A. S. Skinner (Oxford, UK: Clarendon Press, 1976).

Certainly, corporations pursuing maximizing shareholders' wealth do not necessarily fulfill all the various needs of society. Friedman places this responsibility on the government. According to Friedman, it is the responsibility of government to impose taxes and determine expenditures. In a system of democracy, citizens elect government officials to enact and enforce any wealth equalization desires that the society might have. If managers pursue actions that do not benefit shareholders but do benefit other members of society, then they are exercising political power for which they were not authorized. These managers are not voted into office by citizens in order to tax shareholders (which they essentially do by not maximizing shareholder return) and then allocate those revenues to others in the society (for example, charitable donations). Not only do managers *not* have the responsibility to carry out such actions, but they are *not authorized* to do so. To the extent that managers do undertake actions that hurt shareholders and benefit other members of society, they are, according to Friedman, usurping the democratic political process.

Figure 9.1 Efficiency Perspective on Social Responsibility

Shareholders

		Hurt	**Benefit**
Society	**Hurt**	Mistakes Cell 1	Managerially Responsible Cell 2
	Benefit	Cell 3 Managerially Irresponsible	Cell 4 Managerially Responsible

Concerns with the Efficiency Perspective. One of the key premises upon which the efficiency perspective is built is that markets are competitive and that these competitive forces move firms toward fulfilling societal needs as expressed by consumer demand. Firms that do not respond to consumer demands in terms of products, price, delivery, safety, environmental impact, or any other concern to consumers will, through competition, be forced out of business. However, markets are not always competitive and market failures occur. Moreover, corporations can impose externalities (for example, chemical disasters) that may not be correctly priced by market forces. To the extent that market failures occur, societal needs that should be met through normal corporate actions are not met. Under such circumstances, managers may undertake actions that could be placed in Cell 1 (that is, they hurt both society and shareholders). Thus, managers can pursue actions that hurt both groups as a function of market failures or externalities, rather than because of the manager as agent causing problems or making mistakes.

In addition, just as markets can be imperfect, so too can governments. Governments can fail to recognize, fail to act on, and/or fail to successfully implement programs that meet the desires of their citizens. To the extent that governments are imperfect on any one or all three of these fronts, holding to a perspective of strict efficiency raises the possibility that neither government nor business will meet some of society's needs. Because, from the efficiency perspective, the role of business in society cannot be separated from the role of government in society, government failure raises the possibility that the role of business under such circumstance should be redefined.

Social Responsibility Perspective

A report released by the Business Roundtable in 1981 perhaps best exemplifies the social responsibility perspective.[3] This perspective argues that in terms of social responsibility there is a set of roles and constituencies that go beyond those identified in the efficiency perspective. The argument begins with the premise that inasmuch as society grants existence to firms, therefore, it is society as a whole to which firms have responsibilities and obligations, not just shareholders. For instance, the provision of limited liability (which, in turn, makes possible the corporate form as we know it today) whereby shareholders receive downside protection is one example of the society subsidizing the corporate form.[4] Furthermore, if market imperfections and government inabilities leave societal needs unaddressed and unfulfilled, firms have the responsibility to address the legitimate concerns of society which has granted them the right to exist.

Stakeholder Analysis. Beginning with the premise that it is society that grants firms the right to exist, it follows that managers' responsibility is not just to maximize shareholder returns, because shareholders are not the only ones responsible for the firm's existence. Managers must consider the legitimate concerns of other stakeholders in the firm, including the following: customers, employees, financiers, suppliers, communities, society at large, as well as shareholders. According to the Roundtable report, customers have special standing within these stakeholder constituencies because they are the providers of revenue and subsistence for the firm. Shareholders are also given special status, but in the stakeholder approach, shareholders are viewed as providers of risk capital rather than as principals. Consequently, shareholders are entitled to a reasonable return on the capital they put at risk, but they are not entitled to a maximum return because they are not solely responsible for the existence of the firm. To maximize the return to shareholders would take away returns owed to other constituencies. Thus, managers must make decisions and undertake actions that provide a reasonable return to shareholders balanced against the legitimate concerns of customers, employees, financiers, communities, and society at large.

Clearly the efficiency and social responsibility perspectives have low conflict if actions undertaken are in Cell 4 (that is, benefits accrue to *both* shareholders and society). The two perspectives also do not conflict if actions undertaken fall within the domain of Cell 1 (i.e., benefits accrue to *neither* the shareholders nor society). The points of conflict for the two perspectives come into focus in Cells 2 and 3. If actions taken benefit shareholders but hurt the other legitimate concerns of customers, employees, financiers, communities, and society at large, then according to the Roundtable perspective, this is socially irresponsible. Whereas, according to the efficiency perspective, actions classified as falling in Cell 2 would be labeled as managerially responsible. According to the Roundtable report, it is possible for actions that hurt shareholders but significantly benefit other constituencies to be socially responsible. Whereas, from an efficiency perspective such actions would be labeled managerially irresponsible.

Reasons for Considering Stakeholders. The fundamental processes of stakeholder and corporate relations are exchange and influence. For example, customers receive products or service for which they exchange money. Employees exchange work for wages. Because there is a two-way exchange, corporations can influence constituencies but can also be influenced by them. An MNE that emits pollutants into a river may lower its costs and thereby benefit customers, but may hurt surrounding communities that use the water for drinking. Communities can use tax laws, permits, fees, and so on to influence the firm

[3]Business Roundtable, *Statement on Corporate Responsibility,* October, 1981, New York.

[4]K. John, L. Senbet, and A. Sundaram, "Cross-Border Liability of Multinational Enterprises, Border Taxes, and Capital Structure," *Financial Management* (Winter 1991): 54-67.

to stop polluting or to pay for water treatment. The community might also manipulate the local press and influence public opinion, which in turn could influence customer purchases. Because customers, employees, financiers, communities, and society at large can take actions that affect firms, in turn, firms may benefit shareholders by responding to, as well as proactively considering, the needs of other constituencies. Not only can firms avoid or reduce the negative consequences that can result from ignoring the concerns of influential constituencies, but also by responding to and proactively considering their concerns, firms may engender support from customers, employees, financiers, communities, and society at large. This support can lead to greater efficiency in transaction costs and leverage in negotiations with these constituencies.

Concerns with the Social Responsibility Perspective.   One of the key concerns with the social responsibility perspective is that important terms such as "reasonable" returns or "legitimate" concerns are not defined. Given that it is quite possible that reasonable returns to shareholders and legitimate concerns of other constituencies could come into conflict, not knowing exactly what is meant by the key terms reduces managers' ability to find the appropriate balance and undertake actions that are socially responsible. Furthermore, even ignoring the concept of reasonable return to shareholders, it is possible for customers, employees, financiers, communities, and society at large to have conflicting and competing concerns. In such cases, how are managers to determine the most socially responsible action? Customers may be one of the most important constituencies, but how much more important are they than any other (or some combination of the other) constituencies? If customers want plastic bags for groceries but communities in which specific stores and landfills are located want paper bags, how can a manager decide what action is socially responsible?

Summary

It should be clear at this point that there is no universal opinion concerning the social responsibility of MNEs in the international environment. Even if one adopts a strong efficiency perspective, large gray areas remain. For example, Friedman argues that managers should seek to maximize shareholders' returns but must do so within the laws and ethical norms of the society. Which societal norms should be honored? Those of the country of the MNE headquarters? Those of the local subunit? What if the laws and norms of the two societies conflict? Should expatriate managers sent from their home countries abandon their norms and adopt those of the country of assignment?

Moreover, if one adopts a strong stakeholder perspective, equally large gray areas remain. For example, how does one calculate, let alone incorporate, conflicting needs of constituencies across countries? How can needs of the Korean consumer for low price for paper be balanced against the environmental concerns of Indonesian society in which large forests are being cut to produce paper?

In addition to the difficulty of determining the relative weight of different constituencies, MNEs face the challenge of trying to determine the weights of different groups within one category of constituencies across national borders. How are such determinations to be made? For example, MNEs may have employees in a wide variety of countries, and it is quite possible that the concerns of these employees differ by country. Employees in Japan may want the MNE to structure and run itself so as to maximize job security, while employees in England may want the firm to maximize current returns in the form of wages. German consumers may want firms to have high global standards relative to the environment, while Indonesian consumers may have no such concerns. Which standards should be adopted?

At this point, it should be clear that while efficiency and stakeholder perspectives provide different fundamental approaches to questions of MNE social responsibility in the international environment, neither completely answers all the questions and dilemmas that face individual international managers.

ETHICS IN INTERNATIONAL BUSINESS

While corporate social responsibility focuses primarily on business policy issues, ethics focuses on individual managerial behavior. Managerial ethics in the international environment focuses on moral judgments about the "rightness" and "wrongness" of actions. As with social responsibility, there are a variety of schools of thought, but two general approaches provide the foundation for more specific refinements. An understanding of these basic frameworks can help managers examine their personal ethics, as well as help them understand and work more effectively with others who have different ethical perspectives.

Teleological Perspective

Teleological systems of ethical behavior hold that the rightness or wrongness of behavior can be judged by the consequences of those actions. Essentially the good or bad that results from an action for human well-being determines whether the act was right or wrong. Perhaps the most widely known specific teleological system is utilitarianism.

Utilitarianism is often described as "the greatest good for the greatest number." However, this is not an accurate description. More accurately, utilitarianism as an ethical system evaluates actions in terms of the consequences that result "in the greatest good." This is an important distinction, because one alternative could produce the greatest good while a different alternative could produce some good for the greatest number. Within the utilitarian perspective the ethical choice would be to choose the alternative that results in the greatest good compared to the good produced by all other possible choices. The good consequences of an action are determined by the aggregate preferences of those affected by the action. For example, if 2,000 Italian workers strongly prefer to keep their jobs and 100,000 shareholders do not strongly prefer to get an additional 1,000 lira dividend, then, setting aside any legal issues, it would be ethical to pay a 100,000,000 lira bribe to secure a contract that keeps the plant running and the workers employed.

The previous example illustrates one of the criticisms that has been brought against teleological systems of managerial ethics: Individual actions that can be justified from a teleological perspective may in the aggregate produce less good for human well-being. For example, if all workers strongly preferred to keep their jobs and all shareholders had rather weak preferences concerning small additional dividend payments, then all managers could be justified in paying bribes to secure work. However, in the process, bribery rather than cost and quality factors might unduly influence the selection of suppliers and might in turn have a negative effect on product cost, quality, and safety. The aggregate preferences of consumers concerning these aspects of products could easily outweigh the good the bribes bring to workers.

Deontological Perspective

Deontological systems of ethical behavior hold that the rightness or wrongness of behavior can be judged by consequences, but also independent of consequences. From a deontological perspective, one can deduce principles that have moral standing. If the actor's intentions are consistent with the principles of moral standing, then motives—in addition to consequences—must be considered in determining if an action is right or wrong.

Perhaps the best-known deontological system is that developed by Immanuel Kant, who argued for a system based on moral imperatives. His basic imperative was "Act according to the maxim that you would will to be a universal rule." This basic notion has two critical parts. The first addresses universalism: Whatever rule or moral imperative you put forward should apply to all under all situations. The second addresses reversibility: Whatever rule or moral imperative you put forward should be one that you would apply to yourself. The importance of the combination of these two elements can be illustrated with a simple example. You might not object to a rule that required all others to give money to those who ask for it. In fact, if you did a lot of asking, you might benefit considerably from this imperative. However, would you be willing to reverse it—that is, apply it to yourself? This illustrates one of the foundation elements of the Kantian system that "A rational person . . . should treat himself and all others never merely as means but always at the same time as an end."

Beginning with the principles of universalism (would I want everyone to follow a given rule?) and reversibility (would I want that rule applied to me?), Kantian ethics, and other deontological systems deal with the issue of rights. For Kant, the basis of all specific rights stems from freedom and autonomy. For example, the rights of free speech and conscience must be granted, otherwise a person could not be an autonomous entity.

The deontological perspective has a wide variety of implications for managerial behavior and ethics. For example, from a deontological approach, it would be difficult to consider "employment at will" (i.e., the right of an employer to fire an employee for any reason or no reason) as ethical. While one might not object to the application of employment at will to all others, it is unlikely to have reverse appeal. In reverse, one is likely to want to be terminated from employment only for just cause.

However, herein lies one of the common general criticisms of deontological systems of ethical conduct. Most deontological systems fail to explain why a principle or right should be respected or given moral standing. Often, rights are defended in terms of the negative consequences that their violation would produce. Essentially, this is simply using a teleological system to defend a deontological system. Additionally, most deontological systems to not provide sufficient guidance as to which action to pursue when differing rights come into conflict.

Summary

As illustrated in Figure 9.2, both teleological and deontological systems of ethical behavior consider actions and consequences in determining the rightness or wrongness of behavior; however, deontological systems also include the motives of the actor and the moral standing of those motives. Figure 9.3 illustrates the general situations in which the two perspectives would agree and disagree as to whether an action was ethical or not. While Figure 9.3 is a simplification (because from a deontological perspective both motives and consequences must be considered), it does point out that it is in the off-diagonal situations in which the two perspectives generally disagree.

Figure 9.2   Concerns of Teleological and Deontological Ethical Systems

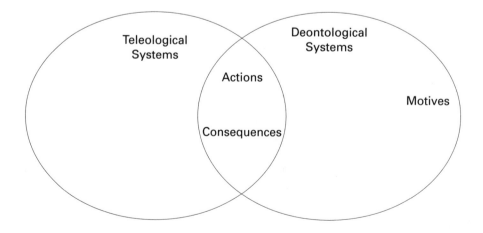

Figure 9.3   Agreement and Disagreement of Teleological and Deontological Systems

Principle with Moral Standing

	No	**Yes**
Good Result **No**	Teleological: *Unethical* Deontological: *Unethical*	Teleological: *Unethical* Deontological: *Ethical*
Yes	Teleological: *Ethical* Deontological: *Unethical*	Teleological: *Ethical* Deontological: *Ethical*

FOREIGN CORRUPT PRACTICES ACT (FCPA)

In the context of international management, few issues of ethical behavior have been given more attention than that of bribes. For US managers, this issue is squarely at the heart of the Foreign Corrupt Practices Act. The FCPA was passed in 1977, primarily in response to the disclosure that Lockheed Corporation had made over $12 million in payments to Japanese business executives and government officials in order to sell commercial aircraft in that country. It was soon discovered that nearly 500 US companies had made similar payments, totaling over $300 million, all around the world.

In the case of Lockheed, its chairman, Carl Kotchian, argued that these payments represented less than 3% of the revenue gained from the sale of aircraft to Japan. Further, these sales had a positive effect on the salaries and job security of Lockheed workers, with positive spillover benefits to their dependents, the communities, and the shareholders. Mr. Kotchian felt that he was in a dilemma, because if he did not make the payments, a competitor would and as a consequence would get the contracts.

The FCPA makes it illegal for US firms and their employees to corrupt the actions of foreign officials, politicians, or candidates for office. The act also makes it illegal for a firm to make payments to any person when there is "reason to know" that the payments made, or any part of them, might be used to corrupt the behavior of officials. Additionally, firms must take steps to provide "reasonable assurance" that transactions are in compliance with the law and to keep detailed records of transactions. The FCPA does not cover payments made to business executives, nor does it cover payments made to low-level employees or clerks. Under the FCPA, facilitating payments (that is, payments made to low-level employees and clerks to perform in a more timely manner the duties they normally would have performed) are not prohibited. Penalties for violation of the FCPA include up to $1 million in fines for the company and $10,000 fines and up to five years' imprisonment for responsible individuals. Clearly, it is not the fines of $1 million—when deals can be worth $50, $100 million, or more—but the jail terms for individuals that provide the real teeth to the act.

Many have argued that the FCPA has put US business at a competitive disadvantage. If US managers cannot pay bribes and others can, then the competitors will, and they will get the business. Data gathered by the US Commerce Department prior to and after the FCPA provide insights concerning the "competitive disadvantage" hypothesis. In 1980, the US Commerce Department surveyed US Foreign Service posts and received responses from 80%, or 51 embassies. Nineteen embassies indicated that the FCPA was an export disincentive; that is, bribes were common in the country, and not being able to pay them would put US businesses at a competitive disadvantage. In addition, Professor John Graham[5] found a high correlation between these countries and reported incidences of bribery in *The Business Periodicals Index* and *Wall Street Journal Index*. In his study, Graham found no support for the competitive disadvantage hypothesis. The change in export growth to the countries for which the FCPA was expected to provide an export disincentive was as good or better than for the other countries both before and after the passage of the act. In fact, his study found no support for the competitive disadvantage hypothesis for industries (aircraft, medical and pharmaceutical products, and machinery) that were thought to be particularly sensitive to the issue of questionable payments.

Global managers can address the issue of FCPA and questionable payments from at least three different perspectives. From a legal perspective, the FCPA provides some guidance concerning questionable payments, but it is not entirely clear as to the difference between bribes and facilitating payments. The jail terms for convicted individuals, however, provide considerable incentive for caution in such situations. From an ethical perspective, it is difficult to justify bribes within a deontological ethical system. A teleological system may provide justification for the payment of bribes, but it hinges on the level of analysis used. If one examines the long-term and broad-based consequences of the payment of bribes, it is difficult to argue that bribes produce more good than does not paying them. Finally, from an economic perspective, there seems to be little justification for paying bribes at an aggregate level (i.e., industry or country level) of analysis. Evidence suggests that the payment of bribes delivers no greater economic returns at the aggregate level than the nonpayment. Thus, it is quite possible that, if individual managers decide to pay bribes, they are paying more for what they desire (for example, a contract, a service, etc.) than they need to pay.

CONCLUSION

The general debates concerning social responsibility or ethics have raged for generations. Consequently, the purpose of this chapter has been not to resolve the debate but rather to help the reader understand the assumptions and rationales of the fundamental perspectives. Hopefully this better enables you to reexamine your own views, so that, when situations arise that require judgments concerning social responsibility or ethics, you will have already thought through what you would do and why, rather than taking actions, under pressure, that you might later regret. Understanding the general framework should also enable you to better appreciate others who have differing perspectives and, thereby, to interact more effectively with them.

[5]John Graham, "Foreign Corrupt Practices: A Manager's Guide," *Columbia Journal of World Business* (Fall 1983): 89-94.

Union Carbide and Bhopal: Diary of a Disaster (A)*

> *"If there ever was a wretchedly undignified, hideously helpless form of mega-death after Hiroshima and Nagasaki, this is it . . . The roses have wilted, leaves have turned black, whole trees have been discoloured, all these new colors are as unnatural and unwholesome, as they are ugly."*
> *Praful Bidwai, Diary from Bhopal[1]*

In 1969 Union Carbide Corporation (UCC), a multinational enterprise in the chemical industry headquartered in Danbury, Connecticut, selected Bhopal as the site for its new pesticide plant in India. Fifteen years later this was to be the location of the worst industrial accident in history (see *Exhibit 1*). Over two thousand people were killed and scores of thousands left permanently injured as a toxic chemical gas enveloped forty square kilometers around the plant. Years after the accident, despite intensive analysis of the events leading to the disaster and numerous court battles, some fundamental questions remain unanswered. Who was at fault—UCC, or its subsidiary Union Carbide of India Limited (UCIL)? Was there negligence on the part of the management of the plant? What was the extent and nature of the cross-border liability of the parent company, UCC, and how, if at all, is it responsible for the actions of its subsidiary UCIL?

December 31, 1969 UK 37, Dow Jones 800**

UCC picks a site outside the northern limits of the city of Bhopal, about two miles from the old city. The railway station, which is an important population center for the area, is located about a mile away and the bus station is about half a mile away.

This case was developed by Nick A. Hall under the supervision of Associate Professor Anant K. Sundaram as a basis for class discussion. © 1993.

[1]"The Poisoned City," Praful Bidwai, *The Times of India,* December 9, 1984.

**The closing stock price of Union Carbide Corporation and the Dow Jones Industrial index on this date (or on the next trading day). Source: *Daily Stock Price Record,* New York Stock Exchange, Standard & Poors Corporation.

EXHIBIT 1

Major Industrial Accidents This Century

Date	Location	Accident	Death Toll
Nov. 19, 1984	Mexico City	Gas tank explosion at the San Juan Ixhuatepec storage facility	452 dead, 4,248 injured
Feb. 25, 1984	Cubatao, Brazil	Gasoline explosion from leaky pipeline	508 dead
1982	Tacoa, Venezuela	Oil explosion and power-station fire	145 dead, 1,000 injured
July 11, 1978	San Carlos de la Rapita, Spain	Overturned propylene truck	215 dead
July 10, 1976	Seveso, Italy	1–22 lbs of poisonous dioxin released after an explosion at the Hoffman La Roche plant	No lives lost, 1,000 forced to flee, children develop a rash called chloracne
June 1, 1974	Humberside, England	Explosion at the Nypro (UK) Ltd. Caprolactum plant	28 dead, 60 acres of buildings destroyed
1956	Minamata, Japan	Mercury discharge into river and bay	250 dead, over 100,000 alleged cases of mercury poisoning
July 28, 1948	Ludwigshafen, Germany	Railway car carrying dimethylether exploded	207 dead, 4,000 injured
Apr. 16, 1947	Texas City, Texas	A boat carrying 1,400 tons of ammonium nitrate explodes setting fire to the Monsanto plant	576 dead, 2,000 injured
Oct. 20, 1944	Cleveland, Ohio	A liquified natural gas tank from the Ohio Gas Co. explodes	131 dead
1942	Tessenderloo, Belgium	Explosion in ammonium nitrate chemicals plant	200 dead, 1,000 injured
Sept. 21, 1921	Oppau, Germany	Workers use dynamite to loosen 4,000 tons of ammonium nitrate	561 dead, houses leveled for 4 miles

Source: "Catalog of Catastrophe," *Time,* December 17, 1984, and *Shrivastava,* pp. 11–13.

Bhopal is an excellent choice of location for UCC. The city is located in the center of India, linked to the major cities Bombay, Calcutta, and Delhi by road, rail, and air. Also, the government of the Madhya Pradesh state, of which Bhopal is the capital, gave the company significant power and water supply subsidies as incentives to establish the plant.

The plant will be designed to produce the pesticides Sevin and Temik. These are UCC trademarks for two carbamate pesticides made from a chemical reaction between a substance called methyl isocyanate (MIC) and alpha-napthol. Under a technology-transfer agreement with the Indian Government, UCC agrees to transfer the capability for the Bhopal plant to make these pesticides from scratch. UCC's initial investment of under $1 million in 1969 would grow to $25 million by 1984.[2]

BHOPAL—A GROWING CITY

Over the next fifteen years the city of Bhopal developed rapidly. Its population grew from 102,000 in 1961, to 385,000 in 1971, and to 670,000 in 1981, a growth rate three times higher than the rest of the country, as people moved towards the potential sources of

[2]"Pesticide Plant Started as a Showpiece but Ran into Troubles," *The New York Times,* February 3, 1985.

employment offered by companies such as UCIL. By 1984, the population exceeded 900,000. There was an acute housing shortage and many shantytowns sprung up as people moved to the area. Although the infrastructure was inadequate to cope with the rapid population growth, it was better than that in many other parts of India.

The government of the region had a great deal of influence over industry in the area. It was the largest employer, producer, and consumer in Bhopal. Over the years, UCIL developed close ties with local government officials. Many officials ended up working in senior positions within the plant and there was a great deal of entertaining of local and visiting officials done to maintain good relations.

December 31, 1974 UK 41$\frac{3}{8}$, Dow Jones 616

UCIL is granted an industrial license to manufacture, rather than just mix and package, up to 5,000 tons per year of Sevin and Temik. A pilot plant is established to manufacture alpha-napthol.

UCC AND UNITED CARBIDE OF INDIA, LIMITED

Union Carbide had operated in India since 1934 when a subsidiary of the Ever-Ready Company in Great Britain became the Ever-Ready Company (India), a subsidiary of Union Carbide Corporation. The company originally made dry cell batteries and, subsequently, flashlights. In 1959, the company became Union Carbide of India, Limited (UCIL) and diversified into chemicals and plastics. By 1984, UCIL was one of fifty international subsidiaries of the Union Carbide Corporation and accounted for about 2% of sales and 3% of profits. The Bhopal plant was one of fourteen UCIL plants in India.

August 25, 1975 UK 61$\frac{3}{8}$, Dow Jones 812

The Bhopal development plan is issued by the commissioner and director of town and country planning for the state, Mr. M. N. Buch. Among other things the plan requires that "... obnoxious industries which are likely to pollute the atmosphere" should be relocated to an industrial zone 15 miles away. Mr. Buch objects specifically to the Bhopal plant but his protests are ignored.

October 31, 1975 UK 58$\frac{4}{8}$, Dow Jones 836

The Government of India's Ministry of Industry grants license number C/11/409/75, giving UCIL the right to manufacture and store MIC at the Bhopal plant. Under the rules of the Indian government, all letters of intent to issue the industrial license require the company to take adequate steps to prevent air, water, and solid pollution as well as adequate industrial safety measures. The rules also state that no new industrial activity should take place within the municipal limits of cities of over 500,000 population.[3]

June 5, 1976 UK 68$\frac{6}{8}$, Dow Jones 958

The local government grants construction permits to Sant Kanwar Ram Nagar, a housing development near the plant. A year later the Madhya Pradesh housing finance corporation grants construction loans to the same area.

---

[3]"Disaster in Bhopal: Where Does Blame Lie?" *The New York Times,* January 31, 1985.

December 30, 1977 UK 41, Dow Jones 831

Indira Gandhi is voted out of office earlier during the year and the new government headed by Janata ("people's") Party passes a law requiring majority Indian ownership of foreign companies located in India. Foreign companies are limited to 40% ownership. As a result, many companies, such as IBM and Coca-Cola, pull out. The Indian government decides to make an exception in the case of UCC, in recognition of the technology the company is bringing to the country and the high potential for exports. UCC is allowed to retain a 50.9% ownership in UCIL, which becomes 49.1% owned by local investors, with its shares quoted on the Bombay Stock Exchange. Of this 49.1%, 25% is owned by the Indian public and 24% is owned by the government. The number of American board members drops from six to four. The remaining seven members are Indian, including the chairman.

After a successful pilot trial, UCIL constructs the world's largest alpha-napthol plant, costing around $2.5 million. The government provides subsidized loans to finance the construction. The manufacture of MIC-based pesticides commences in Bhopal.

December 29, 1978 UK 34, Dow Jones 805

The large size of the new alpha-napthol plant poses problems for UCIL. Other similar plants are only a tenth of the size and the company experiences problems with blocked pipelines and wrong-sized pumps. In November, a fire breaks out in the naptha storage area. The resulting smoke-cloud from the factory damages half a million dollars worth of property in the surrounding towns. The plant is shut down during the year for modifications.[4]

June 29, 1979 UK 37, Dow Jones 842

The UCC Agricultural Product Team proposes to modify the plant to make five other components, one of them being the substance MIC. The Bhopal authorities object to the changes on the grounds that the plant was originally only intended for commercial or light industrial use and that these changes would make the plant more hazardous. But UCIL is an influential company in Madhya Pradesh now, and it manages to use its political connections to secure the necessary approvals for the expansion.

February 29, 1980 UK $40\frac{5}{8}$, Dow Jones 863

The MIC plant is completed and production begins in Bhopal. During the past few years, nearly 100,000 people have settled nearby in the shantytowns of Jayaprakash Nagar and Kali Parade.[5]

THE MANUFACTURE OF PESTICIDE

The chemical process to manufacture Union Carbide's pesticides requires two steps to make the intermediary chemical MIC, and a third step to form the pesticide. The process begins by reacting carbon monoxide and chlorine to form phosgene.[6] Phosgene is then reacted with monomethylamine to form MIC. Finally, MIC and alpha-napthol are reacted

---

[4]"Pesticide Plant Started as a Showpiece but Ran into Troubles," *The New York Times*, February 3, 1985, and *"Behind the Poison Cloud,"* Larry Everest, Banner Press, Chicago, 1985, p. 50.

[5]"It Was Like Breathing Fire. . . " *Newsweek*, December 17, 1984.

[6]Phosgene was used as a chemical weapon during World War I.

to produce Sevin and Temik. MIC is strictly an intermediate input to this process and does not appear in the final pesticide.[7] A 1976 Union Carbide Technical Manual on methyl isocyanate described the substance as "reactive, toxic, volatile and flammable" and "a hazardous material by all means of contact," it is "poisonous by inhalation" and an "oral and contact poison." Exposure to the chemical produces irritation of the skin, nose, and throat. It also produces fluid discharge from the eyes and lungs, and may cause fatal pulmonary edema, a fluid accumulation in the lungs that can drown the victim. US occupational safety rules state that workers should not be exposed to more than 0.02 parts per million of airborne isocyanate during any one eight-hour day.

Because of the hazardous nature of MIC, many plants producing MIC-based pesticides only manufacture it as and when it is needed. For example, DuPont's LaPorte plant in Texas and Mitsubishi Chemical both keep no stock of MIC on-site. Bayer's German MIC plant stores no more than 10 tons (about 2,000 gallons) on-site. UCC, however, was concerned about stoppages in the MIC production process affecting production of Sevin and Temik. Plant production in India could often be held up due to failures in the power supply or water supply and it was difficult to ensure a smooth manufacturing flow. In anticipation of this, the UCC plant design used three 15,000 gallon tanks to hold completed MIC as a way of providing a buffer between the MIC and pesticide manufacture. In the Bhopal plant these tanks were designated E610, E611 and E619. For safety reasons E610 and E611 were only filled to 50-60% of their capacity and E619 was kept empty as dumping storage in the event of failure of one of the other tanks. All three tanks were kept at a temperature of 0-5 °C by a 30-ton refrigeration unit and under pressure to avoid contamination from the air.

The 1976 technical manual had the following warning:

> . . . metals in contact with methyl isocyanate can cause a dangerously rapid reaction. The heat evolved can generate a reaction of explosive violence. When the chemical is not refrigerated its reaction with water rapidly increases to the point of violent boiling. The presence of acids or bases greatly increases the rate of reaction.[8]

December 31, 1981 UK 51$\frac{3}{8}$, Dow Jones 875

During 1981 UCIL finds itself being undersold by small-scale producers who are buying MIC from the plant and using it to make cheaper substitutes to Sevin and Temik. Also, with the country in recession many farmers cut back on their use of expensive pesticides and look for cheaper alternatives, notably new generation pesticides. By the end of 1981, the plant is losing money.

May 28, 1982 UK 45, Dow Jones 819

UCC institutes a safety audit of the plant. They find that many of the plant's basic safety rules are being ignored. Maintenance workers are signing permits they can't read. Some are working in areas without a signed permit at all. The fire-watch attendant was often found to be absent, busy with other tasks.

Among the most serious problems identified are: excessive equipment failure and maintenance problems in the MIC storage area; a lack of sprinkler protection in some areas of the plant; over-filled, over-pressurized, and contaminated MIC storage tanks; inadequate safety valves and inadequate programs for instrument maintenance. Finally, the report comments on the high turnover of plant personnel, especially in operations.

[7]"Methyl Isocyanate: How It Is Made," *Chemical Week*, December 19, 1984.

[8]"The Bhopal Disaster: How It Happened," *The New York Times*, January 28, 1985.

PERSONNEL AT BHOPAL

This last problem, the high staff turnover, got worse as cost-cutting efforts increased. In the early days of the plant, the engineers had been among India's best, selected from the Indian Institutes of Technology. Engineering jobs with UCIL were highly sought after. UCIL paid higher wages than the industry average and provided two years of training before allowing unsupervised duty. Operators were recruited from the ranks of science graduates or people with diplomas in engineering, and given six months of instruction followed by further on-the-job training. As costs were trimmed, however, recruitment standards dropped, training was shortened, and many of the brighter engineers and operators left for better prospects elsewhere. This attrition wasn't limited to the engineering level: Some of the best senior managers and junior executives went elsewhere as career prospects in the Agricultural Products Division declined. In the fifteen-year period before the accident, Bhopal had eight different plant managers, many of them with non-chemical-industry backgrounds.[9]

December 31, 1982 UK $52\frac{7}{8}$, Dow Jones 1047

The last American leaves the plant. Because the Indian government licenses American managers and technicians only for a short time, UCC is expected to train and staff the UCIL plants with Indian employees. By the end of 1982, this process is complete and there are no Americans working at Bhopal. All operational matters are now handled by the UCIL Indian management, although UCC retains the authority to exercise financial and technical control over its subsidiary. The annual budget, for example, still has to be approved by UCC Eastern in Hong Kong, the division of Union Carbide that owns UCIL.

December 30, 1983 UK $62\frac{6}{8}$, Dow Jones 1259

UCC corporate profits for this year are $79M, down from $310M the year before and $890M in 1980 (see Exhibit 2*). Union Carbide, the seventh largest chemical company in the US, now needs to rethink its strategy. For the last few years the company has been divesting itself of petrochemicals, metals, and carbon products and using the cash generated from these sales to move into areas such as specialty products and technology services.*

UCIL faces its own difficulties. Profits are flat (see Exhibit 3*) and pesticide output drops from 2,308 tons in 1982 (Exhibit 4) to 1,647 tons in 1983. Output for 1984 is estimated to be 1000 tons.*

THE PESTICIDE MARKET IN INDIA

The worldwide market for pesticides grew from $8.1 billion in 1972 to $12.8 billion in 1983. India was the tenth largest market in the world. During the periods 1966-67 and 1970-71, market size in India tripled. As a result, a number of manufacturers introduced new pesticide formulations and by the end of that same period, there were over fifty different formulations from two hundred different manufacturers vying for business in India. In the 1960s these companies thrived as the Indian government promoted pesticide use to bolster the nation's agricultural output. However, the agricultural market peaked in 1979 and the combination of an economic recession and a drought in 1982-83 led to falling demand. New and cheaper types of pesticides, known as oganophosphates and synthetic pyrethriods, came onto the market and UCIL found their Sevin and Temik was being undercut from the new generation of products as well as the comparable generation produced more cheaply by their competitors. The cheaper alternatives were welcomed by farmers during the recession and many of those that didn't turn to substitute products stopped using pesticides altogether.

[9]"Bhopal Anatomy of a Crisis," p. 52, *Paul Shrivastava,* Ballinger Publishing Company, Cambridge, MA.

EXHIBIT 2A

Union Carbide Corporation, Balance Sheet 1978–1985

Year ended December 31	1985	1984	1983	1982	1981	1980	1979	1978
Assets								
Cash & equivalents	459	96	118	154	253	243	449	284
Net receivables	1,644	1,512	1,460	1,420	1,513	1,598	1,433	1,259
Inventories	1,422	1,546	1,510	1,740	1,902	1,887	1,774	1,541
Prepaid expenses	145	152	157	187	208	191	155	154
Other current assets	208	0	0	0	0	0	0	0
Total Current Assets	3,878	3,306	3,245	3,501	3,876	3,919	3,811	3,238
Gross plant, property & equipment	10,674	11,131	10,708	10,793	10,047	9,636	8,730	8,050
Accumulated depreciation	4,894	4,748	4,426	4,437	4,253	4,429	4,271	3,931
Net plant, property & equipment	5,780	6,383	6,282	6,356	5,794	5,207	4,459	4,119
Investments at equity	303	288	300	293	307	256	213	178
Other investments	372	306	301	319	298	102	107	113
Intangibles	178	116	69	64	57	NA	NA	NA
Deferred charges	70	119	98	83	91	NA	NA	NA
Other assets	0	0	0	0	0	175	213	218
Total Assets	**10,581**	**10,518**	**10,295**	**10,616**	**10,423**	**9,659**	**8,803**	**7,866**
Liabilities								
Long-term debt due in one year	220	104	91	59	108	51	52	54
Notes payable	847	217	240	328	217	266	156	338
Accounts payable	473	470	492	415	440	432	528	434
Taxes payable	244	82	114	155	173	275	239	220
Accrued expenses	1,271	843	825	788	771	771	766	571
Other current liabilities	0	42	0	9	20	NA	NA	NA
Total Current Liabilities	3,055	1,758	1,762	1,754	1,729	1,795	1,741	1,616
Long-term debt	1,750	2,362	2,387	2,428	2,101	1,859	1,773	1,483
Deferred taxes	333	764	662	765	810	899	953	848
Investment tax credit	0	0	0	0	0	0	0	0
Minority interest	362	355	352	331	329	330	294	281
Other liabilities	1,062	355	203	179	191	NA	NA	NA
Equity								
Preferred stock	0	0	0	0	0	0	0	0
Common stock	751	756	755	739	69	607	557	522
Capital surplus	0	0	0	0	599	NA	NA	NA
Retained earnings	3,434	4,173	4,176	4,421	4,595	4,170	3,486	3,118
Less: Treasury stock	166	5	2	1	0	1	1	1
Common Equity	4,019	4,924	4,929	5,159	5,263	4,776	4,042	3,639
Total Equity	4,019	4,924	4,929	5,159	5,263	4,776	4,042	3,639
Total Liabilities and Equity	**10,581**	**10,518**	**10,295**	**10,616**	**10,423**	**9,659**	**8,803**	**7,866**

Source: Union Carbide Corporation.

Facing a loss of $4 million in 1984, the Bhopal management team instituted a cost-cutting program and in the years preceding the accident the total plant staff was reduced from 880 to 642. The management team faced enormous difficulties in dismissing staff as Indian law forbade dismissing workers except for serious infractions.

EXHIBIT 2B

Union Carbide Corporation, Income Statement 1978-1985

Year ended December 31	1985	1984	1983	1982	1981	1980	1979	1978
Sales	9,003	9,508	9,001	9,061	10,168	9,994	9,177	7,870
Cost of goods sold	6,252	6,702	6,581	6,687	7,431	7,186	6,491	5,580
Gross Profit	2,751	2,806	2,420	2,374	2,737	2,808	2,686	2,290
R&D	275	265	245	240	207	166	161	156
Selling, general and administrative expense	1,289	1,221	1,243	1,249	1,221	1,152	1,053	943
Operating Income Before Depreciation	1,187	1,320	932	885	1,309	1,490	1,472	1,191
Depreciation	596	507	477	426	386	326	470	417
Operating Profit	**591**	**813**	**455**	**459**	**923**	**1,164**	**1,002**	**774**
Interest on long-term and short-term debt	292	300	252	236	171	153	161	159
Nonoperating expense (Income)	173	(77)	(120)	(162)	(164)	(41)	42	(12)
Special items	1,168	0	241	0	0	0	0	0
Pretax Income	(1,042)	590	82	385	916	1,052	799	627
Total income taxes	(441)	227	(10)	58	258	360	205	205
Less: Minority interest	27	39	32	36	47	49	25	33
Plus: UCC share of companies at equity	29	17	19	19	38	30	33	5
Income Before Extraordinary Items & Discontinued Operations	(599)	341	79	310	649	673	556	394
Extraordinary items	18	(18)	0	0	0	217	0	0
Discontinued operations	0	0	0	0	0	0	0	0
Net Income	**(581)**	**323**	**79**	**310**	**649**	**890**	**556**	**394**
Preferred dividends	0	0	0	0	0	0	0	0
Available for Common	**(581)**	**323**	**79**	**310**	**649**	**890**	**556**	**394**
Income per share before extraordinary items	(2.86)	4.84	1.13	4.47	9.56	10.08	8.47	6.09
Extraordinary items	0.08	(0.25)			3.28			
Net income (loss)	(2.78)	4.59	1.13	4.47	9.56	13.36	8.47	6.09
Dividends declared	1.13	3.40	3.40	3.40	3.30	3.10	2.90	2.8
Weighted average number of shares outstanding during the year (000's)	69,693	70,479	70,347	69,306	67,862	66,714	65,674	64,739

Source: Union Carbide Corporation.

EXHIBIT 3A

Union Carbide (India) Limited, Balance Sheet 1978-1982

Year ended December 25	1982	1981	1980	1979	1978
Assets					
Cash & equivalents	52,285	52,173	56,589	53,026	94,482
Net receivables	375,672	244,158	169,015	121,718	78,974
Inventories	327,317	368,606	311,612	292,935	231,945
Other current assets	6,088	9,230	9,277	11,237	12,738
Total Current Assets	761,362	674,167	546,493	478,916	418,139
Net fixed assets	449,546	393,516	405,890	401,422	389,252
Miscellaneous assets	21	21	57	57	57
Intangibles	3,000	3,000	3,000	3,000	3,000
Total Assets	**1,213,929**	**1,070,704**	**955,440**	**883,395**	**810,448**
Liabilities					
Accounts payable	530,641	390,990	341,959	320,942	312,116
Taxes payable	57,739	63,266	60,216	49,000	38,799
Total Current Liabilities	588,380	454,256	402,175	369,942	350,915
Debentures	29,340	54,823	31,315	20,300	
Long-term debt	20,836	34,049	40,420	46,306	33,400
Total Long-term Liabilities	50,176	88,872	71,735	66,606	33,400
Equity					
Common stock	325,830	325,830	325,830	217,220	217,220
Retained earnings & surplus	249,543	201,746	155,703	229,627	208,873
Total Equity	575,373	527,576	481,533	446,847	426,093
Total Liabilities and Equity	**1,213,929**	**1,070,704**	**955,443**	**883,395**	**810,408**

Source: Union Carbide (India) Ltd.

Note: All data shown in Rs. '000 except for per share data. Exchange rate was Rs. 9.00. Inflation rate during this period averaged 11% per year in India, 6.3% per year in the US.

EXHIBIT 3B

Union Carbide (India) Limited, Income Statement 1978-1982

Year ended December 31	1982	1981	1980	1979	1978
Sales	2,075,282	1,854,214	1,615,926	1,449,664	1,111,244
Cost of goods sold	1,720,303	1,518,538	1,307,042	1,190,242	926,958
Gross Profit	354,979	335,676	308,884	259,422	184,286
Operating expenses	136,834	115,550	103,318	83,501	54,592
Operating profit	218,145	220,126	205,566	175,921	129,694
Other income	27,426	26,955	23,528	13,685	10,187
Operating Profit	**245,571**	**247,081**	**229,094**	**189,606**	**139,881**
Interest expense	57,082	30,950	31,468	19,871	15,131
Depreciation expense	41,614	40,913	36,524	32,016	33,340
Pretax Income	146,875	175,218	161,102	137,719	91,410
Provisions for taxes	50,200	80,300	80,000	73,000	41,000
Net Income	**96,675**	**94,918**	**81,102**	**64,719**	**50,410**
Earnings Per Share	2.95	2.91	2.49	2.98	2.32
Dividends Per Share	1.50	1.50	1.40	1.60	1.60

Source: Union Carbide (India) Ltd.

Note: All data shown in Rs. '000 except for per share data. Exchange rate was Rs. 9.00. Inflation rate during this period averaged 11% per year in India, 6.3% per year in the US.

EXHIBIT 4

Production Data for Union Carbide (India) Limited 1978–1982

Products	1982	Production Levels 1981	1980	1979	Capacity 1978	in 1982
Batteries (000s of pieces)	512,200	411,300	458,800	460,300	420,300	767,000
Arc carbons (000s of pieces)	7,000	7,000	6,700	6,200	6,100	9,000
Flashlight cases (000s of pieces)	6,700	7,400	6,900	6,400	5,700	7,500
Industrial carbon electrodes (000s of pieces)	500	500	300	500	200	2,500
Polyethylene (tonnes)	17,290	19,928	19,198	16,324	12,059	20,000
Chemicals (tonnes)	6,331	6,865	7,550	8,511	8,069	13,600
Marine products (tonnes)	649	642	601	648	731	5,500
MIC-based pesticides (tonnes)	2,308	2,704	1,542	1,496	367	5,000
Electrolytic manganese dioxide (tonnes)	3,085	3,000	2,803	2,605	2,700	4,500
Photo-engravers' printing plates (tonnes)	478	431	399	469	506	1,200
Stellite castings, facings and rods (tonnes)	13	16	15	16	18	150

Source: The Stock Exchange Foundation, Bombay, India, The Stock Exchange Official Directory, Vol. XVII/29, July 18, 1983.

February 29, 1984 UK $54\frac{2}{8}$, Dow Jones 1155

James Law, the Chairman of Union Carbide Eastern, proposes to sell the Bhopal plant with the exception of the MIC unit. Five months later the Union Carbide World Agricultural Products Team and UCC management endorses this plan and puts the plant up for sale. Meanwhile, the plant cost-cutting program is continued.

EVENTS PRECEDING THE DISASTER

June 29, 1984 UK 51, Dow Jones 1132

The refrigeration plant used to keep the MIC tanks cool is shut down and drained so that the Freon used in the unit can be used elsewhere in the plant. The Bhopal operating manual specifies that the temperature of the tanks should be no higher than 5 °C (about 41 °F), and a high-temperature alarm was set to go off at 11 °C. Plant officials had the alarms adjusted to sound at 20 °C.

August 31, 1984 UK $54\frac{5}{8}$, Dow Jones 1224

During August, the Bhopal operators experience more trouble with the alpha-napthol plant. The plant is shut down for repair work.

October 7, 1984 UK $49\frac{7}{8}$, Dow Jones 1178

A new batch of MIC production is started and is completed within the next two weeks. At the end of the production cycle, storage tank E610 contains between 11,000 and 13,000 gallons of MIC and tank E611 contains about half that amount. Tank E619 is also in use, it contains 2,400 lbs of MIC (about 215 gallons).[10] Once this production cycle is finished, parts of the plant are shut down for routine maintenance. The flare tower, for example, is shut down to repair a corroded pipe.

[10]"Behind the Poison Cloud," pp. 25-26, *Larry Everest*, Banner Press, Chicago, 1985.

October 21, 1984 UK 49⅝, Dow Jones 1217

The nitrogen pressure in tank E610 drops from a pressure of 18 psi to 4 psi. If the tanks are kept under too little pressure then water and contaminants could enter the tank and mix with the MIC. MIC reacts violently with water to produce heat and gas, and the presence of impurities provides a catalyst for this reaction. Nitrogen, an inert gas, is normally used to maintain pressure in the tanks. Because there is too little pressure in E610, operators start to draw the MIC needed for production from tank E611 instead.

November 7, 1984 UK 50⅚, Dow Jones 1233

The factory is given an environmental clearance certificate in a routine clearance by the state pollution control board, part of the Central Indian Government. The plant is told that only slight modifications are needed to the plant's emission controls.[11]

LOCAL INDUSTRIAL AND ENVIRONMENTAL REGULATION

The activities of the Bhopal factory were controlled by four national laws: the Factories Act of 1984, the Insecticides Act of 1968, the Water Act of 1974, and the Air Act of 1982. The Factories Act was enforced by an inspectorate attached to the department of labor for each state. The inspectorate was responsible for overseeing each factory in its area and prosecuting it for infringements of the Act. Madhya Pradesh state employed a total of 15 factory inspectors to monitor 8,000 plants. The office covering the Bhopal area was based in Indore, 120 miles southwest of Bhopal. The office had two inspectors, both mechanical engineers. They each had a quota of 400 factory visits a year to more than 150 factories. Many of the inspectors were expected to travel to these visits by public transport. The Indore inspectors had made a number of visits to the Bhopal plant and had made some minor recommendations, but mainly they urged the plant to follow the UCC operating procedures more closely.

Industrial pollution control was the responsibility of the Department of Environment. The Department employed around 150 people, of which 25 were scientists, and had an annual budget during 1982 to 1983 of around $650,000 (for a comparison with other countries see *Exhibit 5*). The Department concentrated mainly on the problem of deforestation, India's most severe environmental issue at that time.[12]

November 19, 1984 UK 49⅜, Dow Jones 1185

In a further effort to trim staffing costs, maintenance supervisors are eliminated from the second and third shifts. This is in addition to other cuts that have already trimmed the shift staff from twelve operators to six. There are a number of cases reported of faulty safety devices that have gone unrepaired for several weeks due to staff shortages.

November 30, 1984 UK 48⅞, Dow 1189

Tank E611 also fails to pressurize due to a defective valve. The operators first try to pressurize E610 again but are still not able to do so, suggesting that one of the two pressure equalization valves (the outflow or blow-down valve) is defective. In the end, they repair the faulty valve in E611 and manage to bring the pressure back to normal levels.

[11]"Disaster in Bhopal: Where Does Blame Lie?" *The New York Times,* January 31, 1985.
[12]*Shrivastava.*

EXHIBIT 5

Environmental Management Resources for Selected Countries

Country	Department Established	Total Staff	Scientific Staff	Budget (US $Ms)	1985 GDP (US $Ms)
Bangladesh	1977	52	120	0.13	11,600
China	1984	1,358	413	NA	343,000
India	1980	150	25	0.65	191,600
Israel	1973	36	30	3.50	25,900
Japan	1972	907	374	2.00	1,801,500
Jordan	1980	17	10	0.15	4,900
New Zealand	1972	907	374	1.70	21,700
Philippines	1977	100	50	1.00	42,600
South Africa	1973	280	216	24.00	73,000
Spain	1972	120	20	10.30	382,100
Sweden	1967	640	140	55.00	96,000
USA	1972	12,707	NA	4,000.00	5,007,400

Source: The World Environment Handbook, New York, World Environment Center 1984, the CIA Book of World Facts 1986, and the CIA Handbook of International Economic Statistics 1992.

December 2, 1984 UK 46$\frac{4}{8}$, Dow Jones 1182

Operators during the second shift are instructed to flush out the pipes that lead through the MIC storage tanks to the vent scrubber. When small amounts of water come into contact with MIC the reaction forms a plastic compound called trimer. The flushing was designed to clear out the small accumulations of trimer in the pipes. Flushing begins at 9:30pm.

One of the operators notices that the water is not flowing freely through the pipes but accumulating in the system. The operator stops the water flow and informs the MIC plant supervisor who, nevertheless, tells him to resume the operation. Both the pipes themselves and the overflow lines are so clogged with trimer that the water rises in the system and flows into the relief-valve pipe. At this point the water should have been prevented from going further by a blocking device known as a slip-bind. But no slip-bind had been inserted (this was the responsibility of the maintenance supervisor). Instead the water continues to flow through the system and down hill to the process pipe that leads to tank E610.

The final barrier to the water is the blow-down valve in the nitrogen pressurization system—the system that had been diagnosed as faulty just a few weeks before. Despite this valve being closed 1,100 pounds of water flow into tank E610 and begin to react with the stored MIC. Although this was only a small amount of water compared to the amount of MIC in the tank, a violent reaction starts to take place, perhaps due to the presence of impurities in the tank, and the pressure in the tank begins to build up. At 10:15pm the pressure in the tank reads 2 psi.

At 10:45pm, the third shift arrives and at 11:15, an operator feels a stinging in his eyes and they begin to water—the standard sign at UCIL for detecting a MIC leak. The control room checks the pressure in tank E610, which by now reads 10 psi, but this is still within the normal range of 2 to 25 psi, and the worker is not aware that this is five times the pressure an hour ago. Workers check the tanks to find water leaking from the relief-valve pipe and they inform the control room.

December 3, 1984 UK 46$\frac{4}{8}$, Dow Jones 1182

Just after midnight the control room operator notices that the tank pressure has now risen to 30 psi and is still rising. At 12:30am, it hits the top of the scale. Operators run to the tank which is hissing furiously as gas escapes from the safety valves. The tank pressure and tem-

perature gauges are both at their maximums of 25 °C and 55 psi and, as the operators watch, the concrete around the tanks begins to crack. The control-room operator switches on the vent-gas scrubber and the plant sprinkler system in an effort to neutralize the escaping gases. But the scrubber fails to operate and the water spray does not reach the plume of gas that is, by now, belching from tank E610. The plant superintendent arrives and activates the toxic-gas alarm to sound the warning to the rest of the plant and the residents of Bhopal. But five minutes later it is switched off by the control-room operator in order to make an announcement on the plant's public address system. Afterwards only the internal alarm is switched back on.* A large number of the operators, unfamiliar with any sort of emergency procedure, simply flee in panic. Forty-five tons of methyl isocyanate gas escape into the atmosphere around Bhopal.

The weather is cool and damp and there is no wind. A heavy mist covers the city, preventing the gas from rising into the atmosphere. So, instead of rising or dispersing, the cloud hangs close to the ground, where it has the most devastating effect.[13]

In the shantytowns surrounding the plant the brief sound of the emergency siren meant nothing to the inhabitants anyway. Their first indication of the presence of the toxic cloud is the same burning sensation in the eyes and throat detected by the operator just two hours before, only now it's a thousand times worse. Hundreds of villagers die in their makeshift houses unable to get away in time, drowning as their lungs fill with fluid; hundreds of thousands of others flee, some of them blinded by the gas. At Bhopal station the stationmaster, Harish Dhuney, detects the stinging in his eyes and acts with incredible foresight. He closes the tracks and stops all rail traffic into the city, thus saving many hundreds of further deaths. Harish dies of MIC inhalation while he stands on duty at Bhopal station. By the time the events hit the papers the death toll is estimated to be 410.[14]

December 4, 1984 UK 45$\frac{7}{8}$, Dow Jones 1185

During the next few days the local hospitals treat over 160,000 people and admit 7,400. The number of people reported dead rises to 1,200. There are four hospitals in the Bhopal area with 1,800 beds. Doctors and nurses come from other hospitals but medical supplies and emergency food supplies are in very short supply. Many doctors themselves have been affected by MIC and cannot help with the emergency effort.

December 5, 1984 UK 44$\frac{4}{8}$, Dow Jones 1172**

The estimate of the death toll rises to 2,000. The Union Carbide plant is closed down and locked. The dead are disposed of, some by mass cremation, others by mass burial in graves several bodies deep. So many people are required to provide just basic medical care that there is little time to count the dead. The final estimates of the death toll vary enormously (see Exhibit 6) but it is generally accepted to be somewhere between 2,000 and 5,000. Hundreds of thousands have been injured. Some have been blinded, others have been left with permanent aches in their legs, hands, and chest. Longer term, doctors predict an increased likelihood of sterility, kidney and liver damage, tuberculosis, and even birth defects. Some estimates put the number of permanently disabled at 60,000.

---

*This was supposed to be made impossible in the original plant design, which required the internal and external alarms to sound simultaneously. Frequent minor leaks, however, had led the plant management to have the system altered in 1982 to allow the external alarm to be switched off and avoid the embarrassment from frequent unnecessary panics.

[13]"India's Night of Death," *Time*, December 17, 1984.

[14]"Poisonous Gas Kills 410 in Bhopal," *The Times of India*, December 4, 1984.

**Union Carbide had 70,449,000 shares outstanding during this period.

EXHIBIT 6

Estimates of Bhopal Death Toll

Source of Estimate	Estimate of Deaths and Injuries
Indian government lawsuit filed in New York	1,754 dead, 200,000 injured
Public Relations Review, Spring 1991	More than 3,000 dead, 200,000 injured
Chemical Week, Feb 22, 1989	3,300 dead, 50,000 injured
Delhi Science Forum	5,000 dead, 250,000 injured
Voluntary organizations	3,000 to 10,000 dead, 300,000 injured
Number of shrouds sold	10,000 dead
National Underwriter, Feb 22, 1989	More than 10,000 dead

Source: *Shrivastava* and various news reports.

December 6, 1984 UK $38\frac{6}{8}$, Dow Jones 1170

Union Carbide holds a press conference. Amidst an outcry about the proximity of so many villagers to the plant, a Union Carbide spokesman explains "The plant's location, three or four miles from the center of Bhopal, was selected by Union Carbide India Limited more than 17 years ago. At that time, the area was not densely populated. Land is scarce and the population often gravitates towards areas that contain manufacturing facilities. That's how so many people came to be living near the fences surrounding our property."

A minute of silence is held by all 106,455 UCC employees, and president Alec Flamm orders the American flag to be flown at half mast at all sites for the next seven days.[15]

December 7, 1984 UK $36\frac{7}{8}$, Dow Jones 1163

UCC chairman, Warren Anderson, flies into Bhopal to investigate the scene of the accident. He is arrested at the airport by the local authorities on the orders of Arjun Singh, the chief minister of Madhya Pradesh. Singh charges Anderson with corporate and criminal liability, cruel and wanton negligence, and culpable homicide. Anderson is taken to the UCIL guesthouse overlooking the Narmada river where he is held for six and a half hours. It becomes apparent that Singh has overstepped his authority and the arrest is a source of some embarrassment to the Indian government. The UCC chairman is released at 4pm on a Rs.25,000 bail ($2,100) and escorted to the local airport, where he flies to New Delhi.

December 9, 1984 UK 35 , Dow Jones 1172

A suit for $15 billion in damages is filed by Melvin M. Belli, a San Francisco attorney in a West Virginia Court. Belli specializes in tort cases and his suit is a class action case on behalf of the estates of all those killed in Bhopal.[16]

THE LITIGATION

Belli made it clear that he was filing the suit in America in order to extract higher damages from the courts. Indian courts do not allow punitive damages to be awarded, and American juries are known to be among the most sympathetic in the world. The Belli suit stated that Union Carbide was negligent in its design and construction of the plant, and that it failed to warn the citizens of Bhopal about the dangers of MIC storage, and did this "knowingly,

---

[15]"A Company in Shock," *Newsweek,* December 17, 1984.

[16]"Bhopal: The Endless Aftershocks," *Chemical Week,* December 19, 1984.

willfully and wantonly, or with utter and reckless disregard for the safety of the residents of Bhopal, India." In Belli's mind there was no question of UCC's negligence or that the case should be tried in the US.

Others, however, were not so sure. They believed that since the plant, the location of the accident, the victims, and the witnesses were all in Bhopal then the case should be tried there. Any American court would be likely to throw the case out on the grounds of *forum non conveniens*—that the US was not an appropriate forum to judge the case. Belli would also need to demonstrate that UCC had control or influence over the plant design to create a connection with the US. The final hurdle would be for Belli to get the courts to allow a class action. US courts prefer the victims to come forward and sue separately and Belli had no mandate from the people of Bhopal or the Indian government.

February 27, 1985 UK 38, Dow Jones 1281

In the letter to stockholders in the UCC 1984 annual report, Chairman Warren M. Anderson advises stockholders that he doesn't believe UCC's financial position will be adversely affected by the incident. The company allows for an extraordinary charge of $18 million against earnings ($0.25 per share) to cover "operating, distribution and administrative costs incurred and anticipated relating to the accident."[17]

Over 45 different federal lawsuits against UCC are brought before courts in the US and hundreds more are brought before Indian courts. In addition to suing the parent company, there are 482 personal injury suits brought against UCIL. In all there are 1,200 separate actions brought in India. There is a $1 billion suit filed in Bhopal on behalf of all the victims, and there is a suit filed in the Indian Supreme Court against UCIL, the government of India, and the government of Madhya Pradesh.

March 20, 1985 UK 37, Dow Jones 1265

The Bhopal Gas Leak Disaster (Processing of Claims) Ordinance, 1985 *is passed by the Indian government. The ordinance gives the government the power to represent all the victims in lawsuits and to claim damages on their behalf. The government appoints its own lawyers and from that point on refuses to recognize the private actions that have been brought earlier by lawyers quick to sign up Indian clients.*

UCC issues the results of their investigation into the accident. They say that the plant was being run with standards far below those expected in chemical plants in the US and "not in conformance with established [UCC] procedures." The accident is blamed on the large amount of water entering tank E610 "either inadvertently or deliberately," opening up the possible charge of sabotage.[18]

April 8, 1985 UK 37$\frac{6}{8}$, Dow Jones 1253

The government of India files its action in the United States, which charges UCC with the deaths of 1,700 people and the injury of 200,000. They invoke a new legal claim using a concept they describe as "Multinational Enterprise Liability." The claim says that the multinational enterprise as a whole should be held responsible because:

Key management personnel of multinationals exercise closely held power which is neither restricted by national boundaries nor effectively controlled by international law. The complex corporate structure of the multinational, with networks of subsidiaries and divisions, makes it exceedingly difficult or even impossible to pinpoint responsibility for the damage caused by the enterprise to discrete corporate units or

---

[17]Union Carbide Corporation Annual Report, February 1984.

[18]"Carbide's Report: How Bhopal Happened," *Chemical Week,* March 27, 1985.

individuals. In reality, there is but one entity, the monolithic multinational, which is responsible for the design, development, and dissemination of information and technology worldwide, acting through the forged network of interlocking directors, common operating systems, global distribution and marketing systems, financial and other controls. In this manner, the multinational carries out its global purpose through thousands of daily actions, by a multitude of employees and agents. Persons harmed by the acts of a multinational corporation are not in a position to isolate which unit of the enterprise caused the harm, yet it is evident that the multinational enterprise that caused the harm is liable for such harm. The multinational must necessarily assume this responsibility, for it alone has the resources to discover and guard against hazards and to provide warnings of potential hazards. . .

May 8, 1985 UK $38\frac{5}{8}$, Dow Jones 1250

US District Judge John F. Keenan orders UCC to pay $5 million in interim relief funds. But UCC attaches stringent accounting requirements to the offer to account for each recipient of aid. The $5 million is rejected because the Indian government estimates that the administration alone would absorb half the money. They estimate their expenditure on the disaster to exceed $50 million so far.

June 28, 1985 UK $46\frac{4}{8}$, Dow Jones 1335

A consolidated lawsuit, known as Multi-District Litigation #626, is brought before Judge Keenan that aims to bring together the disparate claims from around 100 different law firms under one hearing. Such is the lack of coordination and agreement between the many different parties. Judge Keenan has to appoint an executive committee to act on behalf of all the plaintiffs. The committee consists of two American lawyers, F. Lee Bailey and Stanley M. Chesley, acting on behalf of the many private actions, plus Michael Cerisi, a Minneapolis lawyer, representing the Indian government. The total value of the claims against UCC is calculated to be $150 billion.

August 11, 1985 UK $48\frac{7}{8}$, Dow Jones 131

There is an accident at Carbide's Institute plant in West Virginia and the chemical aldicarb oxyme leaks from a storage tank injuring 135 people. Soon after the Bhopal accident, the Institute plant—that also manufactures MIC and used a similar process—had been closed down. Union Carbide invested $5 million in additional safety equipment in order to strengthen its message that a Bhopal-style disaster could not happen in the US. On March 28, however, eight people in a nearby shopping mall become sick due to a leak of mesityl oxide and then in August this second leak occurs. Two days later another leak takes place. These accidents, coming so quickly on the heels of Bhopal, result in investigations of the company's operations, which reveal that twenty-eight major MIC leaks occurred from the US-based Institute plant in the five years preceding the Bhopal incident.

August 14, 1985 UK $51\frac{6}{8}$, Dow Jones 1317

GAF Corporation announces 5.6 percent ownership in UCC shares. The corporation is looking for a chemical company to expand its own chemical operations. Despite the fact that UCC is sixteen times larger than GAF, many analysts feel that a takeover attempt seems imminent. Many believe that the uncertainty surrounding the size of the Bhopal damages keeps potential "White Knights" away.[19]

[19]"Who's Afraid of Sam Heyman? Carbide May Be Too Big—and Bitter—a Swallow for GAF," *Barrons*, August 26, 1985, pp. 11–12.

November 26, 1985 UK 60$\frac{1}{8}$, Dow Jones 1477

Judge Keenan orders the $5 million in interim relief money to go to the Indian Red Cross for distribution. Both UCC and the Indian government agree to these conditions.

December 6, 1985 UK 63, Dow Jones 1477

The Citizens Commission on Bhopal and the National Council of Churches file an Amicus Curiae *brief arguing that the case should be tried in the US. The case is set to go before Judge Keenan on January 3, 1986.*

THE FUTURE FOR BHOPAL AND UNION CARBIDE

A year later, the victims of the disaster were still awaiting compensation, many of them no longer supported by the wages that they used to enjoy from the UCIL plant. For these people and for Union Carbide many questions are left unanswered: Where should the case be tried—in the US courts or in India where the damages would be adequate but far lower? Who was at fault—the parent company, UCC, or the Indian managers responsible for the plant's operations? Were those responsible guilty of negligence? What was the responsibility of the Indian government to control the activities of foreign companies in their country? Not only are these questions important to the victims of the disaster and their families, but they also raise far more general questions about the conduct of multinational corporations and their subsidiaries in developing countries.

case 12

Nicolo Pignatelli and Gulf Italia (A)*

Gulf Oil Company had a presence in Italy since 1950 when it received a concession to conduct exploratory operations in Sicily. The Italian oil market was the fourth largest in Europe and was dominated by major players such as ENI-AGIP,[1] Exxon, Shell, and British Petroleum. After a great deal of exploratory and geophysical work, Gulf discovered crude in the Ragusa field in Sicily in 1953 (see *Exhibit 1*). The volume in the ground (120 million barrels) was considered major. The discovery put Gulf Italia on the map overnight and threw open choices that Gulf had not seriously considered before. In addition to this supply, Gulf had 50% ownership of the supply of the Kuwaiti Oil Company, which amounted to one million barrels a day for disposal in Europe and the Far East.

Nicolo Pignatelli, as Gulf's country manager in Italy, was in a position to formulate and implement the plan that would allow Gulf to compete with the big players in the Italian market.

Initially, Pignatelli planned expansion of Gulf's downstream operations in refining and marketing. Pignatelli had a good relationship with the chairman of the board of Fiat, and, in 1961, made a deal to purchase Fiat's oil-related operations for $13 million. This acquisition (called the "Cherry Deal" by Pignatelli), gave Gulf a network of service stations in northern and central Italy as well as in Rome, and included terminals in Rome, Venice, and Livorno.

Recognizing that competing on a cost basis with the market leaders required greater scale, Pignatelli looked to make further acquisitions. Marathon Oil, which, in restructuring, had decided to discontinue operations in Italy, had a network of over 700 service stations in Central and South Italy and on the island of Sicily. Pignatelli knew the Managing

*This case, along with the companion case "Nicolo Pignatelli and Gulf Italia (B)," was prepared by Michelle E. Sparrow with Professors Anant K. Sundaram and J. Stewart Black, as a basis for class discussion rather than to illustrate either effective or ineffective handling of an administrative situation. We are grateful to Mr. Pignatelli for cooperating in case development. © 1991. Revised 1993.

[1]ENI is the acronym for Ente Nationale Idrocarburi, the Italian state oil company. AGIP is ENI's exploration and production subsidiary.

EXHIBIT 1
Map of Italy

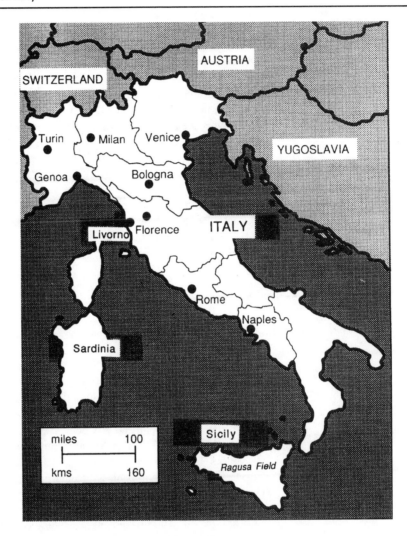

Director well, and made a deal to acquire Marathon's Italian subsidiary. This transaction spread Gulf's distribution network evenly over the Italian territory, increased their number of terminals, and increased Gulf's market share in Italy from 2 to 4 percent.

The other companies in the industry were already well established. Of these, ENI-AGIP had 25% market share; Exxon ("Esso Italiana"), 18%; Shell, 15%; BP, 10%; Total, 8%; and Petrofina, 2%. Although Pignatelli did not expect these competitors to allow him to grow unopposed, he knew that some of them had needs that he could probably leverage for his own purposes. For example, Petrofina needed gasoline and asphalt produced in northern Italy. Mobil was anxious for refining capacity near Milan. ENI-AGIP opposed Gulf's growing presence in the Italian market, but was in need of a partner to share the costs of their CEL[2] pipeline which was only 50% utilized.

THE DECISION TO BUILD

With crude oil coming from the Ragusa field as well as from Kuwait, Gulf had an abundance of supply. The company now faced the decision of whether to build its own refinery

---

[2]CEL is the acronym for the Central European Lines, a rail line owned by ENI-SNAM, ENI's transportation subsidiary.

or contract for the use of existing refining facilities of other oil companies. Contracting would involve paying high processing fees, and could leave Gulf vulnerable to the whims of the host company. On the other hand, building a new refinery would clearly be a daunting regulatory and strategic task, since the Italian refining industry was highly regulated and government permissions would be required along every step of the way.

Even if the regulatory maze in Italy could be negotiated, several other factors had to be considered before the decision could be made: Where should the refinery be located in order to gain leverage for exchanging products? What was the optimal capacity? Could the refinery be built in a timely fashion? How would the crude be transported to the refinery?

In an aggressive first step, Gulf's corporate office, with Gulf Italia, decided to build their own refinery in order to achieve cost advantages. This decision elevated Gulf's stakes in Italy significantly, and represented their aim to go after the industry leaders. As Pignatelli later said,

> Competing in the Italian market was like going to war, and I had to prepare as such. Like any war, this meant I had to learn the weaknesses of my opponents, assess the probability of securing the right allies, and determine a point of attack. It was a confrontation of will, not one of law.

LOCATING THE REFINERY

Pignatelli consulted a business associate, the chief executive of Petrofina, who suggested that Gulf build the refinery in Milan and add an asphalt plant to it. Petrofina offered to purchase asphalt in exchange for supplying Gulf with gasoline in the Roman market where they had a refinery. By placing the refinery close to the Milan industrial region, Gulf would be able to distribute its products throughout Italy at a much lower cost. Such a location would give them control of the Milan market, forcing other companies to come to Gulf in the hope of exchanging refining capacity held elsewhere for capacity in Milan. On the other hand, locating the refinery in Milan would mean Gulf was going straight for the heart of their competitors. Pignatelli knew that this choice of location would ignite strong opposition from everyone: the oil companies, the environmentalists, and the press.

The "war" started with a frontal attack with Pignatelli deciding to go for the Milan location. A deficit of oil supply for industrial production in Milan supported the choice. From this region, Gulf would be able to distribute via their national network of filling stations, storage facilities and distribution centers. Pignatelli noted,

> Most of the production in Italy is in the north, in the Po Valley. That is where the greatest industrial output and energy demand are. If you could position your refinery there, you would be on top of the world.

Environmentalists strongly opposed Gulf's proposal to build in Milan, and campaigned aggressively against the company. The Italian press was generally suspicious of American multinationals, and hostile reports and editorials appeared daily, denouncing Gulf and opposing the construction plans on ecological grounds.

A friend of Pignatelli's from youth was convinced her cancer had been caused by emissions from nearby refineries. As the owner of a newspaper, she was able to voice her opposition to the refinery easily and rallied the support of local communities. However, Pignatelli was able to negotiate with the environmentalist groups by promising to build "the best refinery in Italy." This meant that the refinery's water treatment plant would be of the highest quality, and Pignatelli attested to this with the claim that the effluent water would be good enough to drink; he promised to prove it by drinking the water himself (which he eventually did).

Further plans included a 450-foot smokestack, twice as tall and also wider than others in Italy, which could push heat through the inversion area so that fumes would not be trapped close to the earth's surface. Also, an innovative combustion chamber was designed to contain the ground flare. Ground flares, used to burn waste gas, are typically very noisy and emit dangerous fumes. The combustion chamber would save heat, but would not emit light, sound, or smoke. Finally, Pignatelli planned a landscaped layout which was compatible with the surrounding area. In fact, he asked the environmentalist group to choose the landscape architect he contracted for the project.

Though these expenditures would add $1.2 million to the $81 million budget for the refinery, Pignatelli felt he would set a standard for future refineries and compel other refiners to upgrade at an even higher cost.

OVERCOMING REGULATORY HURDLES

Securing the necessary permits to build the refinery in Milan turned out to be a formidable task. Pignatelli faced barriers to the project at the municipal, regional, provincial, and national levels. Further, his overall strategy had two interdependent parts: If he didn't have a pipeline to transport oil to the refinery, he couldn't build the refinery. He had two options for transporting oil. He could build a new pipeline, which was costly, or he could contract to share an existing line. Amoco operated a small pipeline in Italy which would require construction of a long connecting line. ENI-AGIP owned the CEL pipeline which ran past Milan up to Switzerland and Germany. Based on Pignatelli's ongoing relationship with the state-owned company and its subsidiaries, the probability of success in sharing a pipeline with ENI-AGIP was higher than with Amoco.

In January, 1967, Gulf received a ministerial decree granting a license to install the refinery in Zelo Buon Persico, near Milan. Concurrently, negotiations were initiated for throughput rights to the CEL pipeline with ENI-AGIP.

GAINING THROUGHPUT RIGHTS TO THE PIPELINE

By 1965, Gulf had a surplus of Kuwaiti oil, and their Ragusa supply was no longer vital to the marketing organization. At this point, Pignatelli estimated that the volume still in the ground at Ragusa was 25-30 million barrels. With the help of some imaginative thinking from Mr. Clancy, a senior executive of Gulf in the US, Pignatelli decided to give the Ragusa oil field as a "gift" to the state, in exchange for the state's commitment to buy 10 million tons (70-100 million barrels) of Kuwaiti oil from Gulf Italia. The idea of giving away the oil field was actually in Gulf's interests since ENI had agreed to buy three times more than the volume they could extract from Ragusa. Pignatelli felt that Gulf could make a killing on the deal. In addition to being profitable, the transaction would also create goodwill and set the stage for the upcoming pipeline negotiation.

> I didn't have an ally in AGIP, but they had a weak spot," Pignatelli said, "a half-empty pipeline. It took some time, but I negotiated at length and persuaded them to make a deal.

In February, 1968, Pignatelli secured throughput rights from ENI-AGIP to use the CEL pipeline for twenty years. He also reached agreement with SNAM SpA, the transportation subsidiary of ENI, to construct a connecting line between the CEL pipeline and the proposed Gulf refinery. For the use of the pipeline, ENI wanted an "entrance fee." Gulf, at Pignatelli's request, made a lump sum prepayment of $1,200,000 in US dollars to a Swiss bank account of Hydro-Carbons International Holding Company of Eschen, Liechtenstein, a subsidiary of ENI, in March, 1968. It was customary practice for many Italian businesses to maintain affiliates and banking relationships in Switzerland and to request payments for commercial transactions there. This practice provided efficient transactions processing, as well as the benefit of using a stable currency, although the motive of tax and regulatory evasion also existed.

THE PLUM PROJECT

After securing the initial permit to construct the refinery, Gulf purchased the site, only to run into additional opposition from the public and the press. Newspapers and local citizens called Gulf's proposed refinery "the poison factory." At the same time, the planning law was being changed and, unknown to Gulf, final authority for planning was transferred to a new Ministry. A change in zoning requirements further complicated matters. Construction in the intended area was ultimately blocked and five location changes followed. Each time, Gulf had to purchase options to acquire the land for the refinery, which ultimately cost the company an additional $16 million over the original budget. Finally, in August, 1969, Gulf was granted permission by decree to build in Bertonico, also near Milan.

Gulf built the refinery with an allowed processing capacity of 5.8 million tons annually, and the facility went on line in June, 1972. It had been over five years since the original license for the refinery had been issued. On the opening day, Pignatelli, accompanied by Dr. M.R.J. Wyllie, head of Gulf's Eastern Hemisphere organization, and numerous public officials, drank effluent water from the water treatment facility ceremoniously, illustrating its freedom from pollution.

However, Pignatelli was soon faced with another hurdle. Though the construction permit had been issued for a refinery with the capacity of 5.8 millions tons, the operating permit, based on Gulf's current market share, limited their production to 3.9 million tons annually. Pignatelli knew that production had to be near capacity in order to achieve cost advantages. He was informed by the government that he not only had to obtain a new decree to allow operation at full capacity, but he also had to obtain authorization to implement the decree.

Again frustrated, Pignatelli sought to find an ally. In November, 1972, he began negotiations with Mobil Oil regarding joint operation of the facility. Mobil operated a refinery in Naples and was interested in purchasing refining capacity to supply their northern market. Pignatelli offered to give Mobil an option to purchase 25%, then 35%, and finally 50% of capacity, which would make the two companies fifty-fifty partners. If Pignatelli could get a permit for operating the refinery at full capacity, he knew the arrangement would be extremely profitable for Gulf. "We both would have product with much lower cost," he commented. He called the venture with Mobil the "Plum Project," signifying the desirability of the arrangement.

ANDERGIP, S.A.

In February, 1973, Pignatelli appeared in Pittsburgh before Gulf's Executive Council and made a presentation of the Plum Project. The Executive Council tentatively approved "proceeding with price discussion" and "arrangements to obtain a government permit to increase the licensed throughput of the Milan refinery to 120,000 barrels per day." Later Pignatelli added, "Things were going well, and they just kept saying, 'Nicky, what you're doing is great!'"

Mobil wanted to close the deal prior to the end of 1973. Pignatelli agreed, knowing that "if we don't do it in seven months, we'll drown." He set the goal of securing authorization for operating the refinery at full capacity no later than September, 1973. Given the extreme opposition he had faced in gaining approval for the refinery construction,

Pignatelli felt he needed assistance in expediting the bureaucratic process. Pignatelli hired Andergip, S.A., the consulting company of a former business associate, Mr. Giuseppe Del Bo.

After their negotiations, Pignatelli received a letter from Andergip, S.A., which set forth the basis on which they would assist Gulf in obtaining the authorization. The letter stated (translation):

> In relation to the results of the final tests of the Bertonico Refinery, which have ascertained that it has an installed capacity of 5.8 million tons of crude per year, I wish to confirm to you on behalf of our company that we are prepared to put at the disposal of your company our organization in Italy for public relations consulting at a regional, provincial and local level as well as our necessary technical service in the sector of urban planning and ecology, relative to the application which Gulf Italia will submit in order to obtain the official acknowledgment of the aforementioned processing capacity of the Bertonico Refinery. . . . For our assistance you will credit us an amount of US $870,000 payable at the Bank Institute of the Swiss Confederation, after the aforementioned processing capacity will become operational.

As a caveat to the negotiated price of US $870,000 (equivalent to Italian lire 530,000,000), an oral agreement with Andergip specified that all expenditures would be Andergip's responsibility if Gulf did not receive the necessary permit for expansion of the refinery by September 30th. Fifty percent of the money was earmarked to cover "expenses," and fifty percent was deemed the consultant's "success fee."

DEL BO

In addition to heading up Andergip, Del Bo was the president of Carbonafta, a large petroleum jobber in Italy, and also held the position of Chairman of the National Association of Jobbers. He was considered a man of substantial influence within the industry.

While all applications and formal contacts with governmental agencies were handled by Gulf, a great deal of promotional work was required to support the application. Del Bo's efforts on behalf of Gulf involved transactions with numerous government agencies: the Ministry of Finance; the Ministry for Industry and Commerce; an Interministerial Commission for the testing of Plant and Equipment (composed of representatives of three ministries); an Interministerial Commission for petroleum affairs (composed of representatives of 12 ministries); two bureaus in Milan; the regional government of Lombardy and three of its departments; and the communes of Bertonico, Terranova de' Passerini, and Turano. In addition to obtaining a decree which authorized full capacity operation, implementation would also require additional storage tanks on site, which necessitated further approvals. The new tanks had to be approved by four Ministeries, the regional government of Lombardy and two of its departments, the three communes referred to above, and a Consortium for the Navigation Canal Milano-Cremona-Po. The task of getting all these bodies to acquiesce within a span of months was nothing short of formidable.

Pignatelli was delighted when, on July 4, 1973, the Ministry for Industry and Commerce issued a decree authorizing the processing of 5.8 million tons per year at the Bertonico refinery.

On July 16, 1973, an interim authority for expenditure ("AFE") in the sum of $868,653 was prepared by Wyllie and J. J. Earnest, President and Comptroller, respectively, of Gulf-Eastern Hemisphere, covering the obligation to Andergip. The interim AFE stated:

> Preliminary Expenditures; Note: This AFE will be incorporated into the final AFE for total product cost of about $28 million when finally issued.

The interim AFE was delivered to Z.Q. Johnson, the Vice President of Gulf Oil Corporation, in Pittsburgh for countersignature. He returned it with a handwritten note stating: "I discussed with J. Lee and then advised M. Wyllie that he was to handle some other way." An undated memorandum for file by the comptroller in London stated:

> While Mr. Johnson did not sign AFE there were discussions between Messrs. Wyllie and Johnson on this subject and the Executives were aware that a "special" payment had to be made in order to obtain the permit. . . . In any event . . . the Corporate Director Internal Auditing was in London at the time the payment was being arranged and he was made fully aware of the transaction.

On July 26, 1973, Gulf made a payment of $868,653 to Del Bo. First, the Morgan Guaranty Trust Company of London was instructed to transfer $868,653 to the Swiss Credit Bank of Chiasso for retention pending instruction from Mr. L. Giartosio, Pignatelli's chief assistant. Giartosio, after being identified by his passport, had the funds transferred to Del Bo at the same bank in exchange for an appropriate receipt.

Del Bo issued a receipt which stated (translation):

> This is to certify that the remittance of US $868,853 equivalent to Italian lire 530,000,000 attested by the attached bank receipt . . . represents the agreed full and final settlement of all sums due in reimbursement of any expenses incurred for carrying out preliminary technical, urbanistic and ecological studies and surveys, as well as in payment of consultancy fees for public relations and administrative services rendered at national, regional and provincial levels in preparation of the application and development of information and data in support of the obtainment of the authorization, by means of debottlenecking, to process up to 5.8 million tons per year of crude oil in Gulf's Milan Refinery.

The receipt was forwarded to London by Giartosio with a buckslip stating *"Not for circulation in Italy."* At this time, Gulf Eastern Hemisphere accounted for the payment by charging it to a suspense account. Six months later, the charge was transferred to a fixed asset account for the Milan Refinery. In May, 1974, the charge was transferred back to the Gulf-Eastern Hemisphere suspense account. In July, 1974, the charge was transferred to Gulf Europe, a Liechtenstein corporation, where it was expensed. Mobil ultimately paid Gulf 36.5% ($317,134) of this payment when they purchased an interest in the Milan refinery.

Pignatelli had accomplished his goal within five months. Working with Andergip, he had succeeded in obtaining the favorable opinions of over 20 different government bodies to operate the Milan refinery at full capacity. This meant that he would be able to close the deal with Mobil, the Plum Project, before the end of the year. Gulf Italia was growing rapidly, and Pignatelli's career was rising with it.

But soon enough, Del Bo's success in providing a swift solution led to suspicions regarding the disbursement of the funds which he was paid. Within months, investigations regarding Gulf's payment to Del Bo for consulting services were initiated by the US parent company. Another investigation, by a Special Parliamentary Commission in Italy, followed in 1974. The Commission's task was to inquire into charges of improper corporate contributions to political parties and possibly to ministers of Parliament.

THE US ENVIRONMENT

In the aftermath of Watergate, a number of political contributions by large corporations came to light in the US. Extensive investigations also uncovered evidence of "questionable payments" made abroad in several companies. In this environment, boards of over 400 corporations conducted internal investigations, and filed voluntary reports with the SEC. One such report, prepared for the Board of Directors of Gulf Oil Corporation, received widespread publicity for its revelation of numerous illegal payments.

The McCloy Report, as it was later called, was a 364-page document detailing the investigation of Civil Action No. 75-0324, Securities and Exchange Commission, *Plaintiff* v. Gulf Oil Corporation and Claude C. Wild, Jr., *Defendants*. The report had been demanded by the SEC as part of a consent judgment settling the suit in March, 1975, and was written by a Special Review Committee chaired by John J. McCloy. McCloy, a distinguished lawyer from the New York law firm Milbank, Tweed, Hadley & McCloy, was aided by two outside directors in conducting the nine-month investigation.

Gulf had initiated an internal investigation after Bob R. Dorsey, Chief Executive Officer from 1972 to 1976, disclosed to the rest of the Board in 1973 that Gulf's Washington lobbyist, Claude Wild, Jr., had given $100,000 in corporate cash to Richard Nixon's 1972 campaign. This incident led to a series of meetings with the Watergate Special Prosecution, and subsequently, Gulf and Wild pleaded guilty to violations of the Federal Corrupt Practices Act. Later, Wild was "released from any and all claims" the corporation might have against him in exchange for $25,000 related to a specific contribution. However, Dorsey's revelation opened up a Pandora's box. Investigators later estimated the total amount of payments was closer to $4.8 million, primarily used by Wild to entertain politicians and make contributions. On March 13, 1975, the same day that the SEC issued an injunction that ordered the McCloy investigation, Gulf admitted publicly that they had spent over $10 million of corporate funds on political activities.[3]

When the McCloy Committee began their investigation, Gulf Oil and its subsidiaries were suspected of having made political payments in the US and abroad, both legal and illegal, summing over $14 million. This amount included $4 million paid to a political party in Korea, as well as possible payments to over 20 US senators and congressmen who were implicated.

The Committee made a point of scrutinizing all transactions which they suspected of having real political implications, as well as transactions on which they had been specifically prompted by Gulf management. Consequently, the $2 million paid out in Italy in acquiring the SNAM pipeline throughput rights and expanding the Milan refinery was brought to their attention. Internally and externally, there was considerable disagreement over whether or not the payments constituted political contributions. Gulf's chief financial officer, for one, argued that the sum should be added to the total. After an initial review, the McCloy Committee felt there was sufficient prima facie evidence to warrant a thorough investigation, and proceeded. Throughout the investigation, Pignatelli cooperated by providing detailed information and documentation as requested.

THE ITALIAN ENVIRONMENT

It was the practice in Italy for political parties to solicit financial support from business and industry, and in the case of the oil industry, such solicitations were usually directed to trade organization leaders or ENI-AGIP. Further, giving "omaggi" or gifts to induce local bureaucrats to carry out or to expedite their normal duties or to reward them for extra services was also common. This practice was characterized as tipping rather than bribery and was not considered unlawful. For example, Gulf Italia distributed gas coupons to government functionaries and others as "omaggi."

All of Gulf's contributions to political parties were made following the initiative of ENI-AGIP, Esso, and occasionally Shell. Dr. Vincenzo Cazzaniga, the President of Esso,

---

[3]*Fortune,* "The Directors Woke Up Too Late at Gulf," June 1976, p. 121.

was also the President of Unione Petrolifera Italia (UPI)[4] and received many of these requests. Cazzaniga had been the President of Esso for over 20 years and dominated the affairs of UPI. Pignatelli was Gulf's representative to the UPI and was a member of its Board of Directors. On occasion, Cazzaniga and ENI-AGIP made commitments or contributions to political parties without informing the other companies in advance. They would then determine the amount to be contributed to the political parties by each of the 15 or so members of the organization. Each member company was generally advised of its share, and was given some latitude in selecting the political parties it favored. The payments were usually made after receipt of an invoice from the publications controlled by political parties for "newspaper journalistic services" or words to that effect, and were paid out of corporate funds. Prior to 1974, the corporate political contributions were generally lawful in Italy provided the corporation's stockholders were informed.

Some payments came out of Gulf Italia's "Fondo Nero" or Black Fund. This account was opened in 1962 under the authorization of William Whiteford, then the CEO and Chairman of the Board of Gulf. The purpose of the account was to preserve the confidentiality of recipients of funds dispersed by Gulf, and of Gulf itself, as well as to serve as a vehicle for discretely receiving off-the-books rebates and commissions. Such transactions were apparently quite common.

"WE HAD TO PLAY BIG"

As a result of the investigations, a myriad of civil cases and proceedings were brought by the Italian Parliament against Pignatelli (as well as the Presidents and Chief Executives of ENI-AGIP and other multinational oil companies). The investigations continued for several years. Pignatelli always maintained that he had acted in accordance with the law and argued that his actions were justified by his strategy and the attained results. "I had a strategy, and the strategy made sense; the logic was perfect. If you accept the strategy, you have to accept the way I implemented the strategy. We had to play big, and we were there to win."

---

[4]UPI was a trade association of the private sector of the Italian oil industry of which Gulf was a member.

chapter 10

Country Risk Analysis

Country analysis examines the economic strategy of the nation state. It takes a holistic approach to understanding how a country, and particularly its government, has behaved, is behaving, and may behave in the future. While the government is responsible for establishing the framework—the institutions and rules of behavior—through which the country develops its internal economic, political, and social structure and relates to its outside environment, country analysts study how, and how well, a particular government does its job.

Effective country analysis requires the synthesis of concepts and analytical methods of economics, political science, and sociology. Ideally, country analysis builds upon and integrates those disciplines in the context of today and tomorrow in much the same way that the historian integrates them in studying the past. In a business context, after a general country analysis has been conducted, the analysis must then be related to the industry and particular circumstances of a specific organization. Only when this final step is taken can a country analysis achieve its full value to a firm.

THE USES OF COUNTRY ANALYSIS

A variety of individuals utilize country analyses. Country analysis has long been practiced among government officials as a way to interpret or anticipate the behavior of other governments. Certain industry analysts also have substantial experience in country analysis. For example, petroleum firms have used country analysis because their basic input—crude oil—is generally a natural resource controlled by governments. Since the 1970s, international bankers have increasingly used country analysis as a means of identifying and evaluating the creditworthiness of prospective government borrowers and as a means of anticipating changes in interest rates.

Since World War II, country analysis has spread beyond these core areas and has become an indispensable tool for senior managers in all multinational enterprises. As a result of the General Agreement on Tariffs and Trade (GATT) and the establishment of an international monetary system supervised by the International Monetary Fund (IMF), we have made dramatic progress towards an open world market. Lower relative shipping costs and greater licensing of technology to foreign countries have also contributed to a more global market. As a result, today's multinationals are asking "Where in the world should we build our next plant, raise our next loan, or launch our next product?" All of these decisions represent medium- to long-term commitments and mandate judgments about the future prospects of each country, before a site is selected. Inevitably, senior managers must use country analysis to evaluate and compare countries before they make their decisions; otherwise they risk both passing up opportunities from which they could have profited as well as entering and staying in countries in which they might lose financially.

Economic policy makers in government need a similar perspective. As each country tries to attract investment to create jobs, it becomes increasingly important to appear desirable. Since 1970, this issue has become particularly important for the developed and industrialized countries whose total employment in the manufacturing sector has been dwindling. Multinationals are opting to set up factories in lower-wage sites such as Hong Kong, Korea, Taiwan, Malaysia, and Singapore. In order to promote investment and jobs, especially in sectors exposed to competition from lower-wage sites, the economic policy makers of a country must study domestic variables such as labor costs, tax rates, economic growth, and inflation rates. In doing so, they must use country analysis to gauge how attractive their country will look to potential investors.

No doubt, country analysis is less precise than econometric modeling, but it has an analytical framework of its own. The framework uses a relatively simplified view of an economy in order to relate economic, social, and political phenomena to each other, as well as to evaluate trends and possible aberrations within a particular economy. What follows is a general framework that analysts can use to evaluate the upside and downside risks of operating in a specific country or set of countries.

A FRAMEWORK OF ANALYSIS

Country analysis assumes that a country is a purposeful entity managed by a government. The framework of analysis requires that we sort environmental data into three major areas: performance, strategy, and context. By performance we mean how the economy has been doing along dimensions such as real GDP growth, inflation, unemployment, and balance of payments. Strategy includes the implicit or explicit choice of national goals and policies. And context refers to the institutional, ideological, political, and physical "givens" that shape a government's strategy and its outcome.

Having analyzed a country in terms of its performance, strategy, and context, country analysis relates these data to one another in a three-step process of identification, evaluation, and prediction or scenario generation. The consistencies and inconsistencies that appear provide clues as to what is likely and what is not likely in the future and what those probabilities mean for the firm.

Theoretical Thinking

In order to identify, evaluate, and predict the state of a given country, analysts must utilize systematic and theoretical reasoning. Kurt Lewin, a renowned psychologist, once stated that, "There is nothing as practical as a good theory." This is because a good theory identifies key variables, explains how they relate to each other, and describes how they influence or lead to certain outcomes. The better the theory is at predicting certain outcomes, the more practical and useful it is to managers. Country analysis requires theoretical thinking to guide the selection and correlation of data. Although facts are important to gather in conducting a country analysis, as E. H. Carr observed in *What Is History?* "Facts are like fish in the ocean. They are there in seemingly endless quantities, yet the kind of fish you catch depends on where you fish and what equipment you use." It is theoretical thinking that determines which facts are important, how they fit together, and what outcomes they are likely to produce. Thus, country risk analysis requires theoretical thinking, and good analysts make their theories explicit.

The Role of Values

Evaluation involves values and a point of view, as well as theory. Values, like questions of taste, have only a limited susceptibility to analysis. But it is important to recognize their presence, since analysts' values can cause them to misperceive data or to misinterpret a desirable outcome as a likely one. To keep values from interfering with country analysis, we suggest two key guidelines:

First, the analyst should set aside his or her own views and begin with the perspective of a key actor in the situation. Identify that person's values, since they can have an important bearing on the outcome of the situation. By adopting the point of view of the decision maker (for example, CEO, prime minister, etc.) rather than trying to be both judge and jury, the analyst can make a more meaningful evaluation of the situation.

Second, in evaluating each situation the analyst should look for cause and effect relationships. This should be a value-neutral exercise of attempting to anticipate or explain an outcome. If the analyst is not careful, his or her own values may get in the way of an effective evaluation, perhaps leading to an optimistic or pessimistic assessment rather than an accurate and probable one. Making cause and effect arguments clear and explicit is perhaps the most effective means of guarding against the analyst's own values creeping into the analysis or for helping to identify the values if they do enter the analysis.

IDENTIFICATION: PERFORMANCE, STRATEGY, AND CONTEXT

Performance

Most countries regularly publish data on economic performance. Since the development of the national income accounting system, these data have been reported in a form that permits comparisons over time and across countries. Familiarity with this accounting system is essential for effective country analysis.

The analyst should also be aware of the accounting system's limitations. It measures only economic performance, and generally, only those aspects that show up in the money economy; thus it misses the barter economy and the black market economy. These segments can be particularly large and important in developing or transforming countries. The output measured in GDP includes a car wash purchased from the local garage, but not one bartered in exchange for a few hours' loan of the car. The moonlighting carpenter who insists on payment in cash and fails to report that income is part of a gray market economy not measured by the usual performance statistics.

Performance indicators abound. Which ones should be included in a particular analysis depends on the question at hand. Certain indicators, however, are so important that they should always be examined. The country analyst should always identify external economic performance as measured by the balance of payments statement and exchange rate. Internal economic performance should at least include measures of aggregate results in terms of output, prices, and employment. It should include performance measures on the supply side of the economy such as saving, investment, productivity, wage increases, unit labor costs, and utilization of capacity, as well as demand-side measures such as the distribution of income by various demographic factors (area, age, ethnic group, and so on).

Certain social performance indicators are also important to an in-depth analysis. Income distribution data represent a useful base for social and political as well as economic analysis. Measures of population growth (or decline) and migration can indicate which regions are considered more or less attractive. Net out-migration may reflect a shortage of jobs or political repression. Another important social indicator is educational achievement in particular professional or skill categories, as well as average years of schooling completed. Public health and nutrition indicators can be important too, particularly in low-income countries.

Social indicators are no more precise than economic indicators. Because they are often a focus for media and political attention, they may be subject to controversy and manipulation. For example, with both federal grants and congressional seats at stake, recent US Census figures for some of the large cities in the Northeast were hotly disputed.

Which performance indicators to look for, and in what degree of detail, depends on the questions facing the country analyst. But any compilation should include major social as well as economic indicators.

Strategy

The concept of a unified national strategy is obviously a simplification. For many, it may even seem a contradiction in terms. In countries such as the United States, with a pluralistic, democratic system that includes checks and balances among independent branches of government, one may wonder, "How can there be a national strategy?" Yet for many countries, and particularly in more centralized democracies such as Japan, identification of a national strategy is relatively easy. Americans, who are used to witnessing a continuing battle between the executive and legislative branches, may be at an initial disadvantage in learning to accept this concept and, similarly, in learning how to identify the strategies of other governments.

Goals. In identifying a national strategy, it is important to look for goals as well as policies. A country may have many goals, some more real than others, some more important than others. The analyst should always identify a country's priorities in at least three areas—autonomy, productivity, and equity—and if possible get a sense of their relative importance at a given time.

Autonomy means freedom from foreign domination. For Canada the goal may be autonomy from US economic and cultural influences. For Pakistan or Saudi Arabia it may be defensive capability to withstand foreign diplomatic and military pressures as well as internal security against domestic unrest. For France and Germany it may include not only autonomy from Russian military pressures, but also influence in NATO and the European Union. Goals of autonomy may involve not only territorial integrity but the capacity of the government to continue its rule of the country. The best corporate analogy may be management's desire to avoid a takeover.

Productivity creates wealth and, over time, a rising standard of living. In the short run, however, it requires work, saving, and investment, which may dictate a short-term sacrifice in standard of living. It also requires that performance—work, saving, and investment—be rewarded.

Beyond the baking of the national economic pie, there is always the question of dividing it—the problem of equity. The search for equity can emphasize equality of opportunity or equality of results. Equity and productivity may be partly inconsistent, and tradeoffs may be required. This balancing is like that of a firm making tradeoffs between higher investments for long-term growth and lower investment to boost short-term profitability and cash flow.

Goals are like the motor of the system. Since they are often implicit and somewhat contradictory, it is important to try to be explicit in stating them and in noting which ones appear to have highest priority at a given point in time.

How can one identify a country's goals and priorities? One obvious way is simply to read the public statements of leading politicians. Tracking the behavior of politicians and, in particular, observing their key policy choices is an important second step. When one has to choose between words and behavior, behavior is generally a better bet. Face-to-face interviews with top politicians or their close associates are also valuable, as they both allow the analyst to appreciate nuances as well as give the politicians a chance to explain the compromises they have made. First-rate country analysis requires field work, particularly to identify the priorities of the government in power.

Policies.   The second component of a national strategy is the policies designed to achieve the goals. It is more appropriate to think of a policy mix, implying compromise, because many policies cost money to implement and thus compete with one another for funds. Policy choices are thus constrained by the resources available, but these choices provide important insights about priorities and powerful groups and individuals. The following is a general set of policies that a thorough country analysis should include:

Foreign/defense policy, especially any orientation toward military buildup or downsizing because this can have a dramatic effect on resources

Fiscal policy, especially changes in spending, taxes, fiscal surplus, or deficit

Monetary policy, especially changes in money supply, interest rates, and exchange rates

Income policies, especially those concerning the poor

Foreign trade and investment policies, especially concerning tariff and nontariff barriers, foreign investment and ownership, and capital flows

Industrial policies, especially those concerning growth in specific industries

Social policies, especially concerning labor, education, population control, and religion

Context

Government goals and policies are formulated within a particular context. Hence, the context may be thought of as the "givens," or a country's constraints and resources.

Political Context.   The analyst should note the form or structure of government, the mechanisms designed to guide a transition of power from one leader to the next, key power blocs, and the extent of popular support. In addition, the analyst should note how politicians finance their campaigns—what standards of honesty and/or conflict of interest apply.

In democratic countries the timing of elections and the parliamentary margin held by the incumbents are particularly important to note. Weak governments facing elections are not likely to make unpopular decisions. Dictators or stable majorities, such as the Liberal Democratic Party in Japan, have a better record for taking a longer-term view when economic measures unpopular to important constituencies are involved. In all countries, democratic or otherwise, it is also important to note the coalition of interests that supports government, the opposing interests, the degree of consensus, and the processes through which deals are made and/or confrontations brought about. In many countries, parliament does more to make headlines than to make policy; the analyst should be alert for other "corridors of power."

Institutional Context.   Since the 1930s, if not before, the most significant institution in most countries has been government, an institution with significant military and police powers. In many countries, government has direct responsibility for more than one-third of GNP and sets rules and regulations governing most of the remainder. The analyst should determine the structure of government and, in particular, should note which agencies are more or less independent. The United States, with three independent branches of government, differs sharply from most of the other democracies, which unite executive and legislative functions. The United States is also somewhat exceptional in having a central bank technically independent of the government, although the German central bank is still more "independent." In addition, the analyst should try to develop a sense of the competence and honesty of the bureaucracy and key public officials. In some cases, governments are so corrupt that it is as important to understand the informal government as the official system.

Next, the analyst should consider the business institutions: banking, commerce, transportation, and manufacturing. This analysis in particular should make comparisons of structure, technology, management practices, and financial strength. It should look for any mechanisms that regulate competition, including cartels, informal understandings, or interlocking directorates managed through banks.

The agricultural sector should receive a similar analysis. How large is it, how productive, how much locked in by subsidies to producing high-cost items, how influential a political force?

Labor should be noted as a separate category. What share of the work force is unionized? Through what structure? What changes in unionization are taking place? How are unions financed? How are union leaders chosen? Has collective bargaining been established, or is it still an issue? How do union members and union leaders view attempts to increase productivity—as a threat to jobs? As a necessity for export competitiveness? Perhaps both? At what level do negotiations take place? How politicized are the unions? Finally, are labor relations a strength or a handicap relative to competition?

Ideological Context. A closely related element is that of ideology, or how a society "ought" to be organized. Ideologies spell out the "rights" and "duties" of the members of a society, the powers that should reside in its key institutions, and how these powers should be used.

The analyst should note whether there is broad consensus or serious ideological tension. Where tension exists, the analyst would do well to study the minority's ideologies in order to understand the focal points of tension and how the system might accommodate them.

The country analyst should make a tentative judgment as to whether the ideological component is a strength or a weakness. Normally consensus would seem to be a strength, for it would aid the successful development and implementation of a strategy. But some ideologies may be noncompetitive in themselves, calling either for an "end to progress" or for a redistribution of rights and duties such that the society has more rights than it can afford. Some analysts believe the United Kingdom, and perhaps the United States, may have established more rights than either country can afford, while others have suggested that many of the Moslem revolutionaries in the Middle East would like to halt the spread of Western practices, if not indeed to "turn back the clock."

Physical Context. Having noted geographic and demographic features such as arable land, deepwater harbors, and mineral resources, the country analyst must identify countries' political and economic bearings. Within OPEC, for instance, the countries with "big oil" have small populations, while those with big populations have relatively little oil. Linking these elements is essential to an understanding of the production and pricing strategies of OPEC members. Similarly, a country analysis of Egypt must emphasize the political and economic importance of the Suez Canal.

International Context. Global competition is governed by a framework of rules formulated and enforced by international institutions such as the General Agreement on Tariffs and Trade (GATT), the International Monetary Fund, and the United Nations. The UN was created to develop and enforce rules in the political sphere, but the effect of Security Council vetoes and a General Assembly voting structure that bears little relationship to power realities has been to make the UN little more than a court of world opinion with ancillary, largely noncontroversial development programs.

Hence, real power still rests with sovereign countries, and the international context seems destined to be dominated by the shifting and partially conflicting interests of the industrialized countries, the oil producers, and the less-developed countries.

EVALUATION

At this point the country analyst must review all the performance indicators and make a broad judgment on how well the country is doing. Is performance getting better or worse, and is it better or worse than that of another country or group of countries? The point is not so much to calculate ratios as to note trends and comparisons. For example, inflation that has come down from 6% to 4% might be high compared to another country, yet shows improvement, whereas inflation might be headed up in the comparison country.

Performance can also be evaluated relative to goals. A simple counting of goals achieved or not achieved is a start. But it is also important to evaluate clusters of performance indicators together. For example, a deteriorating trade balance is normally a sign of weakness. If the profitability of domestic firms is also declining, the country is in more serious trouble, like a company that reports declining market share and declining profits at the same time.

Likewise, in evaluating employment data the analyst should note not only the unemployment rate but also the participation rate. Rising participation in the labor force means more people are finding jobs, whether or not more people are involuntarily out of work. On the other hand, rising unemployment in a country with a low and/or declining participation rate suggests much more serious trouble.

Hence, the analyst must evaluate the country's performance with relation to three principal standards: past performance; the performance of other countries, particularly major competitors; and the goals of the government. The second and third standards are particularly important. If performance falls short of both the performance of competing countries and governmental goals, it is likely to produce tensions in the political leadership and demand for changes.

Diagnosing the Causes

Regardless of whether a country's performance is disappointing or exciting, the next step is to attempt a diagnosis of the causes. Sometimes this will be a fairly easy or obvious process. In other cases, there will be competing explanations, often buttressed by competing theories. The situation of Japan is a good one to consider. The following provides an example of a country analysis that might be undertaken.

The Japanese Economy—From Miracle to Mid-Life Crisis

The postwar Japanese economy experienced the fastest growth rate of any country ever. From 1951-1973, the economy grew at an average annual rate of over 10% and GNP increased almost eightfold. This trend has continued so that in terms of unadjusted per capita income, Japan is now the leading industrial power. How does one explain the Japanese miracle?

Historians argue that it is important to remember that the postwar economy of Japan was not starting from scratch, rather it was built on a solid foundation of prewar economic growth. Between 1868 and 1940, Japan's GNP had increased at a rate of 3% per year. During the Meiji Restoration, the country went from dirt roads to trains, from runners to telegraph networks, and from hand-spun to machine-spun silk and cotton. Although in crude economic terms the war cost Japan 20 years of economic growth, the Japanese came out of the war with a critical asset—a well-educated and skilled labor force. Sociologists argue that the people were the key to the Japanese economic miracle.

Economists note that the American occupation brought in approximately $2 billion in aid at a critical time. The Americans paid for two-fifths of all imports into Japan during the occupation. Also, having the Americans pressuring the Japanese government for deflationary programs was absolutely crucial in terms of getting runaway inflation under control and setting the stage for rapid economic growth once recovery had been achieved in the mid 1950s. The American military forces during the Korean War placed special procurement orders of $4 billion from Japan. This came just as US aid was drying up and produced Japan's first postwar boom in manufacturing.

Economists also note that the yen remained undervalued for a long time. It was fixed at 360 yen per dollar in 1949 and stayed there until 1971. This meant that for over 20 years, a period of increasing free trade, Japan enjoyed a tremendous export subsidy.

Political scientists note that, thanks to its alliance with the US, Japan had practically no defense burden. The Japanese government kept an unofficial cap on defense spending of below 1% of GNP. This small military spending allowed Japanese officials to concentrate all government efforts on economic construction and growth.

Labor-relation specialists point out that, by the mid 1950s, businesspersons had succeeded in routing incipient trade unions into automobile and other industries. Hence, the so-called "enterprise" union in which labor cooperated with management became the norm. Moreover, the Japanese practiced lifetime or permanent employment. This contributed to company loyalty and low turnover, and, in turn, created an incentive to train and upgrade the quality of workers. Additionally, a secure job helped rule out workers' resistance to technological progress because there was no fear of technologically driven unemployment.

Fortunately for the Japanese, foreigners were more than happy to sell or license their technology on relatively attractive terms to Japanese companies. In fact, some historians argue that Americans practically gave away many important technologies to the Japanese. This allowed the Japanese to focus on product development rather than basic research.

Economists explain part of the Japanese economic miracle in terms of the unprecedented rate of private capital formation. Over one third of GNP was ploughed back into further expansion. Capital grew at over 9% per year—more than twice the average rate for industrialized nations. One of the major reasons for this rapid investment rate was the high rate of savings induced by the marketing efforts of Japanese banks. Limited retirement pay and a small welfare system necessitated life-long savings for retirement. Another important factor was the way wages were paid. Although the Japanese received monthly paychecks, twice a year (at New Year's and midsummer) special bonuses were paid. Because the average Japanese learned to live on the regular monthly income, these bonuses were easily squirreled away into savings accounts or tax-free "postal accounts," which provided the government with capital to feed economic growth.

Political scientists also point to Ministry of International Trade and Industry and other government agencies and their policies designed to promote growth industries and phase out declining industries as an important explanation of the miracle. But decades after being the miracle economy, Japan has been gripped by a severe contraction. In the year to end December 1992, industrial output fell by more than 8%. Sociologists argue that the social consensus on which Japan has built its success is breaking down. Economic policy has supported long-term growth at the expense of workers and consumers. They consented to this because growth was rapid enough to keep living standards on a sharply rising trend and because Japan had a visibly egalitarian distribution of wealth. But, as future rises in living standards can no longer be taken for granted, this consent is being withdrawn.

Additionally, extraordinary land prices have divided Japan into the haves and the have-nots. Land prices in Tokyo in 1990 were so high that the grounds of the Imperial Palace were calculated to be worth more than all the land in California. Although over the last two years land prices have fallen, such a drop in assets owned by Japanese businesses and people has caused demand in the economy to slump. Many companies, especially those that had gambled on properties, found it difficult to service the debts they had recently taken on.

Figure 10.1
GNP per Head 1990 Prices

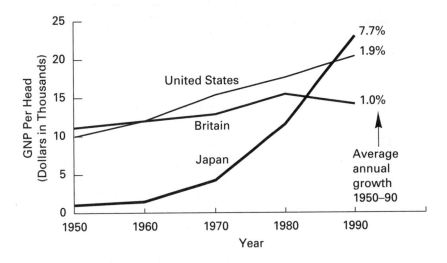

Source: Bank of Japan; CSO; US Department of Commerce; IMF.

The unwinding of the Japanese business paradise has also contributed to the contraction. By 1973, many factors such as favorable exchange rates, easily available technology, and a skilled but cheap labor force had worked their way through the economy. Protectionism has become more common as the US trade deficit with Japan reached over $50 billion. And the younger-generation Japanese are more devoted to themselves and leisure activities than to serving the company.

As this example shows, an analyst incorporates a variety of perspectives from economics, history, political science, sociology, and anthropology. In addition, the analyst must look for inconsistencies between the strategy and the context. A strategy may be internally consistent yet unrealistic in light of the resources at hand or the productivity of the firms. Or it may be politically unrealistic if opposed by farmers or unions or bankers. A strategy may also be unrealistic in the international context—for example, if other countries are reluctant to accept increased imports of particular kinds from a particular country.

No diagnosis is complete without consideration of a country's "quality of management" or political leadership. However intangible or elusive such "quality" may be, competent leadership is likely to adjust effectively to new developments, and inept, corrupt, or unrealistic management is not. Put another way, skillful leaders can do more with less than their less skillful counterparts can.

To complete the diagnosis, the analyst should identify the key problems causing the unsatisfactory performance. In a schematic diagram, for example, one might draw arrows to show inconsistencies or draw circles around particularly troublesome contextual elements or around particularly unrealistic goals or policies.

Evaluating the Future

After looking at performance, strategy, and context in the past and present, the country analyst must project into the future. Skillful country analysts may be able to predict certain immediate developments, such as more or less unemployment. But with a longer time horizon, such as three to five years, few important specific predictions can be made with great confidence, for there are far too many variables and uncertainties. Under these circumstances, the country analyst can formulate alternate scenarios to represent broadly different outcomes. Having done this, the analyst can examine how the interests of the firm or government would be affected by the alternative scenarios, thus developing a practical application of the analysis.

The following example is provided to illustrate briefly some of the basics involved in constructing future scenarios.

PREDICTION OR SCENARIO GENERATION: CHINA

The People's Republic of China (PRC) covers 9.6 million square kilometers and holds a population of over 1.1 billion. However, rugged geography greatly reduces the amount of arable land, and about 75% of China's enormous population is crowded into 15% of the nation's territory, primarily in the lowlands and hills of the coastal provinces and the Manchurian plateau. Many of China's natural resources are located in the interior, but they remain unexploited due to limited capital and technical capabilities, as well as poor transportation facilities. Official estimates claim that oil reserves are high, equal to those in Saudi Arabia, but results of explorations in the South China Sea by Western companies have fallen short of expectations.

The four major political groups are the *radical left,* the *conservatives,* the *pragmatists,* and the *liberals.* The radical left distrusts foreign investment and trade and would like to see their outright elimination from Chinese business. On the other hand, the conservatives, pragmatists, and liberals believe that economic reform is desirable. However, the conservatives differ from the liberals, who would like to see China emerge as a multi-party democracy, and the pragmatists, who are willing to tolerate limited political liberalization as the necessary price for economic development. The conservatives favor state-owned enterprises and centralized planning.

Since Mao's death in 1976, General Deng Xiaoping, a pragmatist, has enjoyed power. He relinquished his last official party post in November 1989 and designated another pragmatist, Jiang Zemin, to the positions of general secretary and chairman of the CMC. However, Deng remains the most influential individual in China, and the pragmatists look up to him as their mentor.

China's biggest social problem is overpopulation. The government's plan to establish the one-child family through education, persuasion, and penalties (such as the withdrawal of welfare benefits when the family has a second child) has not achieved desired success. Unemployment is another major problem, and officials admit that about 100 million Chinese are unemployed. Corruption is pervasive, and although the government reports a low crime rate, many crimes go unreported.

Another growing problem is economic polarization. The regime's open-door economic policy, the establishment of Special Economic Zones in Guangdong and Fujian provinces, and the foreign investment concessions given to 14 cities have widened the gap between peasants and intellectuals.

China's biggest asset is its proximity to Hong Kong. The colony provides an indirect but crucial link by which billions of dollars flow into China's burgeoning economy. The UK and China reached an agreement in 1984 that will return Hong Kong to Chinese sovereignty in 1997. Although Beijing opposes democratization in Hong Kong, it has taken some steps to reassure the population there that it will maintain the special political and economic institutions that have made Hong Kong so prosperous. In July 1991, China and the UK reached an agreement for the construction of a new $16.4 billion airport in Hong Kong. The agreement sets a precedent for Chinese intervention in Hong Kong's affairs even before 1997.

Vital Signs

Gross Domestic Product (92 est.)	$400.2 billion
Real GDP Growth	12.5%
Population (92 est.)	1.1 billion

Source: J. P. Morgan & Co.

China enjoys most-favored-nation trading status with the US and believes that this relationship will keep the door open to financial aid from the World Bank. Relations with the rest of the industrialized world are also bolstered in order to obtain foreign capital, technology, and economic expertise. Nevertheless, trade disputes are an ongoing concern as China contrives to maintain multiple nontariff barriers to US goods.

Official commitment to economic reform has been inconsistent in recent years, but the process continues to lumber along. At least one-third of state companies are overstaffed and in the red. Subsidies on important items such as cooking oil, rice, and steel are being lifted, not so much as part of a belief in market forces but because the state simply cannot afford them. Plans for stock markets have been revived. In the summer of 1991, visiting businesspersons reported being contacted by local Chinese officials offering favorable terms in order to attract investment in their own region rather than anywhere else in China. Moreover, the government has sought low-cost loans from the World Bank, the IMF, the Japanese government, and the Arab Fund for a total of nearly $49 billion (August 1991). And Chinese officials note that most of the joint ventures have now begun to yield returns. Industrial output value of these investments amounted to $70 billion in 1990, accounting for 3.6% of total Chinese industrial production.

The free market economic policies backed by the pragmatists and Deng fostered a sentiment among students for equivalent liberalization in the political arena. This protest culminated in the Tiananmen Square outbreak in Beijing in June 1989. Military suppression of students and the arrest and execution of thousands of critics of the regime followed. After this outbreak, many of the economic reforms implemented in the 80s were withdrawn. The World Bank, the US Export-Import Bank, and foreign commercial banks responded by establishing economic reforms against China. However, normal levels of lending have now been resumed.

Best Five-Year Scenario: Pragmatists

With each day that passes, the position of the pragmatists and Jiang Zemin is strengthened. They would like to reform the economy, reduce the bureaucracy, and integrate China with the global economy, but continue to maintain the Communist party's paramount position. The willingness of the World Bank and other primary lenders to resume loans to China, and the readiness of foreign investors to end their suspension of foreign investment, also strengthens the pragmatists' position. If the pragmatists retain power after Deng's death, while bureaucratic regulation of foreign investment and trade will remain intensive, the regime will ease regulations selectively to encourage needed foreign investment. Investment in high-technology sectors and in export industries will receive the most favorable treatment. The regime will continue to ease trade restrictions to spur economic development, while maintaining those that are integral to security interests.

Real economic growth will have reached 6.5% in 1992 and average about 6% annually for the five-year period as the regime implements its liberalization program. The government will continue to have problems with extrabudgetary investment by local governments, poor quality control, and a poor product mix that cannot cope with market demands. Since a great deal of money now circulates outside the official banking system, inflation will continue and will have reached 8% in 1992 and average 9% annually throughout the forecast period. Shortages of staple items such as salt will continue due to speculation and corruption. Energy production will continue to be a persistent problem.

Discontent over inflation, unemployment, pressure on living standards, and inequality of income will prevent an improvement in the level of turmoil presently experienced in China. A substantial segment of the intellectual community will remain resentful over the lack of freedom. However, foreign firms will remain largely unaffected by such unrest.

The State Agricultural Commission has suggested a gradual commercialization of grain production and an end to state quotas. Under the pragmatists, this plan would be implemented. But it would only be a partial solution to agricultural problems. Soil fertility is declining and cultivated land area has shrunk at an average annual rate of 500,000 hectares over the past decade, and there is no way to end this shrinkage.

More emphasis will be placed on central planning than prior to the 1989 unrest, but reliance on market forces will increase. In spite of many problems, output will continue to expand in both heavy and light industries. Consumer demand will continue to spur growth in light industry.

Worst Five-Year Scenario: Conservatives

Sanctions by the West over human rights issues or problems connected with the transfer of Hong Kong to China could spark a conservative backlash within the party leadership. Soaring inflation or a significant drop in living standards that leads to widespread public disturbances would also increase the chances of a conservative government. Once in power, the regime would establish repressive control over political dissent and economic reform, leading to a highly unstable situation.

Investment and trade restrictions would increase, but many of the economic reforms implemented by the pragmatists would be maintained for economic development. International economic relations would worsen. Foreign investors would be less inclined to provide loans or maintain previous levels of investment. Tourism revenues would drop. Exports would drop as the firms utilize foreign technology and capital. Imports would also drop, but by less than the drop in exports.

Growth would fall to 4% in 1992 and average 4% for the five-year period. Inflation would decline to 6% in 1990 and to 5% for the five-year period. This regime would increase centralized planning and reduce activity in the private sector.

The conservatives would also make strenuous efforts to reduce China's debts, accepting a lower growth rate as a consequence. The current account surplus would drop to $200 million in 1992 and fall into deficit over the five-year period, averaging $300 million.

Regimes	Base	Pragmatists	Conservatives
Turmoil	Low	Same	Less
Restrictions			
Investment	Very high	Slightly less	Slightly more
Trade	Very high	Slightly less	Slightly more
Economic Problems			
Domestic	Moderate	Slightly less	More
International	Moderate	Same	More

Even in light of the best- or worst-case scenarios, the critical next step is to apply the scenario to the firm, because a given scenario will not affect specific firms in the same way. Additionally, the analyst will need to explore how different strategies of a given firm are likely to fare under each scenario (see Figure 10.2). For example, an analyst might find that Strategy A does extremely well under Scenario 1, but is a disaster under Scenario 2, while Strategy B has the opposite profile. The analyst might then find that although Strategy C does better under Scenario 1, it still does acceptably under Scenario 2. Depending on how confidently the analyst feels he or she can predict the future scenario, Strategy C might be the best bet.

Figure 10.2

Alternative Strategies

	A	B	C
1	+++	– – –	+ +
2	– – –	+ + +	+

Alternative Scenarios

CONCLUSION

The keys to useful country analysis are fivefold. First, firms must recognize that without careful country analysis, they are committing both Type 1 and Type 2 errors (not entering a country when they should and being in a country when they shouldn't). Both errors can be quite costly. Secondly, the analyst must accurately and systematically identify contextual and performance factors and explain their causes. Third, the analyst must generate scenarios of the future based on the analysis. Fourth, the analyst must relate those scenarios to a specific industry or firm. Finally, the analyst must examine the pros and cons of various firm strategies across different scenarios in order to provide specific recommendations. This fivefold process will facilitate decision makers' abilities to appropriately navigate the increasingly dangerous, but profitable seas of today's global environment.

SELECTED BIBLIOGRAPHY

BLACK, J. STEWART, and ATEPHEN ERICSON. Working Papers, Amos Tuck School of Business Administration, 1993.

Political Risk Services. "Country Analysis of China," 1991.

SESIT, MICHAEL R., and ROBERT STEINER. "Why Global Investors Bet on Autocrats, Not Democrats," *Wall Street Journal* (January 12, 1993).

case 13

Nike in China

In April 1980 Nike, the leading sports footwear company in the United States, submitted a business proposal to the People's Republic of China (PRC). In a letter of transmittal, Nike founder and president Phil Knight laid out the project's objectives and rationale:

> Primary among our objectives is to establish the means by which we would buy a finished shoe product from the People's Republic of China. We presently target a goal of 100,000 pair per month in the first phase, with growth to 1,000,000 pair per month, or US $30 million per year, by the mid-1980s.

> We feel that the People's Republic of China, with its long tradition of excellence in this field of manufacture, would be an ideal additional source for our product. We see immediate benefits to be derived by each party in this business relationship, with even more important long-term benefits in the future.

Five months later the first production supply contract was signed; by October 1981 shoe production had begun. The rapidity with which Nike had maneuvered through the Chinese bureaucracy was hailed in the business press as "dazzling."

By late 1984, however, production had reached only 150,000 pair per month. Many unforeseen problems had led Knight to comment, "China has got to be about the toughest place in the world to do business." In addition, the rapid growth of the sports shoe market was declining and competition was increasing; this had caused a drop in volume and major cutbacks in Nike's orders from its suppliers in South Korea and Taiwan (which provided 86% of its shoes).

Professor James Austin, Professor Francis Aguilar, and Research Assistant Jiang-sheng Jin prepared this case as the basis for classroom discussion rather than to illustrate effective or ineffective handling of an administrative situation. Copyright © 1985 by the President and Fellows of Harvard College.

David Chang, a Nike vice president and key player in the China project from its beginning, commented, "Unfortunately, China has not come on-stream as we expected. Although there have recently been encouraging changes in the government's policies, with our earnings going down there is pressure to get out of China." However, given the importance of Nike's global sourcing strategy to its past and future success, Chang felt it was time to review the China experience and make recommendations on future actions.

COMPANY BACKGROUND

From a $1,000 investment and a small importing business in 1964, Nike had, by 1984, grown into America's leading sports shoe company, with sales approaching $1 billion. Return on equity averaged 46% over the 1978–1982 period. During these years the business went public, but Knight remained the major stockholder and chief executive officer.[1]

Nike's product line proliferated as the fitness boom created new market opportunities. From high-performance racing shoes, Nike expanded into other sports (soccer, football, basketball, tennis), other user segments (joggers, nonathletes, children), and other product lines (leisure shoes, apparel). The number of basic footwear models increased from 63 in 1978 to 185 in 1983. Including model variations, the number of products totaled 340. Footwear accounted for almost 90% of Nike's 1982 revenues, with running shoes 34%, court shoes 30%, children's shoes 15%, cleated shoes 2%, and leisure shoes 2%; exports added another 6%. Apparel sales were 10% of total revenue.

From its inception, Nike had sourced almost all its shoes from offshore producers. The original Japanese suppliers were replaced by South Korean contract factories, which provided 70% of Nike's needs. Other important suppliers were Taiwan (16%), Thailand, and Hong Kong. The remaining 7% were produced in Nike's own US production and research facilities. China was the most recent supplier. (The Philippines had been phased out due to its political uncertainties. Brazil was no longer considered cost-competitive. Nike owned a factory in Ireland that supplied the European Common Market with 15,000 pairs of shoes per month in 1984—half its earlier peak. Nike also had built a rubber factory in Malaysia, which in 1984 had significant excess capacity.)

Nike held a commanding lead in the US athletic footwear market, with a 30% share. Its strong R&D capacity, high quality, economic offshore sourcing, dependable delivery, and outstanding brand image lay behind its success. Its major competitor, West Germany's Adidas, had a 19% share in the United States and led in the world with $2 billion in sales, of which 40% was in apparel. While Nike's emphasis was on importing and marketing, Adidas developed as a manufacturer. It had its own and contract plants throughout the world, including the Soviet Union. Converse held the next-largest share with 9%; it manufactured 70% of its shoes in the United States and sourced the rest from the Far East. Puma (a spin-off from Adidas) and Keds (a leader in children's sneakers) accounted for 7% each. Several other smaller companies specialized in certain categories; New Balance, for example, had 15% of the running shoe submarket. (*Exhibit 1* shows a breakdown of competitor shares and market segment information.)

The 1970s' rapid market growth began to taper off in the 1980s. Some felt that a shift from a seller's to a buyer's market was in process, and that pricing would become more aggressive. The proliferation of shoe models accelerated; their life cycle in the marketplace shortened. Nike's basic models were expected to rise from 196 in 1984 to 430 by 1986. Seasonality of sales emerged: About 65% of company sales were in the spring and during the August–September back-to-school period. (In the past, Nike had maintained level production year-round.)

---

[1]Data based primarily on the Nike (A)–(E) case series, Harvard Business School, 1984, prepared by Senior Research Associate David C. Rikert and Professor C. Roland Christensen.

EXHIBIT 1

Branded Athletic Footwear Submarkets, 1982 Market Shares (%)

Submarket	Racquet	Running	Basketball	Field	Other
% of total market	35%	30%	15%	15%	5%
Leading competitors (% market share)	Nike 40% Adidas 20 Tretorn 6	Nike 50% New Balance 15 Adidas 10	Converse 36% Puma 30 Nike 20	Puma 30% Adidas 20 Hyde 10	
Comments	Common for street use; tennis has not been growing but may in coming years.	Growth of 6% to 8% expected, depending on how long people continue to run and how many are diverted to home exercise.	Beginning to decline; fewer teens; Title IX[a] bulge over.	Team sports, so depend on increase in industrial leagues; soccer will grow but at expense of football.	Hiking and walking: Small but growing as older people discover walking. Leisure: Moderate growth unless a model captures imagination of young people.

Source: "Nike (A)," HBS No. 9-385-025.

Note: Data based on sales in athletic specialty and sporting goods channels *only*.

a. Title IX, a federal statute, required that educational institutions provide for women athletic programs and facilities similar to those provided for men.

As demand faltered, Nike cut back its orders significantly (by one-third from Korean factories) and closed a US factory. It posted a $2.2 million net loss for the second fiscal quarter ending November 30, 1984. Industry observers projected a 6%–8% growth rate for the rest of the 1980s.

Nike shifted its attention to the apparel line. The Nike name and swoosh logo were believed to be transferable, but apparel, a very different business than footwear, was presenting new problems. Knight commented:

> Adidas sells $700 million in apparel. We should get a portion of this, but with US customs quotas, sourcing is a tough business. The quota on shoes is not so hard on us because we can get it better than our competitors due to our bargaining power with foreign suppliers. This is not true for clothes. Factories prefer to sell ski apparel rather than running warm-ups in their quota because of the higher value. In footwear we source 90% from abroad, but in apparel only 50%. Our apparel sales are growing; in 1984 they grew from $110 million to $180 million, but profit margins are lower this year. We would like to source apparel from China, but their quota is used up through 1987.

CHINA

Before its open-door policy in 1978, the Chinese government had relied on a "lean to one side" (toward the USSR) policy. Mao's Cultural Revolution had stressed self-sufficiency, isolationism, and anti-intellectualism. After Mao's death in 1976 and the Gang of Four's imprisonment, the government under Deng Xiaoping concluded that to modernize, China needed to tap Western technology, management, and capital. In 1979 Foreign Trade Minister Li Qiang described the break with old policy:

> We have made great changes in our trade practices and adopted various flexible policies. Not long ago we still had two important "forbidden zones" in our dealings with other countries: One, we would not accept government-to-government loans; we would accept only commercial loans between banks. Two, we would not consider foreign investments. Recently we have decided to break down these "forbidden zones." By and large we now accept all the common practices known to world trade.

In 1981 Premier Zhao Ziyang described the rationale for the new strategy:

> By linking our country with the world market, expanding foreign trade, importing advanced technology, utilizing foreign capital and entering into different forms of international economic and technological cooperation, we can use our strong points to make up for our weak points through international exchange on the basis of equality and mutual benefit. Far from impairing our capacity for self-reliant action, this will only serve to enhance it. In economic work, we must abandon once and for all the ideal of self-sufficiency, which is a characteristic of the natural economy. All ideas and actions based on keeping our door closed to the outside world and sticking to conventions are wrong.. . . Ours is a sovereign socialist state. In accordance with the principle of equality and mutual benefit, foreigners are welcome to invest in China and launch joint ventures in opening up mines and running factories or other undertakings, but they must respect China's sovereignty and abide by her laws, policies, and decrees.[2]

[2]David G. Brown, "Sino-Foreign Joint Ventures: Contemporary Developments and Historical Perspective," *Journal of Northeast Asian Studies* 1, no. 4 (1982):27.

Foreign investment flow into China in 1981 rose to an estimated $1.2 billion.

Also in Nike's favor was China's shift in emphasis from heavy to light industry, hoping to meet consumer demands and raise the standard of living closer to that of its neighbors. By exporting consumer goods, China would also earn foreign currency needed to achieve its goals of modernization before 2000.

China's Economic System

China's centrally planned economy did not rely on market mechanisms as the major tool for resource allocation. Rather, development priorities were set through decision making at the highest levels of party and government, which then instructed the State Planning Commission to implement these policies through a series of economic plans. These plans were first defined as national programs to meet long-range objectives; later they were specified in short-run, local directives and development targets, based on the various economic units' capacities. The commission allocated resources to ministries and provinces according to these plans. Ministries, organized by economic sector, controlled all important national economic units. Provinces, based on geographic divisions, ran their own economic activities like small nations. The commission had centralized control over the ministries; decentralized power was granted at the provincial level.

The bureaucracy tended to be vertical. Ministries, however, were connected only horizontally by the State Planning Commission. As a result, production sometimes was disconnected, uncoordinated, and difficult to control.

Prices were not based on market needs and demands; instead they were arbitrarily set by the commission to realize national goals. For example, food prices were kept low to meet consumption needs, and luxury items were priced high. Because output was geared to annual targets regardless of market demand, many goods became scarce and others were in oversupply.

Before the 1978 reforms, the Chinese "iron rice bowl" system guaranteed everyone a job and equal pay, regardless of performance. Promotions were based mostly on seniority or politics. With no tools to measure performance, workers had few incentives to produce more. The 1978 reforms, however, provided bonuses to workers based on their performance, but these were still limited. Factory cadres able to institute rewards for their workers had little motivation to do so because they had few incentives for their own performance.

The Chinese Footwear Industry

In the past, most shoes produced in China had been manually made. Although the Chinese experience included the autoclave production technique for manufacturing canvas and rubber court shoes, the process for making more expensive jogging shoes was almost unknown to them. The government had previously neglected the footwear industry.

Workers in Chinese shoe factories generally had only an elementary school education. Also, Chinese factory managers lacked managerial training. Most had begun as workers 20 years earlier and advanced to managerial levels only because of seniority or politics.

Infrastructure

China's transportation and communication infrastructure was quite outmoded. The government had only just begun to rebuild port facilities to handle larger ships, and many new roads were under construction. Only the Beijing-Tianjin highway was close to US standards. There was no direct-dialing telephone system between major cities; capacity within the cities was severely strained.

Cultural Environment

Trust and reliability were especially important components of business relationships in China, since China's formal legal system had yet to be completely institutionalized and channels for the free flow of information were often obstructed. Past experience with untrustworthy foreigners had made the Chinese reluctant to do business with strangers. "Friend of China" had a special meaning implying trust, patience, and understanding. The Chinese insisted that foreigners doing business with them treat them as equals and with respect.

NIKE'S ENTRY STRATEGY AND NEGOTIATIONS

Nike saw sourcing from China as a logical next stage in its global production strategy. It had shifted to South Korea and Taiwan from Japan when rising wages and the value of the yen pushed costs up. As costs in South Korea and Taiwan rose, Nike signed small production contracts in 1980 and 1981 with suppliers in the Philippines (250,000 pair), Thailand (250,000), Malaysia (75,000), and Hong Kong (50,000). A company study on future sourcing indicated India and China as the long-term, lowest-cost suppliers; China won out. (*Appendix A* provides a brief chronological summary of Nike's involvement in China during 1980–1983.)

The company's director of Far East operations, Neal Laurinson, was the first Nike official to visit China; he went to the Canton Trade Fair in October 1979. Knight, deeply interested in Asia and China, waited in Hong Kong two weeks for a visa that never came. Like many other foreign companies, Nike at first found the Chinese bureaucracy impenetrable. To gain access, management hired David Ping-Ching Chang as a consultant.

A Princeton-educated architect, Chang was born in China but left in 1941 at age 10. He was still a favored guest of the PRC and held a rare, multiple-entry visa. His father had been China's ambassador to Czechoslovakia, Portugal, and Poland in the 1930s. The Chinese communists held ancestry in high regard; they also saw political value in dealing with their former class enemies. Before he joined Nike, Chang had helped arrange a deal between a Chinese factory and a US auto parts company. His experience, contacts, language ability (he spoke Chinese but did not read or write it), and personality facilitated Nike's entry.

Chang described the entry period:

> One of the keys to Nike's success so far has been determining ongoing economic sources of supply. The president of the company had determined that China was the last major untapped source for a relatively labor-intensive product. We had to go. It was not a market; it was a production source. But we couldn't help but notice the two billion feet.

> Success in China depends on common sense. The first thing we did was write a proposal to the Chinese, outlining the long-term nature of our commitment, the scope that would indicate to them that we were not just coming in to buy 100,000 pair of rack shoes and then heading over the hill. And we had the common sense to have the proposal translated into Chinese. This probably got our document to the top of the bureaucrats' stack. We wrote the proposal in April 1980 and got an invitation in July to come and hold a seminar. We were directed to the Ministry of Light Industry, which supervises the footwear industry. Our group of six visited 20 to 30 factories in Tianjin and Shanghai.

Negotiations continued in September and November 1980. The Nike team (Chang, the corporate counsel, and production and finance people) met daily with their Chinese counterparts, who numbered 20 to 30—depending on the issues discussed. Supply contracts were signed between two factories each in Tianjin, Guangzhou (formerly Canton), and Fujian province, and one in Shanghai. Ten trips over 12 months were required to complete negotiations involving provincial and municipal officials where the factories were located and the ministries of Light Industry, Chemistry (which controlled the rubber supply), and Foreign Trade.

Christopher Walsh (Nike's first resident managing director in China), who had worked two years in South Korea, three in Taiwan, stated:

> The negotiations were some of the most strenuous exercises I have ever participated in. The major issues we faced. . . were issues we did not expect to arise. The Chinese were not familiar with the standard exclusivity clauses within our contracts. We wanted exclusive rights to these particular factories. We do not have difficulties enforcing these clauses in our other Asian countries and so tried to institute them in China.
>
> The second issue was B-grade production. The Chinese will package almost 100% of what they make. There are certain standards that had to be adhered to which they were not familiar with, so that was a stumbling block for us.
>
> The third issue was defective returns. A great deal of Nike's success today comes from standing behind its product. The Chinese could not accept that particular concept.. . . They felt that once a shoe had been put in the container and was on its way to the United States, that was the end of the production agreement. In Taiwan or Korea that particular clause is long-standing and not questioned whatsoever. What we were able to procure from the Chinese was that they will guarantee the shoes for only 9 months after they depart China. This virtually eliminates that clause, for 9 to 12 months will have passed by the time the shoes reach the consumer.

Pricing was another key issue in the negotiations. Chang described Nike's approach:

> One of the first things we told the Chinese was that their prices had to be more than competitive with our other Far East sources because the cost of doing business in China was so enormous. We opened our books to them and showed what we were paying our other suppliers.

Walsh commented on the results of the price negotiations:

> I think a lot of American corporations are misled in that you go to China expecting to pay much lower prices because people are earning $40 per month. However, the foreign trade corporations are of the opinion that since the standards are the same for them as for Nike in Korea or Taiwan, they deserve equal prices. We gave the Chinese a break on the first pricing round to get started, but we have to be more adamant in the future. The hope is for a 20% price advantage over Korea.

All contract agreements were negotiated with the ministries' staffs and the factory managers, and were based on specific shoe models' price, volume, delivery, and specifications. Because the factories had no foreign currency to purchase equipment, Nike entered into compensation trade arrangements whereby equipment was paid for in shoes. Nike would purchase B-grade shoes at a 20% discount during the first two years, then at a 40% discount. The agreements stipulated that factories could not sign contracts with Nike's competitors; they also granted Nike trademark protection.

Nike agreed to pay for purchases directly to the Ministry of Foreign Trade or its local offices. The factories would then receive Chinese currency at exchange rates higher than the fixed rate—as subsidies from the foreign trade unit (the only organization in China authorized to pay higher exchange rates). In Guangzhou the contracts were signed through the municipal government; new contracts were to be negotiated directly with the factory managers.

Operating Experiences

Walsh recounted the original production plans:

> In July 1981 we established forecasts for 10,000 pair per month in the initial 12-month period, with the gradual increase over 15 months to 100,000 pair. In retrospect those expectations were far too high. In the first 9 months we were able to export a total of only 35,000 pair. Not until 1984 did we reach 100,000 pair per month. We originally thought we would be producing a million pair a month by now.

The annual production figures were 140,000 pair in 1982, 263,000 in 1983 (9 models), and about 700,000 in 1984 (12 models).

Nike had to deal with a multitude of problems in technology transfer, materials, quality control, inventory control, production flexibility, worker and manager motivation, transportation, pricing, plant location, expatriate staffing, and government relations.

Technology transfer. Walsh described the transfer process:

> During the start-up period, we had to arrange for technology transfer. The Chinese are looking for something in return. In the footwear industry the machinery was very antiquated; they expected us not only to import machines but to provide them with technical designs to help them get away from the cottage industry that had existed in China. Normally they would sit in small rooms and do most of the work by hand. A South Korean factory that makes 100,000 pair a day has good systems, so we brought those to China.
>
> We ran into difficulties, however. We did not really recognize what lay ahead for us. Lots of things evolve in these relationships with the Chinese that simply cannot be foreseen from overseas. It takes an on-site presence to get a feeling for the situation. As a result, six individuals and I located in Shanghai. We visited the factories daily. We attempted to institute inventory and transportation strategies. We assessed what these people could actually accomplish relative to our expectations.
>
> Communication is one of the chief liabilities in entering the Chinese market, and we went to great lengths to develop a communications system that would enable us to identify on-site problems and provide solutions to problems that arose in those factories. Only two Nike residents spoke Chinese, and no one at the factory spoke English, so we had to use interpreters.

Managers from the Fuzhou factory visited Nike headquarters in Beaverton, Oregon, in May 1981 and the Hong Kong factory in July 1983; managers from the Tianjin #2 factory visited Nike's Thailand producer in December 1982, and those from the Guangzhou and Quanzhou (Fujian) factories traveled to the facilities in the Philippines and Thailand in November 1983.

Nike considered bringing native managers from South Korea and Taiwan to teach the Chinese the advanced technology. However, the Taiwan factories were much smaller than those in China and the managers were unwilling or unable for diplomatic and political reasons to go to China. South Korean factories, on the other hand, were similar in size to those in China, and their managers were willing to cooperate.

Chang approached the Chinese about bringing South Korean managers to China to help in training. The Chinese leaders agreed, but only if the South Koreans obtained US passports. The Chinese remained obstinate on this issue because of its political sensitivity. Unable to arrange entry for the South Koreans, Nike finally resorted to using videotapes of how the South Koreans operated different equipment. Walsh concluded:

> The biggest problem is that we are the buyers and they have to do it our way. It is difficult to convince them to use our processes and not theirs. For example, the factories need conveyor systems which are not now there. Our shoes, although simple, require a lot of preplanning and coordination on procurement. But their systems can't be changed overnight. There was give-and-take on processing methods. You have to be flexible.

Materials.   The factories continually lacked local materials. Nylon, canvas, rubber, and chemical compounds were essential components in shoe production. Only about one-third of Nike's needs were available locally, and even these were sometimes difficult to obtain. When Nike offered foreign currency for domestically produced supplies, the Chinese were still not forthcoming because of bureaucratic obstacles. For example, although Shanghai had sufficient canvas for all Nike factories, to ship it to Tianjin required prior approval of at least six ministries. Nike found it easier to import canvas from Taiwan and South Korea. Nylon also had to be imported. Suppliers, however, were ambivalent about providing their competitor with materials: shipments often arrived deliberately damaged. This created strain between Nike and its South Korean and Taiwanese suppliers.

Walsh reflected on this aspect of the materials sourcing problem:

> The Taiwan issue went back and forth. Some months Beijing would turn its back on the issue, and some months they would lobby heavily to increase the trade via indirect avenues such as Hong Kong, Tokyo, or wherever, which increased our transport costs. South Korea was another issue. We did not really recognize the posture that the Chinese had on South Korea. The Chinese knew very clearly that South Korea was our base for expansion and R&D in the Far East and that we had to utilize these sources. However, when we brought in material and machinery that was marked properly with "Republic of South Korea" on the outside, it just incurred a lot of wrath from the customs officials, and fines were assessed. But the major difficulties were the resultant delays. These were 60 to 90 days, depending on the moods of the customs people.

Quality Control.   Nike had a worldwide policy that its B-grade shoes could not constitute more than 5% of a supplier's total production during the first year, or 3% thereafter. B-grade shoes had cosmetic defects but were structurally sound. Nike sold them as promotional items or in discount stores, at a 40% discount. However, because of quality-control difficulties in China, Nike offered a 20% discount on all its PRC shoes for the first two years and initially lowered its quality specs. After four years, still only 80% of the Chinese shoes were A-grade. Nike and the Chinese argued constantly about the proper discount for B-grade shoes and the standard measurements for A-grade. Nike felt that Chinese managers used more energy arguing than improving production quality.

Walsh commented on the quality problem:

> The Chinese don't understand the brand concept. They couldn't grasp why C-grade shoes had to be destroyed and not sold locally or in another country. In fact, one batch of these was shipped to Australia without our knowledge.
>
> We are educating factory managers that Korean, Taiwanese, and Chinese shoes are sold as equals and must, therefore, meet international standards. We are also getting the China Trading Company to understand the Nike production and marketing

concept. The trading company staff and factory managers don't communicate enough with each other. Nike's people are physically in each of the factories almost daily. Our role is quality control, but we're looked on as educators. We prepared lots of manuals to define our methods.

Nike hired one Chinese inspector for each factory through the Foreign Services Company, to which it paid $300 a month per inspector. The inspectors received $60 monthly from the services company. They monitored quality, production volume, new model development, and shipping documentation.

One cause of the quality problem was the high level of dust in the cities and factories, which impeded the gluing of insoles to soles. All the Tianjin factory windows had to be shut to keep dust out. However, this made the work area too hot. Since air conditioning was too expensive, the factory had to stop production during the summer. The cleaning procedure was to blow dust off the soles with a squeeze bulb, but workers tended not to do this. Nike took factory managers to the Thailand plants, where they saw the conditions and results of a less-dusty environment and process. Dust-control procedures improved significantly after the visit.

Nike's national accounts, such as J.C. Penney, had been reluctant to take PRC shoes because of their presumed inferior quality. These buyers had at first been similarly reluctant when Taiwan began producing for Nike.

Inventory Control.   Some shoe materials, unavailable locally, had to be imported. Ordering took six weeks. To guarantee normal production schedules, Nike had to know in advance what needed to be imported and when. Chinese managers, however, were unable to relay this information because they did not keep adequate inventory records. Planners did not recognize the importance of the time factor. In the Long March Factory in Guangzhou, the large storage room was on the top floor of the production building. A woman at the door checking materials in and out functioned more as a doorkeeper than as a recordkeeper: She did not know what materials were needed for next month's production schedule and did not regularly coordinate her records with the planners. The planning staff responsible for ordering materials from Nike kept their own records based on a guess method of expected usage; very rarely did they check what materials actually remained in storage.

To remedy this, the Nike staff tried to keep track of materials needed for forthcoming contracts and to coordinate these needs with the supply room records to ensure that supplies were available. They also began teaching Chinese workers how to store the materials correctly to prevent damage.

Production Flexibility.   Flexibility—a primary characteristic of South Korea and Taiwan—allowed Nike to expand production quickly. These factories were able to develop shoe models quickly from written specifications. Chang remarked on the contrasting situation in China: "Decisions in China are cast in concrete. You can't tell them, 'Stop making that shoe next month and start making this one.' Forget it! It's another round of meetings."

To increase flexibility, Nike hoped the Chinese would

- build sample rooms enabling them to produce new models from patterns and specifications. This would require some new advanced equipment, about 19 more people, and an investment equal to about 2% of sales. The Chinese were unwilling to make such an investment.
- produce, rather than import, lasts, molds, dies, and small tools necessary for the construction of each model. The initial investment could cost over $10 million, but individual factories had the authority to invest only $100,000. The Chinese were thus unwilling to accept small orders for different styles requiring different equipment. It was safer and easier for Chinese managers to import materials than to try to develop or purchase local materials. Local suppliers tended to charge high prices

because they did not want to incur losses; under the government's new policies, factories incurring losses risked being closed.

- become more cooperative. Chinese factory managers, however, felt that as yet there was no real commitment from Nike. Furthermore, Nike's efforts to negotiate further price and quantity reductions had antagonized the managers.

Worker and Manager Motivation.   Walsh described the basic, unexpected motivational problems encountered:

> We set out more or less to emulate the South Korean and Taiwan factories. We wanted to get Chinese factories up to where they could compete from development, pricing, and quality standpoints. We didn't realize the problems we would run into from the system. It's a planned economy: There are quotas in all sorts of different areas; pricing stipulations are established in Beijing. But most of all, there's the "iron rice bowl" concept that has long been a thorn in the side of the economy. It is hard to break. The factories are often poorly run because there is just no background in managing factory facilities.
>
> By dangling big numbers we thought it would entice these people. It did not. We'd approach factories in midday and our production would be at a total standstill, and they still had quotas to reach for that particular month. There was no motivation or incentive to increase the production.
>
> A big problem is adhering to schedules. We've brought in graphics outlining schedules, and they don't grasp this. Partially the problem is related to the lack of incentives. There is no difference in pay if they produce more shoes sooner. There is also a lack of talent on production scheduling. The talented business people are in the trading companies.
>
> What we did was to institute our own incentive program. We lined up criteria based on productivity, quality, and delivery. We virtually put money on the table. If they could satisfy our demands, we would reward them with cash bonuses given to the factories. This concept was presented to Vice Premier Huan Lee in November 1981, and he was receptive to the idea. We instituted it in our first year there with mixed results. We saw a great leap forward for about 60 days. After that it was back to the same lack of motivation.

Transportation.   In South Korea, where Nike had dockside factories, the products could be loaded directly into containers and shipped to world markets. In contrast, the PRC shoes had to be trucked to the nearest harbor and shipped to Kobe, Japan, where they were transferred into container vessels. A Japanese trading company, Nissho-Iwai (Nike's primary supplier of working capital), handled all the company's exporting logistics from the Far East.

In Guangzhou, the two factories were close to each other and to the port. They had enough space for containerized trucks to drive in and out. In Fuzhou, however, the factory was on the main street; containerized trucks could not approach the entrance. The factory in Fujian, halfway between Fuzhou and Xiamen on a well-maintained road, also had no access for container vehicles. The dock was outmoded and could not be used on rainy days, causing many loading delays.

Pricing.   Tensions in the initial pricing negotiations continued to exist. The Chinese partners were used to the stable prices of a central planning system. Because of unexpectedly high overhead, the initial price had to be reduced by 25% after two years. Although Nike had to pay extra dollars because of inefficiencies and scarcities in the Chinese system, the Chinese felt that the costs for foreign firms to do business in China were still lower than in South Korea or Taiwan because of lower food and transportation costs. They also disagreed about which side should benefit from the dollar's relative strength. The Chinese felt Nike should first reduce its own costs before asking them to lower theirs. For example, they felt that Nike could reduce costs if Nike employees were to live and eat right at the factories. Managers of one factory were dissatisfied because a price agreement reached with Nike's Shanghai representatives was later rescinded by Nike headquarters.

None of the Chinese participants in price negotiations—staff from the foreign trade bureau, factory directors, and local production bureau leaders—had authority to make price decisions. Everything had to be relayed to authorities in Beijing. Thus, compared with Korea or Taiwan, negotiations were slow. The lack of a cost accounting system and of market prices also made estimating actual costs very difficult. The amount of the government subsidy became a key factor in the costing.

Knight commented on the pricing process: "China has such a cumbersome bureaucracy. In our price negotiations, four ministries were involved. Three said yes, but the fourth wouldn't. Therefore, the agreement was delayed 90 days. In a market that's changing, you can't do this." A further complicating fact in Nike's eyes was that the Chinese did not consider variations in the exchange rate in the price negotiations.

Plant Location. By 1983 Nike concluded that its original plant locations were not optimal. Remarked Walsh: "We were more or less forced to go to Tianjin and Shanghai. We were new to China and did not know which areas would give us the best opportunity and the greatest degree of cooperation. We followed the government's recommendations."

In Shanghai and Tianjin, a major problem was the length of negotiation periods. In Shanghai there was little support from the municipal authorities, who were more interested in larger industrial projects. In Tianjin there was support from the mayor, but product quality was low.

Nike terminated its supply arrangement in 1983 with the Shanghai factory and was attempting the same for Tianjin. In Shanghai, Nike had to make a small compensation payment to close. In Tianjin, officials were quite disgruntled about the original five-year agreement's early termination and, in May 1984, sent a strong letter of protest to Nike. In it, they questioned Nike's sincerity and commitment to China in a slowing world market, charging that Nike had made many unreasonable requests (such as expecting the Chinese to import materials that were unavailable locally, or to develop several new shoe models too quickly). The letter also accused Nike of reneging on its own agreements (such as wanting sudden reductions on "fixed" prices, or reducing orders because of high inventory). The letter concluded that Nike would be responsible for losses incurred if production terminated, and to please reconsider its unfair "way of business." (See *Appendix B.*) Nike risked not being able to recover all its equipment investment.

In the same period, Nike opened two new factories in the south. The Guangzhou and Fujian factories were located in Special Economic Zones, where there was less red tape and more decentralized authority for decision making.

Expatriate Staffing. In September 1981 Nike opened its residential headquarters in Shanghai with a staff of six, all in their twenties and thirties, and all with previous experience in Nike's other Asian operations. The Beijing office was closed in December 1983 because it was deemed no longer necessary and because housing was scarce. Walsh commented on the expatriates:

It's always been Nike's production philosophy to assign expatriates to foreign communities for control purposes. I think that has a great deal to do with our success in the Far East. The expatriate community for Nike in Asia is 80 to 90 people. In Shanghai we represent 20% of the American community. Most of the people are from the State Department, but two other US joint ventures are there. The Americans are a very small but close-knit community.

Shanghai was considered the best place in China for foreigners to live. It was China's commercial center; transportation and communications facilities were relatively more advanced than elsewhere in China. But there were few Western movies; TV consisted almost entirely of programs in Chinese and operated only from 5 P.M. to 10 P.M. It was rumored that the Shanghai city government wanted Nike to remove its office from the city because it had closed the factory. Meanwhile, the Guangzhou and Fuzhou city governments were trying to persuade Nike to move their offices south, but Nike employees resisted because of inferior living conditions and weather.

The Nike staff flew to the factories in the south and stayed for three or four days before returning. More than half the staff brought their families to China. They lived in Western-style apartments built in the 1940s. Nike paid their living expenses and a 30% salary supplement for working abroad. The staff also received a week's vacation every two months, when they could go anywhere with their families—fully paid for by Nike. The staff usually rotated every two years.

Government Relations. From the beginning, Nike tried to establish a positive relationship with the Chinese government through contributions to the country's sports activities (e.g., holding sports clinics and equipping the national 1984 Olympic team). Nike also hosted various Chinese officials visiting the United States.

China received Nike with great hospitality. During banquets, the Nike staff met many high-level Chinese leaders, who listened carefully to its problems. However, this interchange resolved nothing. The Chinese leaders seemed more intent on persuading Nike to sign joint-venture agreements.

Nike often did not know with whom it should talk to solve its problems. The combination of decision makers for different problems was always changing, and it was not always apparent who was in charge of what. Sometimes officials failed to show up for appointments. The local Nike staff often felt it was necessary for high-level managers from Nike headquarters to come to China to get the attention of and gain access to China's higher-level officials. At a banquet given by a city mayor for the Nike staff, one factory manager remarked that he was very happy to see so many leaders for the first time.

Nike sent a report to First Vice Premier Wan Li, reviewing the company's progress and problems in the 1980-1983 period. An excerpt from Knight's letter of transmittal indicates Nike's approach to dealing with the government:

> In my country there is an old belief that in order for any relationship to grow and to develop there must be a mutually candid and beneficial relationship. In our co-equal partnership effort in China, I feel that I should, representing Nike, mention in candor, some of the problems we must face and resolve together if our long-term goals are to be met.

The problems, according to Knight, were

1. nonavailability of local materials (a detriment to both Nike's and China's economic goals);
2. inadequate shipping and transportation provisions (causing Nike's inability to meet delivery dates);
3. inconsistent high quality in China's manufactured goods; and
4. nonmotivation and noncommitment attitudes of Chinese workers (Nike's incentive programs had brought mixed results).

Many factory managers had negative feelings about the $7 million Nike contributed to support the Chinese national sports teams. They felt that such extravagant promotional (PR) expenses did not solve Nike's production problems and only increased Nike's overhead, and that the PR program attracted the attention of only the national leaders, thus fostering good relationships only at the top rather than at the local level. They felt that a Nike joint-venture agreement would be stronger evidence of Nike's commitment to China's modernization program—and at a fraction of the cost. They also noted that the Chinese Olympic team was criticized in the Hong Kong media for wearing Nike apparel rather than Chinese-made clothing.

Chang reflected on Nike's approach to relations with China:

> China historically has been exploited for so long by the West. I, as a Chinese, am perhaps more aware of the sensitivity of the Chinese to the past exploitation. So I want to do everything that we can to come across, for lack of a better term, as good guys. We don't want to be the rapers and plunderers of colonial days, because the Chinese are very, very sensitive to any possible re-emergence of that kind of attitude.[3]

On the political dimension he added:

> You talk about international diplomacy. We are really doing something with the Chinese, not just talking about it. We're pressing the flesh; we're down in the trenches. We're doing every bit as much as the politicians.[4]

FUTURE STRATEGIC CONSIDERATIONS

As Chang deliberated on possible recommendations for Nike's future course of action regarding China, he focused on six areas: (1) the situations of Nike's other suppliers, (2) recent changes in the business environment in China, (3) joint ventures, (4) new factory locations in China, (5) the domestic China market, and (6) Nike's competitors.

Other Suppliers

Chang compared Chinese factories with Nike's primary suppliers, using several criteria:

1. *Development and production start-up time.* The time from when the factory received the shoe model's technical package to the point of shoe production was four months in South Korea and eight months in China (see *Exhibit 2* for timelines).

2. *Quality.* The A-grade to B-grade ratio was 99:1 in South Korea, 98:2 in Taiwan, and 80:20 in China.

3. *Quantity.* Taiwan produced 1 million pairs a month, South Korea 2.25 million (with installed capacity sufficient to double output), and China 100,000 (with current capacity for 180,000).

4. *Raw materials sourcing.* The Taiwanese and South Koreans sourced 100% of their raw materials domestically; the Chinese imported 70%.

5. *Financing.* South Korea and Taiwan provided their own financing and had a straight trading arrangement with Nike; China required compensation trade.

6. *Transportation.* Shipping time from Taiwan and South Korea was 20-25 days; from Shanghai it was 35-40 days.

7. *Labor costs.* For the factories, labor costs as a percentage of total costs were about 30% in Korea, 20% in Taiwan, and 10% in China.

[3]"Nike Builds Firm Foothold in China," *Los Angeles Times,* February 16, 1982.
[4]Charles Humble, "China Connection," *Oregon Journal,* December 23, 1981.

8. *Landed costs.* The landed costs for a pair of shoes from South Korea were $7.86; from the PRC they were $9.87 (see *Table A*). Nike estimated it was losing $1.00 on each pair of Chinese-made shoes.

South Korean shoe manufacturers had been encountering rising labor costs. Between 1972 and 1979 the unit labor cost rose by more than 300% (see *Exhibit 3*), and was still rising in late 1984. In addition, the South Korean government in 1981 discontinued all its support, mostly financial, for the shoe industry. One Korean government official said, "We believe that our shoe industry is now fully developed to compete internationally. Our limited resources for support should be directed to higher-growth-potential industries such as heavy, chemical, and high-tech industries."[5]

EXHIBIT 2

Current Models Development Timelines

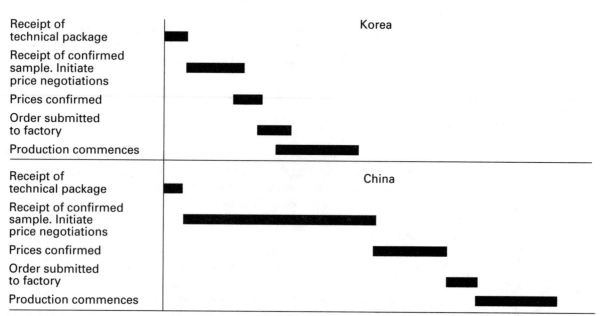

DEC 15 JAN 15 FEB 15 MAR 15 APR 15 MAY 15 JUNE 15 JULY 15 AUG 15

TABLE A

Landed Cost Comparison

	Korea	PRC
Price paid at factory	$6.36	$6.36
Interest	.37	.47
Freight	.23	.45
Duty	.54	.79[a]
Commission	.25	.25
Nike local office overhead	.11	1.55
Total	$7.86	$9.87
Retail price needed to maintain equal margins	$18.75	$23.50

a. Higher duty due to importation of rubber products.

[5]Direct interview by Research Assistant Seok Ki Kim in 1984.

EXHIBIT 3

Comparative Changes in Unit Labor Cost

	1972	1973	1974	1975[a]	1976	1977	1978	1979
Korea	65.4	71.1	85.5	100.0	126.7	149.0	173.2	196.9
Taiwan	65.2	70.5	100.9	100.0	95.3	94.8	90.1	94.3
Singapore	—	71.4	90.7	100.0	99.7	120.4	—	—
USA	74.6	76.7	84.9	100.0	100.7	107.3	115.7	123.2
Japan	59.8	62.0	80.4	100.0	99.4	104.0	102.0	99.1

Source: *Financial Times.*

a 1975=100 in national currency.

An executive from one of Korea's largest shoe-exporting firms (and a Nike supplier) had this to say about his country's rising labor costs:

> In the athletic shoe industry, labor cost must not exceed 24% of total cost to maintain international competitiveness. As of 1984, our proportion of labor costs is between 22% and 24%. This is about 30% higher than in Taiwan. To cope with this problem, we recently modified our production facilities; we reduced the capacity for cheap products [canvas/vinyl shoes] by 25%, and we increased capacity for more expensive products [nylon/leather shoes]. In simple and cheap products, we cannot compete with Taiwan and other countries with cheaper labor such as China, Sri Lanka, Thailand, and the Philippines. Moreover, in response to recent decreases in orders for canvas shoes, we are concentrating in the high-end products such as aerobic shoes. Whatever market segments we may concentrate on, however, I do not think that our international competitiveness with large-scale production can last more than five to ten years from now. We have to get out of this sunset industry successfully and as soon as possible.[6]

In 1983 Korea exported $928 million worth of footwear; in 1984, $1 billion worth. Taiwan exported about 50% more than Korea. About 70% of both countries' footwear exports went to the United States. As of late 1984, most Taiwanese footwear products cost $3 to $4; the Korean products cost $4 to $5.

Most Korean footwear firms were large—employing up to 17,000 people. This size gave advantages in dealing with large foreign buyers, rather than affording technical economies of scale. Almost all companies exported their footwear under foreign brand names.[7]

Chang remembered that "when we first went to China, Korea and Taiwan saw their meal leaving the table." He wondered now if it should be brought back, and if other newer suppliers should be expanded. The two Thai factories' combined output was up to 260,000 pair a month, with a capacity for 400,000. The A:B–grade ratio was 97:3. Delivery time from Bangkok was 30 days. Price negotiations took two weeks. Thailand had been able to reduce its raw material imports to 40% for canvas and nylon shoes; however, it would not be able to supply locally significant quantities of leather if these shoe types were to be manufactured there. Knight looked at Thailand positively but wondered if "it might turn into West Vietnam," given the political dynamics in Southeast Asia. India and Sri Lanka could also be reconsidered for future sourcing.

[6]Ibid.

[7]Yung Whee Rhee, Bruce Ross-Larson, Garry Pursell, *Korea's Competitive Edge: Managing the Entry into World Markets* (Baltimore: Johns Hopkins University Press, 1984).

China's Changing Business Environment

Deng Xiaoping, China's 80-year-old leader, continued to accelerate China's opening to the West. In December 1984 he proclaimed that "China is a good place to invest. China keeps its commitments." He asserted that the PRC would remain open to foreign investors for at least the next 70 years. A proclamation on October 20, 1984, stated that "factory workers will enjoy free-enterprise incentives—including the freedom to change jobs—and a wage scale keyed to the real difficulties of their jobs."[8] The *People's Daily* in Beijing also published an editorial stating that the country could not rely on Marx's and Lenin's doctrines to solve all present problems. This ideological shift was favorable to private and foreign investors, but many traditionalists within the Communist party were reportedly disturbed by it. In late 1983 they mobilized a campaign against "spiritual pollution" caused by the mounting Western presence.

Joint Ventures

The joint-venture form of foreign investment was increasingly favored by PRC authorities: about 20 involving $20 million had been mounted by 1981, and the number increased significantly by 1984. Under the 1979 law, a foreign investor's participation could not be less than 25%, technology contributed was to be "truly advanced and appropriate to China's needs," and exports were encouraged. However, joint-venture companies were allowed to sell their products in China. State subsidies were available to joint ventures, and the foreign partner could screen workers and require new employees to pass skill examinations. Presumably workers could be fired for violating work rules. But some existing joint ventures had met difficulties in exercising these management prerogatives. Salaries were about 20% higher than in local factories.

Such joint ventures, if undertaken by Nike, were estimated to require an investment of $500,000 per factory, which could reduce Nike's flexibility in later shifting production sites if necessary.

New Factory Location

Shenzhen was the most advanced of the Special Economic Zones (SEZs). By October 1984 it had signed 3,316 agreements and contracts with overseas firms, involving a total investment of 6 billion yuan (US $1=2.8 yuan). These SEZs were intended to attract foreign investment, particularly in light manufacturing industries catering to export markets. The Chinese government provided special facilities (infrastructure and services) and preferential tax treatment. Because Shenzhen was administered directly by the provincial authorities, the bureaucracy was simplified, and foreign trade and investment were granted broad latitude to protect investors' legitimate rights and privileges. Other special privileges included favorable consideration in land rent, choice of land sites, corporate income tax of 15% (half the normal rate), and import duties waived on production inputs. There were also favorable personal income tax laws for foreigners working in the SEZs. About 85 of the nearly 100 joint ventures in Shenzhen made profits, with an average rate of 15%. Considerable construction was under way to remedy Shenzhen's remaining infrastructure inadequacies with telephones, power, water, housing, and hotels.

Domestic Market

Visions of two billion feet still floated in Chang's mind. The numbers held inevitable market magnetism, but he was not optimistic about selling Nike shoes locally. The product was made for an affluent consumer, and the Chinese were more interested in Nike's exporting than in selling locally. But still. . . two billion feet.

---

[8]Hobart Rowen, "Deng's Private-Enterprise Initiative," *Washington Post,* December 16, 1984, p. L1.

Competitors

Finally, Chang wondered about the possible reactions of Nike's competitors:

> Puma, New Balance, Adidas, and Bata have visited China; none are sourcing from there yet. Dunlop has been buying canvas court shoes from the PRC, but we don't consider them to be a significant competitor. We are the point man for the industry. They are observing closely our experience and moves.

WHAT RECOMMENDATIONS?

The China project had brought Chang into Nike, and he had made a heavy personal and professional investment in it. Now well-established in the firm and in charge of the company's apparel division, he believed it was important to analyze the China situation objectively and make recommendations that would best further Nike's success. He remembered Knight's words: "Winning is ultimately defined by the scorecard—which is financial results, but in the long run. We've had success, but we have to keep looking forward."

APPENDIX A
Chronological Summary of Nike in China, 1980–1983

April 1980	Nike submits "A Business Proposal Between BRS, Inc., and the People's Republic of China," which outlines Nike's plans to trade with China.
July 1980	A Nike delegation including President Philip H. Knight visits the PRC for the first time for the purpose of entering into a long-term trade agreement with China.
Sept. 1980	Second Nike delegation, headed by Vice President Robert J. Strasser, negotiates and signs the first supply agreements between Nike and factories in Tianjin, Beijing, and Shanghai.
Nov. 1980	Nike delegations return for further discussions with Sports Shoe Factory #2 in Tianjin. Agreements call for a total of about 1.5 million pair of shoes in the first year of production. Nike also signs an agreement with China Sports Service to equip Chinese national men's and women's basketball teams with shoes and apparel. Plans are begun for registering offices in Beijing, Tianjin, and Shanghai, and for establishing long-term residence for Nike's quality control managers in China.
March 1981	Nike's vice president, David Chang, hosts Luo Xin, first secretary of the Chinese embassy in Washington, D.C., at Nike's research and development facilities in Exeter, New Hampshire, and Saco, Maine. Nike signs basketball contract with China Sports Service at head office of Nike in Beaverton, Oregon.
May 1981	Fuzhou factory delegation visits Nike's operations in Beaverton, Oregon.
July 1981	Nike signs supply agreement with Shanghai #4 factory to begin production.
Aug. 1981	Nike's resident teams selected for China under direction of Christopher Walsh, managing director, China operations. Nike sends three US basketball coaches to Shanghai to conduct a clinic and assist in training Chinese athletes. China sends representatives of China National Light Industrial Products Import and Export Corporation to US and to visit Nike.
Sept. 1981	Nike sends three U.S. marathoners to participate in First International Beijing Marathon (placed 7th, 16th, and 25th in a field of 75). Nike's China office established at 65 Yanan West Road, Shanghai. Nike signs supply agreement with Shanghai #5 Rubber Shoe Factory.
Oct. 1981	Nike's One-Line (nylon running shoes) production begins.
Nov. 1981	Nike's president, Philip Knight, heads delegation, including David Chang, vice president, and Richard Holbrooke, former U.S. assistant secretary of state and Nike special counsel, to Beijing and Shanghai to hold high-level discussions concerning Nike's long-term plans for China, and to

	commemorate first "Made in China" shoes. Delegation received by Vice Premier Wan Li at Great Hall of the People in Beijing. Nike signs agreement with Quanzhou Rubber Shoe Factory to begin manufacturing canvas court (tennis) shoes for export. Ribbon-cutting ceremony held in Tianjin by Knight for first production of Nike One-Line shoes.
Jan. 1982	Production schedules mutually agreed upon, calling for over 3,000,000 pairs of athletic shoes to be produced in China by end of 1983.
Feb. 1982	First workers' cash incentive plan begun in Tianjin. Other similar workers' programs are planned.
May 1982	Nike signs supply agreement w/Long March Rubber Shoe (Guangzhou) and Fuzhou #1 Shoe Factories.
June 1982	Nike signs track and field agreement with China Sports Service, wherein Nike agrees to endorse, equip, and help in training Chinese national men's and women's track and field teams.
July 1982	Nike hosts delegation of 10 Chinese coaches to attend clinics held at Washington State University.
Aug. 1982	Nike's coaches conduct a 10-day clinic in Qunming.
Sept. 1982	Nike sends 3 US marathoners to participate in the 2nd International Beijing Marathon (placed 6th, 10th, & 15th). Three US coaches sponsored by Nike conduct track and field clinics in Nanjing, Shanghai, & Beijing.
Nov. 1982	China's national track and field and basketball teams participate in the Asian Games in New Delhi and capture overall title in Nike apparel and shoes. Nike hosts special trip for Shanghai #4 factory personnel to inspect Nike's production facilities in the Philippines.
Dec. 1982	Nike hosts special trip for Tianjin #2 factory personnel to inspect Nike sources in Thailand.
Jan. 1983	First shoes manufactured in PRC arrive in US from Quanzhou factory; second shipment also arrives in US from Tianjin factory.
March 1983	Nike signs supply agreement with Nan Fang factory in Guangzhou.
June 1983	Vice President David Chang meets Zhang Wen Jin, Chinese ambassador to the US, at the Tenth Anniversary Banquet of the National Council for US/China Trade. Former President Richard Nixon is keynote speaker. Zhu Jian Hua, in Nike shoes, breaks the world high-jump record of 2.37 meters at China's fifth National Games at Beijing Workers' Stadium.
July 1983	Delegation from Fuzhou factory inspects Nike operations in Hong Kong. Ron Nelson, vice president-production for Nike, visits factory sources in China with senior executives in charge of all shoe production scheduling and sales forecasting.
Aug. 1983	Nike sponsors Nike China Summit for Foreign Trade Corporation meeting in Shanghai to discuss common problems and seek solutions. Meeting encompasses 24 individuals selected from Nike's source cities of Beijing, Tianjin, Fuzhou, Quanzhou, and Shanghai. High-jumper Zhu Jian Hua captures bronze medal in the World Track & Field Championship Games in Helsinki.
Sept. 1983	Nike chairman Knight visits new factory sources in Guangdong and Fujian provinces, attends 3rd Annual International Beijing Marathon, meets w/board of directors of National Council for US/China Trade in Beijing.
Nov. 1983	Guangzhou and Quanzhou factory personnel visit Nike's operations in Thailand and the Philippines.

中 国 轻 工 业 品
进 出 口 公 司　天 津 文 教 体 育 用 品 分 公 司
中 国 天 津 辽 宁 路 一 七 二 号

CHINA NATIONAL LIGHT INDUSTRIAL PRODUCTS IMP. & EXP. CORP.
TIANJIN STATIONERY & SPORTING GOODS BRANCH
NO. 172 LIAONING ROAD.

CABLE: "STASPORT"　　　　TIANJIN, CHINA　　　　TELEX: 22513 TJSSG CN

In reply please quote our Ref:

TIANJIN

May 10, 1984

Scott Thomas
Managing Director,
NIKE, INC.
Shanghai International Club,
65 Yanan West Road, RM. 304 SHANGHAI,
PEOPLE'S REPUBLIC OF CHINA

Dear Mr. Scott Thomas,

We have read your letter of May 2, 1984 and wish to reply as below: Tianjin and Nike have been cooperating for shoe production for three years. Although we are still behind our designated goal, we have been making progress all the time both in quality and quantity of the products. Now, let us take the last 90 days evaluation period—Jan. 1 to March 31, 1984 as a case in point. The goal was 1,200 pairs of shoes per day for quantity and over 90% of A Grade shoes for quality while the daily output of TJ2 was over 1,000 pairs and A grade shoes was around 90% by the end of March 1984. This means we have created the conditions for further cooperation.

On April 11, 1984 in Tianjin, you talked about the market changes and raised the subjects of price, new models, etc. We clearly expressed our willingness to consider your requests, meaning the prices would be lower and adoption faster for future new models. Our relative department already said we would set up specialized factories to make moulds and materials for large-scale production and quick adoption of new and varied models of NIKE shoes.

However, we must not be divorced from the present reality while considering things in future. In your letter, you definitely asked us to reduce the prices of the present models by 26% and specified the prices of different sizes of all the three models. You asked TJ2 to develop eight new models in September 1984, one new model per month from September to February and two per month after February 1985. Finally, you said that price and adoption of new models were the two prerequisites of our cooperation. If we accept them, our cooperation will continue. Otherwise, you will come to talk with us to cancel the supply agreement. May we ask, even if we accept your requirements on these two points, would you raise further points or put forward higher criteria two months later? We therefore cannot but feel doubtful about your sincerity in the cooperation.

We signed the five-year supply agreement in September 1980. In the spirit of that agreement, we signed the first sales contract for about 80,000 pairs of ONE LINE shoes for which you supplied some of the necessary materials unavailable locally in China. Later on, you said you would not supply the materials and asked us to do the import. That was a great change. But in consideration of our long-term business, we agreed to do so and imported part of the materials enough for the production of 300,000 pairs of shoes. After two years of cooperation, the factory is actually producing only two models—OCEANIA and OLLIE OCEANIA. Production for the third model—DYNO is not started yet. Now you ask the factory to develop eight new models in about four or five months (from May to September). Is this a realistic attitude towards continued cooperation with Tianjin? On more than one occasion, your people said:

(continued on next page)

China National Light Industrial Products
Import & Export Corporation
Tianjin Stationary & Sporting Goods Branch

NIKE is recession proof (not affected by recession) and that your business is expanding very fast while many others in this line collapse because of market changes. With this in mind, we were all very surprised when you said that your inventory of shoes was very high and that you had more shoes than you could sell at the recent FU ZHOU Conference held in March this year. During our talk in Tianjin on April 11, you again said the prices must be reduced since the market was not good. We said we were ready to cooperate relating to the prices of future new models and even to a certain extent for those of the present three models for which prices have been fixed. You should not refuse to let us have orders for the models already in production such as OCEANIA and OLLIE OCEANIA and DYNO of which prices were just confirmed in February. You must be responsible for the losses arising from the suspension of production. So far we have not received any fresh orders from you after P.O. #84-3-5-TJ while in your letter you asked to reduce all the prices for OCEANIA, OLLIE OCEANIA, and even DYNO. For more than one reason, TJ2 has suffered heavy losses owing to the long suspension and abnormal situation of production. For NIKE production, TJ2 has set up new buildings and purchased special equipments and are heavily in debts now. How can a sudden reduction of prices by 26% be possible? Do you really think this is a responsible request? The prices of DYNO were just confirmed in Feb. 1984 by your Shanghai Liaison Office, but you also asked to reduce them two months later on April 11. We expressed on the spot it was not a right way of business while you said it was the decision or instruction of your American Head Office. If your Shanghai Office did not represent your head office and prices confirmed or decision made by your Shanghai Office could be negated by your American Head Office, it would be very difficult for us to accomplish things.In your letter of May 2, 1984, you put forward two prerequisites for continued cooperation with Tianjin, i.e., reduce FOB prices by 26% and develop eight new models in September 1984. If we are not able to accept them, you will come to talk with us to cancel the supply agreement. Does it mean that you are ready to stop NIKE-TIANJIN cooperation?

Finally, we wish to advise that we should cherish our mutual relations already established and abide by the signed agreement. We should have further negotiations on prices, new models, etc. on the principles of mutual understanding and accommodations and in consideration of the market changes and actual situation of the factory so as to reach an agreement on main issues to let our cooperation continue. Cancellation of the supply agreement will be good to neither party, especially to NIKE's reputation. If you intend to terminate the agreement unilaterally by not giving fresh order to the factory while TJ2 has made preparations for the production, you will be held responsible for any loss of the factory arising from the suspension of production, etc.

It is hoped that you will carefully consider the above frank opinions and the five points mentioned by Mr. Li Guang Zeng of Tianjin Second Light Industry Bureau at our last meeting. Please come to Tianjin soon so that we may talk further in detail.

cc: Philip H. Knight of NIKE Beaverton head office, U.S.A.
     David Chang Ping Chong of NIKE Beaverton head office, U.S.A.

China National Light Industrial Products
Import & Export Corporation
Tianjin Stationery & Sporting Goods Branch
General Manager   LI YANJI

chapter 11

Political Risk Analysis

Today's headlines seem to provide a constant flow of tales of political instability. Not surprisingly, managers consistently rank political stability as a major factor in evaluating the business or investment climate in a given country. Despite the fact that managers overwhelmingly believe that "political risk" is a major factor to be considered, very few MNEs have internal assessment mechanisms or have sophisticated teams that can evaluate the usefulness of assessments provided to them by consultants. Consequently, managers often make decisions involving political risk simply on "gut feel."

Civil War Rages in Former Yugoslavia

Czechoslovakia Splits

Students Killed in China

Martial Law Declared in Chile

Another Coup Fails in Philippines

PREVALENT ANALYTICAL TECHNIQUES

There are as many techniques for analyzing political risk as there are firms offering this service. In general though, two major approaches exist—objective, or observational data, and expert-based techniques. The main objective of each is to assess the political stability or instability of a given country.

Observational Data Techniques

The "Political Stability Prospects" model developed by a company called the Futures Group is an example of techniques that utilize observational data in assessing political instability. This technique first constructs a historical index of political stability by assessing (a) destabilizing events and (b) the level of economic deprivation. Economic deprivation is defined as a gap between the economic expectations and the standard of living achieved by the citizens of a country. The two indices are combined, with the most recent data being weighted most heavily. The forecast of political stability is generated by extrapolating from this weighted observational data.

Techniques such as this enable us to gather objective data and generate forecasts for a large number of countries. Thus, comparisons of countries' political stability indices are possible and may be incorporated into the decision-making process. The major shortcoming is that the past is not always predictive of the future.

Expert-Based Techniques

Expert-based techniques are more widely used than observational data techniques. Steve Kobrin offers a categorization of expert-based systems that helps simplify this general category. He categorizes techniques by whether they are unstructured or structured and unsystematic or systematic.

Unstructured/unsystematic. These techniques are generally conceptual, intuitive, and implicit. For example, a large US MNE asked for a political assessment of Brazil. The analyst responsible reviewed available published information on Brazil and interviewed a large number of individuals including US State Department personnel in Washington and Brazil, other government officials, bankers, and academic specialists. The report predicted student protests, tensions between the Brazilian government and military, increased labor unrest, and increased economic nationalism over the following two years. The report also considered the implications for the firm. What the analysis examined, how topics were examined, or how these findings were related to predictions or implications were all left to the discretion of the analyst. This approach is sometimes referred to as the State Department approach.

Unstructured/systematic. An example of this type of approach is provided by a US MNE that prepares its own analysis of a country whenever a new investment is being considered. In this case, the analyst is guided by a set of topics to be investigated (recent political stability, foreign investment, foreign exchange, taxes, domestic economic conditions, and the like). Although the "what" is specified, how the analyst gathers and evaluates it or ties the analysis to predictions and implications is not specified. This type of approach is sometimes referred to as a Listed Issues approach.

Structured/unsystematic. The Business Environmental Risk Index (BERI) represents techniques that are structured but not systematic. The BERI reports on several countries on a quarterly basis. Experts are selected from a variety of institutions including banks, universities, and governments. Each expert rates between 5 and 10 countries on a scale of 0 to 4. The description of each of the five ratings (0-4) is detailed and specific. Also, each expert is given his or her previous rating of a particular country as well as those of all the other experts. This technique provides an evaluation of a set of countries on a regular basis utilizing a fairly stable set of experts, and the description of each of the five ratings is detailed; however, what factors the experts incorporate into their evaluations is not specified. Thus, two experts might each rate Chile as a 2+ on the rating scale but have utilized different factors in arriving at the composite rating. This type of approach is sometimes referred to as an Expert Panel approach.

Structured/systematic.   The World Political Risk Forecast (WPRF) is an example of a technique that is structured and systematic. A consistent panel of experts is asked to assess a specified set of issues (for example, repatriation restrictions, price control, taxation, and so forth) from the perspective of a specified set of "actors" or groups within a country (labor, military, etc.). Each expert scores each actor on each issue (for it, neutral, against it). Then the experts rate each group's ability to influence each issue and the importance of each issue to each group. These scores are factored into a model that assumes that, all else being equal, a group that has a position on an issue, cares about the issue, and can influence the issue has considerable power to affect the policy-making process and future outcomes relevant to that issue. In addition, each expert also rates his or her confidence in each estimate. Thus, probabilities of certain events and policy outcomes are estimated, as well as the confidence interval associated with each prediction. This technique specifies what is evaluated and how it is evaluated, and has an explicit model of relating input factors to outcome predictions.

Summary of Techniques

Several problems are encountered when techniques that assess political stability are unstructured and unsystematic because it is unclear and difficult for the user of the analysis to determine:

- why certain issues are included in the analysis and others are excluded,
- how factors are assessed,
- whether all factors are (or should) be weighted the same, and
- whether the logic relating indices and outcomes is valid.

Techniques that are structured and systematic are not without their tradeoffs as well. For example, they tend to be broad-based and more difficult to relate to a specific firm's particular investment decision. Also, most of these techniques do not make their assumptions about the dynamics of political stability explicit since often they do not specify cause and effect relationships among various political events. It is critical to examine in more detail four particular assumptions that drive structured and systematic models: (1) that past political events predict future events, (2) that economic deprivation predicts political instability, (3) that power affects political outcomes, and (4) that change happens most often during periods of transition.

DYNAMICS OF POLITICAL INSTABILITY

The assumption that past political instability predicts future instability underlies most political stability assessment techniques. For example, between 1985 and 1990, past political instability provided a relatively good prediction of future politically destabilizing events in the Philippines. In contrast, past political events provided a relatively poor prediction of the so-called "velvet revolution" in Czechoslovakia.

When one examines a number of countries cross-sectionally, or a single country over time, a somewhat unusual pattern of political instability emerges. On a continuum from low levels of economic development to high levels of economic development, the pattern of political instability resembles an inverted "U," with political instability peaking in the middle stages of economic development (see Figure 11.1).

This creates, on average, a contradictory relationship between past and future political instability. During the early stages of economic development, past political instability has a slight *positive* relationship with future instability. The greater the instability in the past, the *greater* the instability in the future. However, this relationship holds up only to a certain point. Then, the relationship inverts. That is, past political instability is *negatively* related to future instability. This suggests that past predicts future, but not in a consistent manner. Why might this be so, and what are mitigating factors? It turns out that the major dynamic behind this pattern and the major mitigating factor are both related to the three remaining assumptions.

The second assumption—that political instability is related to economic deprivation—is, in general, supported by existing data and seems to be a major dynamic explaining the inverted "U" pattern of the relationship between these two variables. In the early stages of economic development, the expectations of a country's citizens are focused primarily on survival; economic expectations are low. Also, on average, these basic economic expectations are realized. However, as a country moves toward greater economic development, its citizens' economic expectations rise—often rather quickly and dramatically. As economic conditions and standards of living conditions improve, people increasingly build expectations of even better conditions. As conditions improve, technology such as TV and radio provide people with information about even better standards of living that could be achieved in that country or are being enjoyed in other countries. Generally, however, economic expectations rise more rapidly than actual economic conditions. Consequently, the *gap*—or relative economic deprivation—increases as one moves from low levels of economic development to the middle stages of development. As the gap widens, political instability increases. Interestingly, as one moves toward the high end of economic development, the gap begins to narrow again. Expectations continue to rise but at a slower pace. After all, the argument goes, once you have a house, two cars, an automatic garage-door opener, a VCR, 2 color TVs, a microwave, a dishwasher, an electric can opener, a cordless telephone, and a home computer, how dissatisfied can you be?

The major factor that can mitigate this relationship—involving the third assumption—is the government's administrative power. On the positive side, if the government (through its strategy and policies) is capable of raising the standard of living in line

Figure 11.1   Inverted U-Curve and Political Instability

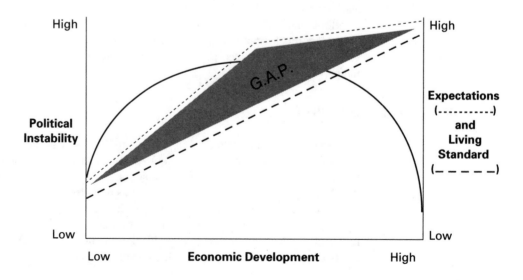

with expectations of its citizens, then the gap remains small and consistent. As a result, the pattern of political instability might look more like a flat line than an inverted "U." In contrast, if the government is not capable of raising the standard of living in line with expectations, then the gap becomes relatively larger than average. As a result, the pattern of political instability might look more like an inverted "J" than an inverted "U." However, even if the government is not capable of raising the standard of living in line with expectations, if they are capable of controlling (by force, disinformation, and so forth) expressions of dissatisfaction, then despite the greater than average economic deprivation or gap, the pattern of political instability might still look like a flattened inverted "U."

The final dynamic of political instability is what we can call the "rule of change": the apparently tautological observation that change is most likely to happen during periods of change. That is, political instability is most common during periods of transition. Transitions tend to "unfreeze" the past ideas and ways of doing things. This notion of "unfreezing" is part of most models of individual as well as organizational change. Transitions in leadership, demographics, economy, and the like can all serve to unfreeze the current situation and thus make it more likely and easier for change in general to take place. Basically, the greater the magnitude of the transition, the greater the array of potential changes that might come into effect, and the more difficult it is to predict which changes will actually take place.

Summary of Dynamics of Political Instability

In summary, there are four key points to keep in mind. First, past political instability may predict future instability, but in an inconsistent manner. The inverted "U" pattern of political instability means that there is a positive relationship between past instability and future instability during the early stages of economic development, an inconsistent relationship during the middle stages, and a negative relationship during the advanced stages of economic development. Second, this pattern seems to be primarily a function of the gap between economic expectations and realizations, which is often largest during the middle stages of economic development. Third, the ability of the government to keep the standard of living close to its citizens' expectations and to control expressions of dissatisfaction with their state of economic deprivation can mitigate the actual pattern of political instability. Finally, more change and greater degrees of change are likely to happen during periods of transition.

POLITICAL INSTABILITY AND POLITICAL RISK

Up to this point our focus has been on gaining a better understanding of the dynamics of political instability and the various assessment techniques. The implicit assumption has been that political instability in a country equals political risk for a company. Although they are related, *political instability is not political risk*.

Political risk is a function of (1) the probability that a given political event will affect a given firm, and (2) the magnitude of the event's impact. Political instability is the probability that an irregular political event will occur. Certainly, the magnitude and discontinuous nature of political events can affect the risk associated with a firm's expected returns. Castro's takeover of Cuba or Hussein's invasion of Kuwait had negative effects on most foreign firms operating in those countries at the time. However, Gulf Oil Company has been profitable in conflict-torn Angola, and most of the foreign toy manufactures in China were unaffected by the student riots and killings in 1989. Not only can MNEs be unaffected by political instability, but they may also benefit. For example, the overthrow of the Peronist regime in Argentina, the demise of Sukarno in Indonesia, and the ousting of the Communists in Hungary, all had positive effects for most MNEs in those countries.

Nature of Political Instability

The examples cited point to an important factor in the assessment of political risk—the nature of the political instability. Evidence suggests that one main issue that is important to examine in this regard is the controllability of the politically destabilizing event. Some politically destabilizing events are inherently more difficult to control than others. For example, a demonstration by students in one city is easier to control than a plan to assassinate the head of state. Two dimensions seem to be the critical components of controllability.

The first dimension is the extent to which an event is overt or covert. Overt events are easier to see in their development and their execution. For example, most demonstrations are designed to gain publicity and, as a consequence, are overt in their planning and implementation. Consequently, countermeasures are easier to plan for and implement. In contrast, assassination or coup attempts are covert, especially in their planning. The implementation of the plan, while often overt, is usually very short. Consequently, it is difficult to form specific contingency or countermeasure plans in advance of covert politically destabilizing events.

The second dimension is the extent to which the event is localized or generalized. A localized event is one in which relative few people are involved and is confined to few places. A generalized event involves many people in a large number of locations. The reasons why localized events are usually easier to control compared to generalized events are obvious—less required resources, easier planning, and so forth.

Control of Instability

There are two other factors that are important to consider—(1) the government's *ability* to control events and (2) its *willingness* to exercise the control. Let us take the example of the overt, localized demonstrations by Chinese students in 1989. Even though a large number of students (and other citizens) participated in the demonstrations, they were largely confined to one area of Beijing. The organizers did not try to keep the demonstrations secret before they occurred, and indeed did all they could to publicize them while they were taking place. In principle, this destabilizing event was more, rather than less, controllable. Why? The government's ability to control the demonstration through a large number of military and police officers and their resources was more than sufficient for the situation. Additionally, their control of internal media further facilitated their ability to keep the demonstrations localized. However, equally important was the government's *willingness* to use the capabilities they had.

Relevance to the Firm

As defined earlier, political risk is the probability that a given political event will affect a given firm. Consequently, the *relevance of the event to a specific firm must also be evaluated.* Not all events affect all industries or firms in the same way. Referring to our example of the student demonstrations in China, it was generally assumed that these politically destabilizing events and the Chinese government's reaction would have a negative impact on foreign firms operating in China. A large number of firms listed on the stock exchange in Hong Kong had subsidiary or joint-venture operations in China, especially southern China. In particular, textile and toy manufacturing firms had extensive operations in China to take advantage of the relative low wages. Most investors thought that the negative impact of the events in Beijing would be severe, the Hong Kong stock market index plunged, and trading was suspended for several days. However, within two weeks after trading resumed, toy and textile stocks recovered most of their losses. In fact, several executives in Hong Kong who determined quickly that production was likely to be largely unaffected by the events in Beijing bought heavily into textile and toy stocks and made significant profits as the stocks rebounded. The point is *not* that it is possible to profit from such unfortunate events, but rather that not all politically destabilizing events have direct economic relevance to a particular firm or industry.

THE POLITICAL RISK ANALYSIS PROCEDURE

We now outline in general terms a procedure for analyzing political risk and avoiding the common error of over- or underestimating such risks at the firm level. The goal of this procedure is to help firms make informed decisions based on the ratio of the return to risk so that MNEs can enter or stay in a country when the ratio is favorable and avoid or leave a country when the ratio *for them* is poor. This procedure involves three major steps.

Step 1: Assessing Issues of Relevance to the Firm

Clearly the relevant issues and the magnitude of their importance will vary by firm even within a given country. For one firm the repatriation of profits (and therefore policies and changes that affect that issue) could be the most important. For another firm in the same country, repatriation of profits may be less of a concern, but product quality (and therefore policies and changes that affect labor, material, or technology) may be of the highest concern. Clearly, there are numerous issues that can affect and are of concern to any MNE. However, an organizing framework for analyzing relevant issues in the context of political risk assessment involves three general constructs.

Ownership-control. When considering the startup or maintenance of operations in another country, the first general area of consideration is ownership and control. All firms must decide in general, or on a case-by-case basis, the form of ownership they desire and the control they want to achieve. These two dimensions often go together, with the form of ownership largely determining the degree and form of control. However, the restrictions, regulations, and associated political risk with respect to ownership varies from country to country.

Inputs. The next general category of relevant issues is inputs. The three basic inputs for all firms are material, capital, and people. The availability, cost, and quality of these three basic inputs also vary from country to country as do the policies and political events that affect them. Additionally, the relative importance of each of the three basic inputs, as well as the desired characteristics of each, varies by industry and by firm. For example, the strategy of one firm may dictate that the cost of material, capital, and people is the most important, while the strategy of another firm may demand that the quality of all three is most critical.

Outputs. All firms have two basic outputs—products/services and profits/losses. Generally, the latter follows from the former. We separate them because the products or services generated by one organizational unit in one country in an MNE can be transferred to another unit in another country where the "real profits" or losses are gained. Thus, the outcome of interest could be just products, just profits, or both for any given organizational unit in a specific country. Firms as well as countries differ in their objectives and desires concerning their products/services and their profits. Consequently, policies concerning the repatriation of profits, restrictions on transfer pricing, regulations of exports, and so forth and their potential change are major determinants of political risk to firms.

Step 2: Assessing Potential Political Events

The general ideas presented earlier concerning patterns of political instability, the role of economic deprivation, the nature of distabilizing events, and government's ability and willingness to control events are all important to incorporate into Step 2. Remember that, in general, political instability is more likely during greater periods of economic deprivation. However, the more the event is controllable (for example, demonstrations vs. coups) and the more government is able and willing to exercise control, the lower the probability that the event will have a direct impact on foreign MNEs.

It is important not only to estimate the probability of a single political event occurring or the confidence with which that prediction is made, but also to model related events. For example, suppose it was highly likely that Russian President Yeltsin was going to be replaced by a new president. Would this have any effect on labor unrest, policies on the repatriation of profits, regulations of exports, and other related issues? The purpose of modeling these relationships is not necessarily to form some formal index of aggregate risk but to make explicit the assumptions and cognitive theories that operate in the analysts' or decision makers' minds. Making them explicit is the only way of assessing their validity before comparing the prediction with the actual outcome.

In addition, modeling can facilitate scenario development, where instead of just estimating the separate probabilities of single events, estimates of the likelihood of *a related series of events* can be achieved. Scenarios are more useful than single-factor forecasts because typically events do not happen in isolation; usually there are both related causes and consequences.

In Step 2 it is also important to keep in mind the government's ability to enforce policy changes. For example, in Indonesia, significant import restrictions were placed on dinnerware. However, the government was not effective in enforcing these restrictions. Thus, for companies such as Corning that would have benefited from a restriction of imports (they had manufacturing facilities in Indonesia), the change in policy did not produce the expected positive impact. For companies that smuggled their products into Indonesia (and therefore cannot be named), the expected negative impact also did not materialize.

Step 3: Assessing Probable Impacts and Responses

Step 3 is really where "political risk" is assessed. Because political instability in a country does not equal political risk for a firm, the same scenario of politically destabilizing events could have very different associated risks for different firms in the same industry or for firms in different industries. For example, after a radical change in government officials, the fact that computer firms are left alone by the government may not reduce the probability that oil-related firms will have their assets expropriated. Or conversely, the fact that transportation firms are likely to be nationalized may have no impact on textile manufacturers in a given country. The fact that firms can be differentially affected by political events because of their unique mix of inputs, outputs, and goals reinforces the usefulness of constructing political scenarios rather than single-item forecasts because scenarios facilitate an MNE's ability to assess separate and related relationships between political factors and facets of the firm.

Finally, there is one additional component to Step 3. Even though the major purpose of Step 3 is to assess the impact of political events, firms can obviously influence and respond to political events. How firms can influence the political events in a foreign country is beyond the scope of this chapter; however, it is important to make a few comments about a firm's response to political risk. Just as the magnitude of political risk varies by firm and by the nature of political events, so too does a firm's response. For example, two firms in the same country in the same industry may be affected in the same way by a particular set of political events, but their abilities to respond to the events may differ, implying that the ultimate impact of risk is different.

This three-step process of political risk analysis is summarized:

Step 1
> Determine critical economic/business issues relevant to the firm.
> Assess the relative importance of these issues.

Step 2
> Determine the relevant political events.
> Determine their probability of occurring.
> Determine the cause and effect relationships.
> Determine the government's ability and willingness to respond

Step 3
> Determine the initial impact of probable scenarios.
> Determine possible responses to initial impacts.
> Determine initial and ultimate political risk.

CONCLUSION AND SUMMARY

First, accurately assessing political risk is important because mistaken assessments can result in two types of costs. MNEs that underestimate the political risks of a country may decide to commit resources to that country and then may suffer direct costs arising from the underestimated risks. MNEs that overestimate the political risks of a country may decide not to commit resources to that country and then may miss out on potential benefits from operations in the country. In either case, the direct costs or lost opportunities can be substantial. Second, political risk and political instability are not the same. A small amount of political instability can have a devastating impact on one MNE, whereas high levels of political instability can have little impact on another MNE. Third, if political risk analysis is undertaken (or purchased) by a firm, to the extent possible it should be structured and systematic. The analysis should consider relevant issues for the particular MNE, the probability of relevant political events happening, the impact of those events, and potential responses by the firm. Only then can MNEs effectively grapple with political risk in a world that is constantly presenting new global threats and opportunities.

SELECTED BIBLIOGRAPHY

BUNN, D.W., and MUSTAFAOGLU. "Forecasting Political Risk." *Management Science* 24 (1978): 1557-1567.

FITZPATRICK, M. "The Definition and Assessment of Political Risk in International Business: A Review of the Literature." *Academy of Management Review* 8 (1983): 249-254.

FRIEDMANN, R., and J. KIM. "Political Risk and International Marketing." *Columbia Journal of World Business* (Winter 1988): 63-74.

HANER, F. T. "Rating Investment Risks Abroad." *Business Horizons* 22 (April 1979): 18-23.

KOBRIN, S. J. "When Does Political Instability Result in Increased Investment Risk?" *Columbia Journal of World Business* (Spring 1978): 113-122.

KOBRIN, S. J. "Political Assessment by International Firms: Models or Methodologies?" *Journal of Policy Modeling* 3(2) (1980): 251-270.

ROBOCK, S. "Political risk: Identification and Assessment." *Columbia Journal of World Business* 6 (July/August 1971): 6-20.

RUMMEL, R. J., and D. A. HEENAN. "How Multinationals Analyze Political Risk." *Harvard Business Review* 56 (Jan/Feb 1978): 67-76.

SIMON, J. D. "Political Risk Assessment: Past Trends and Future Prospects." *Columbia Journal of World Business* (Fall 1982): 62-71.

SIMON, J. D. "A Theoretical Perspective on Political Risk." *Journal of International Business Studies* 15(3) (1984): 123-143.

case 14

Gulfstream and Sukhoi:
The Supersonic Business Jet*

The *New York Times* headlines from the past two weeks were grim:

> K.G.B.–Military Rulers Tighten Grip; Gorbachev Absent, Yeltsin Defiant;
> West Voices Anger and Warns on Aid
>
> Gorbachev Back as Coup Fails, but Yeltsin Gains New Power
>
> Gorbachev Says Coup Will Hasten Reform
>
> Yeltsin Is Routing Communist Party from Key Roles Throughout Russia;
> Forces Vast Shake-Up by Gorbachev
>
> Soviet Congress Yields Rule to Republics to Avoid Political and Economic
> Collapse

Allen Paulson knew that the recent events in the Soviet Union (if it could be called that any-more) would have far-reaching effects, many of which he could not, as yet, anticipate.

It was just over two years since Paulson, Chairman and CEO of Gulfstream Aero-space Corporation, had announced an agreement between Gulfstream and Advanced Sukhoi Technologies of the Russian Republics to explore the possibilities for a supersonic business jet (SSBJ) called the S21-G (named after Sukhoi, the twenty-first century, and Gulfstream) that could fly at twice the speed of sound. Sukhoi, he said, "appears to be years ahead of the rest of the world in the design and development of supersonic aircraft which can be used for business flying." While Gulfstream and many other firms in the aerospace

*This case, along with its companion reading "Note on the Corporate Jet Market and Supersonic Transportation," was developed by Associate Professor Anant K. Sundaram, with assistance from Michelle Sparrow, David Weld, and Professor Stewart Black, as a basis for class discussion. We are grateful to Alvin F. Balaban of Gulfstream Aerospace and Edward Kolcum of Aviation Week & Space Technology for their input. Given the relevant time period, the case refers to the geographical area that is now know as the Commonwealth of Independent States as the "Soviet Union." Support was provided by the Citi-Tuck Global Research Program. © 1991. Revised 1993.

industry long aspired to be the first to introduce twenty-first century supersonic air travel to the business jet market, industry watchers expected that it would take until the year 2005 to do so. But, "the general designer of Sukhoi, Mr. Mikhail Siminov, suggested a much shorter development program. He told us that they could have a supersonic business jet in flight in a few years."

The technological advantage of almost a decade could result in considerable entry barriers in an industry characterized by huge R&D expenditures, long lead times in product development, and steep learning curves. On June 15, 1989, at the Paris Air Show, Paulson and Siminov had signed a Memorandum of Understanding (MOU), to work together on the S21-G project.

GULFSTREAM AEROSPACE CORPORATION

In 1978, Paulson acquired Grumman's corporate aircraft operation, Gulfstream, for $52 million. At that time, Gulfstream was largely an assembly operation. Paulson took the company public in 1983. In 1985, Gulfstream was purchased by Chrysler Corporation for $637 million as part of its diversification effort. After five years as a Chrysler subsidiary, the parent company reversed its earlier decision and divested Gulfstream in an attempt to raise cash and concentrate on its car-making efforts. In March 1990, Paulson, who had been with Gulfstream through the entire Chrysler ownership period, reacquired Gulfstream in conjunction with an equity partner, Forstmann Little, for $825 million.

Over the years, Gulfstream evolved from an assembly operation to a full-fledged producer of corporate jets, designing, manufacturing, and marketing its own products. Also, the company instituted modification programs for current and older aircraft, and began to offer customer support programs for their fleet of business and government operated jet and project planes.

The company's headquarters and principal manufacturing facilities are located at the Savannah International Airport. Additionally, a plant in Long Beach, CA, provides service and support for Gulfstream and other jets.

Gulfstream built its reputation with the G-I, G-II, G-IIB and G-III business jets. Between 1966 and the present, over 650 of these models were sold (*Exhibit 1*). The Gulfstream IV (G-IV) was certified by the FAA in 1987, and is now considered to be the most technologically advanced business aircraft in the world. It is equipped with automated flight operations and voice satellite communications, and is 75% manufactured by Gulfstream in-house.

Selling for $24 million, the G-IV is the world's most expensive business jet; it is also one of the most expensive to operate at about $1600–2000 per hour. The jet has an average cruising speed of 550–600 miles per hour and a range of 4800 nautical miles. With Paulson as captain, the G-IV set around-the-world speed records in both directions in 1987 and 1988. After the first announcement of the jet in 1986, an order backlog built up. This backlog began to be filled in 1988 and 1989 with the delivery of 49 and 40 jets respectively. Thirty-two G-IVs were delivered in 1990, bringing the total to over 150 G-IVs produced and sold by the end of that year (*Exhibit 1*). The company expects to deliver 30 G-IVs in 1991. Backlog in the third quarter of '91 stood at 12 aircraft. Considered by customers to be the premier business jet, the G-IV is laden with amenities such as wet bars and showers. One review called the G-IV "the "Rolls-Royce of corporate jets. . . sleek, fast and posh. . ."[1]

Due to their larger size, Gulfstream jets do not directly compete with all manufacturers of small business aircraft, such as Learjet, Inc., and Beechcraft. Rather, their main competitors are: Dassault (Falcon 900), Canadair (Challenger 601), and British Aerospace (BAe125-800) (see *Exhibits 1 and 2*). Paulson was known to relish the competitive

---

[1]Robert L. Parrish, "Gulfstream G-IV," *Aviation Week & Space Technology,* August 1989, p. 50.

challenge; in an interview with *Interavia Aerospace,* he remarked, "I love to see the other guys selling aircraft because they become stepping stones for people [like us] to move up to something bigger and longer range in the future." However, most of Gulfstream's leading competitors had new products on the anvil for introduction over the next few years (*Exhibit 3*).

In the world of all business jets, 24.8% of those operating in September 1990 were manufactured by Cessna Aircraft, 20.7% by Learjet, 13.0% by Dassault Falcon, 9.6% by British Aerospace, 8.3% by Gulfstream and 23.7% by other manufacturers.[2] Of Gulfstream's fleet of approximately 800 planes, 130 are operated by 29 world governments, including 27 flown by US armed forces. Gulfstream "Special Requirements Aircraft" are offered for specific missions required by governments and military organizations.

Most of the success of Gulfstream is attributed to Paulson, who began his career as a mechanic for TWA in 1941. After serving in the US Army Air Corps, Paulson returned to TWA and was promoted to flight engineer. He later started a company selling parts for airline engines, and then operated a company which converted unused passenger airplanes into cargo aircraft.

EXHIBIT 1

Deliveries of Fixed-Wing Business Aircraft 1986-91

Manufacturer/Type	'86	'87	'88	'89	'90	'91*
JETS						
Beechcraft						
Beechjet 400/400A	17	9	20	10	8	9
British Aerospace						
BAe 125-800	27	31	30	32	29	9
Canadair						
Challenger 601-1A	19	7	—	—	—	—
Challenger 601-3A	—	10	23	20	28	11
Cessna Aircraft	**61**	**62**	**62**	**82**	**101**	**53**
550 Citation IVSII	40	36	47	33	30	16
560 Citation V	—	—	—	33	56	28
650 Citation III	21	26	15	16	15	9
Dassault Aviation	**25**	**47**	**44**	**38**	**34**	**14**
Falcon 100	3	4	7	5	3	—
Falcon 20/100	5	5	1	3	2	1
Falcon 50	14	8	9	11	12	6
Falcon 900	3	30	27	19	17	7
Gulfstream Aerospace	**24**	**30**	**51**	**40**	**34**	**12**
Gulfstream III	14	4	2	—	—	—
Gulfstream IV	10	26	49	40	34	12
Israel Aircraft Industries						
IAI 1125 Westwind 1/2	9	4	1			
IAI 1125 Astra/SP	6	3	6	8	13	5
Learjet	**20**	**16**	**23**	**25**	**25**	**11**
Learjet 31	—	—	5	7	13	5
Learjet 35A	11	12	15	9	7	4
Learjet 36/36A	2		1	3	1	0
Learjet 55/55B/55C	7	4	2	6	4	2
	208	219	260	255	272	124
TURBOPROPS						
Augusta (SIAI-Marchetti)						
SF600 Canguro	—	—	4	3	2	0
Beechcraft	**80**	**90**	**110**	**103**	**122**	**50**

[2]Aviation data sources reported the total number of jets in operation was 6,793 as of 9/3/90.

Manufacturer/Type	'86	'87	'88	'89	'90	'91*
2000 Starship 1	—	—	—	—	11	1
1900E Executive	—	—	—	—	2	0
Super King Air 350	—	—	—	—	34	19
Super King Air 300/300LV	27	37	53	33	10	2
Super King Air 200/200CT	30	32	27	32	41	13
King Air C90/F90	23	21	30	38	35	15
Cessna Aircraft	**82**	**101**	**99**	**101**	**70**	**30**
208 Caravan I	52	21	15	27	22	7
208B Caravan 1B	—	56	75	62	44	11
Grand Caravan	—	—	—	—	—	12
406 Caravan II	2	11	9	12	4	0
425 Conquest I	17	6	) Production			
441 Conquest II	11	7	) Suspended			
Fairchild Aircraft						
SA227AT/TT Merlin	1	1	0	0	0	0
Lake Aircraft						
LA-250 Renegade	22	14	28	23	17	7
TBM (Soccata/Mooney)						
TBM700	—	—	—	—	3	8
Partenavia						
AP68TP-600 Viator	2	4	2	3	3	1
Pilatus Aircraft						
PC-6/B2-H4 Tubor Porter	10	2	3	6	7	7
Pilatus Britten-Norman						
BN-2T Tubine Islander	3	4	4	5	11	3
Piper Aircraft	**20**	**21**	**7**	**5**	**11**	**3**
PA-31T-500 Cheyenne IA	4	1	—	—	—	—
PA-31T-620 Cheyenne IIXL	5	3	—	—	—	—
PA-42-720 Cheyenne IIA	10	12	2	1	9	3
PA-42-1000 Cheyenne 400	1	5	5	4	2	0
Rinaldo Piagglo						
P166-DL3	1	2	4	2	5	2
	221	**239**	**261**	**251**	**251**	**111**
PISTON-ENGINED						
Beechcraft	163	191	194	211	240	120
Bonanza F33A/C	53	105	101	116	126	43
Bonanza A36/AT	5 7	49	63	50	70	53
Bonanza B36TC	16	11	16	12	11	7
Baron 58/58P	37	26	14	33	33	17
Cessna Aircraft	**30**					
T303 Crusader	3)					
402 C Businessliner	5)	Production Suspended				
414A Chancellor	13)					
421 C Golden Eagle	9)					
Pilatus Britten Norman						
BN-2B Islander	11	14	10	10	10	5
Partenavia						
P68C/P68C-TC	10	8	4	2	7	2
Piper Aircraft	**166**	**148**	**114**	**168**	**98**	**25**
PA-31-350 Chieftain	1	—	—	—	—	—
PA-32-301 Saratoga/SP	21	37	20	32	22	14
PA-34-220TR Seneca III	49	57	53	46	50	9
PA-46-310P Malibu	95	54	41	1		
PA-46-350P Malibu Mirage	—	—	—	89	26	2
	380	**361**	**322**	**391**	**355**	**152**

Source: *Interavia Aerospace Review,* September 1991, p. 63.

*January 1–June 30.

A commercial jet and helicopter pilot, Paulson holds five US patents for his aeronautical designs. He has won numerous awards and honorary doctorates, and is known as a man who strives to foster a candid and open relationship with his employees. During the recent buyout negotiations, Paulson informed his employees of his acquisition plans early in the negotiation process. "I risked touching off a bidding war by announcing my intentions," said Paulson, "but no way would I let Gulfstream people suffer through all that uncertainty."[3] Rated by *Forbes* in 1988 as the 187th richest American, Paulson demonstrates his allegiance to his 4,500 employees by sending personally signed Christmas cards every year.

EXHIBIT 2

Sales Breakdown of Leading Business Jet Manufacturers (US $): 1990

Gulfstream	$ 675m
Beech	$ 575m
Dassault	$ 550m
Cessna	$ 520m
Canadair	$ 450m
British Aerospace	$ 260m
Learjet	$ 115m
IAI	$ 95m
Piper	$ 60m
Fairchild	$ 50m
All others	$1,650m
Total 1990 sales approx	$5,000m

Source: *Intervia Aerospace Review,* September 1991, p. 65.

EXHIBIT 3

New Fixed-Wing Business Aircraft

Manufacturer	Model	First Flight	First Delivery	Firm Orders	Base Price ($m)
British aerospace	1000	16/6/90	10/91	21	12.22
Cessna	CitationJet	24/4/91	3/93	130	2.80
	Citation X	3/93	6/95	10	11.85
	Citation VI	6/2/91	6/91	n/a	7.20
	Citation VII	2/2/91	2/92	n/a	8.70
CMC	Leopard	12/12/88	94	—	.85
Dassault	Falcon 2000	3/93	12/94	50*	13.70
Learjet	Learjet 60	13/6/91	10/92	n/a	7.90
	Learjet 31A	9/11/90	8/91	n/a	4.28
Pilatue	PC-12	31/5/91	93	27*	1.63
Rinaldo Piaggio	P180 Avanti	23/9/86	1/8/91	16	4.13
Swearingen	SJ30	13/2/91	6/93	43	2.60

Source: *Interavia Aerospace Review,* September 1991, p. 64.
*Options only

[3]"Letting Employees in the News," *New York Times,* March 4, 1990, Section 3, Part 2, p. 37.

ADVANCED SUKHOI TECHNOLOGIES OF THE RUSSIAN REPUBLICS

Under the direction of Mikhail P. Siminov, the former Sukhoi Design Bureau designed and manufactured fighter jets and bombers which have played a leading role in Soviet military history. While only one of a dozen or so aerospace design bureaus in the Soviet Union, Sukhoi is the youngest and is considered by many in the Soviet Union to be one of the best.

Currently, Sukhoi is best known for its Su-27, a supersonic fighter used in Afghanistan. Observers at the 1989 Paris Air Show were mesmerized by a Su-27's execution of "Pougachev's Cobra," an aeronautical acrobatic feat that no United States fighter jet can manage. Sukhoi aircraft have a reputation for technical and engineering excellence, built up from many years of Soviet defense spending.

Economic and political changes in the Soviet Union between 1988 and 1991 altered Siminov's business environment greatly. Mikhail Gorbachev's drive to dismantle the Soviet military-industrial complex to divert resources to the consumer sector reduced the demand for Sukhoi fighter planes, leaving production facilities idle. Specifically, his "swords to plowshares" policies led to a directive which resulted in Sukhoi being forced into designing food-packaging equipment and a washing machine for tomatoes and apricots. Siminov complied with the directive but, in a typically understated fashion, called it ". . . a gross misapplication of Sukhoi technology."

Still, Siminov did not give up aircraft design. Instead, he aggressively began transforming Sukhoi's military prowess into commercial success, and renamed the design bureau "Advanced Sukhoi Technologies of the Russian Republics." Cutting his military production in half, Siminov replaced fighter plane production with civilian projects which he hoped to market in the West. He remarked, "We want to make a lot of money with some very democratic airplanes."

To provide added incentives, and to retain his engineers and workers, Siminov doubled their salaries.[4] He also attempted to ease their lives by setting up distribution and sales of food and clothing through the company cafeteria so that his workers wouldn't have to spend time waiting in lines. He arranged bank loans and used civilian profits to buy high-tech equipment such as powerful Japanese-built computers for design work. The planned SSBJ is Sukhoi's first aircraft to be designed entirely by computer. Siminov's strategy has been to keep his employees busy with a variety of challenging projects. His ability to bring design, development, and production together under one management, highly unusual in the Soviet Union, has contributed to his success. Vladimir Yakolev, editor-in-chief of the Soviet business weekly *Kommersant,* remarked, "Siminov and Sukhoi were smart enough to get a head start on the competition before we developed real problems with skilled workers leaving the labor force. They have good products and they kept their team intact."

At the 1991 Paris Air Show, Sukhoi exhibited its newest design, the Su-29, a bi-wing, aerobatic sports plane. The high performance aircraft is the successor to the Su-26, a single-seat aerobatic aircraft which has been the leading plane on the aerobatic circuit for the past four years. These planes are loved by aerobatic pilots, airshow junkies, and collectors, for their maneuverability and strength. The Pompano Air Center in Pompano Beach, Florida, an industry leader in aerobatic aircraft sales and training, entered a partnership agreement with Sukhoi to sell their planes in 1989. At the time, the vice-president of Pompano, Brian Becker, said, "We'll do 10–12 airplanes a year, but this is just a foot in the door to do other things with Sukhoi." In 1991, Pompano received an exclusive contract to

---

[4]A typical aircraft engineer in the Soviet Union made about 180 rubles a month in 1990—about $5.60 at the recently set official exchange rate of 32 rubles to the US dollar. Alexander Sarkisov, designer and general manager of a competing design bureau, the Leningrad, Klimov, noted, "We are not paying our people enough, and I would understand it if they are looking elsewhere." However, he proudly noted that ". . . our average salary has gone up to 500 rubles by this July, . . . and my goal is to boost it to 700 rubles per month in 1991."

distribute the Su-29 worldwide. He noted that the aircraft will sell for a price that is "at the top of what the Western market will bear." Pompano officials acknowledged that setting prices is difficult since there is no official exchange rate for converting rubles into dollars. Industry officials value the Su-29 at approximately $200,000, and up to $500,000 including spare parts.

Siminov, 62 years old, graduated from the Kazan Aviation Institute and, in 1959, founded the Sports Aviation Design Bureau in Kazan. While there, he designed and produced more than ten sports gliders. In 1970, Siminov went to the Sukhoi Design Bureau. He rose fast in the organization and soon became the Head of Operational Development and Testing of the Su-24 supersonic bomber. He later became the Chief Designer of the Su-27, and also served four years as Deputy Minister of the USSR Aviation Industry. A true designer as well as an elected official of the Supreme Soviet, Siminov is often seen in Sukhoi's workshops, soliciting ideas and offering encouragement to his staff.

Characterized by the Americans at Gulfstream as a "laid-back, understated type of guy," Siminov doesn't speak English but communicates with them through interpreters. Upon meeting, he and Paulson hit it off immediately. Siminov commented that he "has found a brother" in Paulson, and that the two plan to do great things together.

THE PROPOSED JOINT VENTURE

Independent of each other, Gulfstream and Sukhoi had both been interested in commercial supersonic flight for some time. A June 5, 1989, *Aviation Week & Space Technology* article revealed that Sukhoi might entertain joint venture proposals for the production of a commercial supersonic transport, and specifically mentioned Gulfstream and Dassault as potential partners. The article spurred Paulson to contact Mikhail P. Siminov at the Paris Air Show in 1989. Paulson and Siminov met for 75 minutes on June 15, 1989; on the same day, Sukhoi and Gulfstream signed the MOU to form a joint venture to design, manufacture, and market a supersonic corporate jet (see *Exhibit 4* for the current design of the S21-G).

EXHIBIT 4A
Gulfstream/Sukhoi S21-G
Supersonic Business Jet – 1991

EXHIBIT 4B
Gulfstream/Sukhoi S21-G
Supersonic Business Jet – 1991

The current plans for the S21-G are as follows:

1991: Finalize engine design

Early 1992: Complete market study to
assess demand

1994: Proof-of-concept flight (to take
place in the Soviet Union)

1995-97: Develop three production
prototypes

1998: Obtain certification and start
initial deliveries

Together, it is thought that Gulfstream and Sukhoi possess the complete set of skills required to design a civilian supersonic aircraft, and industry experts have called the collaboration "a near-perfect marriage." As evidenced by the Su-27's "Cobra" move, the Soviets bring exceptional aerodynamic engineering skills to the table. The MOU calls for Sukhoi to conduct research and development, and to design the airframe, with Gulfstream's participation and approval. On their own, Sukhoi is responsible for structural design, airframe manufacture, and Soviet certification. Production of the airframe will take place in the Soviet Union to take advantage of substantially lower wage rates and Sukhoi's "manufacturing muscle." Initial Soviet willingness to come up with the equivalent of US $1 billion in R&D investment made the project possible, which Paulson claims would be uneconomic in the United States without government support.

Gulfstream's competence in electronics and cockpit technology complements the Soviets' design and production expertise. Advanced electronics planned for the S21-G are already available in the Gulfstream IV (which is currently sold in the Soviet Union). "We would take everything from the G-IV—glass cockpit, avionics, etc.—and put all this into the SST with some software changes," Paulson explained. "We want it to have American components."[5] Thus, the MOU calls for Gulfstream to supply aircraft systems, avionics and interior outfitting. In addition, Gulfstream will supply marketing expertise to the venture and product support, in the form of a full line of spare parts, to ensure continuing maintenance and service. Western certification and sales are also Gulfstream's responsibility. Paulson has not revealed the exact manner in which development costs will be split. "We will take care of the dollars, and they'll take care of the rubles," he noted vaguely. Alvin Balaban, Director of Corporate Communications for Gulfstream, suggested that Gulfstream's investment was miniscule in comparison to Sukhoi's.

Cuts in military spending in the Soviet Union and efforts to restructure the economy may impede Sukhoi's efforts to develop and manufacture the SSBJ. "The Soviet defense industry is under enormous pressure to go civilian and equally enormous pressure to come up with hard currencies," said Marshall I. Goldman, the associate research director of the Russian Research Center at Harvard University. Jan Vanous, Research Director at Planecon, a Washington consulting company that specializes in the Eastern Bloc and Soviet economies, said, "I don't think the Soviets are in a position, considering the state of the economy, to stick their necks out on a project that no Western company, even a consortium, would consider doing."

Early in the project, Sukhoi proposed a three-engine design for performance and safety reasons. However, by early 1991, Gulfstream and Rolls-Royce managed to convince Sukhoi engineers that the jet should be run by two engines mounted on the wings. The two-engine model, lighter in weight than the three-engine design, will more easily achieve the speed criteria and range capability sought for the project. Convincing the Soviets to decrease the number of engines from three to two "wasn't easy," Paulson said.

The S21-G will be capable of carrying 8–12 passengers, plus two crew members. At an expected price of $40–50 million, the S21-G will sell for twice the amount of the most expensive corporate jets on the market today. The S21-G will travel at Mach 2.2, approximately three times as fast as any existing business jet, and have the ability to take off and land with only 6000 feet of runway (as compared to 6500 feet for the G-IV). It will cruise at an altitude of 51,000–61,000 feet, and have a flight range of more than 4000 nautical miles.

Though the history of supersonic transport (SST) has been littered with failures and abandoned efforts, the technological challenge of SST is one which few Western aircraft manufacturers can put out of their minds entirely. Most of the industry leaders are now pursuing SST in earnest,[6] and, if on schedule, Gulfstream and Sukhoi's S21-G could emerge ten years ahead of the competition.

The publication of the initial specifications seems to confirm the feasibility of the project, though there are still many challenges to overcome. The production of efficient and relatively quiet engines presents a major technical hurdle to the project. Sukhoi farmed out this part of the project to a joint venture between Rolls-Royce, the British engine manufacturer, and the Lyulka Design Bureau (now called Aero Engine), a Soviet engine manufacturer and one of the largest in the world. The success of this project is crucial to the continued development of the S21-G. "Learning to work together has been more difficult than we expected; [though] Lyulka is comparable to Rolls-Royce in terms of determining engine performance, we have differences in the way we operate," said Brian Lowrie, the chief engineer of Rolls-Royce working on the SSBJ project.[7] Rolls-Royce has been the lead supplier of engines to Gulfstream for over thirty years, and knows the company well.

In 1990, Rolls-Royce and Lyulka signed a 12-month agreement to determine the engine configuration of the S21-G. They plan to work together on the design, development and production of a more fuel-efficient engine. As of mid-1991, Rolls-Royce and Lyulka

[5]*Interavia Aerospace Review,* November 1989, p. 1089.

[6]See the companion case, "Note on the Corporate Jet Market and Supersonic Transportation."

[7]Edward Phillips, "Engine Concept Identified for SSBJ."

appeared to have agreed on a common engine design, and plans were afoot to set up the manufacturing facility in the Soviet Union.

The American and Soviet enterprises were linked in other ways. In December 1990, Gulfstream entered into an agreement with Lyulka to develop an engine noise suppressor, commonly called an aft fan, for the G-II and G-III. Lyulka agreed to deliver to Gulfstream a prototype of the noise suppressor by August 1991, for flight testing. "This is a good start to see what kind of work they can do," Paulson observed at the time. However, as of June 1991, the project was put on hold because, Paulson said, "Upfront research and development costs are too high."[8]

The positions of the US and British governments on the export of potentially sensitive technology may present an obstacle. Currently, the US Department of Commerce and the Coordinating Committee for the Multilateral Control of Exports (COCOM) must approve leasing of low-technology aircraft, such as the Boeing 737, to the Eastern Bloc.[9] According to Gulfstream's Balaban, the Department of Commerce and COCOM have not explicitly approved the technology transfer. Balaban noted that, "if anything, they (Sukhoi) will be transferring technology to us." However, Soviet engineers were having difficulty getting the Immigration and Naturalization Services of the US government to provide visas to visit the US to discuss specifications with Gulfstream. The Soviet officials, on the other hand, were facilitating visits to their country. US officials have been prohibited from issuing the Soviets multiple-entry visas, and requests for visas have often been delayed by 30–45 days.

Gulfstream is also concerned about US export laws on information exchange and the length of time (up to five years) expected for the US Dept. of Transportation and the Soviet Union's Air Ministry to agree on bilateral standards ("Bilateral Airworthiness Agreements"). Before the proposed SSBJ can join the civilian air transportation fleet, the United States and the Soviet Union must reach bilateral agreements on the certification process for the plane's use in the US and elsewhere in the world. Though the two countries allow regularly scheduled flights between Moscow and New York, no certification agreements currently exist between the two countries.

In an effort to confront these bureaucratic hurdles, Paulson testified in front of US Senator Sam Nunn's Armed Services Committee in Washington, D.C. in September 1991. Stating that the existing regulations and interpretations of export control laws are significant enough to bring the joint venture to a standstill, Paulson asked for aid in clearing the "regulatory pathways within government." He specifically focused on the problems of visa delays, multiple export licenses, Bilateral Airworthiness Agreements and restrictions on the peaceful use of technology.

Though US laws on the export of high-technology hardware and knowhow are slowing the project, they haven't diminished enthusiasm on either side. "There are times," says William Murphy, Gulfstream's Director of Product Development, "when we say to the Soviets, 'Look, we know this design is physically possible, but we can't by law tell you how we know it.'" Sukhoi's head of Economic Development, Alexei Komarov, is more philosophical: "The Soviets and the Americans are not going to exact each other's secrets, just ideas."[10] The Rolls-Royce Technical Director, Philip C. Ruffles, anticipates some British security concern with the transfer of engine technology to the Soviet Union.

Several designs were in competition for the SSBJ, and, as planned under the terms of their agreement, Gulfstream and Sukhoi finalized specifications together. At a meeting in August 1991, final decisions on the S21G's configuration were made, and Gulfstream announced plans to proceed with a detailed market study. "Once the design specifications

---

[8]Edward Phillips, "Gulfstream, Rolls-Royce Developing Hushkits to Extend Business Jet Life," *Aviation Week & Space Technology,* June 17, 1991, p. 209.

[9]*Interavia,* December 1988, p. 1222.

[10]Steve Raymer, *National Geographic* News Service, July 29, 1991.

have been completed, we can do our market studies and take deposits from customers," a Gulfstream spokesperson said. The market study, to be conducted by an outside agency, is expected to be completed by early 1992.

Paulson believes that the initial market will support 60 to 100 supersonic transports, though he cautions that his final estimate will hinge upon the market study. Gulfstream and Sukhoi plan to market the jet to corporate and government customers. According to Balaban, Gulfstream has been informally taking polls. "We've had 16 to 18 existing customers, those mainly flying the G-IV, suggesting that they would want to buy the S21-G," he said. Early in the project, the Soviet government expressed an interest in at least 20 jets to transport Soviet ministers and officials across the vast land mass.

Paulson insists he will limit Gulfstream's risk by soliciting orders, backed by deposits, before driving a single rivet. Once he has enough buyer's deposits to use as collateral for financing the project, production can begin.[11] Demand for at least 100 aircraft, Paulson was quoted, will be necessary for the program to be feasible. Other industry experts have estimated that for SST to become economically viable in both the airline and business sectors in the long run, the market would have to bear about 1500 to 2000 aircraft, and that there is unlikely to be room for more than one or two competitors.

Much rests on the market study, and Gulfstream seems to be proceeding cautiously. Sukhoi, on the other hand, is already talking about a line extension in the form of a 50-seater supersonic jet. Gulfstream is reluctant to commit to or comment on the proposal, noting that a jet this large would be outside of the market they know so well. Paulson, however, feels competitive pressure and knows that competitors have approached Sukhoi and other Soviet aerospace enterprises about teaming up on a supersonic jet project. Paulson recently commented that, "If this project. . . is not accomplished by Sukhoi and Gulfstream, it will, most assuredly, be taken away from us by our French and possibly Canadian competitors. . . . They recognize the benefits in employment, in improved trade balances, in aerospace leadership."

Aircraft manufacture is a planner's nightmare. It is traditionally driven by long lead times, vast economies of scale, steep learning curves that make it difficult to retrain or hire new workers, high levels of work-in-process inventory, high R&D expenditures (sometimes equal to the net worth of the company if a new product has to be developed), costly retooling and adjustments once production plans are set, and expensive raw materials. Key questions that have to be answered before manufacturing can begin include what the size and the timing of the market by each category of aircraft is, by sector and geographic region. Planners also typically need to make estimates concerning aircraft retirement schedules, alternative markets, and ways to prolong the life of the product. Finally, some estimates of likely future competition and market share projections were absolutely essential.

Throughout the project's short history, Paulson remained optimistic about the joint venture. ". . . I've had an opportunity to meet with Vice President Quayle and the Secretary of Transportation. In both cases we've been encouraged to proceed with our Gulfstream-Sukhoi business arrangements," Paulson said. His enthusiasm, however, was interrupted by the news in August 1991: The conservative hard-liners of the Soviet Union, including the heads of defense and the KGB, staged a putsch to oust Mikhail Gorbachev from power. Though the poorly planned coup failed within several days, Gorbachev was heavily criticized for using poor judgment in letting former Party members remain in positions of power, and Boris Yeltsin emerged as the new leader of the Russian people. Calling for sweeping economic reforms, dismantling of the Communist Party and an end to corruption, Yeltsin and other newly appointed officials assured that life in the Soviet Union would never be the same. Further, many of the different republics were going their own way economically and politically, and the erstwhile Soviet Union was on its way to breaking apart.[12]

---

[11]Carolyn Geer, "Paulson's Pride," *Forbes* Oct. 29, 1990, p. 156.

[12]Carolyn Geer, "Paulson's Pride," *Forbes* Oct. 29, 1990, p. 156.

Paulson knew the historic events would have a profound effect on the Soviet economy, and in particular, the military-industrial complex. The events could turn the SSBJ project on its head. Further, though significant progress had been made on the project (and though he had the utmost faith in Siminov), Paulson had to admit that all that existed in the form of a contract was the MOU and a handshake. He looked down at the newspapers on his desk. A recent planned trip by Gulfstream engineers to Sukhoi had to be cancelled, though Paulson had been in constant touch with Siminov via fax. He asked himself again: Does this joint venture make sense? Will the economic rewards outweigh the risks? What are the major hurdles to success? Should he go ahead with it?

case 15

Note on the Corporate Jet Market and Supersonic Transportation*

THE CORPORATE JET MARKET

Far more than a status symbol, the corporate jet has evolved into a comfortable and efficient alternative to commercial air travel, allowing corporations to save one of their most critical resources—executive time. The advantage of private plane travel over commercial flights has increased with the crowding of airplanes and congestion of airspace resulting from deregulation, decreasing airline prices, and increasing popularity of air travel.

After strong growth in the '60s and '70s, the business jet market experienced a slump in the 1980s. Jet prices increased dramatically, from $3–7 million to $10–20 million, due to changing regulations, increasing technological sophistication, and higher manufacturing costs. Operating expenses increased due to fuel and insurance costs. Also, older jets proved unpredictably durable, encouraging an active market in used jets. Further, manufacturers faced increasing tort action from product liability lawsuits, and had to raise prices to cover their costs.

By 1989, the industry began to improve. Manufacturers of business and personal jets and turboprops produced 1,535 new aircraft that year, a record for the decade.[1] Thus, industry experts predicted an increase in the purchase of corporate jets in the 1990s. The trend toward lean upper management staffs, which increased the amount of territory an executive must cover, supported the forecasts. In addition, the mergers and acquisition boom in the United States, European conglomeration associated with economic integration, and frenzied activity in the Pacific Rim increased the geographic purview of many top managers.

*This note, along with the companion case "Gulfstream and Sukhoi: The Supersonic Business Jet," was developed by Professor Anant Sundaram, with assistance from Michelle Sparrow (T' 91), David Weld (T' 90), and Professor Stewart Black, as a basis for class discussion. We are grateful to Alvin Balaban of Gulfstream Aerospace and Edward Kolcum of Aviation Week & Space Technology for helping with the case development. Given the relevant time period, the note continues to refer to the geographical area that is now known as the Commonwealth of Independent States as the "Soviet Union." © 1991.

[1] Edward H., Phillips, "GAMA Records Slight Upturn in Light Aircraft Deliveries," Aviation Week & Space Technology, January 29, 1990, p. 55.

Learjet, Inc., and Jet Commander had manufactured the first business jets, which came on the market between 1964 and 1966. Grumman Corporation's aerospace arm, Gulfstream, entered the industry with a turboprop jet, the G-I, in 1966, and eventually sold 201 of these aircraft. By 1969, they had followed with the G-II and IIB, both twin-engine jets. These twin-engine jets were larger than the turboprops, and over 250 were sold for approximately $5 to $7 million each. In 1978, development of the G-III began, and the plane was sold for a price of approximately $12–15 million beginning in 1980. Two hundred two G-III aircraft were manufactured for delivery before production ended in 1987. The intention to build a successor to the G-III had been made public in 1983; the G-IV was certified by the FAA in 1987.

Fortune 500 companies account for a significant portion of sales for business aircraft manufacturers; they operate over 9% of the worldwide business aircraft fleet. In 1988, 332 of the Fortune 500 operated at least one turbine-powered business aircraft. Gulfstream Aerospace Corporation is the lead supplier of business jets to this market segment. Of the 1988 Fortune 500 fleet of 1,294 aircraft valued at $4.99 billion, Gulfstream led in terms of number of customer companies, number of aircraft, and dollar value of aircraft supplied. Of this fleet, Gulfstream provided 218 aircraft worth $1,720 million to 109 companies. Gulfstream competes primarily with Dassault Falcon, Canadair Challenger, and British Aerospace, who manufacture and sell planes in the same category as the G-IV.

Demand by industry segment for corporate jets shifted in the late '80s. Historically, the petroleum industry purchased the most business jets. Then, the service sector increased its purchases of corporate aircraft.[2] The food, forest products, chemicals, petroleum refining, electronics, and aerospace industry groups together operated more than 100 jets in 1989. (*Exhibit 1* shows a breakdown of the Fortune 500 fleet by industry group.)

While business jet sales in North America and Europe had begun to slow in 1990, Oceania (Australia, New Zealand, French Polynesia, and Papua New Guinea), Central America, and South America all experienced double-digit growth in the recent past. The Middle East and Asian markets, which historically accounted for only 30–40% of the business jet market, made up 60% of international sales (*Exhibit 2* provides a breakdown of jets by region of the world). "Another thing that has helped is the opening up of the Eastern Bloc in Europe, which has increased the need for long range aircraft and increased travel," Allen Paulson, CEO of Gulfstream Aerospace Corporation, noted; "It's amazing the number of corporate aircraft you see now in Moscow and Eastern Europe." However, entry into many of these countries is not easy: The availability of landing/take-off slots is not assured in European airports, strict government regulation is a major problem in Latin America and the Pacific Rim, and in Japan, availability of airspace and groundspace for private jets is as scarce as golf courses. Further, despite the increase in the sale of new jets, used jet sales continue to dominate new jet sales.

Despite rosy predictions, actual European and US sales of new and used aircraft were depressed in 1991. Robert H. Cooper, V.P. Marketing for Gulfstream, indicated that potential buyers were hesitant to close the sale due to the troubled world economy and the uncertainty resulting from the Gulf War. James Gormley, president of America's General Aviation Manufacturer's Association, agreed and commented, "In today's uncertain economy, there are few stockholders who would permit the use of general aviation (i.e., business jets) if it were not fully justified." One study concluded that an executive jet is not cost competitive unless it carries at least eight passengers on every flight; most carry two or three.[3]

---

[2]Edward H. Phillips, "Business Jets May Erode Market for Turboprop Aircraft in 1990s," *Aviation Week & Space Technology,* August 21, 1989, pp. 89, 91.

[3]The executive jet also occasionally became a symbol of corporate excesses in the 1980s. One of the more notorious examples was that of Ross Johnson, the former CEO of RJR Nabisco, who according to some press reports used to fly with two executive jets: one for himself, and one for his dog.

EXHIBIT 1

Fortune 500 Business Aircraft by Industry

Industry Group	Companies Operating Business Aircraft	Companies Not Operating Business Aircraft	Total Aircraft Operated
Mining, Crude Oil Production	5	4	13
Food	33	15	113
Tobacco	5	2	24
Textiles	7	4	14
Apparel	5	4	16
Furniture	5	2	17
Forest Products	27	6	100
Publishing, Printing	15	7	37
Chemicals	33	18	108
Petroleum Refining	23	7	196
Rubber Products	9	2	24
Building Materials	9	6	23
Metals	14	10	29
Metal Products	11	6	27
Industrial Manufacturing & Machinery	2	3	4
Electronics	27	17	117
Transportation Equipment	3	3	11
Scientific & Photo Equipment	12	5	48
Miscellaneous Manufacturing	1	0	3
Motor Vehicles and Parts	19	5	86
Aerospace	15	2	123
Pharmaceuticals	14	2	46
Soaps, Cosmetics	5	5	11
Computers, Office Equipment	8	16	37
Industrial & Farm Equipment	17	13	39
Jewelry, Silverware	1	0	1
Toys, Sporting Goods	1	1	1
Beverages	6	2	26
Miscellaneous Investments & Real Estate	0	1	0
Total	**332**	**168**	**1,294**

Source: Aviation Data, Inc., Wichita, KS; *Business & Commercial Aviation.*

EXHIBIT 2

Distribution of Business Jets by Region

The Fleet as of Sept 30 1990			*Distribution*	
Top Models	*Number in Operation*	*% Share of Market*		
Cessna Citation	1,685	24.8	North America	4,753
Learjet	1,405	20.7	Central America	299
Dassault Falcon	880	13.0	South America	328
British Aerospace 125	655	9.6	Europe	915
Gulfstream	565	8.3	Africa	172
Others	1,603	23.7	Asia and Middle East	212
Total	**6,793**	**100.0**	Japan	19
			Oceania	95

Source: Aviation Data Services.

SUPERSONIC TRANSPORTATION

Excessive travel time, especially on long transcontinental United States routes and on transoceanic Pacific routes, spurred demand for a faster mode of transportation. The expectation that Asia's booming markets will increase trans-Pacific travel to 315,000 passengers per day by the end of the decade (15% more than will fly across the Atlantic daily), has intensified the demand. The increase in Pacific Rim/Asia air traffic is estimated at 10 percent per year during this decade, compared to worldwide air traffic growth of 4.5–5.2% per year. Aircraft manufacturers have thus turned their attention to developing supersonic civilian jets, a technology that has been harnessed for several decades in military applications. The company that is successful could earn enormous profits, and because of the potentially high entry barriers, may be able to dominate the aircraft market into the twenty-first century.

The United States and the Soviet Union have both explored civilian supersonic transportation (SST) in the past. Lockheed tried to develop SST in the 1960s, but gave up on the project in 1971. During the period of 1963–1971, Boeing invested over $1 billion in an effort to develop a civilian supersonic transport. Boeing approached the National Aeronautics and Space Administration (NASA) and Congress for funding to bring the program to the next stage, commercial production, but after lengthy appropriations hearings in 1970 and 1971, Congress denied funding for the continuation of the project. A lack of funding, environmental concerns over the impact of supersonic flight on the ozone layer,[4] excess aircraft noise, and a general understanding that the plane would not fly at supersonic speeds over land contributed to the project's demise.

Edward H. Kolcum, an industry watcher and reporter for *Aviation Week & Space Technology,* feels that a "lack of will" on the part of Congress stifled the project. Kolcum indicated that the project held economic potential. Alvin F. Balaban, Gulfstream's Director of Corporate Communications, feels that the US just "dropped out of the race." According to Balaban, US government officials, including some members of the Appropriations Committee, were "running around the country making speeches saying this thing would give you cancer."

The Soviet Union also launched a 1970s effort in supersonic civilian aircraft. However, the plane, the TU-144 (named after the USSR Tupelov manufacturing enterprise), never entered production after a fatal crash at the Paris Air Show in 1973. Though the aerodynamics of the Soviet aircraft were better than that of Western planes, it lagged in engine technology and cockpit electronics. By most accounts, the Soviets did not pursue further efforts for civilian supersonic travel after the '73 crash.

After a lengthy hiatus, the United States began to investigate civilian supersonic transport again. US manufacturers are determined not to be beaten by European or Japanese manufacturers, and the US government is supporting new research. A two-year NASA study on High Speed Civil Transport (HSCT) indicated the technical and economic viability of supersonic transport. In 1989, NASA, Boeing, and McDonnell Douglas teamed up to study various issues surrounding supersonic flight, including engine emissions, the sonic boom, and community noise levels. A study performed by by the Center for High-Speed Commercial Flight encouraged an international approach to the development of this transport to address the attendant concerns of noise pollution and the ozone layer,[5] multilateral certification, and international operating rights.[6] US aerospace manufacturers later aban-

---

[4]To save fuel, SSTs have to cruise at a level of about 60,000 feet, where the atmosphere is quite thin, and close to the ozone layer. The nitrogen oxide emissions produced by jet engines at this height can be more devastating to the ozone layer than chlorofluorocarbons.

[5]Stanley W. Kandebo, "HSCT Propulsion Studies Focus on Reducing Emissions, Noise," *Aviation Week & Space Technology,* July 10, 1989, pp. 34-36.

[6]"Market Studies Indicate Demand for High-Speed Civil Transport," *Aviation Week & Space Technology,* November 21, 1988, pp. 54-61.

doned the coordinated effort, evidently due to lack of continued interest and an aversion to sharing propriety information. However, NASA, Boeing, and McDonnell Douglas continued their research independently.[7]

Most experts acknowledge the job of developing SST is too complex and too costly for one company, and teams of aerospace firms have combined their efforts to share the risk and the financial burden of research and development. In the US, NASA is spending $284 million over five years to study environmental issues surrounding the sonic boom, airport noise levels, and depletion of the ozone layer by jet fumes. The research is intended to aid US aircraft manufacturers in developing technologies that they can apply to their work (NASA has imposed controls on the data to ensure that US-funded research is not supplied to non-US organizations[8]). Boeing and McDonnell Douglas rejoined forces to design an airframe. In early 1991, Boeing announced plans to double the size of its staff for the SST project, to 150, making the project one of Boeing's largest. The manufacturer noted that designers will be focussing on the issue of profitability, as production costs are estimated at $10–15 billion. Pratt & Whitney teamed up with its leading competitor, General Electric, to develop a power plant, or engine, which is quieter, more economical, and burns fuel in a cleaner fashion.[9]

Outside the US, British Aerospace and France's Aerospatiale, the team which built the Concorde, are working on airframes, and, in 1991, invited Boeing, McDonnell Douglas and Deutsche Airbus to join their efforts. The five-company consortium plans to coordinate their efforts so as not to duplicate each others' work. France's SNECMA and Britain's Rolls-Royce have teamed up to develop supersonic engines for a 280-seater SST that British Aerospace has on its design boards.

The Japanese, who currently lack experience in aerospace technology, are investing in European and American ventures in the hope of becoming involved in the next generation of supersonic travel. Further, they hope to learn more about the design and manufacture of SST through their collaborative efforts to produce the FSX (a modified US F-16 manufactured by General Dynamics) fighter in Japan. Many firms in Japan have made significant moves toward the aerospace industry: Nissan is a major producer of liquid-fueled rocket engines, Fuji Heavy Industries is working with Boeing on the development of the 777 aircraft, Mitsubishi is working on aerospace materials technology (and has teamed up with Daimler-Benz), and IshikawajimaHarima Heavy Industries apparently intends to license jet-engine technology from Pratt & Whitney.

The 1976 introduction of the British-French Concorde represents the only successful civilian application of supersonic air travel to date. Fourteen Condordes are in operation today after production ceased in 1980; each carries 100 passengers, has the range of 3500 nautical miles, and flies at Mach 2 (twice the speed of sound, or about 1400 miles per hour). Whether or not the Concorde is profitable, however, is open to debate. The jet can fly from New York to London in three hours and captured almost 50 percent of first-class air travel between New York and Europe in 1985. However, at the current price of over $4000 each way, passenger fares are four times more expensive than conventional fares, and reportedly barely cover the jet's fuel costs.

The British-French alliance is now planning a successor to the Concorde which will be slightly larger with more efficient engines. Over 50 engineers are working to build a supersonic jet which will carry 250–300 passengers at Mach 2.5–3.0, and with a range of 5000–6000 nautical miles. To achieve the higher speed and longer range, the engineers will have to come up with an airframe which is proportionately 30% lighter than the Concordes' and still able to resist temperatures of 600 degrees Fahrenheit. Noise reduction, improved fuel efficiency, and pollution control also must be dealt with.

[7]James Ott, "Lace of U.S. Interest Derails International HSCT Consortium," *Aviation Week & Space Technology,* September 11, 1989, pp. 28-29.

[8]Bill Sweetman, "High-Speed Agreement," *Interavia Aerospace Review,* January 1991, pp. 14.

[9]Jerome Cramer, "Supersonic Boom," *Time,* September 30, 1991, p.48.

CONCERNS WITH SST

The advantage of supersonic air speed is not without cost. The air flow at that speed generates extreme heat, requiring special engineering using modern composites of materials such as silicon and carbon. Also, fuel efficiency is greatly reduced. A plane flying at Mach 2 may use twice the fuel of a subsonic jet of comparable size and cargo. Third, the engines required to reach supersonic speeds generate significantly more noise. This noise, termed the sonic boom, resembles thunder to observers on the ground when a plane flying at supersonic speed passes overhead. The boom is the result of compression waves gathering at the nose of the aircraft and emanating in a dense wave form, and it raises environmental concerns. Over the past decade, increased attention has been focused on aircraft noise. Reduction of the sonic boom is believed to be possible, though many are skeptical the boom can be quieted enough to allow flight over populated areas. Finally, developing an SST that can meet all these concerns and be fuel efficient both subsonically (over land) and supersonically is still an open technological challenge.

Currently, the United States and most Western nations prohibit civilian aircraft from "booming the deck." Supersonic travel is permitted over the oceans, but over 30 countries restrict Concorde flights due to noise levels. The Soviet Union is currently the only country which does not restrict supersonic travel over land. In the US and elsewhere, local activists, especially in communities around airports and military bases where housing values have dropped due to noise levels, have stepped up their efforts. The federal government is considering legislation to require the phase-out of a certain class of older, more noisy aircraft (including Boeing 727 and 737 and the McDonnell Douglas DC-9), a move which would cost the airline industry tens of billions of dollars for replacement.

Environmental concerns about the ozone layer, which protects the earth from harmful ultraviolet rays, are also being examined by engineering crews. Experts estimate that SST emissions of nitrogen-oxide will have to be cut down to one-tenth of the emissions from current conventional aircraft. One concept for reducing emissions involves heating and burning fuel in gradual stages, and requires extensive engine renovation. Finally, there are also other potential threats to the SST, notably from the efforts of Boeing and Airbus to develop a conventional subsonic airplane that would seat 600–700 passengers.

The raw materials to be used for SST include a variety of advanced aluminum alloys, steel alloys, and titanium. Soviet engineers are more experienced in working with titanium than Western engineers, as the material is more commonplace there. Some of the materials to be used bring new challenges to aircraft development since newly developed composites have different weight, strength, flexibility, heat conduction, moisture absorption, and thermal expansion characteristics than traditional metals. While many of the new materials demonstrate significant advantages (e.g., they are lighter, stronger, and can resist higher temperatures), more testing and technical knowledge (e.g., on material aging) are needed before the materials can be used in aircraft. Manufacturers around the world are experimenting with a variety of composites for engine and airframe parts, and looking closely at processing methods and costs. Companies such as Dow Chemical and Boeing, as well as NASA, are enthusiastic about new developments, but are concerned that materials may be chosen for the SST at too early a stage. Development of new high performance materials is thought to be critical over the next 5–10 years.

SOVIET VERSUS WESTERN EFFORTS ON SST

Differences between the economic and political structures of the Soviet Union and the United States help explain the arguable technological lead Soviet aircraft manufacturers reportedly have over Western manufacturers in supersonic technology. Traditionally, Soviet industry has placed its best and the brightest in the military, often to work in technology design bureaus which have been heavily funded by the government. The dozen or more aerospace design bureaus, probably the most sophisticated of Soviet enterprises, invested significant time and money into supersonic transportation. This past devotion to aeronautics and space programs has given the organizations a tremendous advantage. However, large-scale redistribution of authority is expected in the Soviet military-industrial complex. New aircraft programs at all of the design bureaus (i.e., Antonov, Klimov, Mil, Molniya, Sukhoi, Yakovlev, etc.) are expected to face supply problems, the task of retooling factories, inevitable layoffs, competition amongst themselves and from outside, disputes over the ownership of assets, and currency and trade problems. These issues will naturally result from funding cuts and industry reorganization. Given that the Soviet workforce in one of the most highly educated in the world, loss of intellectual base is also feared as highly trained engineers seek better opportunities and higher wages. The problems will be hardest felt in Russia, as 85% of the Soviet aviation industry is within that republic.

Vladimir Koblov, chairman of the Military Industrial Commission, said in 1991 that industries under his command devoted about 45% of their production to the military, down from 65% in the mid-1980s.[10] The space budget is reportedly down 20%, and the aeronautics budget down 50%.

Of the estimated 5 million Soviet workers in aerospace enterprises, it is estimated that 50% could lose their jobs in the next few years.

US aerospace manufacturers have not had the discretionary resources required to fund internal supersonic flight research and development. Their expenditures have typically been for the design of a specific aircraft, either for development of new commercial models or in response to a military request for a new plane design.

EXHIBIT 3

Average Age of Fortune 500 Fleet

Aircraft Type	Average Age	Number of Aircraft
Heavy Jets	9.75	318
Medium Jets	8.96	55
Light Jets	12.07	17

Heavy Jets Include:
Challenger 600,601
Falcon 50, 900
Gulfstream II, II-B, III, IV
JetStar
Airliner-Type Jets

Medium Jets Include:
BAe 125 Series
Citation III
Falcon 20,200
IAI Astra, Westwinds
Lear 55 Series
Sabreliner Series

Light Jets Include:
Beech 400
Citation I, II
Corvette
Diamond I, IA, II
Falcon 10, 100
IAI 1121 A, B, C
Lear 23, 24, 25, 28, 29, 35, 36
MS-760 Paris Jet

Source: Aviation Data, Inc., Wichita, KS; *Business & Commercial Aviation.*

[10]Alan Murray, "Soviet Managers Woo American Investment Against Heavy Odds," *The Wall Street Journal,* September 26, 1991.

chapter 12

The Analysis of MNEs by Countries

Just as MNEs evaluate countries before making significant investment and operational decisions concerning their potential operations in a given country, countries evaluate MNEs and their proposals, because certain conditions can affect the positive or negative value of the proposal for the country. Often, not only can certain aspects of the proposal have differing effects on the value to the MNE and country, but officials of the MNE and government can have different perspectives on variables determining project outcomes. Our purpose is to outline why countries analyze MNEs, and a methodology that they use—economic cost benefit analysis (ECB)—in their evaluation.

WHY GOVERNMENTS WORRY ABOUT MNEs

Governments employ people whose job it presumably is to look out for the welfare of the state. In a world of globally integrated firms, MNEs pose both an important opportunity and a threat to governments. Although most MNE executives are adept at pointing out the opportunities and positive benefits they believe they bring to a given country, they are generally less attuned to the threats they are seen to pose, from the perspective of the government.

General Concern for Independence

Perhaps there is no concern to the nation state other than its independence. The concept of sovereignty is at the heart of why governments exist and operate. When the independence of one nation is threatened by another, it is nearly universally accepted that the threatened nation has the right to respond. Consequently, if entities such as MNEs are seen as posing a threat to the independence of a nation, then one would expect the government to adopt actions that seek to protect its sovereignty.

However, in the case of the interactions between the nation state and MNEs, the threat is more subtle, and so the reaction is usually subtle as well. Despite the subtlety, MNEs are often seen as posing threats to national independence. Governments worry that if MNEs gain control of strategic national assets and resources (oil, gas, metals, forests), they may not be able to control development of their own resources. In the extreme case, governments worry that they might be held hostage and forced to incur costs via lower taxes, or credits and subsidies provided to the MNE. For example, Saudi Arabia sought to ensure that Western oil firms had explicit plans to guarantee the transfer of technical capabilities to local employees, so that foreign MNEs could not have an unacceptable level of influence over oil production in the country. Governments also view MNEs as potential threats to their independence if they become too strong as suppliers of critical resources. For example, after both World War II and the oil shocks of the 1970s, Japan sought to develop a strong domestic nuclear power industry as a means of strengthening its energy independence.

The suspicion of MNEs may be particularly strong among low-income developing countries (LDCs) because of their view that, in the past, MNEs have exploited these countries with an eye to maximizing the benefits to the MNE rather than to the country.

Concerns about Impact on Domestic Firms

The competitive pressures that MNEs can bring into a country's domestic economy can often be severe. Technological, capital, and human resources of domestic firms may not be sufficiently advanced to compete effectively with foreign MNEs. Although many governments acknowledge that domestic firms eventually need to adjust, by either becoming competitive or going out of existence, the dislocations that accompany these adjustments are problematic for most governments. Consequently, governments seem to be particularly concerned about MNEs competing against two types of domestic firms.

First, governments are concerned about firms in declining industries. There may be structural reasons (for example, cheaper natural resources or labor in another country), that may be at the heart of the decline of a particular industry and beyond the control of the government. However, governments often want to ease the transition of workers in these industries. Japan is often cited as an example of direct government intervention in declining industries, such as steel and shipbuilding, in order to ease the transition of workers. We observe similar pressures in the US within the textile and automobile industries. MNEs that pose a threat of accelerating the adjustment of firms in declining industries are likely to be targets of specific government action in an effort to protect what it sees as the best interests of its citizens.

Second, governments are concerned about firms in promising and embryonic industries. If a country's standard of living is to increase, then workers must be able to earn higher incomes and increase their productivity. New industries often are a key source of creating such opportunities. Consequently, MNEs that have the ability to destroy domestic firms in emerging industries represent a substantial threat in the eyes of the local government.

In either of these two categories, MNEs should not be surprised by government policies that restrict their ability to compete profitably in that country.

Concerns about Hidden Value

Governments are concerned about MNEs hiding value. One of the most obvious concerns that governments have about MNEs is that they will hide profits and thereby avoid their tax liability. Because of their global networks, MNEs can move the profits from a high tax-rate country to a low tax-rate country through fees and transfer pricing policies. While this may be attractive to the MNE and benefit the lower the tax-rate country, it is unfair (and often illegal) in the eyes of the other country. In the US, then presidential candidate Clinton made this issue a part of his campaign by promising that foreign MNEs operating in the US would no longer be able to avoid paying US corporate taxes by transferring their profits to other subsidiaries in other countries. Consequently, MNEs should not be surprised when proposals that involve subsidiaries and transfer fees receive special scrutiny by governments.

Governments are also concerned that MNEs will hide value by keeping advanced technologies out of their countries. MNEs can accomplish this in at least two ways. First, they can simply assign low-technology tasks to operations within a certain country. From the government's perspective, this keeps high value-added activities and their benefits from the local economy. Second, MNEs can keep high technology out of the hands of local employees by assigning expatriate managers and technical specialists to the subsidiary. From the government's perspective, while having the technology in the country may provide indirect benefits, preventing local employees from becoming familiar with the technology reduces their ability to earn higher wages and improve their standard of living. Consequently, MNEs should not be surprised when either governments employ policies that require high value-added technology to be incorporated into proposals, or limit the number, type, and duration of expatriate employees.

Concerns about Responsibility

Governments also worry about the social responsibility of MNEs. To the extent that MNEs are viewed as "temporary" visitors in countries, with no long-term commitment to raising the standard of living of citizens, governments worry about these firms exploiting opportunities and not being around for longer-term negative consequences. For example, governments worry about MNEs in natural resource extraction industries (for example, oil, gas, forest products, minerals, and metals) taking resources in the most economically efficient means possible with little regard for environmental consequences, worker safety, or societal health and welfare.

If disasters happen (for example, oil spills, chemical explosions, nuclear meltdowns, hazardous waste dumping, and the like) the individuals responsible may escape the arms of local justice. Those responsible may be transferred out of the country by the MNE before the government can assess responsibility, or the MNE may simply protect the people at headquarters who were responsible for formulating and implementing the decisions that led to the disaster and its consequences. This issue, for example, is at the heart of the continuing dispute between Union Carbide and the government of India concerning the Bhopal tragedy.

All of these reasons provide a broad list of why governments are suspicious of MNEs and why they may look at proposals with different perspectives than do MNEs. However, to the extent that MNEs can understand government viewpoints and their methods of analysis, they will be able to craft proposals that provide a positive return not only to themselves, but to the government and its citizens as well. In the next section, we explore a common method governments use to analyze and evaluate MNE proposals: the method of economic cost benefit analysis.

ECONOMIC COST BENEFIT ANALYSIS

Why might a government not simply be able to adopt the cash flow projections of an MNE, and thereby make a reliable estimate of the worth of the project to the society? In a freely competitive economy in which there are no restrictions on information, prices, entry barriers, both MNEs and governments could use the same set of projections as measures of the project value to both the firm and the society. This is a situation in which private and social valuations are the same. However, when there are externalities or markets cease to be perfectly competitive, private and social valuations can differ, as we shall see below.

In a developing economy, price controls, wage restrictions, subsidies, tariffs, taxes, and other imperfections distort values in such a way that market prices no longer reflect the true value (or opportunity cost) of a resource to society. Consequently, governments need to employ a different method of analysis in order to determine the value of a proposed project to the society. Obviously, if MNEs and governments are using different means of analyzing a common proposal, it is possible that the proposal could have a positive net present value for one party and not the other.

The most common approach utilized by governments assumes that the maximization of national income is its economic objective. In order to examine the extent to which a proposed project adds to or subtracts from national income, governments must value economic costs and benefits at their *opportunity cost* to the society, which, depending on the extent of market imperfections, may differ from existing market prices.

Benefit-Cost Ratio

The first means of examining the value of a proposed project is to examine the ratio of its benefits and costs. Obviously, if benefits exceed costs, the project has a positive value for the country.[1] The basic benefit-cost ratio can be expressed as follows:

$$[\{F + R^* + T\} - O + N]/E$$

where,

F = the local factor payments that the MNE pays to labor, management, and land (e.g., wages, salary, rent),

R^* = the after-tax payments to local capital (e.g., profits, dividends, interest),

T = the taxes collected by the government (e.g., corporate, import, withholding, excise),

O = opportunity costs of local factors,

N = *net* external economies, and

E = payments to external factors of production including technology (e.g., profits, dividends, interest, royalties, management fees, and so on that are transferred out of the country).

Although most of the variables above are straightforward, a brief comment on a couple of them may be helpful. In determining the value of O, we must focus on the opportunity costs to society of local factors utilized *as if they had not been employed by the MNE.* For example, if labor used by the project would have been idle otherwise, the opportunity cost is zero. If the labor used by the proposed project would take workers away from equally productive jobs, the opportunity to the local society cost is equal to what the MNE would have to pay for the labor.

In determining the value of N, we must focus on the *net* sum external economies. The focus must be on the net sum because it is possible for a proposed project to produce both external economies as well as diseconomies. For example, the project may allow other firms to sell products at lower prices or to sell technically superior products. These positive spillover effects are a benefit to the society. However, the same project may produce structural unemployment or discourage local entrepreneurs. These diseconomies must be netted out against the external economies produced by the proposed project.

Once the values for each of the variables is computed, if the ratio is greater than one, the project has a positive value for the society.

Present Value of Costs and Benefits

To calculate the present value of the streams of costs and benefits that occur over time, it is necessary to derive the appropriate discount rate. Just as private and social values differ in a situation of market imperfections, private and social discount rates also can differ.

---

[1]This presumes that benefits and costs occur at the same time. However, benefits and costs occur over time and with different time paths. Once we have examined the static benefit-cost ratio, we will turn our attention to the issues of the net present value of costs and benefits that occur over time and the adjustments that must be made.

Generally, an MNE will select an appropriate risk-adjusted discount rate that is equal to the marginal opportunity costs of its capital (it may also need to add a risk premium to account for political risks that operations within the country may entail). Governments, however, seek to maximize the income effects of proposed MNE projects and therefore select a discount rate that *reflects the marginal productivity of capital in its economy.* Because governments have immediate needs for increased foreign exchange reserves, slower inflation, or reduced unemployment, they often place a higher value on near-term benefits and costs over those in the long term. This leads them to select higher discount rates when examining the present value of proposed projects.

Shadow Price Adjustments and Benefit-Cost Analysis

Because market imperfections can cause the social and private values to differ, governments often make adjustments in the social benefits and costs via the use of *shadow prices.* Shadow prices are intended to measure accurately the opportunity costs of various inputs and the utility of the outputs to the society.

The first potential area of adjustment is the revenue generated by the proposed project. In determining the revenue benefit to the firm, MNEs simply calculate the nominal sales expected to be generated. The value of these outputs to the society can differ from the MNE's estimate of nominal sales in several ways. First, if the output from the project generates goods that would replace imports, then the value of the output is the same as the value of the imports. This value can deviate from the MNE's sales figures for several reasons. One of the most common causes is import tariffs. For example, if the MNE forecasts that first year sales will be $1000 for 1000 units but the same 1000 units would cost $800 on the international market, then the value to the society is only $800. Just as in the case of output that substitutes for imports, output that generates exports should be valued using the international market price rather than the domestic price.

An additional adjustment may be needed in calculating the value of revenues. Governments often have policies in place that control and, hence, distort the real value of their currency. A shadow exchange rate (SER, explained below) rather than official exchange rate (OER) reflects the true value of foreign exchange. For example, suppose the exchange rate of the official US dollar ($) to Mexican peso (P) was 1/10, and the shadow exchange rate was 1/20. In this case, the official exchange rate overvalues the local currency. Consequently, if the official exchange rate is used, the incremental value that foreign exchange would add to the national income would be underestimated. Unfortunately, determining the shadow exchange rate in not easy. In some cases, exchange rates quoted in parallel or underground markets can be utilized; however, because currency exchanges in these markets are usually illegal, these rates often reflect a risk premium. Therefore, a more accurate measure of the shadow exchange rate is probably somewhere between the official and parallel market rates.

Returning to our previous example, in which the value of a proposed project's output is $800 (at world rather than domestic prices), at the official exchange rate ($1 = P10), this translates into a local currency value of P8,000. However, if the shadow exchange rate is used (1 = 20), then the value of these goods to the society is P16,000 rather than P8,000. Because the output would substitute for imported goods and because the official exchange rate overvalues the local currency, using the official exchange rate undervalues the output to the society.

This same process of shadow exchange rate adjustment also would be needed for any factor payments made to MNEs. For example, if any assets were brought in by the MNE, the value of these assets would need to be translated into local currency using the shadow exchange rate. Payments made to MNEs via fees, interest, dividends, profits, and so on would also need to be translated into local currency by using the shadow exchange rate.

In addition to adjustments made via shadow exchange rates, a variety of production factors need to be adjusted using shadow prices. For example, because of government labor laws, union rules, and so on, the market wage paid for labor may not reflect the true value of opportunity cost to society of that labor. The easiest way to estimate the shadow price of labor is to determine the next best relevant alternative use of that labor if it were not used in the proposed project. Similarly, market prices may deviate from shadow prices in the case of production factors such as land and raw materials. In order to estimate the true value of the factor to society, the shadow price rather than the market price should be used.

Example of Differing Valuations

The following example provides a concrete illustration of many of the issues covered thus far. A US MNE is proposing a telephone manufacturing operation in Mexico. In preparing the project's income statement for a representative year, the MNE uses market prices in Mexico to estimate profits or losses. The MNE estimates that it can produce 200,000 telephones and can sell these phones for a total of P20 million. The Mexican government calculates that the same quantity of phones produced by the project could be bought in the international market for 900,000 US dollars, or 9 million pesos at the official exchange rate of $1/P10. However, in order to assess the value of the telephones to the society, the Mexican government translates the value of the phones at international prices using the shadow exchange rate of $1/P20. Based on the shadow exchange rate, the value of the phones in local currency is 18 million pesos.

The MNE's and Mexican government's assessment of the value of inputs also differs. While the MNE estimates that it will pay out P6 million for local labor in the new plant, the government assesses this factor at zero value. This is because the workers who are likely to be employed in the operation would be idle if not for the project; consequently, the shadow price for labor is zero. Next, the MNE estimates that it will import P6 million in raw materials; however, the government calculates the value of these imported raw materials at the preduty international price and translates the value into local currency using the SER. The MNE estimates that raw materials purchased from local suppliers will cost P2 million. The government assesses the value of local raw materials at their international market price in order to remove the price effects of Mexico's import protection policies. Although the MNE estimates that $200,000 will be spent on overhead in the US and translates that into pesos using the OER, the government assesses the overhead expenses incurred in US dollars using the SER. Finally, while the MNE computes the local currency value of interest payments remitted abroad using the OER, the government uses the SER to calculate the value of these interest payments. The government also adjusts its assessment of interest paid locally on a P3 million loan, to reflect the social opportunity cost of local capital, which is estimated to be 20%.

To the US MNE, the project has a positive value; for the Mexican government, it appears to have a negative value (see Table 12.1).

However, the calculations do not incorporate any externalities into the final value. The proposed plant site will require workers to move to a remote location. It is expected that this movement will increase the burden on the local government for improved roads, sewers, water, and other services. However, the MNE has proposed to train ten engineers in their US operations in quality control technology. The MNE has also proposed building a child care facility in town so that women could be employed in the factory with reduced concerns about the care of their children. These and other externalities must also be considered by the government. If the government estimates that the net value of the project's externalities will exceed P2.1 million, then the project's social benefits will exceed its social costs.

Shifting Perceptions over Time

Just as the streams of costs and benefits vary over time, so too does the perception by each party of the value of the project. These perceptions are not necessarily a function of systematic financial or economic calculations similar to the ones we just examined. Rather, they are more a function of intuitive judgments. Unlike the initial calculations that attempt to forecast costs and benefits and then determine their present value through appropriate discount rates, once the project has begun, "real-time" perceptions of value tend to be a function of the moment. Consequently, there is a potential for a conflicting pattern of perceptions by both sides over time.

TABLE 12.1

Item	MNE Value	Government Value
Sales	20.0	18.0
CGS	−14.0	−11.5
Local labor	6.0	0.0
Imported raw material	6.0	10.0
Local raw material	2.0	1.5
Overhead	−2.0	−4.0
Interest	-2.3	−4.6
Remitted abroad	2.0	4.0
Paid locally	0.3	0.6
Profit (loss)	**1.7**	**(2.1)**

For the MNE, although the net present value of the project must be positive in order to justify proceeding, it is quite common for projects to experience losses in the initial stages before profits emerge. Generally, however, there is an upward sloping line that represents an increasingly positive benefit-cost ratio of the project to the MNE. Typically, MNEs make major investment in facilities and equipment early in the project but decrease these investments over its life. Thus, as sales increase and the level of large investments declines, MNEs see an increasingly positive benefit-cost ratio.

Governments, however, have a different perspective. Initially, the benefit-cost ratio is positive for the government as the MNE brings in new capital, training, technology, and so on. Additionally, the MNE takes out relatively low levels of profits, fees, and so on from the project. However, as time passes, the MNE typically reduces or even stops its infusion of new capital, technology, and training, and at the same time it increases the levels of profits that it remits out of the country through dividends, fees, repatriated profits, and so forth. In fact, as the level of technological and knowledge contribution from the MNE declines and local capabilities increase, the government may come to believe that the MNE's operations could be replaced by local operations. A replacement of the MNE would still produce the benefits to society, while avoiding many of the costs associated with MNEs. Figure 12.1 summarizes these ideas.

Up to the point at which the government and MNE perceptions of benefit-cost ratios intersect, few problems are likely to occur between the two parties. However, once the lines cross and the local government views the ratio in worse terms than the MNE, this can lead the government to try to seek new investments or other societal benefits from the MNE. From the MNE's perspective, these demands are tantamount to the government changing the rules after the game is underway.

If the government's perception of the costs and benefits shifts to the point at which it believes the costs outweigh the benefits, it is likely to pursue extreme policies. At that point, if the government cannot cause the MNE to undertake actions that increase its societal contributions, it may pressure or even require the MNE to sell its assets and equity in the operation to local entities. In the most extreme case, the government may simply expropriate the local assets of the MNE. Politically, it is highly unlikely that the government will be able to allow the MNE to continue operations at a level at which the perceived costs to the society outweigh the perceived benefits.

This general shift in perceptions is paralleled by a general shift in power. Initially, MNEs are in a more powerful position than local governments. This is because MNEs have the technology, know-how, money, international sourcing or distribution networks, and so forth to which governments want access. While governments are not entirely powerless (they have local markets, labor pools, natural resources, raw materials, and the like), the balance of power is determined partly by the extent to which the resources on each side are substitutable. The greater the substitutability, the weaker the power position. For example, if the resources the MNE brings can be easily substituted for those of another MNE, this shifts the balance of power in the direction of the government. If, however, the local markets, labor pools, natural resources, and raw materials of the country are easy to substitute, this shifts the balance of power in the direction of the MNE.

In general, it is common for the balance of power to be in favor of the MNE at the beginning. Given that few MNEs will undertake a project that does not have a positive net present value, there are limits to how far the government can push the terms already agreed upon for a proposed project. Additionally, with the exception of rare natural resources, there are generally other countries with similar factors that provide alternative operating locations for MNEs.

Once the MNE has "set up shop" in the country, the balance of power generally begins to shift in the direction of the government, and once operating in the country, the MNE must abide by the laws and regulations of the government. Although the MNE can try to influence these laws, regulations, and policies, it does not have direct control over them. While the MNE is essentially free to leave the country, the resource commitments made at the outset or early stages of the project increase its exit costs. Additionally, as local suppliers, customers, workers, managers, and technicians gain knowledge from the project, they become less dependent upon the MNE. As long as it is more costly to abandon operations than to accommodate the demands of the government, it is likely that the MNE will

Figure 12.1 Divergence of Perceived Economic Benefit-Cost Ratio of Affiliate

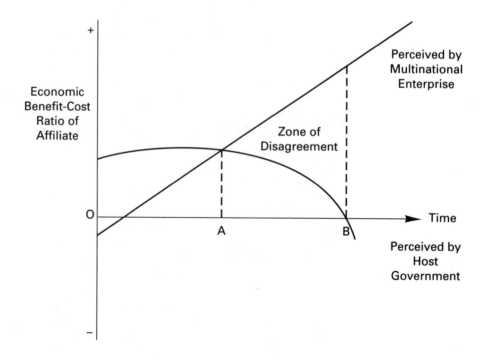

choose to accommodate. However, the government must be careful, because even if there are other MNEs waiting in the wings, their willingness to substitute will be influenced by the government's behavior.

These shifts in perceptions and power are not necessarily true in every case; however, they are common enough for the reasons identified and discussed. MNEs wishing to avoid or alter these patterns must be attuned to the causal factors and proactively seek to influence them. Although it is unlikely that the interests of governments and MNEs will ever be perfectly aligned, there must be sufficiently complementary interests at the beginning and throughout the life of the project in order to motivate both sides to undertake and continue involvement.

In summary, this chapter has provided an overview of why governments are suspicious of MNEs and how they evaluate MNE proposals. Despite the fact that many MNE executives may find the social benefit-cost approach to valuing proposed projects different from (or even strange compared to) traditional corporate approaches, they should realize that governments systematically use such approaches. Inability to anticipate or respond to such analytical methods will compromise MNE's ability to capture and maximize opportunities across the globe.

case 16

Dow Indonesia (A)

In early February 1977, Colin D. Goodchild, the manager of Dow Chemical's Indonesia office, was preparing for the next meeting with Indonesian government officials to discuss Dow's new proposal for a 700-million-dollar petrochemical project based on gas from the Arun gas fields in northern Sumatra. Mr. Goodchild was expecting Mr. Walker, from Dow's regional office in Hong Kong, to arrive within the next twenty-four hours to join in the discussions. Mr. Walker was eager to see some tangible progress in the negotiations, which had been going on for several years.

PREVIOUS DISCUSSIONS

Discussions for Dow participation in a petrochemical facility in Indonesia had begun in 1975 with Pertamina, the state oil company.[1] As originally conceived, the project would have been a joint venture, probably 50-50, between Dow and Pertamina, and had become known as the Aceh petrochemical project. The plant, to be located in Aceh Province, between Banda Aceh and the Arun gas fields (*Exhibit 1*), would produce a range of petrochemicals from ethane, which would be extracted by Pertamina or by a joint venture from the natural gas feeding a liquification plant operated by Pertamina. By 1977 liquified natural gas (LNG) was being sold to Japan and would also be sold to the United States, if US permission was ever granted. The gas was supplied by Mobil Oil from the Arun gas fields, which it operated under a production sharing agreement.

[1]This procedure was unusual. Negotiations for foreign investments in manufacturing were generally handled by BKPM, an investment-coordinating board. Pertamina handled petroleum negotiations, but had also been responsible for negotiating some other large projects.

This case was prepared as the basis for class discussion rather than to illustrate either effective or ineffective handling of an administrative situation. Written by Brizio Biondi-Morra, Research Assistant, under the supervision of Professors James E. Austin and Louis T. Wells, Jr., and Assistant Professor Dennis J. Encarnation.

EXHIBIT 1 Aceh Petrochemical Facility Location Map

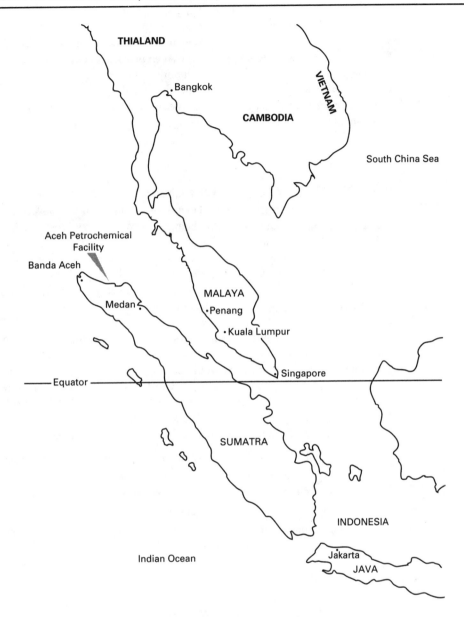

Aceh Petrochemical Facililty Location Map

   The original plans for the LNG project called for a six-train facility. However, in 1976 the plans were changed considerably as Pertamina fell into financial difficulties. The state company had run up over $1 billion in short-term debts to foreign lenders. It had borrowed heavily to finance its expansion into a wide range of activities, including fertilizer plants, a steel plant, and a host of smaller businesses. In spite of higher revenues from increased oil prices, in 1976 Pertamina was unable to meet its debt obligations. The government stepped in to assume the debts of Pertamina. In so doing, it increased its control of the enterprise which, in the past, had been called a "state within a state." Unfinished projects, such as the steel mill and the Aceh petrochemical plant, were taken out of the control of Pertamina and put in the hands of Dr. J.B. Sumarlin, Minister of State for Administrative Reform and Vice Chairman of BAPPENAS, the national planning agency.

In the changes, the plans for expanding the current three trains of the LNG facility were set aside. Minister Sumarlin also mentioned to Dow the possibility of a "Contract of Work," rather than a joint venture, for the Aceh petrochemical project. This was a form of contract common in Indonesia for nonoil mineral projects. Under most such arrangements, the foreign firm provided all the funds and operated the project. As a result of these changes and a scaling down of the forecast of market growth in Indonesia, Dow was now considering a smaller petrochemical plant than originally planned.

THE NEW PROPOSAL

Dow's new proposal (*Appendix*) was contained in a feasibility study made by the company in January 1977. The project proposed that the government of Indonesia grant Dow a "Contract of Work" to manufacture petrochemicals based on the Arun gas/liquids feedstock. Under the auspices of this "Contract of Work," Dow would be given approval to form a "Dow Venture" company that would use some 21,000 barrels/day of ethane to manufacture 600 million lbs./yr. of ethylene, 300,000 million lbs./yr. of low-density polyethylene (LDPE), 150,000 million lbs./yr. of high-density polyethylene (HDPE), and 500,000 million lbs./yr. of vinyl chloride monomers (VCM).

Under this new proposal the government and Dow would have to support the project with their respective resources to ensure the success of the project. The government would sell ethane[2] and fuel gas to the project and provide local know-how and protection from import competition. In turn, Dow would be responsible for the petrochemical technology, training, market development expertise, key expatriate staff, and financial resources. Dow would also have exclusive rights to import LDPE, HDPE, and VCM into Indonesia from the day of signing of the "Contract of Work" until about five years after start-up.

According to Dow, the proposal was guided by four principles:

1. Profitable production of petrochemical products required by industry.
2. Large-scale production with advanced technology to maximize manufacturing economies.
3. Long-term raw material sources to permit extensive growth.
4. Provision of stable sources of petrochemical products for Indonesia with excess product available for export by Dow.

EXPECTED PERFORMANCE

The financing scheme recommended by Dow was based on a projected balance sheet (*Exhibit 2*) and income statement (*Exhibit 3*) that resulted from a joint study by Dow Chemical Pacific and the First National City Bank project finance group. The figures were based on the assumptions that Dow would be responsible for raising the funds and that the interest burden would be carried by the project.

The size of the project was such that the products were destined largely for the Indonesian domestic market, which was currently supplied by imported petrochemicals. The forecasts assumed that tariffs and other taxes on imports would remain at least at their current level of 24%.

In its proposal, Dow noted three characteristics of the project that were thought to be extremely important. First, the project was heavily capital intensive. Second, the manufacturing cost of the Dow Venture's product had a high fixed-cost element. And finally, the

---

[2]The casewriter estimated that each pound of ethane extracted from Arun gas would reduce the export value of the gas by $0.045.

EXHIBIT 2

Dow Venture Pro Forma Balance Sheet
(millions of $)

Assets	1981ᵃ	1982	1983	1984	1985	1986	1987	1988	1989	1990	1991
Cash	1.0	1.1	1.6	1.7	1.9	1.9	2.0	2.0	2.0	2.0	2.0
Inventory	5.4	21.0	27.1	29.1	30.6	31.4	31.4	31.4	31.4	31.4	31.4
Accounts receivable	13.8	39.4	49.0	54.0	57.0	58.4	57.5	57.5	56.7	56.9	54.6
Total current assets	20.2	61.5	77.7	84.8	89.5	91.7	90.9	90.9	90.1	90.3	88.0
Total fixed assets	653.1	614.6	565.3	516.0	466.7	417.5	368.2	318.9	269.6	220.3	174.7
Short-term investment	6.4	18.1	24.2	28.9	37.4	36.7	78.2	112.7	146.6	171.8	208.8
Total assets	679.7	694.2	667.4	629.7	593.6	545.9	537.3	522.5	506.3	482.4	471.5
Liabilities & equity											
Short-term loan	—	—	—	—	—	—	—	—	—	—	—
Long-term loan	480.0	500.0	450.0	369.2	268.4	164.6	131.6	98.6	65.6	30.0	—
Accounts payable	3.9	12.1	20.9	22.9	24.5	25.3	25.3	25.3	25.3	25.3	25.3
Tax liability	—	—	—	—	—	—	31.5	49.1	53.9	56.2	61.7
Equity	248.1	250.0	250.0	250.0	250.0	250.0	250.0	250.0	250.0	250.0	250.0
Retained surplus	-52.3	-67.9	-53.5	-12.4	50.7	106.0	95.3	99.5	111.5	120.9	134.5
Total liability & equity	679.7	694.2	667.4	629.7	593.6	545.9	537.3	522.5	506.3	482.4	471.5

ᵃOne-half year.

EXHIBIT 3

Dow Venture Pro Forma Statement of Income
(millions of $)

	1981(a)	1982	1983	1984	1985	1986	1987	1988	1989	1990	1991
Net sales (b)	27.8	226.6	315.6	348.5(a)	371.7	383.8	388.8	395.3	401.1	402.1	404.6
Cost of good sold (c)	27.0	109.1	146.3	154.7	161.4	164.5	164.5	164.5	164.5	164.5	164.5
Depreciation	18.3	44.8	49.3	49.3	49.3	49.3	49.3	49.3	49.3	49.3	45.6
Gross profit	-17.5	72.7	120.0	144.5	161.0	170.0	175.0	181.5	187.3	188.3	194.5
Royalty (d)	0.8	6.8	9.5	10.4	11.2	11.5	11.7	11.9	12.0	12.1	12.1
Selling expenses (a)	4.2	21.1	28.3	31.1	33.4	34.7	35.6	36.5	37.6	38.1	38.9
General administrative expenses (f)	14.0	14.8	17.5	17.1	18.6	19.6	20.5	21.4	22.3	24.1	24.3
Operating profit	-36.5	30.0	64.7	85.3	97.8	104.2	107.2	111.7	115.4	114.0	119.2
Interest income	3.5	2.1	2.3	2.9	3.6	4.1	6.3	10.5	14.3	17.5	20.9
Interest expense (g)	19.3	47.7	52.6	47.1	38.3	27.6	16.5	13.2	9.9	6.6	3.0
Income before tax	-52.3	-15.6	14.4	41.6	63.1	80.7	97.0	109.0	119.8	124.9	137.1
Tax (h)	–	–	–	–	–	–	35.1	49.1	53.9	56.2	61.7
Income after tax	-52.3	-15.6	14.4	41.6	63.1	80.7	61.9	60.0	65.9	68.7	75.4
Earned surplus beginning	–	-52.3	-67.9	-53.5	-11.8	50.7	106.6	95.9	100.1	112.1	121.5
Total earned surplus	-52.3	-67.9	-53.5	-11.8	51.3	132.0	168.5	155.9	166.0	180.8	196.9
Dividend (d)	–	–	–	–	–	25.4	72.6	55.8	53.9	59.3	61.8
Earned surplus end	-52.3	-67.9	-53.5	-11.8	51.3	106.6	95.9	100.1	112.1	121.5	135.1

NOTES

(a) Half-year only

(b) Domestic sales volume (million lbs.)

Domestic sales volume (million lbs.)										
–LDPE, Tub. process	40	101	112	120	130	140	150	150	150	150
Auto. process	–	60	65	75	84	96	109	135	150	150
–HDPE	20	106	117	129	141	150	150	150	150	150
–VCM	–	83	182	200	220	242	266	293	322	322
Export sales volume (million lbs.)										
–LDPE, Tub. process	–	25	27	30	20	10	–	–	–	–
–LDPE, Auto process	–	40	44	48	66	54	41	15	–	–
–HDPE	–	14	18	21	9	–	–	–	–	–
–VCM	–	105	230	250	260	258	234	207	178	178
Domestic prices ($/lb.)										
– LDPE	0.467	0.520	0.520	0.520	0.520	0.520	0.520	0.520	0.520	0.520
– HDPE	0.455	0.507	0.507	0.507	0.507	0.507	0.507	0.507	0.507	0.507
– VCM	–	0.362	0.362	0.362	0.362	0.362	0.362	0.362	0.362	0.362
Export prices FOB Indonesia ($/lb.)										
– LDPE	0.367	0.367	0.367	0.367	0.367	0.367	0.367	0.367	0.367	0.367
– HDPE	0.357	0.357	0.357	0.357	0.357	0.357	0.357	0.357	0.357	0.357
– VCM	0.286	0.286	0.286	0.286	0.286	0.286	0.286	0.286	0.286	0.286
(c) Imported content of CGS (CIF, $ million)	3.5	44.7	76.5	82.9	88.2	91.0	91.0	91.0	91.0	91.0
Domestic ethane used at pro forma cost of $0.038/lb. ($ million)	1.5	16.3	23.7	25.8	28.2	29.6	29.6	29.6	29.6	29.6

(d) Royalties and dividends are subject to a 20% local withholding tax.

(e) 60% local expenses; 40% to be paid abroad, probably to another part of the Dow enterprise.

(f) 90% local expenses; 10% foreign exchange cost.

(g) Interest and debt repayment go entirely abroad.

(h) The general Indonesian tax rate for corporate income was 45%. Foreign investors were usually granted two years of tax holidays. Investors could apply for an extra year for projects located on islands other than Java, another year for projects with large capital investment, and still another year for significant foreign exchange earnings or savings. High-priority projects could receive an additional year of tax holiday. Contracts of work had, in most cases, governed mining projects. Under recent contracts of work, mining activities had not received tax holidays. Rather, they had been subject to tax rates of 35% to 40% for the first ten years, and rates of 42% to 48% thereafter, with the rates varying by mineral. Such investors had been allowed tax credits in the amount of 8% of the investment outlay.

Dow Venture would produce satisfactory returns only when the levels of sales would enable its plants to operate near capacity. Because of the reduced size of the project, the resulting ethylene scale penalty, and the proportionally high cost of infrastructure, Dow asserted in its proposal that the project offered only marginal returns to the company.

The losses during the initial period of production were considered unavoidable in a project of such magnitude and complexity. Once the project's plants were operating at capacity, however, the Dow Venture was expected to generate sufficient cash to service the debt and yield an after-tax profit. The start-up of the main facilities was phased over a one year period. Supporting services and the infrastructure for the complex would be in place in mid-1981. However, some of the plants they were designed to serve would not be on-stream until the second half of 1982. The ethylene plant, representing a $150 million investment, would operate at capacity only when the plants consuming ethylene would do likewise.

Dow believed that sufficient market existed for the Venture's products so that most plants would be close to capacity operation within two years of start-up. The existence of surplus funds and the ability to borrow short term was thought to provide sufficient "cushion" for the project to meet the long-term loan commitments during any short-term downturn in operating revenue.

Dow's feasibility study provided financial data, but did not present returns on investment or discounted cash flows, since the Indonesian government and Dow would have their own standards for measuring economic viability. The case writer prepared a cash flow of the project, presented in *Exhibit 4*, using Dow's numbers and several assumptions. The casewriter also estimated profits that Dow might earn from production and the exclusive rights to import LDPE, HDPE, and VCM in the early years. These estimates are in *Exhibit 5*.

THE ETHYLENE INDUSTRY[3]

In 1977 the petrochemical industry was a major business in the Western countries and Japan. With total sales in excess of $300 billion, the industry accounted for about one-third of manufacturing investment in the U.S.A., Europe, and Japan. But most producers were experiencing problems of overcapacity.

The bulk of basic petrochemical products was derived from ethylene and its by-products which, in turn, were the primary raw material for making all the major commodity plastics such as LDPE, HDPE, and VCM. These plastics, together with ethylene, accounted for over half the output of the world's petrochemical industry.

During the 1970s many US petrochemical producers barely covered their cost of capital. In Europe, an assortment of state-owned and private companies fought over small increments of the market, earning huge losses in the process. In Japan, a dozen giants, helped into the industry by the government, were also losing money and struggling for positions in a market half the size of markets in Europe or the United States. And in the Middle East, oil producing countries' forward integration plans were likely to complicate an already difficult situation.

Many of the industry's current problems could be traced to its recent history. Although plastics based on phenol and vinyl had been made in the 1920s and 1930s, production of ethylene and the commodity plastics did not take off until the 1950s. Fueled by economic growth and cheap supplies of oil, these plastics rapidly replaced paper, wood, leather, metals, and other materials in many applications. But the world oil crisis of the

[3]Description based partly on "Note on the Ethylene and Commodity Plastics Industries" (0-385-066), Harvard Business School.

early 1970s dramatically slowed this expansion. Raw material and energy costs skyrocketed, demand stagnated, and new, often heavily subsidized producers entered the market. As the plants commissioned in the 1960s and early 1970s came on stream, it became clear that production capacity in most areas far exceeded demand.

Various studies estimated the oversupply of petrochemicals in 1977 at about 20% above demand. It was usually believed that industrialized nations were exporting HDPE and LDPE at prices equal to 70% of their domestic prices, and that these products had been available in 1977 in Southeast Asia at "dumping" prices.

Forecasts made in a few of these studies predicted that the current oversupply would cease around 1985, after which a balanced situation was expected to prevail until 1987. From 1987 onwards, supply—according to these reports—would be tight and prices would increase substantially with incremental changes in demand. Since the demand for ethylene-based products was estimated to increase at about 8% per year worldwide, these studies concluded that the 20% excess capacity would be filled quite rapidly.

Other indications, however, were pointing to a scenario of protracted oversupply beyond 1985. In Southeast Asia, for example, there were indications that a group of Japanese companies was considering the construction of a 660 million lbs./yr. ethylene plant in Singapore, which was already the third largest refinery center in the world and was well positioned to compete with the Aceh petrochemical project. Additional large projects could alter the validity of the optimistic long-term forecasts.

EXHIBIT 4

Cash Flow to Project
($ millions, year-end)

	1977[a]	1978[a]	1979[a]	1980[a]	1981[a]	1982[a]	1983	1984	1985	1986	1987	1988	1989	1990	1991
Sources															
Borrowing		69.0	180.0	165.0	66.0	20.0									
Income after tax					(52.3)	(15.6)	14.4	41.7	63.1	80.7	61.9	59.9	65.9	68.7	75.4
Depreciation					18.3	44.8	49.3	49.3	49.3	49.3	49.3	49.3	49.3	49.3	45.6
Uses															
Fixed investment	34.0	106.0	216.0	235.0	80.4	6.3									
Net working capital					16.3	33.1	7.4	5.1	3.1	1.4	35.9	14.0	5.6	2.1	7.8
Debt repayment							50.0	80.0	100.8	103.8	33.0	33.0	33.0	35.6	30.0

Notes:

[a]For 1977-1980, Dow's additional cash investment equalled the difference between fixed investment and borrowing. In 1981, that investment was $71.1 million, bringing the company's equity in the project up to $248.1 million (see *Exhibit 2*). In 1982, that equity grew to $250 million (again, see *Exhibit 2*), reflecting one final cash investment of $1.9 million.

PROJECT BENEFITS TO INDONESIA

Indonesia, an archipelago comprising five main islands and thousands of smaller ones, is a mountainous region with a land area of 735,000 square miles, almost three times the size of Texas. In 1977 its population was estimated at more than 130 million, making it the world's fifth most populous country. Although 90% of Indonesians were Moslem, in the most populous island, Java, beliefs tended to include elements of Hinduism and animism from earlier days. About 60% of its 51 million labor force was employed in agriculture, forestry, and fishing, and the country faced an estimated 2% to 10% rate of unemployment. Petroleum exports accounted for some two-thirds of Indonesia's export earnings and two-thirds of all government revenues. Far behind petroleum products, agricultural commodities were the next most important export. Indonesia's freely convertible currency, the rupiah, was considered by several economists to be overvalued by at least 20% vis-a-vis the dollar, with the official exchange rate set at Rp 415 to the dollar.

EXHIBIT 5

Profit (Contribution) from Imports
($ millions)

	1978	1979	1980	1981	1982	1983
Indonesian market size[a]	186	207	230	256	284	316
Local production	0	0	0	28	227	316
Value of imports	186	207	230	228	57	0
Contribution at 25% on import exclusivity[b]	46	51	57	57	15	0
NPV at 20% = 140.2						

Source: Casewriter's calculations.

[a]Calculated by taking Dow's assumption of market size for 1983 and reducing the market by 10% each earlier year.

[b]Contribution to Dow's fixed costs was estimated as 25% of the CIF sales prices. This is considered conservative, given Dow's international operating margin of greater than 30% and the excess capacity in world petrochemical plants at the time.

Indonesia's president was General Suharto, who had taken power from President Sukarno in 1965. Although some ministries were headed by military officers, several important economic ministers, including BAPPENAS and the Ministry of Finance, were headed by technocrats who had been drawn from the economics faculty of the University of Indonesia. The Ministry of Industry and some other ministries were headed by people with engineering training.

According to Dow, the benefits of this Aceh Petrochemical Project to Indonesia were manifold and encompassed foreign exchange savings and earnings, value added to hydrocarbons in Indonesia, employment, education, and local business opportunities. The project would be located in a province noted for its strict Moslem beliefs and with a history of efforts to break away from Indonesia. Dow felt that the rewards to the Indonesian people, the government of Indonesia, and Dow were such that the project had to be considered a top priority of the government.

Dow estimated that ten years after the start-up of the first plants the project would have saved Indonesia a cumulative net foreign exchange sum of US $1,450 million (see *Exhibit 6*). This amount was calculated by adding the total capital spent in Indonesia, the earnings from export sales, and the CIF value of petrochemicals sold domestically, under the assumption that they would otherwise have been imported. From this total were then subtracted the imported raw materials, the FOB value of Indonesian raw materials consumed by the project, the principal and interest repayments on loans, and the dividends paid to Dow.

Dow also pointed out that at full capacity the chemical complex proposed in Aceh would add an annual value of US $190 million to the hydrocarbons used as feedstock and fuel. This was consistent with the government's stated policy of upgrading energy resources to petrochemicals rather than selling energy in its less-refined state as was currently being done by Indonesia.

Dow also estimated the employment that would be generated by the proposed project. During the peak construction period there would be about 3,800 people employed at the plant site. Permanent employees were expected to number 1,600.[4] Employment was also expected to be created as a result of local business opportunities in servicing the needs of the complex. Dow claimed, however, that the most significant effect on employment would be in the plastics fabrication and chemical consuming industry in Indonesia. Dow estimated that 50,000 jobs would be created in the downstream sectors.

---

[4]Casewriters later assumed that wages would equal approximately US $1,000 per worker per year.

Dow also explained that Indonesia would gain technology for operating the plants. This technology would be passed on to Indonesians by training them in Indonesia and in Dow's US and European operations prior to start-up. Similarly, personnel would be trained in Dow's laboratories to learn technical applications and laboratory techniques. Additional skills would include those acquired by instrument and electrical technicians, fitters, welders, mechanics, and carpenters. Dow was certain that some of the people and skills employed during construction would be utilized in other projects in Indonesia. And it expected many additional skills to develop in the downstream plastics fabricating and chemical consuming industries.

EXHIBIT 6

Net Cumulative Foreign Exchange Earned by Project for Indonesia
(as calculated by Dow)

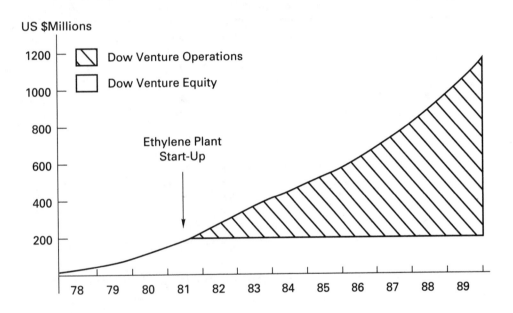

APPENDIX

Excerpts From Dow Proposal

INTRODUCTION

Major changes have occurred in Indonesia which have had a significant effect on the Aceh project economics. These changes have resulted in a reduced project scope and a forecast lower growth rate of the Indonesian domestic markets.

In addition there has been a significant downturn in world economic conditions such that the growth rate in the chemical industry has slowed. This has affected the potential export markets and the rate of new investment in the industry.

In Dow's view the project economics and financial performance are marginal at best, and some additional incentives are necessary for the project to proceed.

The economics presented in this study have incorporated assumptions which have a high element of risk not the least of which is the required Indonesian market growth. Before any negotiations proceed Dow would request a response from the Government of Indonesia (GOI) on the following "Dow Proposal."

The "Dow Proposal" would be incorporated into a "Contract of Work" to be negotiated between Dow and the GOI for petrochemical manufacture based on the Arun gas/liquids feedstock.

As part of this "Contract of Work" Dow would request that a two-year period be allowed to evaluate the Arun gas reserves, negotiate the essential elements of the project, and implement a market building program in Indonesia.

Only when this total project package is completed could Dow expect to obtain a commitment from financing institutions that would allow the project to be financed under the necessary conditions to proceed.

THE DOW PROPOSAL

A. The GOI form a company to extract ethane from the natural gas feed to the liquid natural gas (LNG) facility.

B. Dow be given approval to form a "Dow Venture" Company/Companies to manufacture ethylene, LDPE, HDPE, vinyl chloride, power/stream as an initial phase of a petrochemical project and as a later phase, ethylene dichloride, chlorine, caustic soda, ethyl benzene, styrene monomer, polystyrene, and additional ethylene and power steam.

C. The "Dow Venture" would have the right to manufacture these products, select equity partners, determine financing sources, and market products in Indonesia and for export.

D. Ethane and fuel gas must be sold by the GOI to the "Dow Venture" at prices such that the venture can be economically competitive.

E. The GOI approve the project and identify it as a high priority of the Government.

F. Confirm that the benefits currently available to foreign investors will be available to this project, and specifically that all capital goods, equipment, and raw materials may be imported free of all customs duties and taxes.

G. Develop a way to extend the period of foreign investment licenses beyond the 30 years maximum period now permitted.

H. Dow will require OPIC or similar insurance on its investment.

J. Dow needs sufficient access to data validating the deliverability of ethane and fuel gas from the Arun field.

K. Confirm that the existing levels of tariff and border-crossing taxes will remain effective for products manufactured in the complex and necessary steps will be taken to protect the investment from import substitute products.

L. Allow Dow exclusivity in the Indonesian market for LDPE, HDPE, and vinyl chloride from the day of signing the "Contract of Work" until the commercial debt is repaid, which is estimated to be five years after start-up.

M. Grant Dow the right to manage the "Dow Venture" for the life of the project.

N. Dow would require that a utility company be established to operate the ethylene and power/steam plants as well as the town site infrastructure. This utility company would operate at 15% return on total cost before taxes (ROTCBT) on a long-term basis.

P. Dow would request that to nullify the effects of possible Rupiah devaluation that the assets of the "Dow Venture" be in US dollar accounting and that pricing to the Indonesian market be on a US dollar basis.

Q. The project would require the establishment of a substantial polyvinyl chloride (PVC) industry. To this end, the GOI and Dow would work together to identify suitable PVC producers and establish appropriate incentives for these producers to develop and invest in the Indonesian market.

R. The GOI would make every effort to have this project recognized as an Association of South East Asian Nations (ASEAN) project and have access to ASEAN markets.

Dow Indonesia (B1)

In February 1977 Colin D. Goodchild and other Dow managers met with Indonesian government officials in a conference room of BAPPENAS, the Indonesian national planning agency. [For background, see Dow Indonesia (A).] The meeting was conducted by Dr. Mooy, Dr. Sumarlin's deputy. Fifteen or twenty Indonesians were present, coming from BAPPENAS, Pertamina, and the Ministry of Industry. None of the Indonesians had been involved in earlier discussions of the project. In addition to Dow managers and Indonesian officials, there were two Americans present who were consultants to the Indonesian government.

Dr. Mooy opened the meeting by welcoming the Dow managers and inviting them to present their proposal for the petrochemical project. After a presentation by Dow executives, the meeting was opened for discussion. A number of Indonesians present asked technical questions about the plant and the process to be used. One asked how the royalty proposed by Dow had been determined. Mr. Walker of Dow responded that the amount was negotiable, but that the rate in the presentation was based on Dow's total R&D expenditure over Dow's total sales. In response to a further question, Mr. Walker responded that the company has not charged all licensees the same percentage royalty. In response to a question about the importance of the assumed ethane price, Dow managers responded that the returns were not terribly sensitive to the exact figure for ethane. The American consultants asked a number of questions about the economics of the proposed project, including questions about the prices proposed for the output of the plant, the needs of the project for imports, and the efficiency of the plant at the proposed scale. There were several references on the part of Indonesians to a "Third Generation Contract of Work." Dow managers understood that the form and terms of contracts of work in Indonesia had undergone changes from the original contract for copper mining with Freeport Sulphur, signed in the late 1960s soon after President Suharto took office. The so-called "Second Generation Contracts" had demanded more of the foreign investor. The proposed "Third Generation Contract of Work" was, officials explained, not quite ready for distribution. Dow managers felt that the Indonesians had not met in advance to coordinate their questions and that the meeting ended without giving Dow any clear signs of how the Indonesians might view their proposals.

This case was prepared as the basis for class discussion rather than to illustrate either effective or ineffective handling of an administrative situation. Written by Brizio Biondi-Morra, Research Assistant, under the supervision of Professors James E. Austin and Louis T. Wells, Jr., and Assistant Professor Dennis J. Encarnation. Copyright © 1985 by the President and Fellows of Harvard College. No part of this publication may be reproduced, stored in a retrieval system, or transmitted in any form or by any means—electronic, mechanical, photocopying, recording, or otherwise—without the permission of Harvard Business School. Distributed by HBS Case Service, Harvard Business School, Boston, MA 02163.

After the meeting, Mr. Goodchild ran into the two American consultants on the steps of the BAPPENAS building. They suggested that the Indonesians did not know what the company wanted as the next step in discussions. Mr. Goodchild responded that management hoped for answers to the requests included in the company proposal. [See Appendix of Dow Indonesia (A).] He added that Dow did not expect a "yes" to every point, but it also did not anticipate a "no" to every item. One of the consultants proposed that Mr. Goodchild join the two consultants and Dr. Mooy for lunch. Over lunch (paid for by Dr. Mooy) the conversation covered Dow's activities elsewhere and a few more questions about the economics of the proposed plant. Still, Mr. Goodchild felt that he had little sense of the Indonesians' reaction to the proposal.

In March, less than a month after the initial meeting in BAPPENAS, Mr. Goodchild received a letter from Dr. Sumarlin, Minister of State for Administrative Reform. The letter (in the *Appendix*) raised a number of economic and policy issues.

APPENDIX

REPUBLIC OF INDONESIA
NATIONAL DEVELOPMENT PLANNING AGENCY
JAKARTA, INDONESIA

No.: 601/WK/3/1977.-   Jakarta, March 17, 1977.-

Mr. Colin D. Goodchild
Regional Director
DOW Chemical N. V.
Jakarta.-

Dear Mr. Goodchild,

The Government has now completed its analysis of the revised petro-chemical project as summarized in the document "Aceh Petrochemical Project Feasibility Study" (undated) submitted to the Government in late January and discussed between Dow and the Government in early February.

The result of this analysis of the project's benefits can be briefly summarized as follows:

The discounted cash flow return to Dow as a corporate entity is significantly more attractive than the economic benefits to Indonesia. The social benefits to Indonesia, in fact, are quite marginal. I would emphasize that for the calculation of both the private and the social returns Dow's figures and assumptions were used throughout.

In addition, the proposal as it now stands, if we understand it correctly, raises very serious policy issues that are difficult for the Government to accept without substantial modifications.

We believe economic issues can probably be resolved to the satisfaction of both sides if further discussions are pursued in a spirit of constructive give and take. The policy issues are more difficult. In particular, the Government finds it very difficult to accept granting Dow a two year "grace period" during which the Government is asked to accord Dow a number of important facilities, while Dow, on the other hand, assumes no obligations to proceed with any project whatsoever. This feature of your proposal as it stands is unacceptable.

Therefore, the comments on Dow's specific proposals as set out below are, at this stage of our discussions, to be interpreted as replies "in principle" and as fully contingent upon a successful prior resolution of the more important economic and policy issues now unresolved.

A. If it were determined to be more appropriate not to integrate ethane extraction with the petro-chemical project, the Government would have no objection to arrangements to have ethane extracted from the natural gas feed to the LNG facility by a third party.

B. The project would be implemented under a Joint Venture Agreement or Contract of Work which would require Dow to form a company or companies under Indonesian Law, and would specify the products to be produced by such company(s).

In principle there is no reason why the products listed by Dow would not be so included.

C. A Joint Venture Agreement or Contract of Work would authorize Dow to manufacture the products agreed upon, to select foreign equity parties acceptable to the Government of Indonesia provided such equity partners fully accepted all owners' obligations jointly with Dow, and to market the products in Indonesia and for export.

D. Obviously, if there is to be a project, ethane and gas must be sold to the project at a price that allows the project to be economically competitive _and_ at the same time affords gas production and ethane extraction a sound rate of return.

E. The Government has already stated that the petro-chemical industry is of high priority and is proceeding as quickly as possible in its efforts to conclude a mutually acceptable agreement.

F. This project naturally would be eligible for benefits currently available to foreign investors in Indonesia in a similar situation.

G. The Government is willing to consider any proposals from Dow on arrangements for the long term participation of Dow in the petro-chemical industry.

H. The Government has no objection to Dow's seeking insurance on its investment.

J. The Government is proceeding to make data available to Dow on the gas from the Arun field. It is understood that such data are being provided on a confidential basis and that Dow will make available to the Government of Indonesia all results of its analysis.

K. The Government does not currently see the need to change the tariffs of the products to be manufactured by the petro-chemical complex.

L. The Government believes that all the ramifications of arrangements that would afford Dow any assured market position in Indonesia for LDPE, HDPE, and VINYL CHLORIDE must be thoroughly explored. Any further comment on this request must await further discussions with you. In any event, any such arrangement must be precisely circumscribed in time and must include adequate protection to assure that products will be sold to Indonesia at prices not higher than those prevailing on the world markets and the arrangement must be consistent with any contractual commitments outstanding at the time an agreement is reached.

M. The Government would expect the benefits of Dow's management skills in operating the project and in training Indonesians.

N. The Government sees no objection in principle to an establishment of a separate utility company to operate the ethylene and power/steam plants as well as the town site infrastructure if such arrangement assists Dow in financing the venture, provided such an arrangement does not dilute the Dow's tax liabilities to Indonesia.

P. The venture can request authorization to maintain its accounting in U.S. Dollars and to tie its pricing to world market prices as expressed in U.S. Dollars. Such requests have been granted when desirable for a high priority project.

Q. The Government would welcome the development of a substantial PVC industry in Indonesia. It is Government policy to constantly review the need for and nature of appropriate incentives it could provide to encourage the development of such down stream industries based on indigenous national resources.

I am sure that you are as anxious as we are to push ahead with a discussion of both the economic and policy issues that must be resolved. You will be hearing soon as to a date and agenda for the next meeting.

                    Sincerely yours,

                    (Signed)
                    B. Sumarlin
                    Minister of State/Vice Chairman
                       of BAPPENAS.

Dow Indonesia (B2)

To aid in preparing Indonesia's response to Dow's proposal for a petrochemical project in Indonesia, consultants prepared a cost/benefit analysis for Dr. J. B. Sumarlin, Minister of State for Administrative Reform. [See Dow Indonesia (A) and (B1).] The Appendix presents an adapted and abbreviated version of this analysis.

The consultants' report concluded that the proposed project showed a negative return for Indonesia.

APPENDIX

Cost/Benefit Analysis*

The first step[1] was to calculate the domestic value added at international prices. To do this, the sales were converted to reflect F.O.B. value (for export sales) and the C.I.F. equivalent value of imports (for domestic sales). Export volumes were multiplied by export prices (Dow Indonesia (A), *Exhibit 3* Note b). Domestic prices were converted to C.I.F. import equivalents by multiplying the domestic sales prices by 0.80 (i.e., by 1.00/1.24) to eliminate the 24% border taxes assumed by Dow. These calculations appear in *Exhibit 1*.

This case was prepared as the basis for class discussion rather than to illustrate either effective or ineffective handling of an administrative situation. Written by Brizio Biondi-Morra, Research Assistant, under the supervision of Professors James E. Austin and Louis T. Wells, Jr., and Assistant Professor Dennis J. Encarnation. Copyright © 1985 by the President and Fellows of Harvard College. To order copies, call (617) 495-6117 or write the Publishing Division, Harvard Business School, Boston, MA 02163. No part of this publication may be reproduced, stored in a retrieval system, or transmitted in any form or by any means—electronic, mechanical, photocopying, recording, or otherwise—without the permission of the Harvard Business School.

Source: Adapted from a report done by a consultant to the Indonesian government.

[1] Various techniques, with their corresponding terminology, exist to adjust market prices and correct existing distortions between private and public values of benefits and costs.

This appendix follows the method and terminology used by a consultant to the Indonesian government. Its step-by-step procedure is consistent with the "Economic Cost-Benefit Analysis" note 9-379-073 published by the Harvard Business School.

First, Dow's sales, or the firm's revenues, are adjusted to calculate the benefits of the investment to Indonesia (*Exhibit 1*, and line 1 of *Exhibit 2*).

Second, the enterprise's costs, both investment and operating, are subtracted from revenues after they have been divided into two categories. Costs involving foreign exchange transactions (*Exhibit 2*, lines 2-8) are separated from those originating from purely domestic operations (*Exhibit 2*, lines 10-13).

Third, all numbers (*Exhibit 2*, lines 1-13) are converted from dollars into rupians (*Exhibit 3*) using a shadow exchange rate when appropriate. Dow Indonesia (A) suggests (page 254) a possible conversion rate of 1.2 between the official and the shadow exchange rate.

Finally, the project's return on investment to Indonesia is computed by discounting the project's life stream of benefits and costs to their present value (*Exhibit 3*, last lines).

From the resulting values of product the following items were subtracted:

1. Cost of imported raw materials, as estimated in meeting with Dow negotiators.
2. Ten percent of G&A, which was an estimate of the foreign exchange component of these costs.
3. Interest payments, assumed to go entirely abroad.
4. Dept repayment, assumed to be all foreign exchange expenses.
5. Forty percent of sales expenses, the fraction estimated to be paid abroad.
6. Eighty percent of dividends. This represents the portion remaining from cash flow after the payment of a 20% withholding tax.
7. Eighty percent of annual royalties. This represents the remainder after the payment of a 20% withholding tax.

The next figure as calculated above was taken as the value added domestically, at international prices, to the ethane. Lines 1-9 of *Exhibit 2* show the calculations.

The next step was to calculate the domestic resources used in producing the value added. The following domestic expenditures were taken as measuring the use of local resources:

1. Ninety percent of G&A, representing Dow's estimate of the goods and services purchased locally under this heading.
2. Sixty percent of sales expenses, representing Dow's estimate of local expenses for sales efforts.
3. The local content of cost of goods sold, except for the ethane bought from the government. This figure was calculated by taking Dow's estimate of CGS (Dow Indonesia A, *Exhibit 3*) and subtracting the imported content and the ethane at the cost assumed by Dow ($0.038/lb.).
4. The opportunity cost of the ethane used, calculated to be $0.045/lb. (Dow Indonesia A, note on page 248). Lines 10-13 of *Exhibit 2* show these calculations.

Exhibit 2 was then converted into rupiahs, using a shadow rate in lines 1-9 and 13, and the official exchange rate in lines 10-12. *Exhibit 3* shows the calculations, which yield a negative NPV at a 10% discount rate.

APPENDIX EXHIBIT 1 Value of Sales

	1981	1982	1983	1984	1985	1986	1987	1988	1989	1990	1991
Domestic Sales: C.I.F. Equivalent											
1 LDPE—Tub. process Millions of lbs.	40.ᵃ	101	112	120	130	140	150	150	150	150	150
2 Value in millions of $	15.0	42.3	46.9	50.3	54.5	58.7	62.9	62.9	62.9	62.9	62.9
3 LDPE—Auto. process Millions of lbs.		60	65	75	84	96	109	135	150	150	150
4 Value in millions of $		25.1	27.2	31.4	35.2	40.2	45.7	56.6	62.9	62.9	62.9
5 HDPE—Sol. process Millions of lbs.	20.ᵃ	106	117	129	141	150	150	150	150	150	150
6 Value in millions of $	7.6	43.4	47.9	52.8	57.7	61.4	61.4	61.4	61.4	61.4	61.4
7 VCM—Millions of lbs.		83ᵃ	182	200	220	242	266	293	322	322	322
8 Value in millions of $		24.2	53.1	58.4	64.2	70.7	77.7	85.5	94.0	94.0	94.0
Export Sales: F.O.B.											
9 LDPE—Tub. process Millions of lbs.		25	27	30	20	10					
10 Values in millions of $		9.2	9.9	11.0	7.3	3.7					
11 LDPE—Auto. process Millions of lbs.		40	44	48	66	54	41	15			
12 Value in millions of $		14.7	16.1	17.6	24.2	19.8	15.0	5.5			
13 HDPE—Sol. process Millions of lbs.		14	18	21	9						
14 Value in millions of $		5.0	6.4	7.5	3.2						
15 VCM—Millions of lbs.		105	230	250	260	258	234	207	178	178	178
16 Value in millions of $		30.0	65.8	71.5	74.4	73.8	66.9	59.2	50.9	50.9	50.9
17 **Total Value in Millions of $**	22.6	193.9	273.3	300.5	320.7	328.3	329.6	331.1	332.1	332.1	332.1
18 **Total Value in Millions of Rp(b)**	9,379	80,468	113,419	124,767	133,090	136,244	136,784	137,406	137,821	137,821	137,821
19 **True Value to Indonesian economy in Millions of Rp (c)**	11,254	96,561	136,102	149,648	159,708	163,493	164,141	164,887	165,385	165,385	165,385

ᵃHalf year only.
ᵇ$ x OER OER = Official Exchange Rate $1.00 = Rp 415.00.
ᶜ$ x SER SER = Shadow Exchange Rate=OER x 1.2 = Rp 498.

APPENDIX EXHIBIT 2 Dollar Figure for Cost/Benefit Analysis (millions of dollars)

	1981	1982	1983	1984	1985	1986	1987	1988	1989	1990	1991
1 Sales (see *Exhibit 1*)	22.6	193.9	273.3	300.5	320.7	328.3	329.6	331.1	332.1	332.1	332.1
2 Cost of imported raw materials	(3.5)	(44.7)	(76.5)	(82.9)	(88.2)	(91.0)	(91.0)	(91.0)	(91.0)	(91.0)	(91.0)
3 10% of G&A using foreign exchange	(1.4)	(1.5)	(1.8)	(1.8)	(1.9)	(2.0)	(2.1)	(2.1)	(2.2)	(2.4)	(2.4)
4 Interest payments	(19.3)	(47.7)	(52.6)	(47.1)	(38.3)	(27.6)	(16.5)	(13.2)	(9.9)	(6.6)	(3.0)
5 Debt repayment	0.0	0.0	(50.0)	(80.8)	(100.8)	(103.8)	(33.0)	(33.0)	(33.0)	(35.6)	(30.0)
6 40% of sales expenses	(1.7)	(8.4)	(11.3)	(12.4)	(13.4)	(13.9)	(14.2)	(14.6)	(15.0)	(15.2)	(15.6)
7 80% of dividends	0.0	0.0	0.0	0.0	0.0	(20.3)	(58.1)	(44.6)	(43.1)	(47.5)	(49.5)
8 80% of annual royalties	(0.6)	(5.4)	(7.6)	(8.3)	(9.0)	(9.2)	(9.4)	(9.5)	(9.6)	(9.7)	(9.7)
9 Domestic value added at international prices, to the ethane[a]	(3.9)	86.2	73.5	67.2	69.1	60.5	105.3	123.1	128.3	124.1	130.9
10 90% of G&A purchased domestically	(12.6)	(13.3)	(15.8)	(15.9)	(16.7)	(17.6)	(18.5)	(19.3)	(20.1)	(21.7)	(21.9)
11 60% of sales expenses	(2.5)	(12.7)	(17.0)	(18.7)	(20.0)	(20.8)	(21.4)	(21.9)	(22.6)	(22.9)	(23.3)
12 Local content of CGS except ethane	(22.0)	(48.1)	(46.1)	(46.0)	(45.0)	(43.9)	(43.9)	(43.9)	(43.9)	(43.9)	(43.9)
13 True value of ethane bought from GOI[b] (lbs. × $0.045)	(1.8)	(19.3)	(28.1)	(30.5)	(33.3)	(35.1)	(35.1)	(35.1)	(35.1)	(35.1)	(35.1)

Notes

[a] 9 = 1 − (2 + 3 + 4 + 5 + 6 + 7 + 8).

APPENDIX EXHIBIT 3 Cost/Benefit Analyses (millions of Rp)

	1981	1982	1983	1984	1985	1986	1987	1988	1989	1990	1991
1 Sales (*Exhibit 1&2*) $×415×1.2	11,254	96,561	136,102	149,648	149,708	163,493	164,141	164,887	165,385	165,385	165,385
2 Cost of imported raw materials $×415×1.2	(1,743)	(22,260)	(38,097)	(41,284)	(43,923)	(45,318)	(45,318)	(45,318)	(45,318)	(45,318)	(45,318)
3 10% of G&A using foreign exchange $×415×1.2	(697)	(747)	(896)	(896)	(946)	(996)	(1,046)	(1,046)	(1,096)	(1,195)	(1,195)
4 Interest payments $×415×1.2	(9,611)	(23,755)	(26,195)	(23,456)	(19,074)	(13,745)	(8,217)	(6,574)	(4,930)	(3,287)	(1,494)
5 Debt repayment $×415×1.2	0	0	(24,900)	(40,238)	(50,198)	(51,592)	(16,434)	(16,434)	(16,434)	(17,729)	(14,940)
6 40% of sales expenses $×415×1.2	(846)	(4,183)	(5,627)	(6,175)	(6,673)	(6,922)	(7,071)	(7,270)	(7,470)	(7,569)	(7,769)
7 80% of dividends $×415×1.2	0	0	0	0	0	(10,119)	(28,924)	(22,191)	(21,474)	(23,625)	(24,621)
8 80% of royalties $×415×1.2	(299)	(2,689)	(3,785)	(4,133)	(4,482)	(4,582)	(4,681)	(4,731)	(4,781)	(4,831)	(4,831)
9 Domestic value added, at international prices, to the ethane[a]	(1,942)	42,927	36,603	33,465	34,411	30,129	52,439	61,303	63,893	61,801	65,188
10 90% of G&A purchased domestically $×415	(5,229)	(5,519)	(6,557)	(6,598)	(6,930)	(7,304)	(7,677)	(8,009)	(8,341)	(9,088)	(9,088)
11 60% of sales expenses	(1,037)	(5,270)	(7,055)	(7,760)	(8,300)	(8,632)	(8,881)	(9,088)	(9,379)	(9,503)	(9,669)
12 Local content of CGS ethane $×415	(9,130)	(19,961)	(19,131)	(19,090)	(18,675)	(18,218)	(18,218)	(18,218)	(18,218)	(18,218)	(18,218)
13 True value of ethane bought from GOI ($0.045×lbs.)×415×1.2	(896)	(9,611)	(13,994)	(15,189)	(16,583)	(17,480)	(17,480)	(17,480)	(17,480)	(17,480)	(17,480)
Net Value	**(18,234)**	**2,566**	**(10,134)**	**(15,172)**	**(16,077)**	**(21,505)**	**183**	**8,508**	**10,475**	**7,512**	**10,733**
NPV @ 10% = negative											
IRR = negative											

[a]g = 1 − (2 + 3 + 4 + 5 + 6 + 7 + 8).
Official Exchange Rate (OER):$1.00 Rp 415.00
Shadow Exchange Rate (SER): OER×1.2= Rp415 × 1.2=Rp498

chapter 13

The Cultural Environment of International Business*

Navigating through different cultures and their various norms can be a difficult task for MNE executives. For example, General Electric (GE), in an effort to increase its global strategic position in medical technology, took control of the French company, Cie. Generale de Radiologie (CGR) in 1988. The company was owned by the state and manufactured medical equipment with a specific emphasis on X-ray machines and CAT scanners. GE acquired CGR and received $800 million in cash from state-controlled Thomson S.A. in return for GE's RCA consumer electronic business. The acquisition of CGR was viewed by many as a brilliant strategic move. GE projected a $25 million profit for the first full year of operations; however, things did not turn out as the strategic planners projected.

One of the first things GE did was to organize a training seminar for the French managers. GE provided T-shirts with the slogan "Go for One" for each of the participants, and although the French managers wore them, many were not happy about it. One manager stated, "It was like Hitler was back forcing us to wear uniforms. It was humiliating."[1]

Soon after the takeover, GE also sent American specialists to France to fix CGR's financial-control system. Unfortunately, these specialists knew very little about French accounting or financial-reporting requirements, and consequently tried to impose a GE system that was inappropriate for French financial-reporting requirements and for the way CGR had traditionally kept records. This problem (and the working out of an agreeable compromise) took several months to solve and resulted in substantial direct and indirect costs.

GE then tried to coordinate and integrate CGR into its Milwaukee-based medical-equipment unit in several other ways. Because CGR had racked up a $25 million loss instead of the projected $25 million profit, an American executive from Milwaukee was sent to fix things at CGR. Several cost-cutting measures, including massive layoffs and the closing of roughly half of the 12 CGR plants, shocked the French workforce. Additionally,

*Part of this chapter is reprinted with permission from a chapter written by J. Stewart Black in *Global Assignments: Successfully Expatriating and Repatriating International Managers* (San Francisco: Jossey Bass, 1992).
[1]"GE Culture Turns Sour at French Unit," *Wall Street Journal,* July 31, 1990, A11.

the "Be number 1 or 2," profit-hungry culture of GE continued to clash with the "state-run, no competition" history and culture of CGR.

GE's efforts to integrate CGR into the GE culture through putting up English-language posters everywhere, flying GE flags, and the like were met with considerable resistance by the French employees. One union leader commented, "They came in here bragging, 'We are GE, we're the best and we've got the methods.'" The reaction was so strong that a significant number of French managers and engineers left GE-CGR, and the total workforce shrank from 6,500 to 5,000. Although GE officials estimated that GE-CGR would produce a profit in 1990, the expected loss was another $25 million.

As this example illustrates, even companies that have reputations as experienced and savvy MNEs can run aground on unseen cultural reefs. In order to avoid the negative consequences of cultural clashes, it is vital to understand what culture is and how it can be systematically analyzed.

THE ESSENCE OF CULTURE

Many people think about culture as though it is something a country, region, or firm has, something that you can see, hear, touch, smell, or taste. Consequently, people who take this view often point to ceremonies, clothing, historical landmarks, art, and food as examples of a country's culture. Clearly these differ substantially from one country to another. The interesting question, however, is "Why?"

The answer lies in a much more complex view of culture.[2] Although a team of anthropologists identified over 160 different definitions,[3] it is possible to cite some common elements. First, all cultures emerge as a group of people face and then respond to the challenges of life. Consequently, culture is *learned* through experience and is not inherited. To the extent that people believe certain responses to be successful enough to teach them and the underlying values and assumptions to others, they become shared among the members of the group. Because circumstances change over time, responses once considered successful can change; as a consequence, culture is also adaptive. Finally, the key factor that allows culture to be transferred from one generation to another or shared within a family, community, region, or country is the human capacity for symbolic representation and communication. The creation and interpretation of symbols, primarily through words and pictures, allow stories, speeches, discussions, novels, poems, art, and so on to be effective means of learning, teaching, sharing, and adapting the multiple dimensions of culture.

Culture can be thought of as having three levels. The tangible aspects of a culture—things you can see, hear, smell, taste, or touch—are artifacts or manifestations of underlying values and assumptions that a group of people share. The structure of these elements is like that of an iceberg, as in Figure 13.1. Artifacts are what you can see, but what you can see is only a small fraction of what is there; and what you cannot see—the values and assumptions—are what can sink your ship if you mistakenly run into them.

Culture, however, is not simply the total collection of a group of people's assumptions, values, or artifacts. It consists of a common set of assumptions and values that consistently influence artifacts, especially behavior, and are passed on from older to younger members of the group. Because there are a limited number of problems that all people must solve, such as how to communicate, educate, feed, clothe, and govern, methods and ideas that prove successful are passed on to future generations and become the invisible but powerful dimensions of culture; they become the rules that exist in people's minds.

[2]E. Schein, "Coming to a New Awareness of Organizational Culture," *Sloan Management Review* (Winter 1984) 3–16.

[3]A. L. Kroeber and C. Kluckhohn, *Culture: A Critical Review of Concepts and Definitions* (Cambridge, MA: Harvard University Press, 1952).

Figure 13.1
The Iceberg of Culture

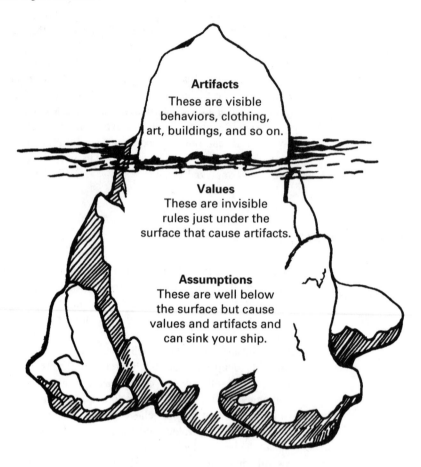

Source: Reprinted with permission from *Global Assignments* by J. Stewart Black, Hal B. Gregersen, and Mark E. Mendenhall (San Francisco: Jossey-Bass, 1992).

In essence, culture is a mental road map with traffic signs and signals. The road map tells you what the important and valued goals are, and what "highways" or "lowways" can get you there. The traffic rules tell you who has the right-of-way, when to stop, how to signal a left turn, when U-turns are allowed or prohibited, and so on. Imagine being put in the middle of the heart of a Tokyo freeway with no map, no road signs, and no idea of the rules concerning speed, changing lanes, following distance, or even which side of the road to drive on. Suddenly, trustworthy social and interpersonal road maps and traffic rules of the past are now useless or, in the worst case, deadly.

However, just as in the case of the violation of traffic rules, not all rules of culture have equal punishments or rewards attached to them. A helpful way of thinking about this is to conceptualize the rules along two dimensions—the extent to which they are widely shared among group members and the extent to which they are deeply held—illustrated in Figure 13.2.

Those assumptions, values, or rules of the culture that are widely shared and deeply held are generally those that are accompanied by substantial rewards or punishments, depending upon whether they are violated or honored. For example, one widely shared and strongly held rule in the US is that you do not talk to yourself constantly or loudly. When others see a person doing this, they become nervous and concerned even if the person poses no physical threat to anyone—after all, it isn't normal.

Figure 13.2
The Matrix of Culture

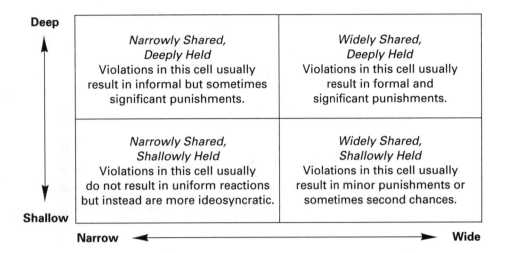

Narrowly Shared, Deeply Held
Violations in this cell usually result in informal but sometimes significant punishments.

Widely Shared, Deeply Held
Violations in this cell usually result in formal and significant punishments.

Narrowly Shared, Shallowly Held
Violations in this cell usually do not result in uniform reactions but instead are more ideosyncratic.

Widely Shared, Shallowly Held
Violations in this cell usually result in minor punishments or sometimes second chances.

What about the case in which the rule is one that is deeply held but not widely shared? In this case, the rewards and punishments are often informal. For example, in the US, burping after a meal is considered by some to be a serious violation of proper behavior, but not by all. Consequently, you are unlikely to be put in jail for burping; however, you might be cut out of particular social circles. In certain other cultures, a very effective way to offend a host is by not burping after a meal.

In the case of widely shared but not deeply held rules, violations of the rules often carry with them uniform but rather mild punishments. In many cases, infrequent violation of these rules may carry no punishment at all. For example, not interrupting someone who is talking to you is a generally accepted rule of conduct in the US. However, if one occasionally interrupts, it is unlikely that this behavior will be accompanied by any punishment.

The Nature of Assumptions about the World

Because assumptions are the source from which values, rules, artifacts, and behaviors flow, it is important to touch briefly on the nature of these assumptions and how they differ from one culture to another. The basic underlying assumptions can be divided into a five-part categorization.[4] Figure 13.3 provides a summary of the general nature of these assumptions and examples of the specific forms they might take, as well as their management implications.

Humanity's Relationship to the Environment. The first set of assumptions concerns those made about the relationship of humanity to nature. For example, in some cultures (the US for example), the assumption is that humans are here to dominate nature and utilize it for their wealth and benefit. In other cultures, the assumption is that humans and nature are to coexist harmoniously. The implications of these differing assumptions can be quite significant. In the US, the dominance assumption is an important basis for the building of dams, the mining of minerals, and the logging of trees. However, the implications may reach beyond these basic activities to strategic planning or management practices

[4]E. Schein, "Coming to a New Awareness of Organizational Culture," *Sloan Management Review* (Winter 1984): 3–16.

in business as well. Consider how most US firms view their business environment and how they strategically approach it. Is the business environment viewed as something that people must accept and with which they must try to harmonize? Or is it viewed as something that must be mastered and dominated if possible? Americans' assumption that the business envi-

Figure 13.3
Basic Assumptions and Their Implications

Nature of Assuption	Specific Assumptions	Management Implications
Environment (assumptions about the relationship between humans and the environment)	People are meant to dominate the environment.	Strategic plans should be developed to enable the firm to dominate its industry.
	People must be submissive to the environment.	Firms should seek positions that allow them to coexist with others.
Human nature (assumptions about human nature)	People are generally lazy.	Implement procedures for monitoring behavior and establish clear punishment for undesired behaviors.
	Work is as natural as play for people.	Provide people with opportunities and responsibilities and encourage their development.
Relationships (assumptions about how humans should relate to each other)	Individuals have certain rights and freedoms.	Individual performance should be measured and rewarded.
	People exist because of others and owe an obligation to them.	Cooperation with and contributions to the group should be rewarded.
Activity (assumptions about the proper types and targets of human activity)	People create their own destinies and must plan for the future.	People who fail to plan should plan to fail.
	People should react to and enjoy whatever the present provides.	Planning the future only gets in the way of enjoying the present.
Truth (assumptions about the nature of truth and reality)	Truth objectively exists.	Facts and statistics are presented to convince and influence people.
	Truth is what is socially accepted.	Opinion leaders are utilized to influence decisions.

Source: Reprinted with permission from *Global Assignments* by J. Stewart Black, Hal B. Gregersen, and Mark E. Mendenhall (San Francisco: Jossey-Bass, 1992).

ronment is something to be dominated is evident in the purpose of antitrust laws. Antitrust laws and regulations in the US are in place not because Americans feel they must be submissive to or harmonize with the environment, but rather to counteract some of the negative outcomes of domination by a single firm.

The Nature of Human Nature. Different cultures also make different assumptions about the nature of people. Some cultures assume people are fundamentally good, while others assume they are inherently evil. The relevance of this area of assumptions was made clear by Douglas McGregor in his classic book, *The Human Side of Enterprise.*[5] McGregor argued that every manager acted on a "theory" or set of assumptions about people. Theory X managers assumed that "the average human being has an inherent dislike for work and will avoid it if he can" (p. 33). Consequently, managers accepting this view of people believed that "people must be coerced, controlled, directed, and threatened with punishment to get them to put forth adequate effort toward the achievement of organizational objectives" (p. 34). On the other hand, Theory Y managers assumed that "the expenditure of physical and mental effort in work is as natural as play or rest" (p. 47). Consequently, managers accepting this view of people believed that "external control and the threat of punishment are not the only means for bringing about effort toward organizational objectives. Man (sic) will exercise self-direction and self-control in the service of objectives to which he is committed. Commitment to objectives is a function of the rewards associated with their achievement" (p. 47).

The Nature of Human Relationships. This area of assumptions really deals with a variety of questions. "What is the right way for people to deal with each other?" "How much power and authority should any one person have over another?" "How much of individuals' orientation should be toward themselves versus others?" A large study by Gert Hofstede found significant differences among 40 countries in terms of the answers to these questions.[6] For example, he examined the degree to which people accepted power and authority differences. In his study, people from the Philippines, Venezuela, and Mexico had the highest levels of acceptance of power differences; in contrast, Austria, Israel, and Denmark had the lowest levels of acceptance. Hofstede's study also found that, in terms of individual versus group orientations, people from the US, Australia, and Great Britain had the highest individual orientations, while people from Venezuela, Colombia, and Pakistan had the highest group orientations.

The Nature of Human Activity. This set of assumptions concerns issues of the right activities for people and whether they should be active, passive, or fatalistic in these activities. In the US, people brag about working 80 hours a week, about having no time for vacations or watching TV, and about doing several things at the same time on their computers. They believe in phrases such as "People who fail to plan should plan to fail," and "Plan to work and work the plan." In other cultures, such "high-strung" activity is not valued and may even be seen as a waste of time and energy. Such cultures believe that preoccupation with planning only gets in the way of enjoying the present.

The Nature of Reality and Truth. Different cultures also form differing assumptions about the nature of reality and truth and how they are verified or established. For example, the adversarial system in US criminal law is based on the assumption that truth exists and that the heat generated by opposing views will ultimately illuminate what really happened. The famous CEO of ITT, Harold Geneen, always talked about "the unshakable facts," or

[5]D. McGregor, *The Human Side of Enterprise* (New York: McGraw-Hill, 1960).
[6]G. Hofstede, *Culture's Consequences* (Beverly Hills, CA: Sage, 1980).

those that would hold up even after intense scrutiny. In other cultures, reality is much more subjective and dependent upon what people believe it to be. Consequently, opinion leaders or persuasive stories, rather than "unshakable facts," are utilized as means of influencing people and business decisions.

The purpose of discussing these five areas of assumptions is to illustrate two key issues. First, as mentioned earlier, assumptions are the source from which values and behaviors flow. In order to understand the visible artifacts of culture, one must understand the invisible values and assumptions. Second, fundamental assumptions by their very nature not only are invisible but are generally taken for granted. Their being taken for granted means that they are not easy to uncover or understand, because the people who hold them are not generally conscious of them, and therefore cannot easily identify and explain them to foreigners. They are as unaware of how their cultural assumptions affect their behavior as they are about the oxygen in the air around them. Breathing and following cultural norms are natural and almost automatic processes. Furthermore, the taken-for-granted nature of cultural assumptions means that they are not easily changed. Behaviors may be changed (Japanese may discontinue wearing "kimonos" and instead wear Western clothes), but underlying values and assumptions determining those behaviors remain and are not easily or quickly changed.

In the context of international business, the observation that cultures differ is important because of the impact these differences have. Because MNEs send executives and managers from one country and culture to another as a means of managing their global international operations, the impact that cultural differences can have on the successful adjustment of these expatriate managers is important. In addition, it is vital to examine the impact that culture can have on managerial behaviors such as communication and negotiation, as well as decision making.

CROSS-CULTURAL ADJUSTMENT: THE PROCESS

Many global managers and their families experience adjustment difficulties when they are sent on overseas assignments. Estimates are that nearly one in five US expatriates have such difficulties adjusting that they return home early, at a cost to their companies of over $150,000 per person.[7] Unfortunately, while the term "culture shock" is recognized by most, its underlying process is understood by very few. Consequently, the primary purpose of this next section is to describe the dynamics of the process of cross-cultural adjustment.

Routines, Ego, and Self-Image

Almost no one wants uncertainty in life. In fact, most people want a reasonably high degree of certainty and predictability, which is primarily why we establish routines. For example, the global success of McDonald's is testimony to the general human need of a certain level of predictability. A Big Mac is a Big Mac. The taste does not vary much by the day of the week, different locations within a given country, or even across countries. People not only like the product, they also like the predictability of the product.

Routines affect all aspects of people's lives, from the mundane to the critical. For example, people establish routines concerning what they do when they wake up in the morning—smash the alarm, get up, take a shower, get dressed, eat, run out the door, and buy a new alarm clock. But people also establish more serious routines, such as how they

---

[7]J. S. Black, H. B. Gregersen, and M. E. Mendenhall, *Global Assignments: Successfully Expatriating and Repatriating International Managers* (San Francisco: Jossey-Bass, 1992).

form or develop relationships, how they deal with conflict in those relationships, and what they expect from relationships.

As mentioned, the first and most obvious function that routines serve is that they provide a level of predictability and certainty in people's lives and provide a "psychological economy." Because you know what a Big Mac will taste like, you save the mental energy of wondering. The disruption of routines means that more mental time and energy must be devoted to processing these disruptions. To the extent that mental time and energy are limited, the disruption of routines means that there is now less mental time and energy for other things. But all disruptions are not created equal. The severity is a function of three dimensions.

Scope. The first dimension is the scope or total number of routines that are disrupted. All other things being equal, the greater the number of routines disrupted, the more difficult the process of dealing with these disruptions, and the greater the level of frustration, anger, and anxiety that are likely to follow. For example, it is one thing to have your morning shower routine disrupted, but it is quite another to have your eating, sleeping, commuting, and working routines all altered by a new cultural environment. Or it may be an inconvenience to have to give up the "good old Texas handshake" for a bow in greeting someone, but it can be quite upsetting to have to alter most of the dimensions of how you delegate authority, make decisions, influence people, plan and organize your workday, and motivate your subordinates.

Magnitude. The second dimension is the magnitude of the disruption. The continuum of disruption for any given routine could range from a slight alteration to a total and complete destruction. The greater the magnitude of the disruption, the greater the time and energy required to deal with it, and the greater the level of frustration, anger, and anxiety that is likely to follow. For example, if a shower was previously the first order of the day, having to take a bath would be somewhat of a lesser disruption compared to not being able to do either without going down to the public bathhouse. Or it may be somewhat irritating to have to switch from cash bonuses to days off as motivation incentives, but it can be totally frustrating to have your ability to administer rewards and punishments as tools of motivation completely removed from your hands and placed in those of a labor ministry.

Criticality. The third dimension is the criticality of the disrupted routine. Not all routines are equal in importance. Some are critical, while others are trivial. The greater the criticality of the routine disrupted, the greater the time and energy required to deal with it, and the greater the level of frustration, anger, and anxiety that is likely to follow. For example, not having the reserved parking spot you are used to is probably not as frustrating as having to change from a "tell and sell" style of leadership to one of consulting and joint decision and execution.

Despite the importance of understanding the dynamics already described, it does not totally explain the deep level of frustration, anger, and anxiety that is commonly associated with culture shock. Isaac Newton claimed that for every action there is an equal and opposite reaction. If this is true, then logically one would also expect the reverse to be true. That is, for every reaction, there is an equal and opposite cause. In terms of culture shock, one would expect that for every level and severity of culture shock there is an equally powerful cause. This assertion is perhaps most important for the most severe cases of culture shock.

The powerful cause of severe culture shock stems from something that is generally quite sensitive for everyone—ego, self-image, identity. The most important underlying process in cross-cultural adjustment is the maintaining and repairing of one's ego and self-image. For most people there is nothing so fragile and important as their ego and self-image. Though it may not seem obvious, routines are a great source of maintaining one's self-image. In a sense, a routine is a demonstration of a level of proficiency, a proficiency that by the nature of its routinization is usually taken for granted. There is nothing like living in a foreign culture, however, to challenge these basic proficiencies and raise them from a "taken-for-granted" to a "very conscious" level. In fact, often the more taken-for-granted the proficiency, the more severe the reaction to its loss.

Although unfamiliar situations are encountered from almost the moment expatriates step off the plane, it takes a while before they build up enough courage to overpower the defense mechanisms with which everyone defends ego and self-image. As the number and magnitude of these incidents build up over time, people get worn down and can no longer ignore them. Although the specific symptoms vary across individuals and even within individuals from week to week, emotions such as anger and frustration are common. In addition, feelings of anxiety and depression are also prevalent, as the positive self-image people try to maintain gets battered and their confidence crumbles over time. Quite often, the mechanisms people have developed to defend and maintain their ego cause them to direct their frustration toward others. This is a primary cause behind the common culture-shock symptom of blaming others. Stop by any gathering center for Americans, such as the local American club, and you are likely to find conversations peppered with statements such as the following:

> I can't believe how stupid these Japanese are. Their addresses make absolutely no sense.
>
> Europeans think they're so superior to the rest of us.
>
> Headquarters has no idea of how things should be run in this country.
>
> The locals are just plain lazy. It's impossible to motivate them, and they feel no loyalty to the company.
>
> This whole thing is my spouse's fault. She has no appreciation for what I'm going through. She has her comfortable little cocoon at the office.

Unfortunately, many people never recover from culture shock. Some return home, but not all. Many who never recover from culture shock stay for the duration of their overseas assignment, usually fearful of the negative consequences of returning early or sometimes in hope that things will get better with time.

Most who stay eventually work their way through the culture-shock stage and gradually adjust to living and working overseas. Although the pain of making mistakes is the primary source of culture shock, it can also be the source of adjustment as well. If you make a mistake and notice important, negative consequences, you are less likely to repeat that mistake in the future. Gradually, through making mistakes, and recognizing the mistakes, as well as observing how others behave appropriately and successfully in the foreign culture, people learn what to do and not do and when to do or not do it.

In summary, several general statements about the cross-cultural adjustment process can be made. First, people establish routines in order to obtain a certain level of predictability in their life and to achieve a certain level of "psychological economy." These routines also provide an important means of preserving and maintaining egos and self-images. Living and working in new cultures generally disrupt these established routines. The more routines that are disrupted, the more severely any given routine is altered, and the more critical the disrupted routines, the greater the time and mental energy required to cope with the change and the greater the feelings of frustration, anger, and anxiety associated with culture shock. Most important, however, is the fact that the disruption of routines is generally accompanied by situations that challenge an individual's confidence, ego, and self-esteem. It is primarily threats to these sensitive aspects of all people that create the strongest reactions associated with culture shock—depression, anger, denial, and even hatred. In principle, then, factors that increase the disruption of routines and uncertainty tend to inhibit cross-cultural adjustment, while factors that reduce disruption and uncertainty tend to facilitate cross-cultural adjustment.

THE IMPACT OF CULTURE ON MANAGERIAL BEHAVIORS

Culture not only has an impact on a manager's ability to adjust to living and working in a foreign country, but it also can affect managerial behavior and create counterproductive clashes when managers from different cultural backgrounds must interact. Three vital areas of managerial behavior affected by culture are general communication, negotiations, and decision making.

Communication

Culture can affect communication styles in a variety of ways, but two aspects of communication have been found to differ rather dramatically by culture. The first is the extent to which the context affects what is said or how it is said.[8] Cultures that are considered "high context" tend to change what is said and how it is said significantly depending on the context. For example, Japan is considered a high-context culture and has three distinct levels of language that one utilizes depending on one's status relative to the other person. As an example, there are actually five different words for "you," depending on rank and status. In contrast, low-context cultures tend not to vary what is said or how it is said as dramatically in response to the situation. In fact, low-context cultures often interpret dramatic adaptation of the language as a negative characteristic and use labels such as two-faced, insincere, hypocritical, and chameleon to describe the speakers. On the other hand, individuals from high-context cultures often view low-context behaviors as a sign of immaturity or a lack of sophistication.

The second dimension of communication that can vary by culture is the extent to which communication is explicit or implicit. In explicit-language cultures, managers are taught that to communicate effectively you should "say what you mean, and mean what you say." Vague directives and instructions are seen as a sign of poor communication abilities. The assumption in explicit-language cultures is that the burden of effective communication is on the speaker. In contrast, in implicit-language cultures, the assumption is that the speaker and listener both share the burden of effective communication. Implicit communication also helps avoid unpleasant and direct confrontations and disagreements.

For global managers, trying to determine what is better—low context or high context, explicit or implicit communication—is not the relevant issue. However, realizing that these two key dimensions of communication can vary significantly by culture is critical because it allows managers to anticipate potential problems and to be proactive in making adjustments if they choose.

Negotiation

Research on international negotiation has identified important similarities and differences across cultures. One of the most important similarities is that, generally, negotiations seem to have five distinct stages. The first stage involves the planning that takes place prior to face-to-face negotiations. It is in this stage that individuals or teams conduct background research, gather information, plan their strategy, and make initial decisions about what they hope to achieve and are willing to give during the course of the negotiations. The second stage is commonly referred to as "nontask time"—the time at the beginning of the negotiations devoted to introductions and getting acquainted. The third stage involves exchanging information in an effort to provide background, establish common facts, and set the context of the negotiations. The fourth stage focuses on attempts to influence the other party to accept your desired set of exchanges (for example, to accept a certain price in exchange for a certain quantity and quality of a good or service). The final stage is reached if a mutually acceptable exchange is agreed upon.

[8] E. Hall, *Beyond Culture* (Garden City, NY: Doubleday, 1976).

Although research has found that these five stages are common across a wide variety of countries and cultures, it has also found important differences in terms of their content and timing. Although it is impossible to provide a comprehensive discussion of the important cultural differences along these dimensions for even the major cultures of the world, it is possible to provide a general framework and to identify the key dimensions that characterize significant differences.

Timing of Stages.   Although most cultures seem to follow the model of negotiations just described, the length of each stage seems to vary widely by culture.[9] For example, Americans generally spend relatively little time in the nontask stage of negotiations. Phrases such as "I know you're busy so I'll get right to the point," or "Let's cut straight to the chase," illustrate the general tendency for Americans to spend little time getting acquainted. In contrast, cultural norms in Mexico and Japan require significant time in this early stage. In these countries, much of the determination of whether a deal will be struck is a function of the relationship that is formed between the two parties. Consequently, the nontask stage plays a critical role in establishing this relationship. If one party is ready to "cut to the chase," while the other wants to spend more time getting acquainted, the potential for conflicts is obvious. The difference between Japanese and American norms concerning the nontask stage may also be reflected in the agreement stage. Typically, Americans rely on long and extremely detailed contracts that explicitly spell out the obligations of each party and the penalties for noncompliance; the length of contracts for complex issues can be in the hundreds of pages. In contrast, in Japan, where relationships play a bigger role than contracts, written agreements are often quite short in length and spell out only the general intentions and obligations of each party. Often the final sentence or paragraph simply states that, if disagreements arise, both parties will seek to resolve them in good faith. These examples illustrate that, before entering negotiations with individuals from an unfamiliar culture, it is important to research the norms of that culture concerning the length and significance of each stage of the negotiations.

Locations of Stages.   Just as the length and importance of stages can differ by culture, so too can the location in which each stage or portions of a given stage occur. For example, in the US, almost all stages could occur in a formal setting such as an office or conference room. In contrast, in Japan, at least some portion of the nontask stage is likely to occur in a more informal and nonwork setting such as a restaurant or golf course. The location and setting for closing the negotiations (that is, the signing ceremony in some cultures) can also differ. In Korea, for example, the contract is likely to be signed in a much more formal and public setting than someone's office.

Participants.   Team composition, team size, and the relationship between two parties can also differ significantly by culture. In countries that are sensitive to status and ranking (for example, Japan, Singapore, Mexico, Korea, India, Venezuela) having team members of both parties that are similar in status, position, age, and authority is much more important than in countries that are not as sensitive to these issues (for example, United States, Australia, New Zealand, Canada). Team size can also differ significantly by culture. In the United States, where such "go it alone" heroes as John Wayne are admired, team size is generally much smaller than in more collectivist-oriented cultures such as Taiwan, China, and Japan. Moreover, a mismatch in team size can be misinterpreted by both sides. Taiwanese might interpret a single individual or small team size as a sign that the other party does not consider the negotiations to be of sufficient importance to send a "regular" team. On the other hand, Americans might interpret the presence of a large team as an attempt to intimidate with numbers. Finally, the assumed relationships between parties can also differ

---

[9]J. Graham, The Influence of Culture on the Process of Business Negotiations in an Exploratory Study, *Journal of International Business Studies* (Summer 1983): 81–96.

significantly by culture. For example, many negotiations involve buyer/seller relationships. In countries such as the United States, buyers generally have more power and slightly more status than do sellers, but in countries such as Japan, buyers have significantly more status and power—so much so that there are fairly rigid norms of what language sellers must use and the behaviors and attitudes they must exhibit.

Influence Tactics.   Influence tactics can also differ significantly among cultures. For example, in one study of Japanese, American, and Brazilian negotiators, it was found that Brazilians tend to make significantly fewer promises and commitments than do Americans and to say "no" much more frequently.[10] Japanese negotiators were much more likely than either Americans or Brazilians to use silence as a means of responding, and Brazilians were nearly twice as likely as either Americans or Japanese to begin talking before the other party had finished.

Clearly these general tendencies and differences should not be taken as valid for all individuals from a specific culture. However, they do point out that while most cultures seem to move through five stages of negotiations, cultural norms vary significantly concerning the length and location of these stages, the number and type of people involved in negotiations, and the tactics utilized to influence the other party. Consequently, when one is preparing to negotiate with individuals from a culture different from one's own, at a minimum, research into these topics of difference should be a key component of a team's preparation.

Decision Making

Culture can also have a significant impact on by whom and how decisions are made. Research has identified at least three fundamental aspects of decision making that differ significantly by culture.[11] One of the first dimensions is who makes the decision. Collectivist-oriented cultures such as Japan are well known for efforts to make decision by consensus. In fact, executives from more individualistic-oriented cultures such as Australia and the United States often complain about how long decisions in Japan take because of the involvement of so many people in the decision.

In addition to who makes decisions, how decisions are made also varies by culture. One of the key factors that influence decisions is the role of information in the decision-making process. In the United States and Sweden, managers emphasize rationality and utilize quantitative information. By contrast, French, Italian, and Argentinean managers emphasize past experience and qualitative information over quantitative data in making decisions. These examples further illustrate that the type of information that managers pay attention to and utilize in decision making can vary. And these variations may, in fact, be a function of more fundamental assumptions about the nature of truth, discussed earlier.

Culture also seems to play a significant role in the extent to which managers are comfortable in making decisions in uncertain environments. For example, managers from the United States, Germany, and Scandinavia seem to have the highest tolerance, while managers from Italy, Iberia, and Japan seem to have much lower tolerance for making decisions in circumstances of uncertainty. These differences in tolerance can have a variety of implications. For example, if managers from Germany and Iberia are trying to come to an agreement concerning a joint venture in the context of significant uncertainty, they may clash and differ in their willingness to make decisions.

[10]J. Graham, "Brazilian, Japanese, and American Business Negotiations," *Journal of International Business Studies* (Spring 1983): 47–61.

[11]S. Ronen, "Managerial Behaviors and Leadership Style," *Comparative and Multinational Management* (1986), 187–231.

CONCLUSION

This chapter has provided a systematic conceptualization of culture and a means of assessing the underlying assumptions and values of unfamiliar cultures. Furthermore, it has provided examples in three critical areas of managerial behavior—communication, negotiation, and decision making—that illustrate how culture can influence managers as well as cause conflicts and clashes when managers from different cultures have to interact. Although it is impossible to examine all the areas in which culture can influence managers or all the various cultures and their specific influences, the framework does provide a general road map to help managers plan and more successfully navigate the unfamiliar territory of international business environments.

West Coast University and Hamamatsu Chemical*

The vice-chancellor of health services of West Coast University, Dr. Edward Quinlin, sighed in frustration and called for a break in the negotiations. This was the third official meeting between West Coast University and Hamamatsu Chemical concerning a joint venture. The agreement should have been fairly easy to conclude but things were going nowhere fast despite the presence of Dr. Yamanouchi, the president of Hamamatsu Chemical. Ostensibly, Dr. Yamanouchi was at the meeting because he was on business in the United States anyway, but Dr. Quinlin sensed he had made a special trip to try to facilitate the negotiations. As people got up from the table, Dr. Quinlin wondered if he could get the negotiations back on track and, more importantly, if he *should* get them back on track.

BACKGROUND

West Coast University and Hamamatsu Chemical first crossed paths in the early '80s when the research of Dr. George Nakayama, a professor of biochemistry at the university, caught the attention of Hamamatsu Chemical scientists in Japan. They were intrigued by Dr. Nakayama's research on microbes and met with him several times to discuss his findings. Hamamatsu Chemical saw great commercial potential in some of Dr. Nakayama's research findings and consequently proposed to provide some funding for his research. This funding was funneled to the professor through the West Coast University contracts and grants department. Dr. Nakayama's research continued to produce interesting results, and many of the scientists at Hamamatsu Chemical thoroughly enjoyed their interactions with him.

*This case was written by J. Stewart Black as a basis for class discussion rather than to illustrate either effective or ineffective handling of an administrative situation.

Two years after the first meeting between Dr. Nakayama and Hamamatsu Chemical officials, the Japanese firm decided to offer scholarship money to doctoral and post-doctoral students to enhance the relationship between the two institutions. A large sum of money was donated to West Coast University to underwrite several scholarships. The doctoral scholarships were awarded to deserving students in the usual fashion. A few of the post-doctoral scholarships, however, were awarded to Hamamatsu Chemical scientists, most of whom were young and had just received their Ph.D.s. These "post-docs" worked primarily with Dr. Nakayama during their stay in the US. When these Japanese scientists returned to Japan, they were full of enthusiasm and a host of new research ideas. Unfortunately, some soon lost their zeal because of the rigid and hierarchical structure and process of the Japanese research labs. Still, as a result of these initial positive contacts, in 1984 Hamamatsu Chemical gave $600,000 to endow a research chair for Dr. Nakayama. This donation continued to solidify the relationship between West Coast University (particularly the biochemistry department) and Hamamatsu Chemical.

Background on West Coast University

West Coast University is one of the largest university systems in the entire United States. It has several major campuses on the West Coast and is governed by a president, a board of regents, and several senior vice-presidents over such functions as budget, administration, and academic affairs. The administrative structure of the southern California campus is presented in *Figure 1.*

Background on Hamamatsu Chemical

Hamamatsu Chemical is a wholly owned subsidiary of Hamamatsu Ltd., a large Japanese conglomerate that operates in over seventy countries across a wide variety of industries, including power systems and equipment, industrial machinery, consumer products and electronics, information and communication systems, wire and cable, metals, and chemicals. The chemicals firm had sales of $1 billion across several areas, including electronics and electrical materials (41%), organic chemicals (14%), synthetic resins (13%), inorganic chemicals (7%), and housing and environmental facilities (25%). Hamamatsu Chemical is marginally profitable and generally spends 6 percent of sales on R&D (approximately $62 million in 1987).

All the presidents of the various subsidiaries within Hamamatsu Ltd. meet every third Thursday to discuss coordination and cooperation issues among the various firms, though Dr. Yamanouchi, who heads Hamamatsu Chemical, has a fair amount of autonomy to run his operation as he and his senior management team see fit. The general decision-making style within Hamamatsu Chemical reflects the consensus style of the larger parent company; Dr. Yamanouchi, however, has somewhat a more directive and charismatic style than many of his counterparts at other Hamamatsu subsidiaries.

CURRENT PROJECT

In 1986 Dr. Yamanouchi was on campus and met with West Coast University Chancellor John Petersen. At that time Dr. Yamanouchi mentioned the idea of a joint research facility on West Coast University land similar to a joint venture recently completed by WCU and a US laser technology company. The general idea was that Hamamatsu Chemical would construct the building and occupy a portion of it; West Coast University would occupy the remainder. It seemed to be a very appealing idea to both sides with significant benefits to West Coast University and Hamamatsu Chemical.

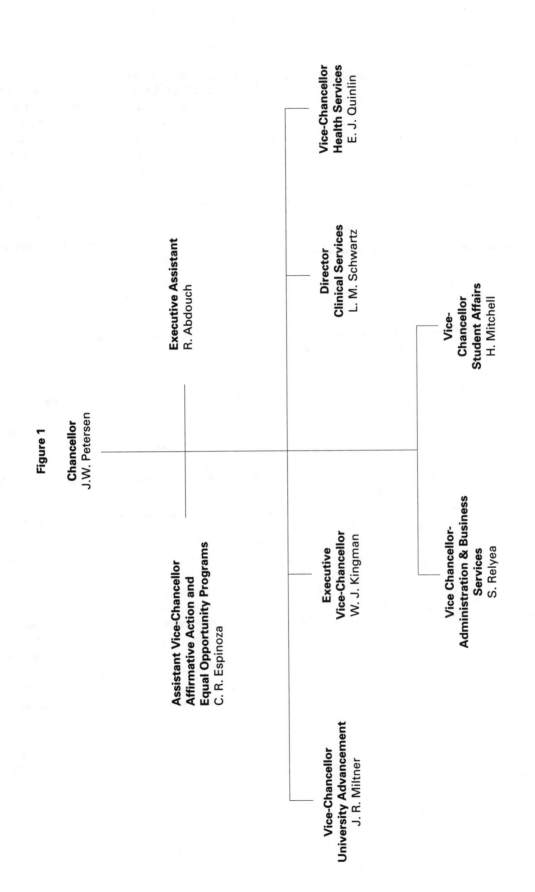

Figure 1

Chancellor
J.W. Petersen

Executive Assistant
R. Abdouch

**Assistant Vice-Chancellor
Affirmative Action and
Equal Opportunity Programs**
C. R. Espinoza

**Executive
Vice-Chancellor**
W. J. Kingman

**Vice-Chancellor
University Advancement**
J. R. Miltner

**Vice Chancellor-
Administration & Business
Services**
S. Relyea

**Vice-
Chancellor
Student Affairs**
H. Mitchell

**Director
Clinical Services**
L. M. Schwartz

**Vice-Chancellor
Health Services**
E. J. Quinlin

Later in that year there was an exchange of letters between Vice-Chancellor Walter Kingman and Dr. Yamanouchi. In one of these letters, the general purpose of the joint venture was described by the Japanese as follows:

> The purpose of this proposed venture is to broaden and deepen the relationship between Hamamatsu Chemical and West Coast University which was initiated by a donation of the Hamamatsu Chemical to the Nakayama Biological/Chemistry Research Fund. In order to make this relationship even closer, Hamamatsu Chemical plans to construct a chemical research facility on the university campus. This plan, including an offer of space to the university, will develop a closer relationship and interaction between Hamamatsu Chemical and the University which we believe will contribute to widen and deepen research activities for both parties. This should also further enhance the good relationship which exists between the United States and Japan.

Following this exchange of letters, a meeting was set up for June 1987 to begin talking in detail about the proposed joint venture.

FIRST MEETING

In addition to the correspondence between Dr. Yamanouchi and Vice-Chancellor Kingman that preceded the June 1987 meeting, Dr. Quinlin, Vice-Chancellor in charge of health services, which included the biochemistry department, sent a letter to Hamamatsu Chemical. He wrote that university officials were looking forward to the first official meeting and that representatives from the school would be from the Office of Physical Planning, one of several offices reporting to Vice-Chancellor Kingman. This initial team consisted of Paul Carter, manager of advanced planning; Laura Knight, project manager for special projects; and Dennis Neven, associate vice-chancellor and campus architect.

After receiving the letter from Dr. Quinlin, the Japanese began to organize and prepare their negotiation team. The Hamamatsu Chemical team for this first meeting consisted of Mr. Nomura, executive managing director and general manager, Research and Development Division; Mr. Kinoshita, manager, International Division; Mr. Kanda, architect; Mr. Suzuki, manager, Saitama Research Laboratory; and Mr. Konishiki, architect.

The Japanese arrived on a typical warm and sunny southern California day. After the Japanese team was welcomed and invited to the meeting room, a series of introductions took place—the Japanese presenting their business cards to the Americans and the Americans fumbling for business cards and presenting them, in some cases upside down, to the Japanese. After this rather awkward start, each team sat on either side of a very long rectangular table. Mr. Carter opened the meeting by asking for greater clarification of the purpose that Hamamatsu Chemical saw in the proposed joint facility. Mr. Nomura, the team leader for Hamamatsu Chemical, reiterated what was contained in a previous letter written by the president of Hamamatsu Chemical to Vice-Chancellor Kingman. This letter indicated that the basic purpose of the joint facility was to enhance the good relationship between Hamamatsu Chemical and West Coast University and to facilitate the interaction and research of both parties.

At this point the Japanese mentioned that they had several questions and points of clarification. Mr. Kanda, the architect, withdrew from his briefcase a rather large file of detailed plans for the building (the plans presented by Mr. Kanda are provided in *Exhibits 1-6*), and then presented an initial drawing of the facility (see *Exhibit 1*). The proposed facility was a three-story structure of approximately 40,000 square feet. The proposed site of the new facility was on a 1.5-acre spot just behind the medical science buildings (see *Exhibit 2*). Mr. Kanda continued by stating that approximately one-third of the building would be allocated to West Coast University, and Hamamatsu Chemical would occupy the other two-thirds (see *Exhibits 3, 4, 5, and 6* for detailed drawings of the proposed facilities). Mr. Kanda then asked several questions about building codes in the state of California, particularly regarding the Uniform Building Code, Seismic Code, Uniform Plumbing Code, Uniform Mechanical Code and Standards, National Electrical Code, California Administrative Code, and National Fire Protection Administrative Code. Mr. Kinoshita, manager of the International Division, asked about legal issues concerning animal rights and the use of animals in laboratory studies. The Americans were surprised by this level of detailed questioning. In their minds, the basic purpose of the joint facility had not been clearly established, and there were many prerequisites before a detailed discussion of building codes or square footage could be addressed fruitfully. Consequently, Mr. Carter suggested that his staff look into these specific questions and get back with the Japanese team within two weeks. The meeting ended.

THE SECOND MEETING

In advance of the second formal meeting, both sides attempted to exchange detailed information about the joint facility. West Coast University officials calculated that there were 8,660 assignable square feet for their portion of the building based on the detailed drawings that were presented at the first meeting. Hamamatsu Chemical estimated total construction costs would be $7 million. Hamamatsu Chemical also provided a general research building construction schedule (see *Exhibit 7*) and detailed finish schedule (see *Exhibit 8*).

West Coast University in turn explained that the ground lease proposal for the West Coast University/Hamamatsu Chemical research facility would be based on space for land analysis conducted by the Office of the Treasurer. In principle, the campus would lease a portion of the newly constructed building rent-free (except for operating costs) as consideration for the ground lease. Analysts at the Office of the Treasurer estimated that the present value of the foregone ground rent on the Hamamatsu-allocated share of the building would equal the construction cost of the rent-free space occupied by West Coast University after approximately 10 years. This estimate was in part based on commercial rents in the area near West Coast University of approximately $0.89 per square foot per month. West Coast University proposed to allow Hamamatsu Chemical to occupy their portion of the building for another 15 years before the entire building would revert to the university. Hamamatsu Chemical, however, preferred to occupy the building for an additional 30 rather than 15 years.

The second meeting between Hamamatsu Chemical and West Coast University took place in the fall of 1987. The Japanese team consisted of seven individuals including two new members from the Accounting and Finance Department: Mr. Yamaguchi, deputy manager, and Mr. Saito, manager. The American team consisted of the same three individuals who were in attendance at the first meeting, as well as Martha Lennard, director of Research and Program Development Office within the College of Medicine, and Donald Singer, assistant dean, Office of Research and Graduate Studies, a legal representative whose specialty was patent issues.

The meeting once more opened with awkward introductions and exchange of business cards. After everyone was comfortably seated, Mr. Carter of West Coast University asked for clarification of the purpose for the joint facility. The Japanese were somewhat surprised that this question surfaced again and reiterated that the purpose of the joint facility was to build upon the relationship between Hamamatsu Chemical and West Coast University, to augment the research activities of both parties, and to enhance the good relationship between the United States and Japan. After this the Japanese had several questions about the ground lease, the difference in return times, and the differences in return value assessed by both parties in the building. Mr. Carter indicated that he would be happy to talk about these issues but that he first needed greater clarification of the purpose of the joint facility.

At this point Mr. Singer indicated that he had specific concerns regarding patents. He presented a document to the Japanese team that outlined several key issues in terms of research and patents within the West Coast University system (see *Exhibit 9*). The response from the Japanese was a long period of silence.

Uncomfortable with the silence, Mr. Carter asked more probing questions about the nature of the research that Hamamatsu Chemical hoped to pursue. The director of the Saitama Research Laboratory, Mr. Suzuki, indicated that Hamamatsu Chemical hoped to pursue research in four categories: (1) human medicine, (2) diagnostic systems and diagnostic agents, (3) industrial bio-reactors, and (4) electronics. Mr. Carter probed further to find out exactly what was meant by these four categories. Mr. Suzuki explained that development of human medicine for illness and diseases related to aging were important because of the increasing aging population in Japan; Hamamatsu Chemical was interested especially in neurological disorders such as Alzheimer's disease. The firm also was interested in pursuing research in diagnostic systems and their reagents, in particular using DNA probes. Additionally, since wastewater treatment systems were among Hamamatsu Chemical's major products—pure water to help in the well-being of the community was a high priority to the company—Hamamatsu officials were interested in broadening its scope of research in this area, utilizing industrial bioreactors and highly efficient enzymes and bacteria in disposing of waste. Finally, said Mr. Suzuki, the electronic materials category focused on development of various kinds of novel materials and systems that were important for biology and medicine.

Mr. Singer then revived the patents issue and asked the Japanese for clarification in the role of patents in the proposed joint facility. The Japanese responded with another long period of silence. Frustrated by and somewhat suspicious of their silence, Mr. Carter suggested that the negotiation be concluded for the time being and that later negotiations be scheduled. A third meeting was set up for December 1987.

While the second meeting was going on in the US, Dr. Yamanouchi was involved in a meeting in Japan with his board of directors. Dr. Yamanouchi assured them that within a very short period of time the joint facility contract with West Coast University would be signed and the building would be completed and occupied by 1989.

THE THIRD MEETING

One week before the scheduled third meeting, Dr. Quinlin was informed by the Japanese that Dr. Yamanouchi would be present for the negotiations since he was in the United States on business anyway and wanted to attend the negotiations to finalize the agreement as soon as possible. In preparation for the negotiations, the Americans concentrated on the issue of interaction between Hamamatsu Chemical personnel and University personnel. The detailed drawings presented by Hamamatsu Chemical had focused their attention on this issue and they were determined to discuss and resolve this topic before moving on to any other issue such as the land-lease agreement.

At the beginning of the third meeting, Hamamatsu Chemical President Yamanouchi reiterated his desire to solidify the company's relationship with West Coast University and his view of the potential benefits of the research activities within this joint facility. Mr. Carter followed these remarks by asking again about the nature of the expected interaction between Hamamatsu Chemical personnel and University researchers. The Japanese indicated that they had several questions and points that needed clarification. For example, when university and Hamamatsu personnel jointly made use of the lecture room, would West Coast University regard this as research space? Also, when West Coast University granted the title of adjunct professor to a Hamamatsu scientist, would this constitute employment by West Coast University? If a Hamamatsu researcher utilized funds provided through the research grant given by Hamamatsu Chemical to West Coast University, would *this* constitute being a West Coast University employee? In response to these picky questions, Mr. Singer indicated that all of these could be answered specifically; however, he and the rest of the group were interested in the general expectations of interaction that Hamamatsu Chemical had for their personnel and the university researchers. Again the Japanese responded with silence. It was at this point that Dr. Quinlin decided to call for a recess.

EXHIBIT 1

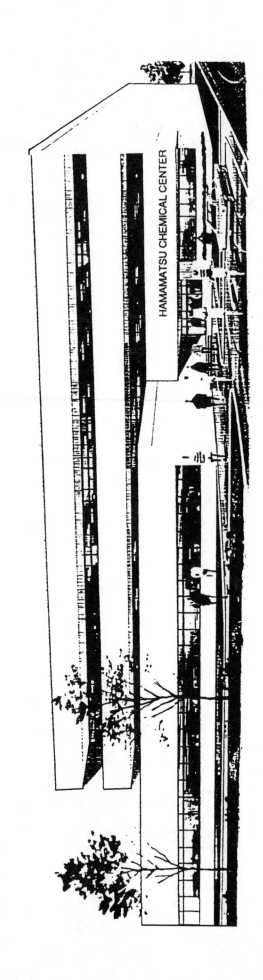

HAMAMATSU CHEMICAL CENTER

EXHIBIT 2

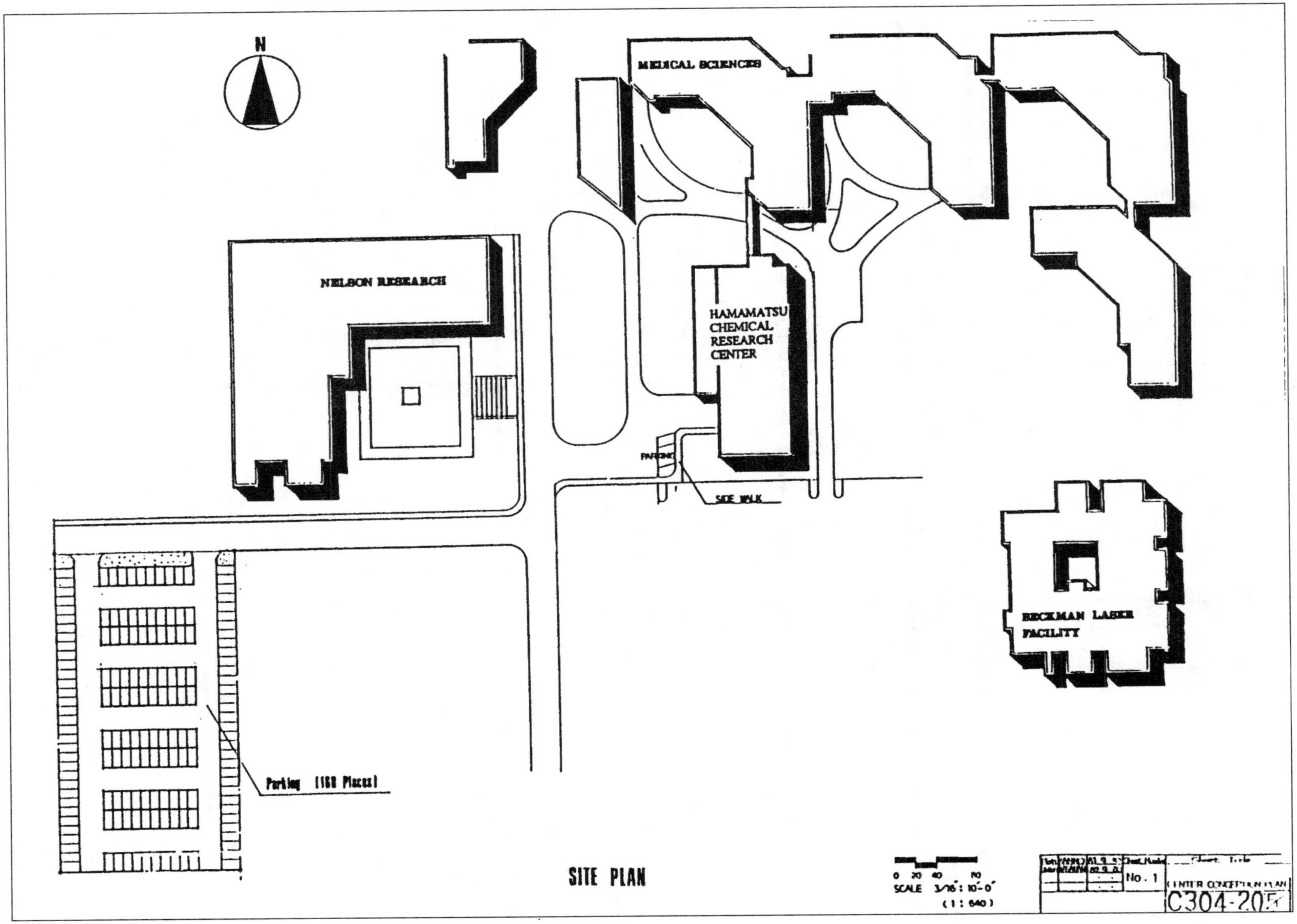
N
MEDICAL SCIENCES
NELSON RESEARCH
HAMAMATSU
CHEMICAL
RESEARCH
CENTER
PARKING
SIDE WALK
BECKMAN LASER
FACILITY
Parking (168 Places)
SITE PLAN
0 20 40 80
SCALE 3/16" : 10'-0"
(1 : 640)
No. 1
C304-205

EXHIBIT 3

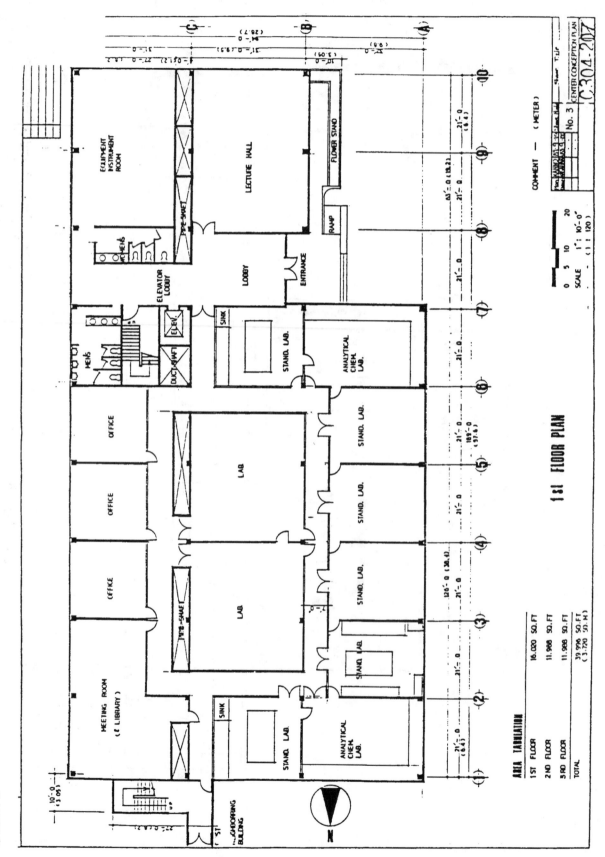

288

EXHIBIT 4

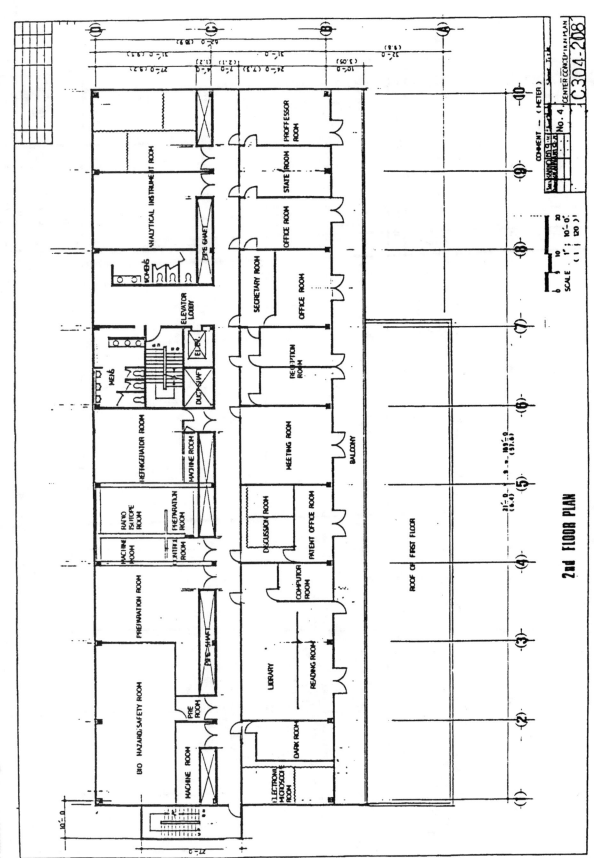

2nd FLOOR PLAN

EXHIBIT 5

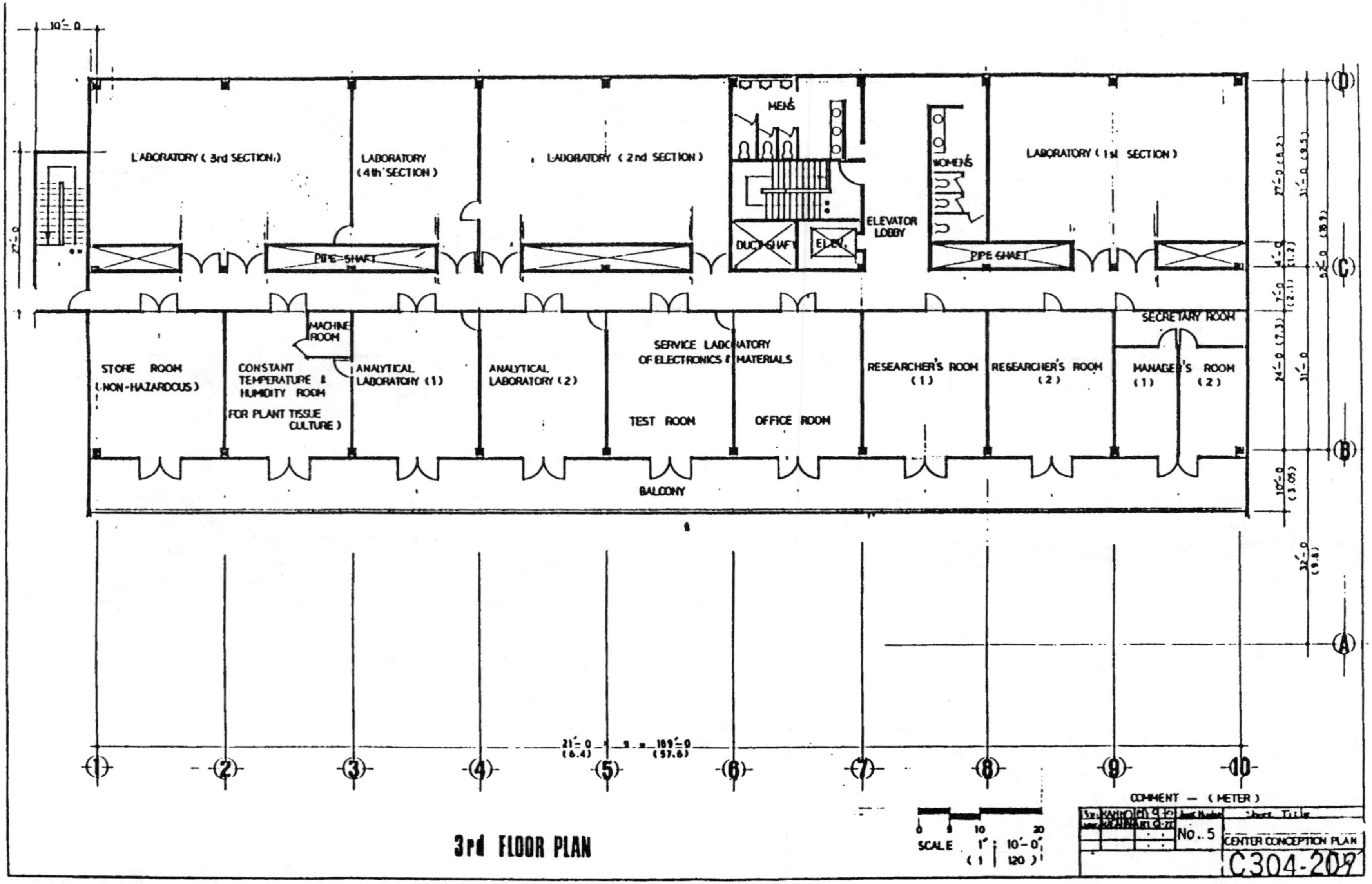

290

3rd FLOOR PLAN

EXHIBIT 6

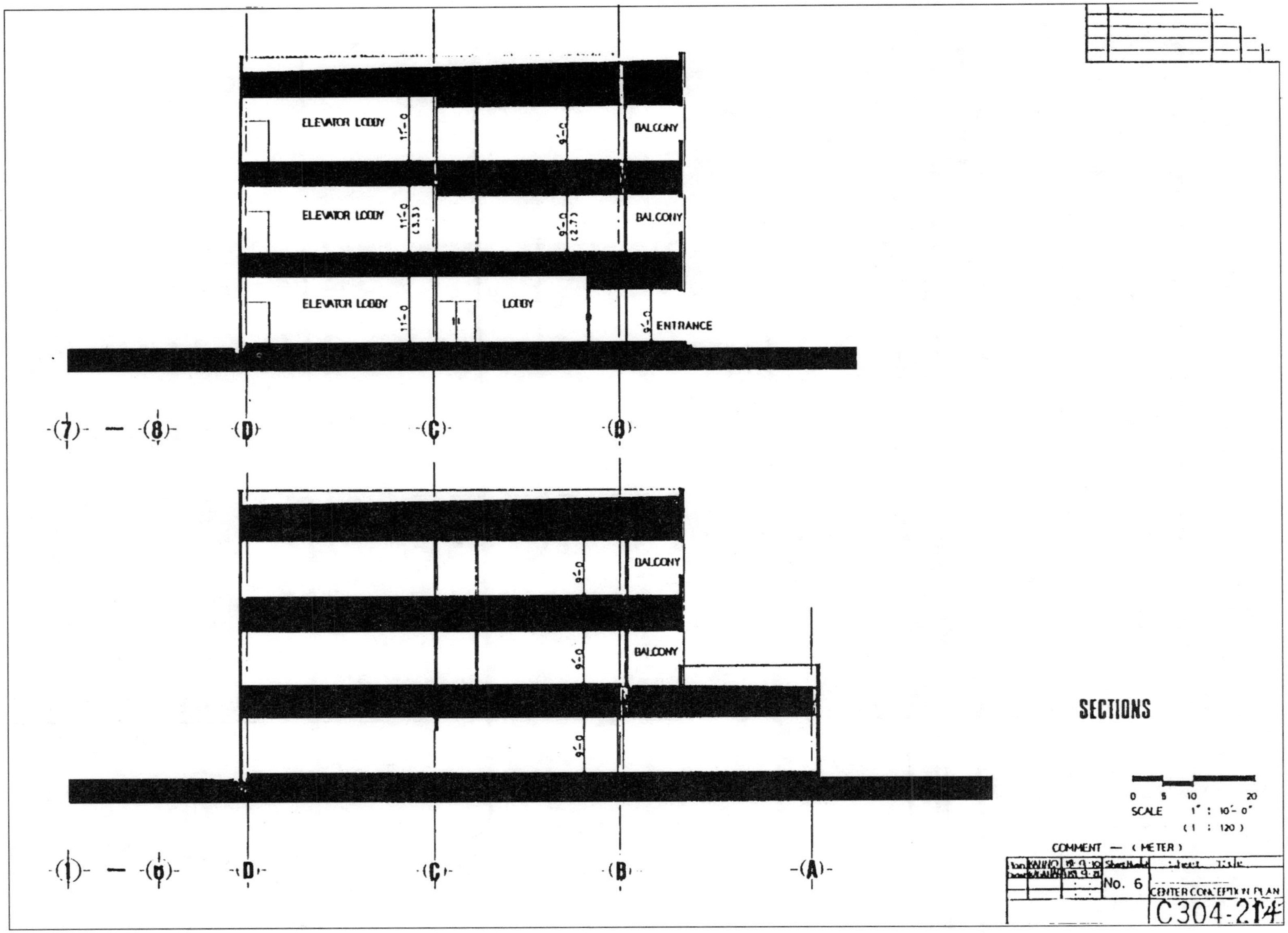
ELEVATOR LOBBY
BALCONY
ELEVATOR LOBBY
BALCONY
ELEVATOR LOBBY
LOBBY
ENTRANCE
11'-0
9'-0
(3.3)
(2.7)
(7) — (8)
(D)
(C)
(B)
BALCONY
BALCONY
(1) — (6)
(A)
SECTIONS
0 5 10 20
SCALE 1" : 10'-0"
(1 : 120)
COMMENT — (METER)
No. 6
CENTER CONCEPTION PLAN
C304-214

EXHIBIT 7

Research Building Construction Schedule

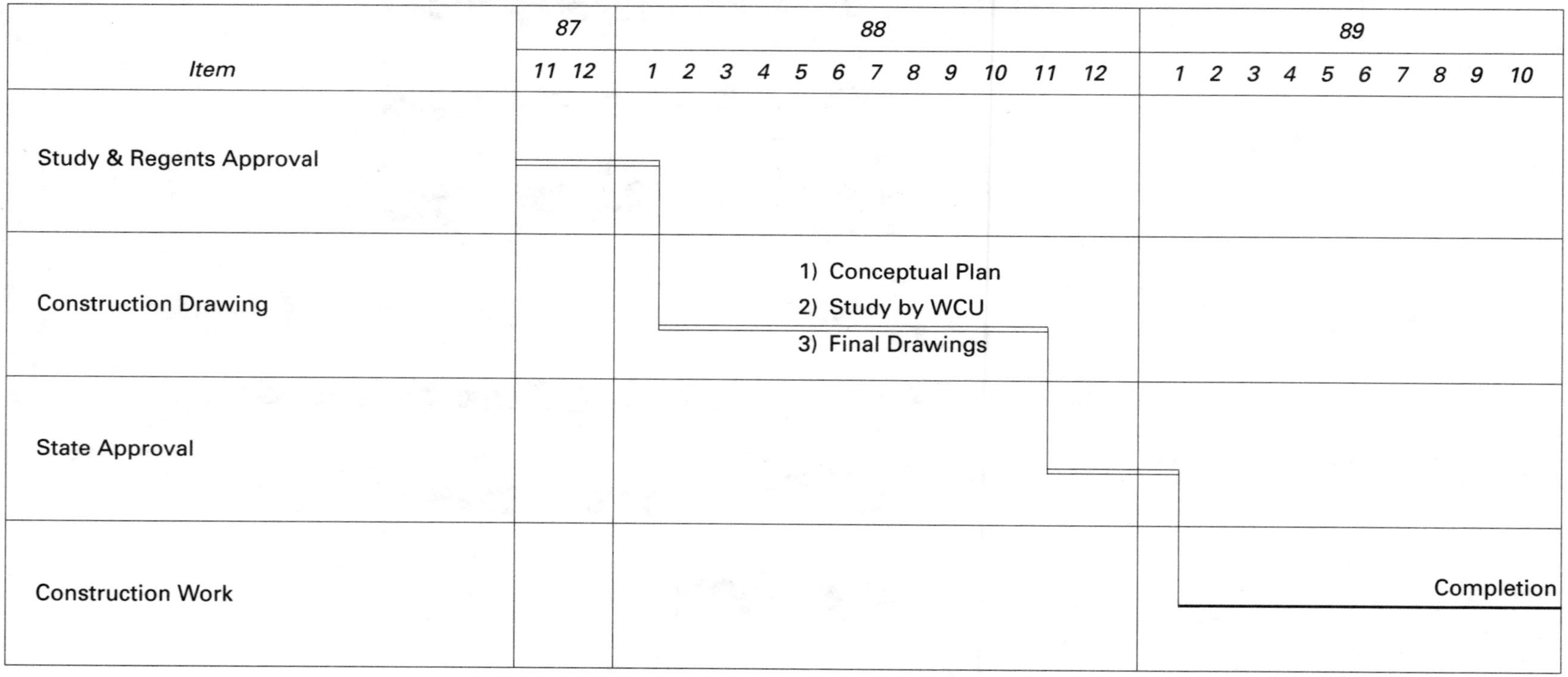

Item	87		88														89										
	11	12	1	2	3	4	5	6	7	8	9	10	11	12		1	2	3	4	5	6	7	8	9	10
Study & Regents Approval																										
Construction Drawing							1) Conceptual Plan 2) Study by WCU 3) Final Drawings																		
State Approval																										
Construction Work																									Completion

EXHIBIT 8

Room Finish Schedule

Room	Floor		Walls		Ceiling
	Material	Finishing	Base	Material	Finishing	
Lobby Elevator Lobby	Concrete	Quarry Tile	Quarry Tile	Gypsum Board	Coating	Acoustic Board
Rest Room	Concrete	Ceramic Tile	Ceramic Tile	Gypsum Board	Ceramic Tile	Gypsum Board, Coating
Stairs	Concrete	Vinyl Tile	Vinyl	Gypsum Board	Coating	———
Machine Room	Concrete	Coating	———	Concrete	———	———
Lecture Room	Concrete	Vinyl Tile	Vinyl	Gypsum Board	Coating	Acoustic Board
Office Guest Room, etc.	Concrete	Carpet	Vinyl	Gypsum Board	Vinyl Leather	Acoustic Board
Reasearch Lab.	Concrete	Coating	Vinyl	Gypsum Board	Coating	———

EXHIBIT 9

Hamamatsu Chemical Co.   November 11, 1987
Re: PATENT

1. Excerpts from WCU RESEARCH ADMINISTRATION'S POLICY AND PROCE-
   DURES MANUAL ON PATENTS
   A. Persons in the following categories must sign a University Patent Agree-
      ment which provides that the signers agree to assign their patents and
      inventions to the University:
      i. All employees hired by the University.
      ii. Any person using University research facilities, exclusive of libraries.
      iii. Any person who uses contract or grant funds obtained through the
          University.
   B. The following persons are exempted from signing the University Patent
      Agreement, but the exemptions are limited in each case to only those
      persons who are not covered under A. ii–iii above:
      i. A member of the military service who is non-University compen-
         sated.
      ii. A teacher and lecturer of University Extension who is not a regular
          University instructor.
      iii. A visiting scholar on special short-term assignment of one year or
           less. (If the individual is reappointed, a Patent Agreement must be
           signed.)
      iv. A lecturer making a one-time appearance or a series of appearances.
      v. A non-University compensated clinical appointee who does not use
         University research facilities.
   C. The following is a guideline of Agreement regarding West Coast Univer-
      sity Patent Rights to be executed between the University and potential
      industrial (for profit) Sponsors of Research:
      i. A written agreement, having detailed terms and conditions, must be
         executed between the University and the Sponsor.
      ii. When the sponsor pays all direct and indirect costs for the research
          to be undertaken, the Sponsor may be granted a right of first refusal
          to an exclusive or nonexclusive license to the inventions resulting
          from that research. Right to sublicense may be granted under the
          exclusive license only.
      iii. When the sponsor pays less than all direct and indirect costs for the
           research to be undertaken, the Sponsor may be granted a right of
           refusal to a nonexclusive license to the inventions resulting from that
           research.

chapter 14

Competitive Strategy and the International Business Environment

How a firm matches or betters its competition lies at the core of its success. This, in turn, is often determined by how a firm *plans* to compete—that is, its competitive strategy. Although few will argue against the importance of careful strategy formulation and implementation, there is a great deal of debate as to what constitutes a good strategy, and how to formulate or implement an effective one. Answers to these questions are even more complex in the cross-border setting.

Acknowledging the breadth of domain that the topic of competitive strategy covers, our objective in this chapter is modest. We first summarize two basic views of strategy, followed by the commonly accepted principles of strategy formulation. We then discuss the traditionally used concepts in identifying strategies adopted by MNEs—notably those of coordination and configuration of the various elements of the MNE's "value chain"—and see how they provide us a taxonomy to understand the cross-border firm as either being "multidomestic" (at one end of the spectrum), or "global" (at the other). We then link these forms of the MNE to the role played by factors in the international environment. We shall see that strategies that work—and prescriptions that seem to be optimal—in the traditional contexts may require substantial modification, to take into account the two unique aspects of the international environment that we have discussed in this book: multiple sources of external authority (MA) and multiple denominations of value (MV).

TWO DOMINANT VIEWS OF STRATEGY

One dominant view of strategy is the view that it is a *plan* of purposeful action—that is, it is the outcome of a carefully managed process of translating a firm's strategic intent into a systematic and well-communicated plan of action. The idea is that a firm should systematically formulate and implement a plan of action in order to exercise control over its environment—its existing and potential competitors, customers/markets, suppliers, government, and so forth—and, in implementing this strategy, the firm should marshall its internal resources and capabilities. The number of scholars and managers talking about "the strategic planning process" and the factors to include systematically in formulating a strategic plan is testimony to the "purposeful" nature of strategy for guiding intended actions.

Others have argued that strategies emerge from *patterned* behavior rather than from planned and intended actions. It has been pointed out that observers and managers alike impute a strategy to a corporation based on observed patterns of actions, whether these actions were intended or not. That is, observers may simply assume that what they perceived is a function of what was planned, but often, the observed pattern may simply be a function of the consequences of a series of actions, rather than specifically planned intentions. Certain actions may be reinforced by positive consequences; these actions are then repeated and expanded only so far as positive consequences continue, and patterns in these actions are subsequently interpreted by observers as intended. Indeed, the patterns may have been retrospectively interpreted even by those who performed them as "strategic" and "intended" from the outset.

Therefore, we need to recognize the existence of both *deliberate* (planned) strategies and *emergent* (patterned) strategies. Deliberate strategies focus our attention on analyzing factors in the international environment, and on trying to predict (and, therefore, plan for) the future. In contrast, emergent strategies focus our attention on the consequences of past and present actions, how these have shaped decision-making processes and cultures within organizations, and how strategies have been implemented. Whether they are deliberate or emergent, there are certain commonly accepted principles that help a manager to systematically think through how a firm may formulate or interpret its competitive strategy.

PRINCIPLES OF COMPETITIVE STRATEGY FORMULATION

The most widely accepted views of strategy formulation are owed to the ideas of Michael Porter, who argues that whether strategy is deliberate or emergent, it is the *relative* position of a firm and its products within its industry that ultimately determines its success or failure. The strength or weakness of the firm's relative position, he argues, requires us to understand three aspects of the firm's operations in the context of its industry:

- The external forces that drive a firm's *industry structure*
- The type(s) of "generic" strategy that determines a firm's *competitive positioning* within this industry structure
- The internal organization of the firm as embodied in its "value chain," or its internal *sources of competitive advantage*

As we shall see, Porter argues that a combination of these three aspects of the firm in the context of its industry structure optimally determines how the firm structures itself and competes globally.

Industry Structure

The structure of any industry consists of five competitive forces that shape a firm's strategy: (1) the firm's buyers/market; (2) its suppliers; (3) its competitors; (4) products or services that may be substitutes for what the firm offers; and (5) the threat of new entrants. Each of these five forces is working to put downward pressure on the profits (or economic rents) that a firm can earn. Moreover, these five forces determine the prices that firms can charge for their products, the costs they incur, and the investments they have to make in order to create and sustain entry barriers in the industry.

The power of buyers is a determinant of the prices that a firm can charge in the marketplace; the greater the buyer power, the lower the firm's ability to price high. The power of suppliers is a determinant of the costs incurred by the firm for its inputs; again, the higher the supplier power, the higher the costs that the firm will incur. The breadth and depth of competitive rivalry determine profits not only by constraining a firm's ability to price, but also by constraining its costs (competition for factor inputs) and its investment spending (R&D, capital, and advertising, for example). The presence of close substitutes determines—and often limits—what the firm can charge for its goods and services without inducing substitution and market-share erosion. Finally, any industry that offers profits is always a magnet for potential new entrants, thus raising the question of how a firm can erect entry barriers, and the investments and costs that will be incurred in erecting these barriers.

The strength and importance of each of the five forces vary from industry to industry, but they all matter to a greater or lesser degree in every industry. For instance, buyer power tends to be higher in industrial as opposed to consumer products; supplier power tends to be higher in industries such as airplanes, since the supplying firms are large and few in number (although competition even among a couple of firms in the commercial airframes industry has lowered profits in that industry); commodity chips offer an example of an industry in which competitive rivalry is intense, and firms are often forced to price their products at razor-thin margins; all industries are affected by the presence of substitute products to some degree (for example, the arrival of the fax turned out to be a substitute for the services offered by the overnight delivery industry); and many industries incur huge costs in R&D and advertising in order to try to continuously impede the entry of potential new entrants.

The first step in the formulation of competitive strategy is, therefore, to undertake a systematic audit of how each of the five forces affects the profitability—pricing and costs—in a particular firm, given the structure of the industry in which it competes. The next step is to determine the *positioning* that the firm seeks within that industry structure: In other words, what approach should the firm adopt in competing in a particular industry, once it has figured out what the five external forces and their impacts are?

Competitive Positioning

A firm's performance, given the five forces and the industry structure, is determined by the competitive positioning that it adopts with respect to its competitors. Porter suggests that there are two broad types of competitive advantage that determine a firm's positioning within an industry: They are the "generic" strategies of cost leadership and differentiation; in addition, the firm should also determine its competitive scope, or the breadth of operations that it seeks to be involved in—the range of products, the types of buyers or market segments, the geographic areas it will serve, and the like.

Cost Leadership.   With the generic cost leadership strategy, a firm seeks to be the lowest cost producer of a product or provider of a service. To the extent that the cost leader can provide products or services of sufficient value to command prices near the industry average, it can achieve above-average profits. If a low-cost producer priced its product relative to competitors at a level equivalent to its cost advantage over competitors, it generally would not be more profitable in the short run; however, it might achieve above-average profits in the long run if its pricing practices increased its market share and drove competitors out of the business, and consequently, allowed it to increase prices later. For cost leadership to lead to sustainable above-average profits, the firm's products must: (1) achieve parity with the industry average in quality and other attributes valued by customers, and (2) have a source of cost leadership that is not easy for other firms to imitate or otherwise match.

Differentiation.   A firm using this strategy seeks to differentiate its product or service on dimensions that are highly valued by customers. If the firm can uniquely differentiate itself in this manner and has costs that approximate the industry average, then the premium price it can command allows it to earn above-average profits. Any number of characteristics might provide the basis for differentiation. These characteristics might be directly related to the product or service itself or might be indirectly related through any of several aspects of the firm's value chain. Eveready batteries might command a premium price because they provide longer-lasting power. In contrast, Caterpillar tractors might command a premium price because of available 24-hour service and spare parts delivery anywhere in the world. To the extent that customers highly value a number of product attributes, there is the potential for several firms to pursue a differentiation strategy if they attempt to differentiate their products from each other on diverse attributes. If, on the other hand, for a given product or service, there is only one attribute that customers highly and widely value, there will be less room for firms pursuing a differentiation strategy. The most successful firm in this setting would be the one that is best able to distance its product from that of its competitors on the attribute valued by customers and can, at the same time, keep a superior cost position. For a differentiation strategy to lead to sustainable above-average profits, products must achieve unique advantage on attributes highly valued by customers, and the source of the differentiation must be one that is not easy for other firms to imitate or otherwise match.

Scope. Relative to both these generic strategies, a firm can choose to limit the scope of its strategy. For example, a firm could pursue a differentiation strategy by creating a product or service with an attribute that is highly valued by a narrow set of customers. While the restriction in scope reduces the total volume and revenue the firm can obtain from that product, to the extent it can differentiate its product and maintain a superior cost position, it can earn above-average profits in this "niche." This would also apply to a focused-cost leadership strategy. To the extent that the cost leader can provide products or service of sufficient value to command prices near the industry average for some targeted segment of customers, it can achieve above-average profits. Whether pursuing a cost or differentiation strategy, for either of these generic strategies to work in a focused scope, there must be differences among targeted customers or segments of the market.

Sources of Competitive Advantage: The Value Chain

A variety of ways of examining the internal aspects of a firm and how they are the sources of the firm's competitive advantage have been proposed. However, the "value chain" approach proposed by Michael Porter is arguably one of the most cited and widely utilized. Porter separates the internal components of a firm into five *primary* activities and four *support* activities (see Figure 14.1). Primary activities are those that are directly involved in the creation of a product or service; support activities facilitate the creation of the product or service and its transfer to the customer.

Porter stresses that, rather than the cost of these activities, it is the value that they add to the product or service that must be assessed in order to truly understand the firm's relative position. The value of a product or service is a function of how much customers are willing to pay and how many customers are willing to purchase the product or service. The firm makes a profit if it can produce something whose value exceeds its costs. Determining value activities internal to the firm requires a separate examination of each of the nine primary and support internal activities.

Inbound Logistics. This component of the value chain consists of activities that are designed to receive, store, and then disseminate various inputs to the products. Raw materials, delivery, transportation, inventory, and other issues are commonly a part of inbound logistics.

Operations. A wide variety of activities are conceptualized as being within the operations component of the value chain. Activities that transform the inputs into the products and services of the firm are at the heart of operations. In addition, activities (such as

Figure 14.1
The Value Chain

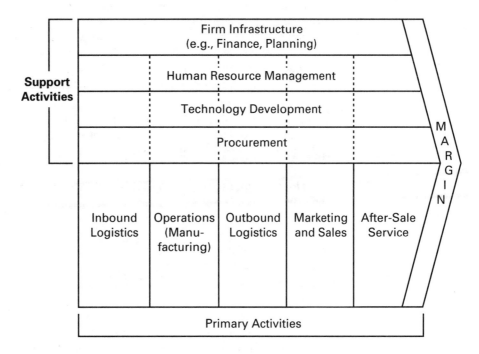

Source: Porter (1985).

maintenance) that keep the machines in working order would also be included in the operations segment of the value chain.

Outbound Logistics. Outbound logistics include those activities that get the product from the firm to the customers. This might involve transportation, vehicle scheduling, warehousing, and order processing.

Marketing and Sales. Marketing and sales activities are designed to let customers know about the products and services available and to entice them to purchase what the firm has to offer. Activities such as advertising, promotion, direct sales, and pricing would all be included in this component of the value chain.

Service. These activities are designed primarily to keep the product in the hands of the customer after the purchase, and to increase the probability of a repeat purchase. Service activities may involve repair, supply of parts, installation, or product warranties and adjustment.

Each of these primary activities has associated costs. They enhance the firm's positioning and profitability if a customer is willing to pay more for them than they cost. The importance of the various activities changes and depends on the products and services, and the preferences of the customers. For example, in the fashion industry, customers often want the latest styles, colors, and fabrics as soon as possible. This places a premium on both inbound and outbound logistics to ensure that what is produced can be delivered in a timely fashion to customers.

As illustrated in Figure 14.1, the four support activities cut across all five primary activities; that is, elements of a given support activity can be found facilitating each of the five primary activities.

Procurement.   The activity of procuring usable and consumable assets can be found in each of the primary activities. For example, not only must raw material be purchased within inbound logistics but procurement within inbound logistics may also involve the purchase of delivery trucks and scheduling software for the fleet. Purchases of machinery and replacement parts are examples of specific procurement activities within operations.

Technology Development.   This support activity of the value chain revolves around know-how and the tools or equipment related to the exercise of that know-how. The technology may be as simple as a pencil manually recording information or as complicated as a supercomputer. While technology development may be concentrated on product development or process innovation, know-how and the means by which that knowledge is applied to tasks is present in all five primary activities.

Human Resource Management.   Given that there are no activities that are completely independent of humans, the process of acquiring, training, evaluating, compensating, and developing human resources is present in all five primary activities. Given the impact that capable and motivated people can have on all activities of a firm, human resource management is potentially the key support activity. In service industries such as law, consulting, or accounting, the quality of the people determines the quality of the service, and, therefore, this component of the value chain is significant.

Firm Infrastructure.   Firm infrastructure has less to do with brick and mortar and more to do with functions that support all primary activities. Infrastructure consists of planning, finance, accounting, legal, government relations, among other activities. It is principally the information supplied by these functions to the various primary activities that is of concern. For example, legal information concerning worker safety standards may be needed in operations, while legal information on truth in advertising standards may be needed in marketing and sales.

Just as each of the primary activities had associated costs, so do the support activities. The support activities enhance the firm's positioning and profitability to the extent that they contribute to valued primary activities and the final product or service purchased by the customer. The importance of the support activities changes and depends on the products and services and the preferences of the customers. Returning to our earlier example of the fashion industry, the preference for customers for the latest styles, colors, and fabrics as soon as possible may reduce the importance of legal information as a component of the firm's infrastructure, but might increase the importance of planning information as related to specific buying seasons and purchasing cycles. This might also increase the importance of the technology development support activities that specifically allow fabrics to be colored after they have been assembled into a sweater, rather than as separate yarns, so that the latest color preferences by customers can be incorporated.

All activities in the value chain are a source not only of costs but also of buyer value. A firm is profitable if the collective value of performing activities in each element of the value chain exceeds the costs of performing those activities. Firms gain their competitive advantage from constantly innovating and upgrading every aspect of the value chain, and by figuring out new ways to conduct each of these activities.

Global Strategy: Coordinating and Configuring the Value Chain

The way in which a firm coordinates and configures its value chain is an important determinant of how the firm creates value and incurs costs in each part of its value chain. Each element of the firm's value chain is linked to other elements of the chain, and therefore requires coordination. In the global context, this coordination is rendered more complex because of the differences in languages and cultures, differences in the five competitive forces in the different parts of the world, and, often, the sheer geographical distance that is involved in the delivery of goods and services. Second, the firm has to decide how to configure the various elements of the value chain globally: Should the value chain be dispersed across the countries in which the firm conducts business, or should it be concentrated in one location? In other words, where and in how many locations should each activity in the value chain be performed?

The optimal coordination and configuration needs of the value chain across the world are often determined by the industry structure and industry economics. In capital- and scale-intensive industries (for example, manufacture of commercial airframes or earthmoving equipment), the optimal configuration of production activities may be concentrated, with the finished goods or components being exported to foreign markets. In less scale-intensive industries that require a great deal of product differentiation by location, the optimal configuration may be dispersed; an example of such an industry may be soaps and detergents, or the cosmetics industry. In such industries, both production and sales activities may be undertaken locally.

Certain industries require a great deal of coordination—information sharing and effort alignment—among the various elements of the firm's value chain. Again, the example of such an industry is the manufacture of earthmoving equipment. In such industries, optimal configuration may have to be concentrated because of the extensiveness of such linkages. In other industries—for example, retailing—coordination needs may be lower and, hence, different parts of the value chain could optimally be located in different parts of the world.

In general, industries that require a concentrated configuration of activities and have high coordination needs among the various elements of the value chain are "global" industries. Such industries are characterized by largeness of scale, capital intensity, a high ratio of exports from a home base, and careful coordination of advertising and R&D strategies worldwide. Examples of such industries include commercial airframes, automobiles, semiconductors, earthmoving equipment, and electrical distribution equipment. Industries that require a dispersed configuration of activities and have low coordination needs among the various elements of the value chain are "multidomestic" industries. Such industries are characterized by lower capital intensity, a low ratio of exports from the home base, less R&D intensity, and overall lower linkages between what happens in one part of the world and another. In other words, the multidomestic MNE is structured as a set of autonomous subsidiaries—or a portfolio of activities—worldwide, with most parts of the value chain being replicated in most of the places that a firm does business. Examples of such industries include consumer packages goods and food processing.

In summary, strategy formulation requires the manager to undertake at least the following four steps of analysis (see Figure 14.2): (1) What is the industry structure, and how do the five forces affect the industry that the firm competes in? (2) What should the firm's competitive positioning in this industry be? Should it be based on cost leadership or differentiation, and if so, should its scope be narrow or broad? (3) How do the various elements of the firm's value chain create buyer value and what costs do they incur in the process? How can the firm manage its value chain so that every part enhances buyer value and lowers the firm's costs? (4) How should the various parts of the value chain be configured and coordinated? Should the firm adopt a global strategy or a multidomestic strategy?

Moving from analysis of stage (1) to stage (4) reflects the recognition that industry structure shapes strategy; however, it is important to recognize that a firm's choice of strategy can also shape industry structure, as effective strategies are imitated or bettered by competitors.

We turn to how answers to these questions are influenced by the effects of multiple sources of external authority (MA) and multiple denominations of value (MV).

Figure 14.2
Steps in MNE Strategy Formulation

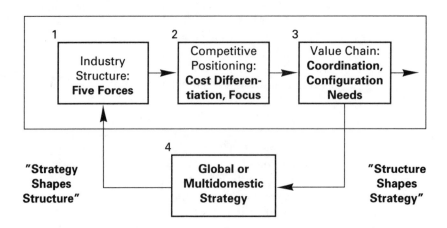

THE EFFECTS OF MA AND MV ON COMPETITIVE STRATEGY FORMULATION

As we discussed in Chapter 1, multiple sources of external authority (MA) and multiple denominations of value (MV) are the two crucial aspects that differentiate international and domestic environments. Since sovereignty is the underlying principle in cross-border relationships and allows states the authority to influence events inside its borders, as we said in Chapter 8, multinational enterprises face a void at the intersection of national borders. Manifestations of this sovereignty include laws, language, cultural norms, and currencies. The uncertainty that a multinational enterprise faces in terms of MA and MV can have an impact on both its competitive positioning—that is, its choice of generic strategies—and its choice to compete as a global or multidomestic firm.

The Effects of MA and MV on Competitive Positioning

Firms seeking competitive advantage through cost leadership strive for efficiency in order to control costs but at the same time must control prices. Firms that seek competitive advantage through differentiation focus on nonprice factors such as quality, technology, brand name, after-sales service, and R&D. The greater the MA as manifested by extreme differences in legal, political, and cultural structures among the countries in which a given firm operates, the greater the risk to firms pursuing a cost-leadership strategy. Why? Since MNEs that rely on cost-based strategies typically venture abroad to capitalize on productive efficiency, their competitive advantage is affected by their ability to adopt both aggressive pricing policies and operations that emphasize ability to achieve economies of scale, scope, and experience. The greater the MA, the greater the vulnerability of a cost-based strategy to the influences of external authority such as changes in tariff or taxation systems in host countries, rules that specify local content in manufacturing, rules that require the firm to undertake investments in the host country in order to compete there, and so forth.

However, firms that rely on differentiation strategies would be less subject to the influences of such external authority. There are two reasons for this: (1) Since such firms often compete on the basis of their ability to tailor their products to local tastes, there is less of a mismatch between the MNE's global product-market needs and the host country's local product-market needs; and (2) Since nonprice factors are relatively more important in value-based competition, external influences that affect prices abroad will matter less in the MNE's ability to sustain its competitive advantage.

This rationale suggests that firms which choose to pursue a cost-leadership strategy have three options. First, they can choose to operate in countries in which MA is low. That is, they can reduce risks to their strategy by operating in countries that have fairly stable governments, laws, norms, and so forth, and in a set of countries that are similar to the home country. Second, such firms can choose to limit their cost leadership to products and services for which the firm's value chain resides primarily in the given country. Some would view this as a "multidomestic" cost-leadership strategy. Because the cost-leadership strategy and the value chain is self-contained within the countries in which the strategy is pursued, it significantly reduces the void at the intersection of sovereign boundaries resulting from MA. Third, firms pursuing a cost-leadership strategy for all products in all countries will find that, as MA increases, they will be pushed in the direction of the adoption of a differentiation strategy.

Multiple denominations of value (MV) affect a firm's cash flows as unanticipated shifts in real exchange rates occur in a given firm's home country relative to host or competitor country currencies. A real appreciation of the home country currency would make products produced in the home country less competitive relative to the rest of the world. In general, changes in currency values matter more when demand is sensitive to price changes. We have already argued that cost-based strategies are more dependent on price competition than are differentiation strategies, which are more dependent on nonprice factors and the MNE's ability to create entry barriers. As a result, unanticipated changes in real currency values matter more in the case of cost-based, rather than differentiation, strategies.

The impact of currency values on the firm's costs is similar. In general, cost-based strategies are likely to produce lower per-unit profit margins, resulting in smaller pricing leeway. Consequently, if there is a real appreciation of the currency in which costs are denominated, there is the risk that profit margins will be reduced even further. And worse, an appreciation could push the firm's costs above the price that the market will bear, resulting in negative profit margins. This risk is lower for differentiation strategies, given the likelihood of higher per-unit profit margins.

Unlike the case of MA, MV presents only two options to firms that choose to pursue a cost-leadership strategy. In the presence of floating exchange rates, even if a firm tries to reduce the risk of MV by operating only in countries with fixed rates of exchange, this would do very little to reduce the risk posed by competitors operating in countries with variable exchange rates and gaining cost advantages through depreciation in cost-denominated currencies. Thus, MNEs pursuing a cost-leadership strategy for all products in all countries cannot insulate themselves from MV risk by choosing to operate only in countries for which MV is low.

Firms pursuing cost leadership can choose to disperse the firm's value chain and duplicate components of the firm's value chain across a wide variety of countries. To the extent that components of the firm's value chain are dispersed and duplicated, it can then simply shift emphasis to the value chain components in the countries that have gained cost advantage through real currency movements. These arguments suggest that, to the extent that a firm pursuing cost leadership as a generic strategy for all its products in all countries does not disperse or duplicate its value chain components, it will find that as MV increases, it will be pushed in the direction of adopting a differentiation strategy.

In summary, while traditional models of strategy formulation might suggest that a firm, based on its industry analysis, should optimally choose a cost-leadership strategy, the impact of the international environment, through MA and MV, could result in the firm having to rethink its generic strategy.

The Effects of MA and MV on Coordination and Configuration of the Value Chain

The Porter framework argues that MNEs that require concentrated configuration and high coordination among the various elements of the value chain are optimally structured as global firms, while those with dispersed configuration and low coordination among the various elements of the value are optimally structured in a multidomestic fashion. However, MA and MV can alter this prescription.

With respect to MA, the more important the lack of a superstructure to mediate differences between sovereign boundaries (arising from political risk, country risk, cultural and legal risks, and the like), the greater the potential risk to the MNE of dispersing its activities across sovereign boundaries. Furthermore, the greater the risk of a particular location, the greater the potential risk to the MNE if it locates activities there that it performs nowhere else. For example, if the MNE's single manufacturing operation produced all of the product for the MNE's worldwide operations, the potential risk from MA to the MNE would be much higher compared to a situation in which such a site was duplicated elsewhere. In other words, the risk of MA pushes a multidomestic firm toward a more concentrated configuration of its value chain. Put simply, higher MA favors a global strategy, even if industry economics might argue otherwise.

With respect to MV, as we saw in Chapter 5, the greater the economic exposure to exchange rates, the greater the potential threats of having the firm's value chain configured in any one country. Dispersing the value chain serves to diversify the firm's risks arising from unfavorable real exchange rate movements relative to otherwise concentrated value activities. Consequently, greater MV is associated with a more dispersed configuration of the MNE's value chain. Put simply, higher MV favors a multidomestic strategy, even if industry economics might argue otherwise.

In summary, the impact of MA and MV may require the MNE to rethink, and perhaps backtrack on, strategy prescriptions that result solely from consideration of its industry economics. With respect to a firm's competitive position, cost-leadership strategies can run into difficulties in a situation in which MA and MV are high, and they may push the firm toward adopting a more differentiated strategy. With respect to the optimal configuration of the firm's value chain, MA and MV work in opposite directions: High MA pushes a firm toward a global strategy, while high MV pushes a firm toward a multidomestic strategy, all else equal. This requires us to modify the generalized approach to strategy formulation that we discussed earlier, and this is summarized in Figure 14.3.

CONCLUSION

Multiple sources of external authority and multiple denominations of value are two factors that differentiate the impact of the international environment on MNE strategy. While the pursuit of either generic cost leadership or differentiation strategies is possible, MA and MV have important implications for the configuration of the firm's value chain and its ability to sustain above-average profits by pursuing one or the other. MA and MV make it imperative for the MNE to simultaneously pursue different strategies in different locations for the products within its portfolio. It is also possible that an MNE could pursue different strategies for the same product in different countries. Substantially different industry and competitor configurations might provide a firm with a significant cost advantage in one country, and a differentiation advantage in another country. The optimal configuration of its value chain—the choice to be global or multidomestic—is similarly affected.

In conclusion, it is important to emphasize that, in addition to many of the factors that domestic firms must analyze, such as competitor position or internal capabilities, MNEs must consider the impact of MA and MV on strategy decisions and the configuration of their value chain.

Figure 14.3
How MA and MV Affect MNE Strategy Formulation

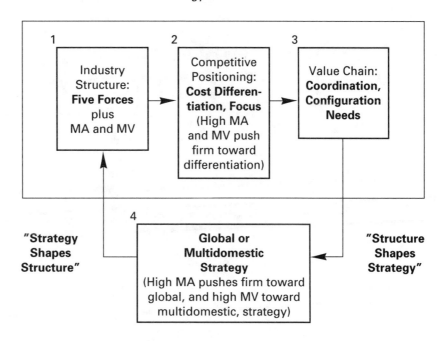

SELECTED REFERENCES

ADLER, NANCY. *International Dimensions of Organizational Behavior.* Boston, MA: PWS-Kent, 1992.

MINTZBERG, HENRY. "The Strategy Concept: Five Ps for Strategy." *California Management Review* (Fall 1987).

PORTER, MICHAEL E. *Competitive Advantage.* New York: Free Press, 1985.

PORTER, MICHAEL E., ed. *Competition in Global Industries.* Cambridge, MA: Harvard Business School Press, 1986.

PORTER, MICHAEL E. *The Competitive Advantage of Nations.* New York: Free Press, 1991.

SUNDARAM, A. K. & J. S. BLACK. "The Environment and Internal Organization of Multinational Enterprises." *Academy of Management Review* (October 1992).

case 18

The Honda-Yamaha War (A)*

Yamaha has not only stepped on the tail of a tiger, it has ground it into the earth. Yamaha wo tsubusu! [Crush, break, smash, squash, butcher, slaughter, destroy Yamaha!]

—Battle cry issued by Honda's President Kawashima, January 1982.[1]

What had Yamaha done that caused such a violent reaction from Honda's President Kawashima? The explanation begins in the early 1950s when there were 50 competitors fighting for position in the Japanese motorcycle market. Demand was growing steadily at over 40% per year. Honda was the number two competitor with a market share of 20%. Its arch enemy was Tohatsu, the number one motorcycle manufacturer with a 22 percent market share. By most measures, Tohatsu, like the Shoguns whose military might allowed them to rule supreme, dominated the Japanese motorcycle landscape. Tohatsu's after-tax profits were 8% of sales compared with Honda's 3.4%. It's debt-to-equity ratio was 1.5 to 1, while Honda's was 6 to 1. In 1955, the widely held view of the competitors in Japan's financial community was:

Tohatsu: With Honda, one of the two largest motorcycle manufacturers. However, it is considerably more profitable and its financial condition is superior.

Honda: High growth contributed to Honda's market share, but overexpansion deteriorated its financial condition because of excess borrowings.[2]

---

*This case was prepared by Research Assistant, Sonali Krishna, under the direction of Associate Professor J. Stewart Black, as the basis for class discussion.

[1]Richard Winger, "Fast Means Tough in the 90s," *The Executive Speaker,* vol. 11, no. 3 (March 1990): 1.

[2]Kaisha-Yoran (Company Handbook) (Tokyo: Diamond, March 1956), 212-13.

However, in the space of five short years, Honda emerged as the undisputed leader of the Japanese motorcycle industry. Tohatsu took a more conservative approach to the competitive battles in Japan and grew at a slow and controlled rate. From 1955 to 1960, it did not significantly increase production capacity. Honda, on the other hand, fought aggressively and grew at 66% per year in a market growing at 42% per year. In doing so, Honda established a "winner's competitive cycle." High growth led to greater sales revenues and decreased costs through economies of scale. With increased revenues and decreased costs came increased profitability and financial strength. More cash was available internally and from external sources to fund growth. This cash was reinvested in the business in ways that yielded further increases in market share and a replay of the "winner's competitive cycle."

To wage this aggressive battle Honda borrowed heavily. Although these borrowings carried high interest rate penalties, they were critical to Honda's expansion and growth. As complacent competitors such as Tohatsu lost ground, Honda's profits increased and it became even more aggressive. Tohatsu's market share dropped to less than 4% while Honda's soared to 44%. In 1960, Honda reported an after-tax profit of 10.3% of sales while Tohatsu registered losses of almost 8% of sales. Honda's balance sheet had strengthened and the company had a debt-to-equity ratio of 1 to 1. Tohatsu's balance sheet deteriorated with a debt-to-equity ratio of 7 to 1 as it borrowed to offset losses. With market growth slowing to 9% per year, this new competitive positioning appeared to be permanent.

The financial community in Japan, somewhat belatedly, reassessed its opinion of the two companies:

> Honda: It has the largest production capacity for motorcycles in the world, and is still aggressively expanding production at its Suzuki plant. Rapid growth is expected in both domestic and overseas markets.
>
> Tohatsu: Business has been deteriorating because of intense competition. The company is currently being restructured with the support of Fuji Electric.[3]

Finally, in February 1964, Honda's enemy was destroyed. Tohatsu filed for bankruptcy. Its sales had decreased sharply, its funds were exhausted, and its bills were unpaid. Tohatsu had fallen from number one position to bankruptcy in less than 10 years. And it was not the only casualty; other motorcycle manufacturers also went bankrupt or exited the industry. The original 50 manufacturers had shrunk to 30 by 1960, 8 by 1965, and by 1965 to four—Honda, Yamaha, Suzuki, and Kawasaki.

Honda's battle for market share is a classic example of aggressive *kaisha* or Japanese corporate tactics. Like Shogun generals of the past, *kaisha* executives battle ferociously for territory and the right to proclaim themselves *ichiban* or number one in the country. The winners seemed to be those *kaisha* that, like Honda, get the winner's cycle going for themselves by boosting their share of the market faster than their rivals. To lose in this battle often meant corporate death, and this was the fate Tohatsu suffered. Hence, in this commercial equivalent of jungle warfare, *kaisha* executives sharpen their strategic thinking and competitive skills.

Over the next ten years, as a sharply growing number of Japanese became more interested in purchasing luxury goods over durable goods, growth in the Japanese motorcycle industry slowed. Honoring the rule of the *kaisha* to never rest on your laurels, Honda diversified into automobiles. To reduce the risk of failure, the company deployed its strongest forces in the automobile venture. This meant that all available cash and technical capabilities, along with the best troops, had to be directed toward the automobile business. Honda's high level of investment in the auto industry had to be supported by the resources and cash

[3]*Kaisha-Yoran* (Company Handbook), 233-34.

generated from its motorcycle business. At the end of the 60s, Honda's share of the Japanese motorcycle market had reached 65%. Despite efforts by the powerful Ministry of International Trade and Industry to persuade Honda to get out of the automobile business or merge with one of the much larger car makers such as Toyota or Nissan, the company ignored this "administrative guidance" and, by 1975, was obtaining more revenues from autos than from motorcycles. Profits continued to soar and its balance sheet steadily strengthened throughout the 1970s.

As Honda began focusing on the automobile front, Yamaha saw an opportunity to attack and take territory in the motorcycle market. However, rather than begin with an all-out direct assault on Honda's motorcycle troops, Yamaha borrowed a chapter from the ancient *Ninja* warriors and decided to launch a sneak attack. It began by quietly increasing its motorcycle production capacity in Japan. Yamaha took advantage of the fact that its enemy's attention was focused on its automobile business, and began gnawing away at Honda's market share. Honda's production share declined from its peak of 65% to 40% by 1981. In contrast, Yamaha increased its share from less than 10 percent in the mid-1960s to about 35 percent by 1981. Basically, the territory that Honda lost went directly into Yamaha's hands.

By the end of 1981, Yamaha and Honda had nearly equal shares of the Japanese motorcycle landscape. Honda's domestic market share in motorcycles had declined to 38% while Yamaha's had risen to 37%. Yamaha was within reach of toppling Honda as Japan's market leader and proclaiming itself *ichiban,* the world's number-one motorcycle producer. The sentiments of Yamaha's top general are reflected in the following quotes:

> At Honda, sales attention is focused on four-wheel vehicles. Most of their best people in motorcycles have been transferred [into cars]. Compared to them, our specialty at Yamaha is mainly motorcycle production.
>
> —Yamaha's President Koike, 1979.

> If only we had enough capacity, we could beat Honda.
>
> —Yamaha's President Koike, 1981.[4]

During this period, Yamaha's profitability compared favorably with Honda's. Both companies had operating profits of about 7% to 10% of sales in the late 1960s and about 3% of sales in the early 1980s. Honda's profitability was depressed in part by its heavy investments in R&D for its young auto business. Its R&D expenditures increased steadily from approximately 2% of sales in 1970 to 5% in 1983. Yamaha spent slightly more than 1% of sales on R&D throughout the entire period.

Yamaha was able to push into Honda's territory and capture market share by focusing all of its resources on motorcycles and related products. The first phase of Yamaha's battle plan, the *Ninja*-like sneak attack of quietly increasing capacity and being able to supply dealers with more product quicker than Honda, had been successful. The second phase of Yamaha's strategy involved a more direct, frontal attack. In the early 1970s, Yamaha had about 18 different products in its product line compared to Honda's 35. By 1981, Yamaha offered 60 models compared to Honda's 63. Although, in the early 1970s, Honda had introduced two new models on the market for every one introduced by Yamaha, in 1981, Yamaha introduced 18 models to Honda's 17.

Indifferent to this direct attack by Yamaha on the motorcycle front, Honda continued to exhibit a preoccupation with autos as it began investing in large-scale automobile production in the United States. By 1979, Honda had more than $1 billion invested in automobile and motorcycle production facilities in Marysville, OH. Most of its production was devoted to building the Honda Accord but some capacity was also directed toward manufacturing large "cc" motorcycles.

---

[4]*Nihon Keizai Shimbun,* July 28, 1979, pp. 7.

Despite Yamaha's massing of troops on the motorcycle front, Honda did not seem to be significantly redeploying its troops in order to protect this weakened flank. Yamaha interpreted this as an unexpected chance to strike and gain even more ground on Honda. As a result, in 1981, totally disregarding the arrival of a "low pressure economy," Yamaha embarked on a breakneck production spree.

In August 1981, Yamaha announced plans to construct a new motorcycle factory with an annual capacity of one million units. This factory would increase its total capacity to four million units, exceeding Honda's capacity by 200,000 units. If the new factory's total production were sold in Japan, Yamaha's domestic market share would approach 60%. The opening of the new factory would shift the balance of power and make Yamaha the world's largest motorcycle manufacturer, the prestigious position that Honda had won from Tohatsu and held for almost 20 years.

> The difference between us and Honda is in our ability to supply. As primarily a motorcycle producer, you cannot expect us to remain in our present number two position forever.
>
> —Yamaha's President Koike announcing new factory plans, August 1981.

> In one year we will be the domestic leader, And in two years, we will be number one in the world.
>
> —Yamaha's President Koike at a shareholders' meeting, January 1982.[5]

With these words, President Hisao Koike laid down the challenge and publicly launched Yamaha on a heady campaign to surpass Honda. Koike anticipated a quick, decisive victory. Yamaha had enjoyed the spoils of hard fought battles and had seen its sales increase 20% in 1982 to ¥516 billion. Its pretax profits also hit a record high of nearly ¥ 15 billion.

Yamaha's management was betting its company could achieve leading market share in motorcycles. Since Yamaha had no other business with significant growth potential it was prepared to invest heavily in motorcycles. But Yamaha invested at a rate far higher than its internal cash generation could support. As the company turned to banks to make up the difference, its debt burden increased steadily. Although it was as profitable as Honda, Yamaha and its affiliated companies had a debt-to-equity ratio of almost 3 to 1, while the Honda group's ratio was less than 1 to 1.

Although Yamaha thought its overt and public challenge had gone unnoticed by Honda, they were mistaken. As early as 1978, President Kawashima of Honda said, "As long as I am president of this company we will surrender our number one spot [in motorcycles] to no one." In 1979, he admitted, "From the late 1960s until recently we have concentrated our efforts on product development of four-wheel vehicles. The fact that another [motorcycle] maker could pull so close to us was an unavoidable situation."

But when the words of Koike's statements at the Yamaha shareholders' meeting reached the ears of Honda's president, he was incensed.

> Yamaha has not only stepped on the tail of a tiger, it has ground it into the earth.
> Yamaha *wo tsubusu*! [Crush, break, smash, squash, butcher, slaughter, destroy Yamaha!]
>
> —Battle cry issued by Honda's President Kawashima, January 1982.[6]

And so Honda rapidly redeployed its forces. Over the next eighteen months, as the Honda-Yamaha War raged on, Honda's production share increased from 40 percent to 47 percent while Yamaha's decreased from 35 percent to 27 percent. Honda gained more

---

[5]*Shukan Toyo Keizai,* July 28, 1979, pp. 7.

[6]Richard Winger, "Fast Means Tough in the 90s," *The Executive Speaker,* vol. 11, no. 3 (March 1990): 1.

ground and increased its domestic market share from 38% to 43% while Yamaha's share collapsed from 37 percent to 23%. Honda's simple and innovative counterattack was funded by the company's auto division which brought in two-thirds of the company's sales (Honda's total revenues exceeded ¥2 trillion), and continued to prosper during the motorcycle war. The strategy included massive price cuts and increases in promotional funds and field inventories. At the time of the heaviest competition between Honda and Yamaha, retail prices for popular models had fallen by more than a third. In the summer of 1982, it was possible to buy a 50 cc motorcycle for less than the cost of a 10-speed bicycle. About 75% of all Yamaha models were smaller than 700 cc and sold domestically while its larger bikes were exported to overseas markets. In spite of this heavy discounting, Honda was able to provide products to its dealers at costs that enabled the dealers to earn profits that were 10% higher than the profits they could earn by selling Yamaha motorcycles.

The innovative element of Honda's counterattack was the use of product variety as a competitive weapon. Honda devoted considerable resources toward new model design and production.

Changes in Product Line

	New Models		Discontinued Models
	1981	1982-83	1982-83
Yamaha	18	34	3
Honda	17	81	32

Source: James C. Abegglen and George Stalk, Jr., "The Japanese Corporation as Competitor," *California Management Review,* vol. 28, no. 3 (Spring 1986): 14.

The effects of Honda's two-pronged attack of new model proliferation and price cutting were devastating for Yamaha. New model introductions offered greater technical and design appeal to customers, thereby increasing demand, and dealers had incentives for pushing them. But increased volumes of new models came at the expense of older ones; therefore the life cycles for existing models were shortened and demand for them declined sharply.

Yamaha's sales of motorcycles plummeted by more than 50 percent, and the company incurred heavy losses. By early 1983, Yamaha's unsold stock of motorcycles in Japan were estimated to be about half of the industry total of unsold stock. At the then-current Yamaha sales rate, its inventories were equivalent to about one year's sales. The only way to move stocks was to forward promotional funds to dealers and allow cuts in prices. But Yamaha could not afford to do this and even considered a scrapping program for unsold motorcycles. Yamaha's debt-to-equity ratio increased from less than 3 to 1 in 1981 to 7 to 1 in 1983. In contrast, buoyed on by its continuous success in automobiles, Honda's balance sheet gained further strength.

The Battle for Marketshare

Production in Million Units (Domestic Market Share in %)

	1980	1981	1982	1983
Yamaha	2.24 *(35)*	2.79 *(36)*	2.66 *(33)*	0.82 *(29)*
Honda	3.09 *(43)*	3.59 *(39)*	3.64 *(46)*	2.61 *(49)*

Source: *Financial Times,* November 16, 1983.

The Honda-Yamaha rivalry pushed 1982 worldwide inventories of Japanese motorcycle makers to more than 2.5 million bikes, and alarmed the US manufacturer Harley-Davidson. Harley worried that this excess inventory would be dumped in the US market, which historically, had taken in about 20% of Japan's output. In April 1983, Harley-Davidson persuaded the US International Trade Commission (ITC) to give it import protection.

> Frankly, we were scared that nationwide fire sales would spell the death knell for Harley.
>
> —Harley-Davidson spokesperson, July 1983.[7]

President Reagan approved a recommendation by the ITC, raising the initial import tariff on heavyweight motorcycles (with engine displacements over 700 cc.) from 4.4% to 49.4%. The ITC's recommendation was based on its finding that imports of heavyweight motorcycles posed a "threat of serious injury to the domestic industry."[8] The ITC defined domestic industry to include any producer assembling motorcycles in the US. This ruling was another lost battle in a war that Yamaha feared might spell its end.

In January 1984, Yamaha's parent company Nippon Gakki, which had a 39.1% stake in Yamaha, called for an emergency board meeting. The company could no longer hold the fort. A new strategy had to be developed urgently. The board members pondered over their options:

1. Make further drastic production cuts.
2. Publicly apologize to Honda and call for a truce and "cease fire."
3. Expand into new overseas markets and set up offshore production facilities.
4. Dump excess output into established overseas markets such as the US.

Drastic action was needed in part because losses at Yamaha for 1984 were estimated to be ¥ 19 billion.

BIBLIOGRAPHY

Abegglen, James C. and George stalk, Jr. "The Japanese Corporation as Competitor." *California Management Review,* vol. 28, no. 3 (Spring 1986) 9-27.

"Altitude Sickness on Wall Street." *The Financial Times,* October 13, 1983, 20.

"A Burned Out Yamaha Pulls in for an Overhaul." *Business Week,* July 11, 1983, 41.

Chakravarty, Subrata N. "Economic Darwinism." *Forbes,* October 6, 1986, 52-56.

Flanagan, William G. "Zen and the Art of Cyclemakers." *Forbes,* April 9, 1984, 158-160.

Grant, Alison. "Budding Technology Speeds Products to Market." *United Press International,* June 4, 1990.

Nihon Keizai Shimbun, April 2, 1985, 21.

Stalk, George Jr. "Time—The Next Source of Competitive Advantage." *Harvard Business Review* (July-August, 1988).

"To Survive Low Pressure Consumer Economy; Producers Need to Exactly Size up Changing, Diversified Demand Trends." *Nihon Keizai Shimbun,* August 9, 1983.

"Yamaha Retrenches After Its Costly Battle Against Honda, the Top Motorcycle Maker." *Wall Street Journal,* July 7, 1983.

[7]Bob Woods, "Wheeling & Reeling," *S&MM,* May 16, 1983, pp. 43-50.

[8]*Heavyweight Motorcycles and Engines and Powertrain Assemblies Thereof,* Report to the President on Investigation N. TA-201-47, USITC Publication 1342, February 1983, pp. 1.

chapter 15

Designing Organizations for International Environments

The fundamental purpose of organizational design and structure is to facilitate organizational survival and prosperity. To survive and prosper, MNEs need to (1) acquire necessary resources, (2) transform products and services efficiently, (3) produce valued outputs, (4) effectively coordinate activities, (5) adapt to changing conditions, and (6) satisfy multiple constituencies, including employees, investors, customers, and government and regulatory agencies.[1]

Organizational design for international environments facilitates the accomplishment of these six requirements through two basic processes. The first process—referred to as differentiation—divides various tasks into subtasks, which then are performed by individuals with specialized skills. The second process—referred to as integration—integrates these subtasks around the completion of organizational goals. In addition to differentiation and integration, we will see that other aspects, namely the extent of formalization and centralization, play important roles in organizational design.

Although the fundamentals of dividing things up and then putting them back together again may sound simple, the specifics of how this is done effectively, given the international environments faced by MNEs, are complex. This chapter begins by outlining the key principles of organizational design, examines common MNE organizational structures, and concludes with a discussion of the contingencies that govern effective organizational design for international environments.

BASIC PRINCIPLES

Traditionally, the processes of dividing and then putting things back together has been referred to as differentiation and integration.[2] Differentiation refers to the difference in tasks as well as the cognitive orientation of managers in different areas of an organization.

[1]R. Steers and J.S. Black, *Introduction to Organizational Behavior* (New York: HarperCollins, 1993).
[2]P. Lawrence and J. Lorsch, *Organization and Environment* (Boston: Harvard University Press, 1967), 16.

Task differentiation refers to the differences in what tasks are done and how they are completed. Cognitive differentiation refers to what and how the doers of the tasks think. For example, accountants and marketers typically undertake different tasks, but they might also think about things differently. Accountants might think about the internal organization through financial ratios, while marketers might focus on the external environment and customers through qualitative surveys of customer satisfaction. In contrast to differentiation, integration refers to the extent of collaboration and coordination that exists within an organization. Prior to discussing alternative organizational structures and the factors that determine appropriate MNE design, it is important to understand clearly several key aspects of organizational design, including differentiation vs. integration, formal vs. informal structures, and centralized vs. decentralized configurations.

Differentiation vs. Integration

The smallest unit of analysis in an organization is the individual. Consequently, the origin of differentiation lies in the decision of how specialized the task is that individuals perform. In most organizations there are financial, accounting, marketing, sales, production and other tasks. The greater the specialization of these tasks and the greater the differences in the cognitive orientations of people performing these tasks, the greater the degree of *horizontal differentiation*. Although separate departments such as marketing and accounting usually correspond to greater horizontal differentiation, it is not only the differences in the tasks that accountants and marketers perform that contribute to differentiation, but also the differences in their thinking. Insights into the extent of cognitive differentiation can be obtained by answering two basic questions: What responsibilities do individuals think about and how do they think about them?

Task specialization can also be accomplished through *vertical differentiation*. Vertical differentiation is characterized by differences in organizational levels or hierarchy. Just as with horizontal differentiation, overall vertical differentiation is a function of not only the differences in tasks, but also how people think about them at varying positions in the organization's hierarchy. Organizations with high vertical differentiation are likely to be characterized by first-line supervisors and top executives who not only perform different tasks but also think differently about their business and its environment. In contrast, less vertically differentiated firms are likely to be characterized by first-line supervisors and top executives who perform some similar tasks (for example, talking to customers) and think similarly about their business and its environment.

The factors that contribute to both horizontal and vertical differentiation will become clearer later, as we discuss common types of organizational structure and the contingencies that affect effective organizational design. For now it is sufficient to recognize that both the behavioral (that is, task specialization) and the cognitive (that is, differences in thinking) components of horizontal and vertical differentiation play a role in organization design.

The largest unit of analysis, and the origin of integration, is the entire organization. One of the key driving forces of integration is *interdependence*. There are three types of interdependence. *Pooled interdependence* occurs when various groups are largely independent in their functions but collectively contribute to a common output, such as when Product Division A and Product Division B both send products to the shipping department to be sent to a single customer. *Sequential interdependence* exists when the outputs of one group become the inputs of another group, such as when the raw materials provided by the purchasing department become the inputs of the manufacturing department, whose outputs become the inputs (that is, products) sold by the sales department. *Reciprocal interdependence* occurs when two or more groups depend on one another for inputs, such as when new product development relies on marketing research for ideas to investigate and marketing research relies on new product development for new products to test on customers. In principle, the greater the interdependence, the greater the need for integration.

The other factor that can influence the need for integration is uncertainty. Uncertainty for a firm refers to the extent to which future input, throughput, and output factors can be forecasted accurately. For example, to what extent can the firm accurately anticipate the needed quantity and price of material or labor inputs? To what extent can the impact of specific throughput activities and tasks be anticipated? To what extent can output factors such as market demand be predicted accurately? The greater the difficulty in accurately forecasting these types of factors, the greater the uncertainty the firm faces, and the more integration that is required.

Integration, however, can be achieved through a variety of mechanisms.[3] The appropriateness of the mechanism is a function of the level and type of interdependence and the extent of uncertainty.

Rules.   The more task interdependence is pooled or sequential in nature and the lower the uncertainty (for example, tasks are predictable and routine), the more rules can be used as an effective coordination mechanism. Precisely because routine tasks and their outcomes are predictable, rules of behavior and procedure can be set in advance with predictable outcomes.

Goals.   As task uncertainty and interdependence increase, the probability that preset rules can effectively coordinate tasks declines. Consequently, goals become a more effective coordination mechanism. Instead of specifying what individuals should do, goals specify what outcomes individuals should achieve. Effective goals tend to be specific (that is, define quantitative outcomes) and difficult (that is, require high levels of effort to achieve). Specifying the outcomes, but not the process, maximizes individual flexibility in how things get done, and yet facilitates integration by ensuring what the output is that individuals are working toward.

Values.   In cases of high task uncertainty and interdependence, values become an important coordinating mechanism. Values specify underlying objectives, such as customer satisfaction, but unlike goals do not specify quantitative outcomes. Shared values can facilitate coordination under conditions of high task uncertainty more effectively than rules and goals, which because of changing conditions would inconsistently facilitate the accomplishment of organizational objectives.

Formal vs. Informal Structures

During the process of differentiation and integration, MNEs can vary substantially in the utilization of formal or defined structures and systems in decision making, communication, and control. Formal systems specify clear lines of authority within an organization. MNEs with strong formalization rely on the chain of command for decision making, communication, or control.

Informal structures of decision making, communication, and control are often not represented in objective descriptions of the organization such as organizational charts and yet pervade the day-today functioning of many organizations. One study that compared US and Japanese MNEs found that Japanese relied much more on informalization.[4] Much of the decision making, communication, and control was accomplished through informal, face-to-face meetings. In Japan, this process is referred to as *nemawashi*. This is a gardening term that is used to describe a process of transplanting a tree or shrub by incrementally cutting the plant's roots over time so that by the time the final root is cut, there is no shock

---

[3]R. Cyert and J. March, *The Behavioral Theory of the Firm* (Englewood Cliffs, NJ: Prentice-Hall, 1963). J.R. Galbraith, "Organization Design: An Information Processing View," *Interfaces* 4(3) 1974: 28-36.

[4]Y. Rhy-song, and T. Sagafi-nejad, "Organizational Characteristics of American and Japanese Firms in Taiwan," *National Academy of Management Proceedings,* 1987: 111-115.

to the plant's system. In Japanese organizations, *nemawashi* takes the form of informal conversations in which incremental decisions and attempts at influence are undertaken such that by the time a meeting is held to make the formal decision, the decision is in fact already made.

Centralized vs. Decentralized Structures

Centralization and decentralization refer to the extent to which decisions are made at the top of the organization or pushed down into lower levels. For instance, European MNEs tend to be decentralized and allow units in different countries to make decisions in accordance with the local conditions. Often this enables them to better adapt to host government demands or shifting consumer preferences.[5]

Japanese MNEs, on the other hand, exhibit a stronger degree of centralization and tend to delegate decisions far less than either European or American MNEs.[6] Most Japanese MNEs operate like centralized hubs into which information flows, and from which decisions are announced. In fact, recent complaints by host nationals in local subsidiaries about the "bamboo ceiling"—or the exclusion of host nationals from the strategic decision-making process by Japanese expatriates and headquarters executives—may stem from the centralized orientation of many Japanese MNEs.[7]

ORGANIZATIONAL STRUCTURES

As firms expand across borders, they adopt a variety of organizational structures in order to meet the demands of the international business environment. Although a variety of specific MNE structures exist, seven structures represent the most common forms. These will be described in their general format, though it will be obvious as we progress that it is possible to combine some of these general structures. A graphical illustration and a summary of the key strengths and weaknesses of each type of structure are provided in Figure 15-1.

International Division Structure

Often upon their initial entry into the international environment, firms have few products for international markets or little understanding of foreign customers and governments. Consequently, it is common for MNEs at this point to establish an international division, which is responsible for all functional activities relative to international markets. A variety of functions such as accounting, finance, marketing, and sales are generally conducted within the international division. Typically, production activities are not part of the international division. Products are produced within the normal "domestic" organizational structure and then modified or simply turned over "as is" to the international division.

Strengths.   The international division structure has a number of advantages. First, it is an efficient means of dealing with the international market when an MNE has limited experience with the international environment. The focus on international activities and issues within the division can foster a strong professional identity and career path among its members. It also allows for specialization and training in international activities. The focus on international markets, competitors, and environments can also facilitate the development of a more focused international strategy. Further, because the top officer of the

---

[5]C. A. Bartlett and S. Ghoshal, "Organizing for Worldwide Effectiveness: The Transnational Solution," *California Management Review* (Fall 1988): 54-74.

[6]J. R. Lincoln, M. Hanada, and K. McBride, "Organizational Structures in Japanese and U.S. Manufacturing," *Administrative Science Quarterly* 31 (1986): 338-364.

[7]J. Schachter, "When Hope Turns to Frustration: The Americanization of Mitsubishi Has Had Little Success," *Los Angeles Times,* July 10, 1988, 1.

international division often reports to the CEO (or similar senior executive), international issues can receive high-level corporate consideration and support.

Weaknesses.   One of the major weaknesses is the international division's dependence upon other divisions for products and support. Because international sales of a particular product are often only a small percentage of the product's overall sales, low priority may be given to international sales. Also, other parts of the firm that supply products and services to the international division may be unwilling to make modifications that would facilitate greater international sales.

Figure 15.1
Alternative MNE Organizational Structures

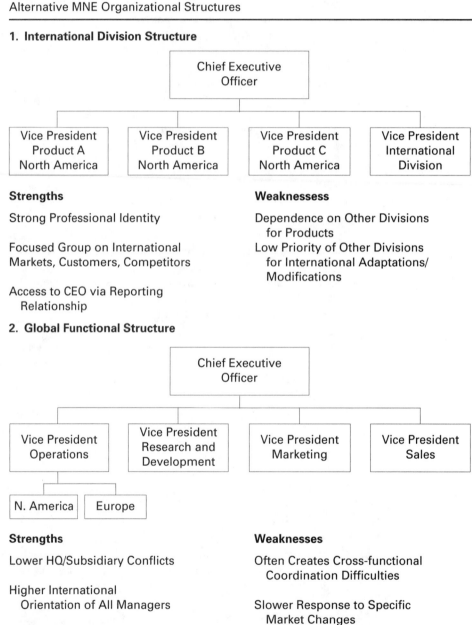

1. International Division Structure

Chief Executive Officer

| Vice President Product A North America | Vice President Product B North America | Vice President Product C North America | Vice President International Division |

Strengths

Strong Professional Identity

Focused Group on International Markets, Customers, Competitors

Access to CEO via Reporting Relationship

Weaknessess

Dependence on Other Divisions for Products

Low Priority of Other Divisions for International Adaptations/ Modifications

2. Global Functional Structure

Chief Executive Officer

| Vice President Operations | Vice President Research and Development | Vice President Marketing | Vice President Sales |

N. America   Europe

Strengths

Lower HQ/Subsidiary Conflicts

Higher International Orientation of All Managers

Facilitates Global Coordination within Function

Effective when International Market Demand Is Similar

Weaknesses

Often Creates Cross-functional Coordination Difficulties

Slower Response to Specific Market Changes

Ineffective when International Market Demands Differ

3. Global Area Structure

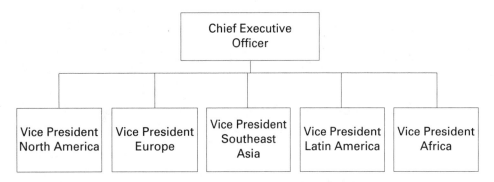

Strengths

Facilitates Local
    Responsiveness

Develops In-depth Knowledge
    of Specific
    Regions/Countries

Accountability by Region

Facilitates Cross-functional
    Coordination within Regions

Weaknesses

Often Creates Cross-regional
    Coordination Difficulties

Can Inhibit Ability to
    Capture Global Scale
    Economies

Duplication of Resources and
    Functions Across Regions

4. Global Product Structure

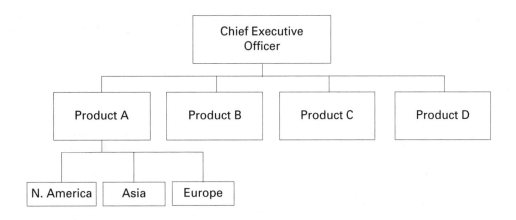

Strengths

Facilitates Cross-functional
    Coordination for a Given
    Product

Facilitates Ability to
    Capture Global Scale
    Economies by Product

Weaknesses

Duplication of Resources
    by Product Division

Can Inhibit Cross-product
    Coordination

5. Global Division Structure

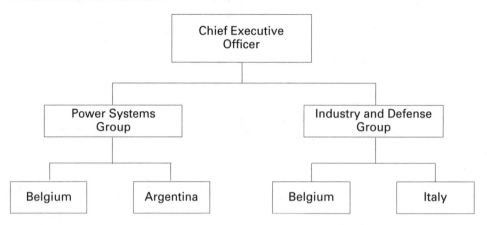

Strengths

Reduces Resource Duplication

Facilitates Cross-product
   Coordination

Facilitates Cross-regional
   Coordination

Weaknesses

Can Inhibit Cross-divisional
   Coordination

Can Obscure Global Scale
   Economies

6. Global Customer Structure

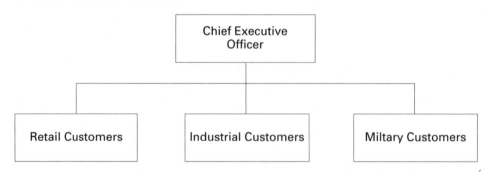

Strengths

Facilitates Coordination
   across Functions and Regions
   by Customer

Effective if Customer
   Classifications Are
   Significantly Different

Weaknesses

Less Effective if
   Differentiation between
   Customers Diminishes

Less Effective if Differences
   Exist within a Customer
   Category across Countries

7. Global Matrix Structure

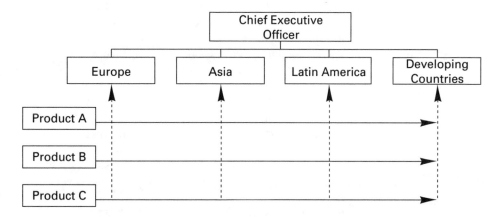

Strengths	Weaknesses
Increased Information Flow throughout Organization	Increased Conflict Potential
Balanced Orientation	Ambiguity of Authority

Global Functional Structure

The global functional structure organizes the MNE around traditional functional departments such as accounting, finance, marketing, operations, and so forth, but each functional area has worldwide responsibilities. This structure is most common when the technology and products that the MNE produces are similar throughout the world.

Strengths. The major advantages are that this structure reduces potential headquarters-subsidiary conflicts because operations throughout the world are integrated into their respective functional areas, and functional area executives are charged with global responsibility. This, in turn, enhances the overall international orientation of managers. The global functional structure can also facilitate centralized global coordination and control since all function heads are charged with worldwide responsibility.

Weaknesses. The weaknesses of this structure are most prevalent when the firm has a wide variety of products and these products have different environmental demands (for example, government restrictions or standards, customer preferences, performance qualities). This weakness is exacerbated when different functional areas experience different demands by geographical area. For example, if the accounting practices are similar between the US and Japan but the advertising approaches differ, this will tend to exaggerate coordination difficulties arising from different environment demands via governments, customers, and so on.

Geographic Area Structure

MNEs can structure themselves around various geographical areas or regions in the world. Within this structure, area or regional executives are generally responsible for all functional activities in their regions.

Strengths.   One of the strengths of this structure is that it facilitates the development of an in-depth understanding of the market, customers, governments, and competitors within a given geographical area. The fact that area managers are responsible for all activities within their region also fosters a strong sense of accountability for performance, and regions are often treated as profit centers. Placing all functions under a regional umbrella also facilitates the coordination of functional activities under the region.

Weaknesses.   One of the major weaknesses of this structure is that it can inhibit coordination and communication between regions. Additionally, placing separate production activities in each region has the potential for causing MNEs to miss economies of scale in manufacturing products common to different regions. Placing all functional areas within each region can also lead to duplication of resources such as accounting, finance, human resource management, and so on. Finally, regional structures can foster competitive behavior among the regions, leading to suboptimization of outcomes relative to common customers across regions.

Global Product Structure

In a global product structure, the MNE is organized around specific products with global scope. Each global product division is generally treated as a profit center. Typically, each product division contains all the traditional functional departments such as accounting, finance, marketing, operations, human resource management, and so on.

Strengths.   Because all functions are placed within the product division, this focuses all departments on the common product and thereby facilitates coordination among departments. Focus on the product also enhances knowledge about the product and how the product needs to be adapted in order to maximize its potential in different markets. This, in turn, facilitates the identification of elements of the product that are global in nature and those elements that are local. Further, a global product structure can facilitate capturing economies of scale and making optimal location decisions to leverage a country's comparative advantage in such things as labor cost or raw materials.

Weaknesses.   The major disadvantage of the global product structure is that resources are duplicated. For example, both Global Product A and Global Product B have accounting, finance, operations, marketing, human resource, and sales personnel. Also, structuring by product can inhibit coordination across product divisions, which, in turn, can create problems when a single customer purchases products from two or more global product divisions.

Global Divisional Structure

The global divisional structure places all functional activities within each division and charges each division with worldwide responsibility. In a sense, the global divisional structure is an extension of the global product structure. Typically, a division is formed by grouping several, related products together. As a consequence, it has many of the same advantages and disadvantages as global product structures. However, there are a few differences.

Strengths.   One of the strengths of a global divisional structure over a global product structure is that the duplication of resources can be reduced by having common functions for all products within the division. Also, for customers who tend to make purchases within a related set of products, coordination across products is easier and can facilitate customer service and satisfaction.

Weaknesses. Whereas the product focus in the global product structure can facilitate the determination of global and local elements of a product, the more diversified focus created by a global divisional structure can inhibit this determination. This can increase costs by obscuring opportunities to leverage global advantages in raw materials sourcing, production, marketing, or advertising.

Global Customer Structure

As the name implies, global customer structures are organized around categories of customers. Typically, this structure is utilized when different categories of customers have separate but broad needs. For example, industrial customers might purchase a different set of products from retail customers.

Strengths. The primary strength of this organizational form is that it facilitates in-depth understanding of specific customer segments. Even if general categories of customers differ by market location, the focus on the customer segments can facilitate adaptations in design, manufacturing, advertising, and so forth.

Weaknesses. The primary weakness is that to the extent that the differentiating lines between categories of customers begins to diminish, suboptimizing competition, as well as duplication of resources, between divisions can occur.

Global Matrix Structure

A global matrix structure consists of two organization structures superimposed on each other. As a consequence, there are dual reporting relationships. These two structures can be a combination of the general forms already discussed. For example, the matrix structure might consist of product divisions intersecting with functional departments or geographical areas intersecting with global divisions. The two intersecting structures will largely be a function of what the organization sees as the two dominant aspects of its environment, such as product and functions, or product and region.

Strengths. Because of the dual interaction, global matrix structures can facilitate the flow of information throughout the organization. Before key decisions are made, the structure brings to bear the two intersecting perspectives. This tends to balance the orientation of the MNE so that no single perspective dominates.

Weaknesses. The weakness is that by bringing two perspectives together, the level of conflict is likely to rise. To the extent that effective conflict resolution mechanisms are not in place, increased levels of conflict can inhibit the organization's ability to quickly respond to changing conditions. Further, this structure means that many managers have two bosses. To the extent that they receive conflicting information or directives from dual sources of authority, employees may choose a variety of suboptimal alternatives such as avoiding conflict, siding with one boss over the other, and the like, based on factors other than what is best for the organization as a whole.

Mixed Organizational Structures

As we mentioned earlier, while these are pure forms, any combination of different forms is possible. The general intent of these mixed or hybrid organizational structures is to gain the advantages associated with one structure and reduce the disadvantages by incorporating the strengths of a different form. For example, in an effort to turn itself around, IBM recently reorganized into 13 divisions. Eleven of the divisions are product or service based (such as personal computers or network services) but two are regional (Europe and Asia Pacific).

CONTINGENCIES IN ORGANIZATIONAL DESIGN

An important question that arises at this point is what determines which organizational structure (or combination) is most effective and which principles of differentiation/integration, formalization/informalization, and centralization/decentralization need to be incorporated into the organizational design? For example, a crucial determinant of appropriate organizational design is the internal and external environment of the organization. In this section, we describe these determinants and develop a heuristic that can be utilized in making specific organizational structure and design decisions.

Organizational Uncertainty

Organizations do not exist in a vacuum. As we discussed in Chapter 1, the environment of an MNE has unique aspects that influence its internal components, including its structure. A variety of important factors exist in an MNE's internal and external environment.[8]

The key factor in the MNE's environment is the level of uncertainty it faces. Environmental uncertainty has two critical components: The first has to do with the extent to which the environment is simple or complex, and the second concerns the extent to which it is static or dynamic.

Simple environments result in few variables that need to be incorporated into decision making. Also, these variables are similar to each other. Obviously, the greater the number and the more dissimilar the variables that can affect decision making, the more complex the environment. For example, when Boeing puts together a 747 jumbo jet, it must assemble over six million parts that range in characteristics from a simple metal bolt to a panel composed of rare composite materials.

Static environments may have few or many factors, but these factors tend to remain stable over time. In contrast, factors in a dynamic environment change rapidly. Fashion is an example. The colors, fabric, styles, and so forth change from year to year and season to season. Technology in the semiconductor industry is another example.

Combining the dimensions "simple-complex" and "static-dynamic" produces a four-cell matrix that begins to provide a broad backdrop against which the heuristic of designing appropriate organizational structures can be placed (see Figure 15.2). However, we must examine the internal and external components of an MNE's environment in order to get a clearer idea of what factors lead to one of these four general environments.

Internal Environment. There are three general categories of factors that are important in an organization's internal environment. The first is the organization's personnel. Specific issues of importance include employees' educational level, technological sophistication, and managerial competence. The second category is the organization's functional and staff units, including interdependence among units and technological characteristics. Finally, the nature of the organization's product or service and its related goals play a critical role in the internal environment. Obviously, the greater the number of people, levels of education, and managerial competencies required and the greater the dissimilarity within and between these elements, the more complex the organization's internal environment. Additionally, the greater the interdependence among organizational units, technological requirements, and organizational products and services, the greater the complexity. Finally, the more people, technologies, interdependencies, products, and so on change, the more dynamic the organization's internal environment.

External Environment. There are also a number of factors that contribute to the complexity and dynamism of the MNE's external environment. As discussed in Chapter 1, one of the unique external factors MNEs face is economic exposure to exchange rates. The

---

[8]R. Duncan, "What Is the Right Organizational Structure?" *Organizational Dynamics* (Winter 1979): 59-79.

Figure 15.2
Business Environment Matrix

	Stable	**Dynamic**
Simple	Few factors Relatively stable	Few factors Relatively dynamic
Complex	Many factors Relatively stable	Many factors Relatively dynamic

greater the number of countries and the volatility of economic exposure, the greater the environmental uncertainty. Multiple sources of authority also poses a unique environmental factor for MNEs. The greater the number of countries in which MNEs operate, the greater the dissimilarities between these countries (their governments, laws, customer preferences, language, and so forth), and the greater the changes in these countries, the more complex and dynamic the MNE's external environment. The number, dissimilarity, and changes among competitors in various international markets also contribute to environmental uncertainty for MNEs. Finally, the number, dissimilarity, and changes among suppliers as well as among technologies in various markets contribute to the complexity and dynamism of external environments.

Globalization vs. Localization

In addition to factors that can directly contribute to the uncertainty in an MNE's environment, there are also factors that contribute to the globalization or localization demands of the international environment. When benefits can be gained from worldwide volume, this pushes toward a more globalized environment. These benefits could include economies of scale for production, greater leverage of high-cost distribution networks, greater leverage of intensive research and development requirements, and so forth. In a variety of industries the minimally efficient production scale is beyond that which could be supported in a single market. For instance, the minimally efficient scale for a semiconductor plant approaches half a billion dollars in sales; it requires between $100 and $200 million to develop a new drug; the breakeven point for a new commercial aircraft is 600 planes, with each plane costing in excess of $50 million. Technology intensity and scale economies such as these push toward globalization and concentrated configuration of the upstream components of a firm's value chain.

By contrast, differences among countries and customer preferences are two key factors that push toward localization. For example, the fact that Germans prefer front-loading washers and believe that boiling whites is the only way to clean and sanitize them, while French prefer top-loading washers and do not hold such beliefs about cleaning whites, pushes toward localization of these products.

Obviously, it is possible for forces to simultaneously push toward both globalization and localization, requiring MNEs to be both globally integrated and locally responsive.[9]

Information Exchange

In general, as uncertainty and the simultaneous demands for globalization and localization increase, the need for improved information flow also increases. For example, as the complexity and pace of change in the environment increase, so does the need for timely sharing of information throughout the organization in order to make appropriate decisions. As MNEs face greater pressures for global integration and local customization, they need more information in order to determine which specific aspects of the organization to try to integrate and which elements to modify to local demands. These increased information needs can be met in a variety of ways.[10]

Direct Contact.   Often, direct contact is an important means of sharing information. One of the largest MNEs in the world, Matsushita, has an interesting way of accomplishing this. Because R&D is of vital importance in the consumer electronics industry, Matsushita has a large central R&D lab. In an effort to make sure that managers know what is going on in the lab and to ensure that lab scientists know what the emerging market needs are, Matsushita holds an annual, internal trade show. Senior managers throughout Matsushita's worldwide operations gather and examine research results and potential new products. Managers also feed back information about market differences, customer preferences, and competitor positioning to R&D scientists. The result is a massive sharing of information that has helped keep Matsushita ahead in a highly competitive industry.

Liaison Roles.   Liaison roles are designed to enhance the link, and therefore information flows, between two or more groups, be they teams, departments, divisions, or subsidiaries. Part of Matsushita's success in the VCR market is due to its purposeful use of liaison roles. The vice president in charge of Matsushita's US subsidiary was also a member of the senior management committee of the parent company in Japan and spent about a third of his time in Japan. This facilitated the link between headquarters and the most important consumer market for VCRs. In addition, the general manager of the US subsidiary's video department had previously worked for 14 years in the video product division of the production and domestic marketing organization in Japan. This created a strong link between the product division in Japan and the US subsidiary. Also, the assistant product manager in the US subsidiary had spent five years in the central VCR manufacturing plant in Japan. Through these three individuals, Matsushita succeed in ensuring that vital links at the corporate, product, and factory levels were established between Japan and the US.

Teams.   When integration needs arise across a wide set of functional areas, teams can be an effective integration mechanism. N. V. Philips is an example of a firm that utilizes teams as an integrative mechanism. This may stem from the fact that the firm was founded by a team of two brothers, one an engineer and the other a salesman, who worked together in charting Philips's early strategic course. Whatever the origin, Philips has long had an "office of the president" (as opposed to a single CEO) composed of a technical, commercial, and financial executive. Furthermore, for each product there is a team of junior managers from commercial and technical functions. These teams integrate various perspectives

[9]Anant Sundaram, and J. Stewart Black, "Environment and Internal Organization of Multinational Enterprises," *Academy of Management Review,* 17 (1992): 729-757.

[10]J. R. Galbraith, "Organization Design: An Information Processing View," *Interfaces* 4(3) 1974. C. A. Bartlett and S. Ghoshal, "Organizing for Worldwide Effectiveness: The Transnational Solution," *California Management Review* (Fall 1988): 54-74.

and information around a single product to ensure that interfunctional differences are resolved early and that necessary design, manufacturing, and marketing issues are integrated from the outset in an effort to increase the success of the product.

Contingency Heuristic

We now outline a heuristic that managers can use in making decisions about the most effective organizational design and structure.[11] However, given all the different environmental demands that any given MNE might face, it is difficult to spell out by every level and by every department how a specific firm should be organized. Instead, the heuristic presented here provides a framework that can guide managers through the general questions and rules of thumb to determine the most appropriate organizational structure.

The first question managers must address is the extent to which the environment they face is simple or complex. Although most managers tend to believe that their environment is complex, this complexity needs to be placed in a relative context. For example, a manager might examine the level of technological intensity in the business. One crude measure of this is R&D expenditures as a percent of sales. In low-technology-intensity firms, R&D expenditures will represent less than 5% of sales. In high-technology-intensity firms, R&D expenditures can represent more than 20% of sales. A manager may also want to examine the number and similarity of the countries in which the firm operates. Having operations in say, just the US, UK, and Canada is less complex than the case of N. V. Philips, which operates in over 50 countries around the world. Additionally, a manager might examine the number and complexity of products produced. For example, assembling 6 million parts into a commercial airliner is more complex than assembling 132 parts into an office chair.

Assuming that the MNE environment is relatively simple, the next question is the extent to which the environment is static or dynamic. Again, few managers want to categorize their environment as static. After all, nothing in this world of change remains the same forever. On this dimension as well, managers must determine the relative level of stability or dynamism of their environment. Product life cycles and the half-life of technology are two simple means of assessing the dynamism of the environment.

Simple and Stable environments. To the extent that the environment is relatively simple and stable, the level of uncertainty is relatively low (see Figure 15.3). Low uncertainty reduces the need for quick and widespread information flows within the MNE, which in turn reduces the general need for high levels of integration. Most decisions can be handled through formal structures without significant decentralization. To the extent that international sales represent only a small percentage of the MNE's overall sales (for example, less than 15%), the international division structure is appropriate. It provides all the advantages previously discussed but in a relatively simple and stable environment, and results in few of the disadvantages mentioned.

As the percentage of international sales increases, the global functional structure is an appropriate match for relatively simple and stable environments. Because MNEs in this environment typically have few products in a limited number of similar markets, the structural divisions between functional areas are relatively unimportant. In contrast, the global functional structure facilitates the development of strong functional expertise within a global perspective, since each functional area has worldwide responsibilities. Consequently, each functional area can maximize its effectiveness by placing particular departments in locations that leverage comparative advantage. For example, operations might place one of its two factories in the UK in order to take advantage of labor costs and government tax incentives, while R&D might locate its basic lab near a leading academic institution in order to draw on faculty expertise and a supply of young scientists.

---

[11]R. Duncan, "What Is the Right Organizational Structure?" *Organizational Dynamics* (Winter 1979): 59-79.

Figure 15.3
Basic International Structures

	Stable (Slowly Changing Factors)	Dynamic (Constantly Changing Factors)
Simple (few and similar factors)	Low uncertainty Low information needs Structure International division structure (especially if percentage of international sales is small)	Moderate uncertainty Moderate information needs Structure Global functional structure Cross-functional teams

Simple and Dynamic Environments. If the environment is simple and dynamic, the ambiguity and the need for information increases. This context places a greater emphasis on integration and generally requires formal integration systems for key decisions. A global functional structure with mechanisms such as cross-functional teams is appropriate for this environment. Because the environment is dynamic, information will need to be gathered and shared across functional areas. The example of Philips illustrates how this can be accomplished at two levels. At the corporate level, the key executives in the team would be those whose functional areas are most affected by the changing environment. For example, if the dynamism of the environment stems largely from real exchange rate movements, then executives from areas such as finance, manufacturing, and marketing/sales would be logical members of the corporate level team. In addition, teams can be formed at the product level. If the dynamism of the environment is in part due to shifting customer preferences, then marketing research, product design, manufacturing, and sales are natural areas from which to draw product-team members.

Complex Environments. Environments that are judged to be complex require an additional assessment before their stability or dynamism is evaluated (see Figure 15.4). Once an environment has been judged complex, it is necessary to determine if the source of the complexity in the environment can be traced to clear categories such as geographic region, market/customer, or products. This determination will be largely a function of the globalization and localization forces discussed earlier. For example, to the extent that factors such as customers, governments, and competitors differ significantly by geographical area, this will push in the direction of utilizing a regional organizational structure. Once a determination about the segmentability of the environment has been made, the next step is to assess the stability or dynamism of the environment.

Complex, Segmentable, Stable Environments. Environments of this type have moderate levels of uncertainty, and, therefore, MNEs have moderate information needs. Global product or division structures, regional structures, and global customer structures are all appropriate in this context. The choice is a function of the dominant variable

Figure 15.4
Advanced International Structures

	Stable (Slowly Changing Factors)	**Dynamic** (Constantly Changing Factors)

Segmentable	Moderate uncertainty
	
	Moderate information needs
	
	Structure
	  Decentralized
	  Global product/division
	  structure
	  Global customer structure
	  Regional structure
		High uncertainty
		
		High information needs
		
		Structure
		  Highly decentralized
		  Global product/division
		  structure
		  Global customer structure
		  Regional structure
		
		    Direct contact
		    Teams
		    Liaisons

Not Segmentable	Low uncertainty
	
	Low information needs
	
	Structure
	
	  Global functional structure
	    Rules
	    Goals
	    Personnel transfers
		Moderate uncertainty
		
		Moderate information needs
		
		Structure
		  Somewhat decentralized
		  Mixed global functional
		  Structure
		    Teams
		    Direct contact

*(Left margin label: **Complex** (many dissimilar factors) spanning both rows)*

along which the environment can be segmented. However, the complexity of the environment means that it is impossible for senior executives to have all the information necessary to make effective centralized decisions. Consequently, even within each of the appropriate structures mentioned, formal as well as informal efforts are required to push authority and decision-making responsibility down the organization. As an example of decentralized decision making, even though the headquarters for Philips is located in Europe, its first color TV set was built and sold in Canada, its first stereo color TV was developed in Australia, and its programmed word-processing typewriter was developed in the United States.

Complex, Segmentable, Dynamic Environments. Environments of this type have high levels of uncertainty, and, therefore, MNEs have high information needs. As in the previous case, global product or division structures, regional structures, and global customer structures are all appropriate in this context. Again, the choice is a function of the dominant variable along which the environment can be segmented. However, the complexity and dynamism of the environment mean that a variety of managers throughout the organization need to gather and share information and that centralized decision making will not be effective. Consequently, formal as well as informal efforts are required to decentralize authority and decision-making responsibility. The complexity and dynamism of the environment implies that a variety of coordination and information exchange mechanisms will be needed in order for the organization to function effectively. MNEs in this type of environment not only may need to send expatriate executives out from headquarters, but also will need to bring nonparent nationals into headquarters as a means of both establishing common goals and values and sharing information throughout the MNE. Teams that bridge not only functional areas but also geographic regions will be necessary if the MNE is to coordinate its activities in a complex and changing environment.

To the extent that two particular aspects of the environment dominate, such as region and product, a global matrix organizational structure may also be appropriate. However, as previously discussed, global matrix organizations are inherently difficult to manage and require conflict-resolution skills, interpersonal skills, and power and influence abilities significantly greater than those required in alternative organizational structures. Consequently, the global matrix structure should be selected only after a careful assessment of both the fit between the structure and the environment, as well as the ability of organizational members to meet these higher demands and skill levels. At the very least, if organizational members do not have the requisite skills and abilities, specific steps must be taken to train members in order for the implementation of a global matrix structure to succeed.

Complex, Nonsegmentable, Stable Environments.   MNEs facing complex, nonsegmentable, and relative stable environments have low uncertainty and low information needs. Consequently, the global functional structure is an appropriate structure. Although MNEs in this environment may have many products in a number of markets, the similarity of markets or products renders the structural divisions between functional areas relatively unimportant. Formal rules, goals, and personnel transfers are likely to be all that is necessary to coordinate organizational activities effectively. The global functional structure will facilitate the development of strong functional expertise and foster a global perspective. The lower information need pushes in the direction of greater centralized decision making. The more the particular functional areas find that their activities are similar across countries, the more the centralized decision making can be effective.

Complex, Nonsegmentable, Dynamic Environments.   The final type of environment to consider is one that is complex, nonsegmentable, and yet dynamic. The complexity and dynamism of the environment place an emphasis on integration over differentiation. Furthermore, in this type of environment, it is unlikely that key decisions can be made centrally or implemented effectively without formal integration systems. Since the environment is dynamic, information will need to be gathered and shared across functional areas. A mixed global functional structure with mechanisms such as cross-functional teams is appropriate for this environment. The mixture of what remains in the traditional functional divisions and what moves toward decentralization is a function of the particular globalization and localization demands of the environment. For example, to the extent that the MNE has a wide variety of products and different customer preferences, the MNE may keep a global functional structure for areas such as finance, human resource management, and accounting, but may imbed design, operations, marketing, and sales in each of several operating divisions.

WARNING SIGNS

A key question concerning organizational design is "What happens if you have the wrong structure, and what are the warning signs?"

With the wrong structure, managers increasingly make the wrong decisions. MNE managers have to make decisions about what products to produce, what quality standards to set, how to reduce costs, how to advertise, how to position products against competitors, and the like across the globe. In the absence of timely, relevant information, effective decisions are unlikely. The more complex the decision, the more the information that is generally needed. Inappropriate organizational structures block needed information sharing, focus attention away from information that needs to be gathered, and consequently, hurt decision quality, organizational prosperity, and perhaps even survival.

Given that inappropriate organizational design and structures can severely inhibit organizational effectiveness, what are some of the key warning signs that a mismatch exists?[12]

One of the first warning signs is the decision maker's inability to anticipate problems. If problems caused by competitors, governments, customers, suppliers, and so forth consistently arise without advance notice, this is a warning sign that the organizational structure is inhibiting environmental scanning, data gathering, or information dissemination. To the extent that the organization is not designed or structured to correct this problem, decision makers will have to react to—rather than anticipate—the environment and will be placed at a competitive disadvantage relative to other organizations with appropriate structures.

Another key warning sign is an increase in conflict that prevents decisions from being effectively implemented. This sign, in particular, can indicate that the limits of a global functional structure are being stretched and that information exchange mechanisms, such as cross-functional teams or liaisons and other lateral relations, are needed.

There may also be signs at the individual level. When the number of individuals who do not know what is expected of them (high role ambiguity) or who receive conflicting expectations (high role conflict) increases, this is an early warning sign that the organizational structure is not appropriate for the environment. In general, the higher the level of individual role ambiguity and conflict and the larger the numbers of individuals experiencing these problems, the more severe the mismatch between the organizational structure and its environment.

CONCLUSION

Designing MNEs for international environments is one of the most critical activities of global executives. In the early chapters, we discussed many of the unique problems that multiple denominations of value and multiple sources of authority pose for MNEs. In this chapter we have examined how these factors affect organizational structure. It is important to keep in mind that inappropriate structures and designs restrict the timely flow of needed information and consequently hurt strategic decision making. By understanding the aspects of the international environment of business that affect structure, executives can more effectively formulate and implement global competitive strategies and design their organizations for competitive advantage.

---

[12]J. R. Galbraith, "Organization Design: An Information Processing View," *Interfaces* 4(3) 1974. C. A. Bartlett and S. Ghoshal, "Organizing for Worldwide Effectiveness: The Transnational Solution," *California Management Review* (Fall 1988): 54-74.

ABB ASEA Brown Boveri (A): The Merger

I'm anxious to set an example. ABB will be a success story. We have no choice. There is no way back.

Percy Barnevik[1]

While most families in Stockholm enjoyed the serenity of the Christmas season in December 1987, Percy Barnevik, age 46, prepared for his family's move to Zürich, where he would take charge of a new company to be born on January 5, 1988. The new company, ABB Asea-Brown Boveri, was the result of a merger that Barnevik had engineered between Asea AB of Sweden, where he was chief executive officer, and BBC Brown Boveri Ltd. of Baden, Switzerland. The merged entity would constitute "the world's leading supplier in the $50 billion electric power industry, surpassing such household names as Westinghouse, General Electric, and Japan's Mitsubishi.. . . [ABB would control] as much as a third of Europe's business and more than 20% of the world market."[2]

The prospect of steering such a powerful entity into the 1990s was exciting for Barnevik. He intended ABB to join the elite club of successful cross-frontier mergers, including the Anglo-Dutch groups of Unilever (consumer products) and Shell (integrated oil). With the excitement, however, also came the responsibility for successful integration of 850 subsidiary companies and 180,000 employees operating in 140 countries. Barnevik believed that the popular phrase "think globally, act locally" would be his new corporate call to arms, and he relished the challenge of turning the slogan into profits.

This case is the first in a series of cases exploring the creation and management structure of the Asea Brown Boveri Group. The case was prepared by Eran Gartner, MBA '92, under the supervision of Andrew Boynton and Mark Eaker and with support from IBM's Advanced Business Institute. Copyright © 1992 by the Darden Graduate Business School Foundation, Charlottesville, VA.

[1]Jules Arbose, "ABB: The New Energy Powerhouse," *International Management,* June 1988, pp. 24-30.

[2]Jonathan Kapstein and Stanley Reed, "The Euro-Gospel According to Percy Barnevik," *Business Week,* July 23, 1990, pp. 64-66.

BARNEVIK AT ASEA AB

Barnevik was born in 1941 in the western coastal town of Uddevalla, Sweden. He learned a disciplined work ethic that would guide his career as one of Sweden's most famous business leaders while working long hours in his father's printing shop.[3] He was educated in economics and computer science in Sweden, and ultimately earned his MBA from the Gothenburg School of Economics. He later spent two years studying at Stanford University in California before entering Swedish industry with the specialty steelmaker Sandvik AB in 1969 as group controller.

Sandvik was one of several companies controlled by Swedish industrialist Peter Wallenberg and his family. Through a complicated web of leveraged cross-holdings, Wallenberg was thought to control an empire worth nearly 300 billion Swedish kronor (SKr) or US $50 billion. After his position as group controller, Barnevik moved to run Sandvik's US operations. Between 1975 and 1979, Barnevik rattled the underperforming North American subsidiary and tripled sales to $226 million. After his five years in the United States, Barnevik returned to Sweden as executive vice president of Sandvik AB.

Barnevik's decisive and determined style at Sandvik caught the attention of Asea's Chairman Curt Nicolin and Asea's largest shareholder—the Wallenbergs. In 1980, following success at Sandvik, Barnevik was asked to work a similar miracle at Asea AB, a sleepy industrial jewel of Sweden. Asea's business was broadly defined as "the generation and application of electric power." The company manufactured such diverse items as steam turbines for power plants and high-speed electric locomotives for passenger railroads.

In his first two years at Asea, Barnevik carved the amorphous company into rational divisions, each with clearly defined product and market responsibilities. Then he concentrated on focusing the company's resources on profitable lines of business in which the firm had some discernible technical or market advantages. At headquarters, Barnevik slashed staff from 2,500 to 100 in less than two years; he told those not retained to find a job in the operating companies or go home.

In a highly decentralized format, managers had direct accountability for annual budgets reported to headquarters and for complete balance sheets that reflected the health and profitability of their operating companies. Each unit, therefore, also had an opportunity to develop an identity beyond the parent company, which strengthened management and employee commitment.

In 1986, Asea announced the successful implementation of its Nordic Strategy, an attempt to extend the firm's engineering and manufacturing operations beyond Sweden in order to gain economies of scale—both in manufacturing and in raising capital. The big step forward had been the acquisition in Finland of Strömberg AB with its 7,000 employees, which was followed in late 1987 by the acquisition of 63% of EB Corporation in Norway. By 1987, Barnevik had realized his plan, radically altering Asea "from a Swedish-centered into a pan-Nordic electrical multinational." The strategy worked wonders: Revenues tripled, earnings grew fivefold, and market capitalization increased an incredible 15 times during Barnevik's tenure (see *Exhibit 1*).[4]

The experience with Asea had given Barnevik a thorough understanding of the electrical-power equipment industry in Scandinavia and the rest of Europe. In particular, it gave him a sense of the dimension of change that the industry as a whole needed to undergo in order to match the impressive results Asea had achieved under new, lean management:

> When Europe in 1986 pledged to create a single, deregulated market, Barnevik knew he was hearing the death knell of the coddled European power industry.. . . Few industries nurture a cozier relationship with governments and state utilities than the equipment makers.[5]

[3]Kapstein and Reed, pp. 64-66.

[4]"Asea- Brown Boveri: Power Play," *The Economist,* May 28, 1988, pp. 19-22.

[5]Kapstein and Reed, pp. 64-66.

As for Asea, Barnevik decided the company needed to look beyond Sweden's population of 8.5 million, and even beyond the Nordic countries, in order to continue realizing improvements in productivity and profit margins.

BBC BROWN BOVERI LTD.

While Barnevik's discipline had brought an admirable level of profitability to Asea by the late 1980s, the same was not true of other firms in the industry. Serious problems plagued Asea's fiercest European competitor, BBC Brown Boveri Ltd.

By the late 1980s, Brown Boveri had become one of Europe's most prestigious engineering firms, but engineering mastery had also become one of Brown Boveri's greatest liabilities. The company tended to respond more to the whims of its technical staff than to the requirements of the market. Rather than leverage experience from previous designs, Brown Boveri engineers were more inclined to build new and innovative solutions to suit customer specifications. The constant turnover of designs, and lack of shared components among them, led to reliability problems and high costs.

Dr. Fritz Leutwiler, appointed chairman in 1985 after a career in central banking, intended to redirect the company's energies toward the paying customer and to improve profit margins from their dismal levels (see *Exhibits 2* and *3*).[6] He outlined a series of "measures designed to pull the group out of its unsatisfactory profit position," including a new organizational structure, elimination of unprofitable businesses, and weaning the company of its excessive dependency on power generation.[7]

By 1986, Leutwiler was confident that "[t]oday's Brown Boveri Group has Business, Regional and Functional Divisions, standing shoulder to shoulder, each with clearly defined missions and responsibilities." These groupings paralleled the organizational lines Barnevik had drawn for Asea (see *Exhibits 4* and *5*).

By 1987, Leutwiler's next challenges were to overcome the independent directions pursued by the engineers, and the divergent course charted by Brown Boveri's German subsidiary. The Mannheim-based BBC Brown Boveri Aktiengesellschaft had, over the years, outgrown its parent company. Brown Boveri had followed the federalist model established when the Swiss cantons formed a federation of states in the 13th century. The states ceded no more authority to the collective central government than the powers needed for maintaining a common defense and facilitating trade among them. Brown Boveri had granted maximum independence to its foreign subsidiaries in order to encourage aggressive pursuit of local contracts and to develop relationships with governments, utilities, and suppliers. The proliferation of product variety in an industry with excess capacity had, however, taken its toll on Brown Boveri's cost structure. Most rebellious of the subsidiaries was the German affiliate, which Leutwiler intended carefully to rein in.

ELECTRICAL POWER: BRACING FOR DEREGULATION

Leutwiler's letter to the shareholders opened the BBC Brown Boveri annual report for 1987 with a gloomy forecast for his own company and the industry as a whole:

> The electrical market has essentially stopped growing, at least in the industrial countries. Demand remains high in the developing countries, but sales are hampered by financial problems and high debt. Overcapacities prevalent throughout the electrical manufacturing industry make retrenchment and restructuring measures inevitable.

[6]"Asea Brown Boveri: Closing the Generation Gap," *The Economist,* August 15, 1987, pp. 53-54.
[7]Fritz Leutwiler, "Chairman's Letter," *BBC Brown Boveri Annual Report,* 1986.

In the coming years, Leutwiler predicted, the fragmented and localized industry would be exposed to extensive global competition, but electric-power generation was simply too capital intensive to continue to support such a fragmented market. It would be forced into significant consolidation. By 1993, EC (European Community) governments were expected to open their national bidding policies to foreign-owned companies, which would force the weaker players to seek mergers or fail. In the United States, new plant construction had slowed considerably; nuclear orders had stopped altogether because of excessive litigation, the 1978 Three-Mile Island accident, and the specter of the meltdown at Chernobyl. In response, the century-old US manufacturers, Westinghouse and GE, were busy diversifying away from the troubled power industry.

The situation facing electric-power equipment makers was similar in related lines of business, most notably, car and locomotive manufacturing for electrified railroads. Unlike Americans, Europeans had not abandoned passenger rail services in favor of air travel. The rail infrastructure remained pervasive in the 1980s. Suppliers were fragmented, however; 24 domestic manufacturers supplied Western Europe's national railroads with locomotives and cars built to custom specifications. Some manufacturers built only 10 or so locomotives annually.[8] With the introduction in 1981 of high-speed train service between Paris and Lyons, however, the industry changed forever. The race was on throughout the European continent to match the French TGV. European governments committed their national railways to high-speed projects whose construction would cost $200 billion through the year 2000. They were motivated not only by national pride but by economic necessity. To be left off the high-speed main line was to forgo the economic development that the new train routes promised to bring.

In this atmosphere, small rail equipment manufacturers could not match the resources of the big players (Alsthom, Siemens, GEC, BBC, and Asea). In rail equipment as in electric-power generation, the smaller national companies would be forced to seek international partners with broad bases for capital investment in order to keep pace with the accelerating rate of technological development.

Global Markets

Harmonization among the 12 EC members had ramifications for the electric-power industry beyond rationalization of capacity. The EC encompassed a total market of 345 million people generating a collective gross national product (GNP) in excess of $6 trillion and accounting for nearly 40 percent of world exports. The EC member countries had announced in 1987 their intent to complete legislation for integration of the European Common Market by the end of 1992 to allow the seamless flow of capital, goods, and people among the member states. Companies from nonmember countries could not know for certain whether the Common Market would bring new opportunities from the opening of national markets or shut the doors on existing businesses within a Fortress Europe:

> National preference is such an ingrained habit that local favorites always have a definite and usually a decisive advantage everywhere—GEC and Northern Engineering in Britain, Siemens and AEG in West Germany, General Electric and Westinghouse in the United States, Hitachi in Japan and so on.[9]

The fortress phenomenon was pronounced in Asia, where some of Asea's fiercest competitors—Hitachi, Mitsubishi, Toshiba, and Daewoo—dominated their protected home markets and used government export incentives to capture market share from Western firms. In addition, in reaction to the growing regionalization of Europe and Asia, North

---

[8]William Taylor, "The Logic of Global Business: An Interview with ABB's Percy Barnevik," *Harvard Business Review,* March-April 1991, p. 92.

[9]"Asea Brown Boveri: Power Plan," pp. 19-22.

American leaders had begun talking of a free trade zone encompassing Canada, the United States, and Mexico. These regional trading blocs could herald a new age of global trade or a new era of protectionism.

As a counterweight to the EC, neutral Sweden and Switzerland had joined the European Free Trade Association (EFTA), whose other members included Austria, Iceland, Finland, and Norway. To prevent being shut out of the more lucrative EC union, EFTA had opened negotiations to form a "European Economic Area" with the EC. Discussions on the form and operational details of such an association had so far failed to yield substantive results, and businesses within EFTA countries had begun to realize that presence in the EC countries would be the only way to guarantee access to EC markets. With respect to such investments within the EC, *The Economist* reported,

> Four factors help explain the sudden Swedish shopping spree: a tiny home market, an ailing domestic economy, the chance to tap new markets in the EC—and a rising fear of what is brewing in Brussels.. . . They have already set up shop in as many countries as possible so that they can present themselves as local manufacturers.[10]

Local Pressures

The domestic scene posed further problems for Swedish firms. The Swedish brand of socialism, which had enabled a period of growth and prosperity in the years since the Second World War, had recently soured. Government revenues consumed more than half of the GNP, a rate 50% higher than the EC average.[11] With a pervasive welfare system and extensive government employment, many Swedes lacked motivation to increase individual productivity. The local brand of social capitalism had muted employer-worker tensions and allowed uninterrupted national development, but it seemed in 1987 that Swedes would have to abandon some of their traditional social principles in order to maintain and improve the standard of living (as measured by worker productivity).

In Switzerland and Sweden, the small domestic markets had always created pressure on domestic to export in order to remain competitive. In 1987, Asea had reported that 70% of its business was carried on outside Sweden; Brown Boveri sold 95% of its turnover outside Switzerland (70% outside Switzerland and West Germany).

In addition to pressure to export, both firms felt the pressures of environmentalism years earlier than many of their competitors in other countries. Despite the cost of meeting such stringent regulations in the short term, this heightened consciousness could, however, become an advantage in the long term. When foreign markets adopted new environmental controls, competitors required years to gain the experience ABB engineers had accumulated in their home markets. In his annual report message, Leutwiler pointed out another silver lining in environmental and other pressures on the power-generation business:

> The brighter side of the [electrical-power industry] picture is that new user needs and new technology are opening up new opportunities for future growth in the industry. The electrical industry is becoming an electronics industry. Energy-saving and non-polluting technology is in demand, and so are better means of transportation and modern factory automation equipment. Exploitation of these growth opportunities requires a great deal of additional research and development expenditure coupled with first-rate manufacturing performance.

[10]"Swedish Firms Set Sail for Europe," *The Economist,* September 1, 1990, pp. 59-60.

[11]John Burton, "Fine-tuning Reforms," *Financial Times,* October 23, 1991, Special Survey on Sweden, p. 6.

TRANSNATIONAL MERGER

Barnevik and Leutwiler intended their new company to be among the survivors of the industry shake-out. Asea and Brown Boveri were of roughly equivalent size in many respects (annual sales, net worth, number of employees) and had adopted similar lines of decentralized command. The companies also complemented each other in their geographical concentrations and in management strengths (see *Exhibit 6*). *The Economist* reacted to news of the merger by concluding that "[t]he merger will combine Asea's reputation for tough management with Brown Boveri's technical know-how and marketing name."[12]

Leutwiler was confident that a marriage of equals with Asea would bring to bear the resources necessary to stay at the technological edge in the power industry:

> The new Asea Brown Boveri Group has what it takes to meet these challenges successfully. It has the resources to finance research and development and can utilize production plants in many countries to make most of the advantages of international specialization. No competitor has comparable omnipresence in the world's markets.

To Barnevik, upheavals in the electrical-power equipment industry were a signal of potential rather than a cause for concern. In a market where contracts would be won by managerial skill, low cost, and technological leadership, Barnevik's lean and innovative company looked forward to significant order bookings:

> Mr. Barnevik observes with satisfaction that ABB's main competitors are fast diversifying into consumer electronics, defense equipment, even medical products to reduce their dependence on electrical-engineering in general and the power industry in particular. . . (for Mr. Barnevik the way to make money in manufacturing, as in the stock market, is to invest when everybody else is fleeing).[13]

QUESTIONS

As Barnevik prepared to leave Stockholm, he thought about how to apply the lessons he had learned in his years at Asea to the grander organization of which Asea was now a part. Barnevik believed that, "ABB is on its way to becoming an entirely new breed of corporation, breaking ground for the post-multinational company of the 1990s."[14] Only the question of how to organize this new company remained. What would be his role at the center of the organization with respect to the operating companies around the world? How could he track the developments of ABB around the world in sufficient detail to make decisions without introducing delay, bureaucracy, and hierarchy? What would be the optimal organization for the diverse operations of ABB: along functional lines, product lines, or geography? His experience had taught him that decentralization was a powerful force in developing a high-performance organization, but which dimension of the organization was most important? What structure would allow adequate investment in basic research but also support quick commercialization of new technologies?

Finally and immediately, Barnevik was aware that the downfall of many mergers had been their inability to conduct business as usual during a prolonged merger process. He was eager to act quickly and decisively in structuring the new company to avoid any such paralysis.

[12]"Asea Brown Boveri: Closing the Generation Gap," pp. 53-54.

[13]"Asea Brown Boveri: Power Play," pp. 19-22.

[14]Kapstein and Reed, pp. 64-66.

EXHIBIT 1

The Asea Group, Five-Year Review of Financial Position (in Swedish kronor[1]; millions, except as noted)

	1983	1984	1985	1986	1987
Order bookings	27,255	35,635	39,358	47,438	56,165
Invoiced sales	30,589	36,600	41,625	46,601	52,271
Earnings after financial income and expense	1,970	2,337	2,413	2,425	2,724
Adjusted stockholders' equity	6,593	7,419	8,635	10,532	11,570
Total capital	32,175	37,087	41,618	47,154	59,040
Capital expenditures for property, plant, and equipment	1,077	1,063	1,427	2,069	2,097
Capital expenditures for acquisitions	358	260	1,009	2,137	2,111
Average number of employees	56,660	58,434	60,979	63,124	72,868
Operating earnings/invoiced sales, %	7.9	7.6	6.4	6.1	6.7
Return on capital employed, %	16.5	17.8	16.8	18.2	16.2
Return on equity, %	18.3	18.8	16.7	15.0	15.0
Debt/equity ratio	1.07	0.98	1.18	1.01	1.36
Interest-coverage ratio	2.80	2.92	2.85	2.40	2.74
Net income per share (SKr, 50% tax)	16.00	18.90	19.60	19.60	22.10
Net income per share, fully diluted (SKr, 50% tax)	–	–	18.70	19.30	21.60
Dividend per share (SKr)	4.00	4.70	6.00	7.00	8.00

Source: Asea AB annual report, 1987, p. 4.

[1]Translation rate on December 31, 1987: $1.00 = SKr 5.84.

EXHIBIT 2

BBC Brown Boveri Ltd., Five-Year Summary of Consolidated Balance Sheets[1] (Swiss francs; millions)

	At December 31				
	1983	1984	1985	1986	1987
Assets					
Current assets					
Cash and marketable securities	1,999	2,722	3,048	3,133	3,275
Trade receivables	2,851	3,556	3,600	3,297	2,697
Other receivables, prepayments, and accrued income	764	938	970	760	571
Advances to suppliers	819	690	517	235	154
Inventories	7,833	8,786	7,217	4,421	4,238
Total current assets	14,266	16,692	15,352	11,846	10,935
Fixed assets and investments					
Property, plant, and equipment[2]					
At book value	1,685	1,903	1,786	1,773	1,740
Revaluation to current value	2,099	2,180	2,355	2,254	2,098
At current value	3,784	4,083	4,141	4,027	3,838
Investments and intangible assets	348	323	281	285	393
Total fixed assets and investments	4,132	4,406	4,422	4,312	4,231
Total assets	18,398	21,098	19,774	16,158	15,166

(Exhibit continued on following page)

	At December 31				
	1983	*1984*	*1985*	*1986*	*1987*
Liabilities and equity					
Liabilities					
Short- and medium-term borrowings	1,363	1,468	1,400	1,233	1,230
Long-term debt	1,318	1,484	1,426	1,336	1,023
Accounts payable	1,471	1,639	1,867	1,900	1,334
Accrued expenses	878	1,281	1,673	1,829	1,694
Advances from customers	6,621	7,489	5,574	2,799	2,755
Total liabilities	11,651	13,361	11,940	9,097	8,037
Provisions and adjustments	2,275	2,481	2,602	2,233	2,260
Equity					
Capital of BBC Baden	501	553	553	553	720
Reserves of BBC Baden	445	459	475	488	777
Retained profit of BBC Baden at beginning of year	3	5	5	12	24
Consolidation reserve	3,575	4,154	4,089	3,679	3,163
Net earnings/loss	(52)	85	109	96	186
Total equity	4,472	5,256	5,232	4,828	4,870
Total liabilities and equity	18,398	21,098	19,774	16,158	15,166
Equity attributable to minority shareholders	797	980	840	627	523
Contingent liabilities	311	406	565	491	365

Source: BBC Brown Boveri Ltd. annual report, 1987, pp. 74-75.

[1]Balance sheet and income statement are reproduced here as presented in annual report.

[2]Insured value (at December 31): 1983—8,722; 1984—9,176; 1985—9,403; 1986—9,056; 1987—9,236.

EXHIBIT 3 BBC Brown Boveri Ltd., Five-Year Summary of Income Statements[1] (Swiss francs; millions)

	1983	*1984*	*1985*	*1986*	*1987*
Orders received	10,501	12,431	12,977	11,032	10,994
Income					
Sales	10,658	11,214	13,876	13,826	10,369
Changes in work in process and finished goods	615	916	(1,493)	(2,502)	127
Gross production income	11,273	12,130	12,383	11,324	10,496
Other operating income	377	395	402	409	378
Nonoperating income	234	487	436	321	334
Total income	11,884	13,012	13,221	12,054	11,208
Expenses					
Expenses for materials and goods	4,958	5,166	5,521	4,679	4,131
Personnel expenses	4,152	4,421	4,590	4,515	4,371
Depreciation	516	565	521	537	495
Interest and other financial charges	418	424	336	202	169
Other expenses and taxes	1,892	2,351	2,414	2,025	1,856
Total expenses	11,936	12,927	13,112	11,958	11,022
Net earnings/loss	(52)	85	109	96	186
Net earnings/loss attributable to minority shareholders	13	18	17	16	18
Cash flow	464	650	630	633	681

Source: BBC Brown Boveri Ltd. annual report, 1987, p. 76.

[1]Balance sheet and income statement are reproduced here as presented in annual report.

EXHIBIT 4

BBC Brown Boveri Ltd., Business Segments, 1987

Business Segment	Divisions	Revenue (%)
Power Supply	Power Plants Power Transmission Transformers Medium Voltage Equipment Power Systems Control Power Lines	20.6 27.0
Transportation	High-Energy Batteries Transportation Systems	7.1
Standard products	Low Voltage Apparatus Supercharging	10.4
Electronics	Factory Automation Measurement and Control Information Technology Electronics Components	9.1
Installation	Installations District Heating Systems Cable and Wire	11.9
Industry	Mining and Metallurgical Industries Process Industries Oil, Gas, and Marine Industries Electrical Drives	11.2
Other products and services		2.7

Source: BBC Brown Boveri Ltd. annual report, 1987.

EXHIBIT 5

Asea AB Business Segments, 1987

Business Segment	Divisions	Revenue (%)
Power plants	Hydro Power Nuclear Power/Nuclear Fuel Thermal Power	5.3
Power transmission	Installations Protection Relays High Voltage Apparatus Transformers	13.4
Power distribution	Distribution of Electricity Cables Capacitors Copper and Aluminum Wire	9.5
Transportation	Railway Equipment All-Terrain Carriers[1] Hydraulics[1] Forklift Trucks[1]	7.0

(Exhibit continued on following page)

Business Segment	Divisions	Revenue (%)
Industrial equipment	Metallurgical Industry Process Control Motor Drives Electronic Components Industrial Robots Industrial/Shop Refrigerator	11.7
Financial services	Asset Management Stockbrokerage Insurance Trading and Countertrading Leasing	7.7
The Fläkt Group (environmental)	Air Pollution Control Industrial Processes Components Gadelius (Japan) Service Indoor Climate	22.6
Standard finished goods	Electrical Wholesale Buiness Household Appliances Low-Voltage Apparatus Electric Motors	10.0
Other operations	Industrial Plastics Power Utility Operations Service and Installation Castings Telecommunications	12.8

Source: Asea AB annual report, 1987.
[1]Not included in Asea Brown Boveri merger.

EXHIBIT 6

Sales by Geographical Markets

Asea AB	%
Sweden	29.7
Nordic countries	20.6
Western Europe	19.8
Eastern Europe	1.9
North America	10.9
Latin America	2.0
Australasia, Asia	14.2
Africa	0.9
SKr (millions) 52,271	100.0

BBC Brown Boveri Ltd.	%
Switzerland	5.4
West Germany	24.2
Rest of Europe	32.9
North America	8.8
Latin America	6.3
Australasia, Asia	17.2
Africa	5.2
SFr (millions) 10,369	100.0

Index

All page numbers that are followed by an *n* refer to a footnote on that page.